AMERICAN ARCHITECTS AND THEIR BOOKS, 1840–1915

Frontispiece John Calvin Stevens in his library, ca. 1900. Courtesy of the Maine Historic Preservation Commission.

AMERICAN ARCHITECTS
AND THEIR BOOKS, 1840–1915

Edited by Kenneth Hafertepe
and James F. O'Gorman

UNIVERSITY OF MASSACHUSETTS PRESS
Amherst and Boston

Printed in the United States of America

LC 2007016248
ISBN 978-1-55849-602-6

Designed by Dennis Anderson
Set in Adobe Caslon Pro
Printed and bound by Sheridan Books, Inc.

Library of Congress Cataloging-in-Publication Data

American architects and their books, 1840–1915 / edited by Kenneth Hafertepe and James F. O'Gorman.
p. cm. — (Studies in print culture and the history of the book)
Includes bibliographical references and index.
ISBN 978-1-55849-602-6 (cloth : alk. paper)
1. Architects—Books and reading—United States. 2. Architectural writing—United States—History—19th century. 3. Architectural writing—United States—History—20th century.
I. Hafertepe, Kenneth, 1955– II. O'Gorman, James F.
NA710.A45 2007
720.973—dc22
2007016248

British Library Cataloguing in Publication data are available.

This book is published with the financial assistance of the
Grace Slack McNeil Program in the History of American Art at Wellesley College
and the College of Arts and Sciences, Baylor University.

To the Memory of
William H. Jordy (1917–1997)
Historian, Critic, Teacher

CONTENTS

ILLUSTRATIONS

INTRODUCTION

Architects and Their Books, 1840–1915

"'What is the use of a book,' thought Alice, 'without pictures or conversations?'" Lewis Carroll surely hadn't architects in mind when he wrote that memorable line; nonetheless, Alice's question can overarch the following studies. Pictures in architectural books and the conversations such books include or engender are two of the most important ingredients of the genre, the one illustrating content, the other directing its effect. (And surely there have been clients who thought of their architect's office as located down a rabbit hole and presided over by a hookah-smoking caterpillar.) Architects' books, in all the dimensions that phrase implies, including pictures, text, and the conversations they inspire—the visual and the verbal, that is—are the subjects addressed here.

This gathering of papers is a sequel to our previous volume of similar title.[1] Here as there, the collection began with a public symposium, this one held as part of the annual meeting of the Society of Architectural Historians in Providence, Rhode Island, in April 2004, although it is augmented by several studies not read at that event. Here as there, the authors have applied a broad definition to the category of architectural books. This is a group of papers on various aspects of architects' relationship to print culture, of the literary works that past architects collected, used, read, criticized, discussed, argued over, wrote, illustrated, designed, printed, were inspired by, cribbed from, educated clients with, advertised their services through, polemicized by means of, designed libraries for, or just plain enjoyed. Once again our collection demonstrates a wide variety of approaches to the topic. And once again the result is a volume that represents the intersection of the history of architecture, the history of ideas, and the history of the book. Changes wrought in nineteenth-century print culture had an impact upon the architectural profession as elsewhere in society.

Our earlier volume covered the years between the eighteenth century, when architects' books were imported from abroad, and the 1840s, when homegrown works on architecture began to seem common and a history of architecture written by an American first appeared. It was the period in which architects began to split from the building trades to establish themselves as professionals, as the third party in the triangular relationship that includes client and builder. Two visible signs of this development were the proliferation of architectural drawings in the wake of the Industrial Revolution (along with borrowing from an increasingly rich menu of historical styles), and the appearance in architectural offices of collections of publications ranging from technical manuals to treatises on the history of architecture and theories of design. The decorative title page to a reference work much used in the nineteenth century, the Pugins' *Examples of Gothic Architecture*, places this development in historical perspective (figure INTR. 1).[2] It is a contemporary conception of a medieval draftsman plying his compass amid stores of source books. Large professional libraries were rare before the mid-nineteenth century—Ithiel Town's large collections at New York and New Haven being the notable exception—but the possession of drawing skills and the trappings of learning became in the early nineteenth century the signs and symbols of emerging professional status, and they often appear in portraits of architects. They also appear in advertising. The Connecticut architect Henry Austin (1804–1891) inserted notices in the *Hartford Courant* around 1840 in which he stressed the value of drawings and books in the wooing of clients. "All who feel an interest in Architectural improvement," he stated, "are invited to call at his office, where he will be happy to offer them every opportunity of examining, gratuitously, his collections of books and drawings. Persons who contemplate building ... may find it for their benefit to call and examine before they commence."[3] From the pictures in these books certainly came conversations.

The development of the profession quickened after midcentury with the establishment of the American Institute of Architects (1857); the founding of the first school of architecture at the Massachusetts Institute of Technology (1865, to be immediately followed by others at various institutes of higher learning); the appearance in Boston of the professional journal *American Architect and Building News*

FIG INTR. 1 A. W. Pugin, decorative title page. From A. Pugin and A. W. Pugin, *Examples of Gothic Architecture*, vol. 2 (1836).

(1876); the proliferation of books published by and for architects; the inclusion of architectural criticism in books and periodicals; the founding of large architectural firms; and the gathering of significant libraries in the offices of architects.

Such office libraries were a real schoolhouse for aspirants before and long after the universities began to educate prospective practitioners. As Earle Shettleworth tells us in this volume, John Calvin Stevens (see Frontispiece) said of the office he entered in the 1870s, "Mr. [Francis H.] Fassett had an excellent library, and his boys had ample opportunity to make use of it, so that the office boy had only him self to blame if he did not profit by what was at his hand."[4] A prime example of such a library is the large collection of professional books and photographs amassed by H. H. Richardson at his office in Brookline, Massachusetts, and housed by the 1880s in a fireproof sanctum at the end of a string of drafting cubicles (figure INTR. 2).[5] He encouraged his staff to browse there in search of pictures to inspire office conversations about how to design original works based on traditional forms and technology. The object was not to copy the past but to create within its spirit.

Pictures and conversations: the architect seeks inspiration in pictures or illustrates his own publications as a form of advertising his wares; books inspire conversations among professionals, critics, theorists, students, and, perhaps most important, between architects and their clients or would-be clients. The following pages investigate some—but of course not all—the ways in which architecture and print culture intersected in the United States through the second half of the nineteenth century and into the early twentieth. The architects included were purposely selected to represent the rural as well as the urban, the barely known as well as the famous. The gathering is miscellaneous; the intent is to demonstrate a variety of approaches.

Kenneth Hafertepe uses Downing's readings—and the readings of those whom Downing read—to fix his role as a tastemaker but also more broadly as a cultural figure. In his works on rural domesticity—from the *Theory and Practice of Landscape Gardening* of 1841 to *The Architecture of Country Houses* of 1850—he pictured an America in which all people could occupy a tasteful cottage, farmhouse, or villa. Hafertepe argues that the conversation in which Downing attempted to engage Americans was deeply rooted in Enlightenment aesthetics, particularly of J. C. Loudon and Archibald Alison. Yet what Downing saw as a democratic vista was criticized by his rivals as an elitist cul-de-sac. More objective observers such as Susan Fenimore Cooper admired Downing's picturesque aesthetic while creating a more realistic theory of how domestic architecture evolved in the absence of big cities and brand-name architects. Hefertepe suggests that although Downing was

FIG INTR. 2 The library of H. H. Richardson, Brookline, Mass., ca. 1885. Courtesy of Historic New England.

perhaps not as egalitarian as he imagined, his books had a significant influence on the developing American scene, and in so doing he offers a major revision of recent scholarly theories about Downing's place in American history.

Downing wrote for both rural and urban audiences—for those who lived in the Hudson River Valley and those who lived in the metropolis at the mouth of the river; his perspective was that of a northeasterner. A very different perspective was that of Oliver P. Smith, who was born near Utica, New York, but went west first to Buffalo and then to Detroit. One might expect Smith to have carried the traditional mental tool kit of the carpenter-architect, bringing eastern styles to frontier places, but Ted Cavanagh argues that he was a progressive, freed from the strictures of eastern taste and open to new architectural ideas. Analyzing both

Smith's surviving buildings and his publications, Cavanagh suggests that he was an exemplar of the rural capitalist, not tied down by agrarian responsibilities, willing to engage in domestic-scale enterprises, and thus both mobile and innovative. His entrepreneurial spirit led him to publish a lecture titled "The Science and Progress of Civil Architecture." His building guide and pattern book, *The Domestic Architect*, first appeared in 1852. It included original designs for Grecian and cottage (i.e., Gothic) styles, detailed directions to builders, and rules for drawing and shading, all illustrated in more than two hundred engravings. Smith made quite clear that builders should not rely solely on pictures for their understanding of a building, without studying the explanations of the designer. Alice, had she been a rural architect at midcentury, would have found this a useful package, but the mantle of progressivism would soon pass to urban designers and large-scale industries.

The big-city, midcentury professional occupies our next two contributors. Jhennifer Amundson profiles T. U. Walter's indulgence in books as well as the changing complexion of his library across his long career. His passion went far beyond professional literature. A deeply religious man, he saw reading as the broad road to personal enrichment. Bunyan, the Bible, moralistic novels, and Milton, among others, inspired him as they did so many members of his generation. Though numerous colleagues and rivals happily sent manuscripts to publishers, he disliked "bookmaking while we have so many more good books than we read." Not surprisingly, then, his literary output was, in Admunson's estimate, unremarkable. It was the use of books both lay and professional, not the making of them, that fueled his life and work. Pocket notebooks record his architectural perusal, ranging from Palladio's orders to the standard technical manuals coming out of England. As Amundson writes, Walter understood the essential position of books in the architect's office. He, along with Frank Lloyd Wright and Charles Sumner Greene, among those included in this volume, also understood that not all inspirational reading had to be professional.

If Walter eschewed the role of author, his Philadelphia rival, Samuel Sloan, exemplified the midcentury urban authorial voice in his first book, *The Model Architect* of 1852–53. Like Downing, Sloan addressed the consuming public, focusing on the role of the architect in the marketplace; Elspeth Cowell contends that he used his books specifically as a tool for building his client base. At the same time she shows that the men for whom Sloan designed houses were not unlike their architect. They were entrepreneurs who began by practicing a trade but became industrialists, possessing both business sense and a spirit of innovation. She concludes that *The Model Architect* provides insight into the "transitional period for the

American architectural profession, when the roles and relationships of architects, builders, and clients had not yet been fully formulated."

If the conversations—texts—of Sloan's books stand out in Cowell's discussion of his published works, Daniel Reiff and Chris Szczesny-Adams fix upon Alice's desired pictures. With their chapters on little-known Enoch A. Curtis and Edward Townsend Mix, we move into the later nineteenth century. Reiff begins by canvassing the pages of *The American Architect and Building News* for the editors' recommendations of professional publications essential to the architect's library either for solutions to specific problems or for the general knowledge of the practicing architect. He then turns his attention to Curtis's practice, using a myriad of details about buildings documented to have been designed by Curtis to infer the contents of his professional library. Fully in keeping with the architectural age usually called eclectic, Curtis, informed by his pictorial sources, created building facades somewhere between pastiches and collages. Szczesny-Adams traces the professional path of Edward Townsend Mix from bookish old New Haven to nascent Milwaukee, where he became a leading architect. She uses a collection of twenty-one books owned by the architect and now at the Milwaukee Public Library to explain how Mix arrived at his distinctive style. Where Curtis looked back to the cities of the East, Mix drew on English and especially French sources as key elements in his design process.

Back in Philadelphia, Gothicist Henry A. Sims was accumulating his own, unsystematic library before the nation's centennial celebration. Michael Lewis concerns himself with how Sims used his sources. A lively assessment of this unusual collection reminds us that not all architects at the time read—or collected—the same books; that not only books but magazines were prime sources of architectural pictures and conversations; that, speaking of pictures, photo collections such as those of Sims and H. H. Richardson were as important as bound volumes; and, speaking of conversations, not all of them were accessible to an English-reading practitioner. The texts of German books, especially, were slighted in favor of their illustrations. Lewis provides context for the careers of Curtis and Mix. His characterization of how architects of the first half of the nineteenth century differed from those of the post–Civil War era in the way they used, or copied from, the works in their libraries—whole buildings were appropriated by the former, whereas the latter limited "copyism" to "incidental details"—seems a key to understanding the historicism of the earlier period as opposed to the eclecticism of the later one.

Among the more prolific collectors of professional publications in the years spanning the turn of the twentieth century was Maine's John Calvin Stevens. Earle Shettleworth traces the continuous growth of that collection from its birth after the Civil War in the Portland office of Francis H. Fassett to the late years of Stevens's life during the Great Depression. Stevens's reputation rests on his works in the Shingle Style and the English Colonial Revival, and the weight of his four-hundred-volume library—now preserved at the Maine Historical Society in Portland—clearly reflects those stylistic tracks, although he did find room for Louis Sullivan's *System of Architectural Ornament*. His contributions to the bookish life did not stop at collecting, however, for he supplied the lively pictures that illustrated the *Examples of American Domestic Architecture*, which he copublished during his brief partnership with Albert Winslow Cobb. And he, like Bertram Grosvenor Goodhue, turned his hand to the design of ornamental initials and bookplates as well.

In the early years of Goodhue's career, James O'Gorman finds a man whose energies were divided between his work as a designer of buildings and that of an illustrator as well as designer of books, typeface, and bookplates. Where specialists in the history of one or the other of these métiers have so often discussed them as separate, this chapter makes an attempt to join them. Goodhue's evolution in architecture from Puginesque Gothicist to protomodernist found a parallel development in his book work. And as a gifted draftsman he was capable in either realm of making pictures to warm Alice's heart. His death at a relatively young age leaves us to ponder the possible climax of his bifurcated career.

In contrast, the long career of Frank Lloyd Wright led to a number of climaxes. His life is much studied, but there is still room for conversations about his reading and the impact it may have had. Elaine Harrington contributes to that discussion by walking us through Wright's literary interests as a young man in Oak Park. He not only read voraciously; he illustrated and helped print William C. Gannett's *The House Beautiful* of 1896–97, and he was continually occupied with providing suitable settings for books and reading not only in his own home but in those of his clients as well. James O'Gorman returns with a brief essay that shows how a short story by Herman Melville, whom Wright listed in his autobiography as someone he had read, describes the kind of domestic environment that Wright was to make his ideal. This case study points to the fact that Wright's early career—despite rhetoric to the contrary—was well bedded in the nineteenth-century context.

The paper on Charles Sumner Greene by Edward Bosley and Anne Mallek closes this collection. With his brother Henry Mather Greene, Charles produced some of the finest domestic architecture of the early twentieth-century Arts and Crafts movement. The content of his library ranged broadly over publications on Japanese architecture, arts, and crafts, as one might expect, but went on to include books on the history and spirit of the Japanese people. The same inclusiveness marked his library in general. As the authors write, it "encompassed science, aesthetics, religion, the building arts, and—to a more modest degree—literature." As he grew older, works on religion and mysticism came to occupy his shelves, and one, Claude Bragdon's *The Beautiful Necessity: Seven Essays on Theosophy and Architecture*, connected inspiration to building. Greene, like Henry Sims before him and many others, augmented his books with periodicals. In the early years of the twentieth century he read and annotated *The International Studio*, an American descendant of an English journal dedicated to the spirit of William Morris and early modern movements in Europe. As the authors show, Greene drew heavily from the pictures and conversations in his library for forms and ideas in his work. And, as the chapters gathered here seem to suggest, the broader the architect's literary perusal, the richer his achievement.

As did our previous volume, this collection takes us from the drafting room through the looking glass into the world where print culture and architecture intersect. Both volumes are intended as guides for the investigation of that world, guides along a little-explored mode of access to architectural history which enriches our understanding of the creative context. In fact, since both volumes demonstrate a variety of approaches to this broad subject, we do not suggest that any one of the essays presented here is definitive; what we do hope is that the pictures we have provided will generate further conversations about the literary input and its relationship to the creative output of architects' careers, conversations that may include, as part of our national heritage, the preservation of the material world of architects' books as well as the physical world of architects' buildings.

KENNETH HAFERTEPE
JAMES F. O'GORMAN
Waco, Texas, and Windham, Maine

NOTES

1. Kenneth Hafertepe and James F. O'Gorman, eds., *American Architects and Their Books to 1848* (Amherst: University of Massachusetts Press, 2001).

2. A. and A. W. Pugin, *Examples of Gothic Architecture*, vol. 2 (London, 1836). The plate is signed "A. W. Pugin Invent." Cf. figure 8.8.

3. In this he was following in the footsteps of A. J. Davis. See Mary N. Woods, *From Craft to Profession* (Berkeley: University of California Press, 1999), 83–84, 209.

4. John Calvin Stevens II and Earle G. Shettleworth Jr., *John Calvin Stevens: Domestic Architecture, 1890–1930* (Portland, Maine: Greater Portland Landmarks, 1990), 5. See also Shettleworth's chapter in this collection.

5. James F. O'Gorman, "An 1886 Inventory of H. H. Richardson's Library, and Other Gleanings from Probate," *Journal of the Society of Architectural Historians* 41 (May 1982): 150–55. Richardson's collection is now housed in the Loeb Library, Graduate School of Design, Harvard University.

AMERICAN ARCHITECTS AND THEIR BOOKS, 1840–1915

I

DOWNING'S READINGS—AND READINGS OF DOWNING

Kenneth Hafertepe

A. J. Downing was one of the most influential American architectural writers of the nineteenth century, setting the pattern, so to speak, for a generation or more of books aimed at American builders and their potential clients. Though many have hailed him as an arbiter of American taste and as a prophet with honor, others have castigated him as an elitist masquerading as a man of the people. Such assessments have drawn on Downing's own writings, the writings of his nineteenth-century competitors, and the architectural treatises that influenced him. I suggest that the method of Downing scholars has fallen short in situating Downing and his works in the context of American and British cultural history. A closer analysis of the books that he read, the ideas that he found inspiring, and the ideas that he rejected, shows that he found inspiration in Enlightenment aesthetic philosophy, as had Thomas Jefferson, Benjamin Henry Latrobe, and Charles Bulfinch before him. Further, I examine the issue of his influence on readers: how were his works received, and what did readers get out of them?

* * *

The career of A. J. Downing as an author, architect, and tastemaker was remarkably brief but also remarkably fruitful. He published his first book, *A Treatise on the Theory and Practice of Landscape Gardening, Adapted to North America*, in 1841, when he was twenty-five years old. Although largely devoted to landscape gardening, the book focused a later chapter on rural residences. The success of this volume was such that he followed it the next year with *Cottage Residences*, which was specifically devoted to picturesque houses and their rural and suburban settings. His continued interest in gardens and orchards led to the publication of *The Fruits and Fruit Trees of America* in 1845. The next year he undertook the editorship of a journal, *The Horticulturist, and Journal of Rural Art and Rural Taste*, a task he continued until his death in 1852. His most fully developed consideration of the American house came in 1850, with *The Architecture of Country Houses*. Two years later Downing was dead at age thirty-seven. Selections of his writings from *The Horticulturist* were published in 1853 under the title *Rural Essays*. Numerous editions of his books appeared after his death, a testament to the continued popularity of his architectural writings.[1]

Downing harbored ambitions to produce a volume on landscape gardening and rural residences from an early age, as has been noted by most of the leading Downing scholars: George B. Tatum, William H. Pierson Jr., Jane B. Davies, and, most recently, David Schuyler. In December 1838, when he had recently turned twenty-three, Downing wrote to the New York architect Alexander Jackson Davis: "I am at present busily engaged in preparing a work for the press on Landscape Gardening and Rural Residences with the view of improving if possible the taste in these matters in the United States. My friend, R. Donaldson, Esq., has informed me that he has mentioned my name to you and that you were so kind as to offer to show me any work, views or plans in your possession which might be of any service to me."[2]

This oft-quoted letter to Davis emphasizes the pragmatic and visual character of Downing's enterprise. It suggests that his interest was not in great works of architecture from ages past but in the contemporary architectural scene, as could be found in the current projects of A. J. Davis. Moreover, the letter suggests the degree to which his writings were inspired by the Hudson River estates of wealthy friends such as Donaldson, as well as by the works of talented architects such as Davis.

Davis had worked with Robert Donaldson on his Hudson River estate, developing plans for a new house but ultimately remodeling an earlier house and designing a new gate lodge in the Gothic style. Downing would have been familiar with the image of the "Gate-house in the Rustic Cottage Style" that Davis had illustrated in his book *Rural Residences*, a lavish 1837 publication featuring hand-colored engravings of Davis's own work (figure 1.1). Davis's unbuilt design for a new Gothic villa for Donaldson would also have been of great interest to the youthful Downing (figure 1.2). In the images of both the gate lodge and the main house, Downing would have

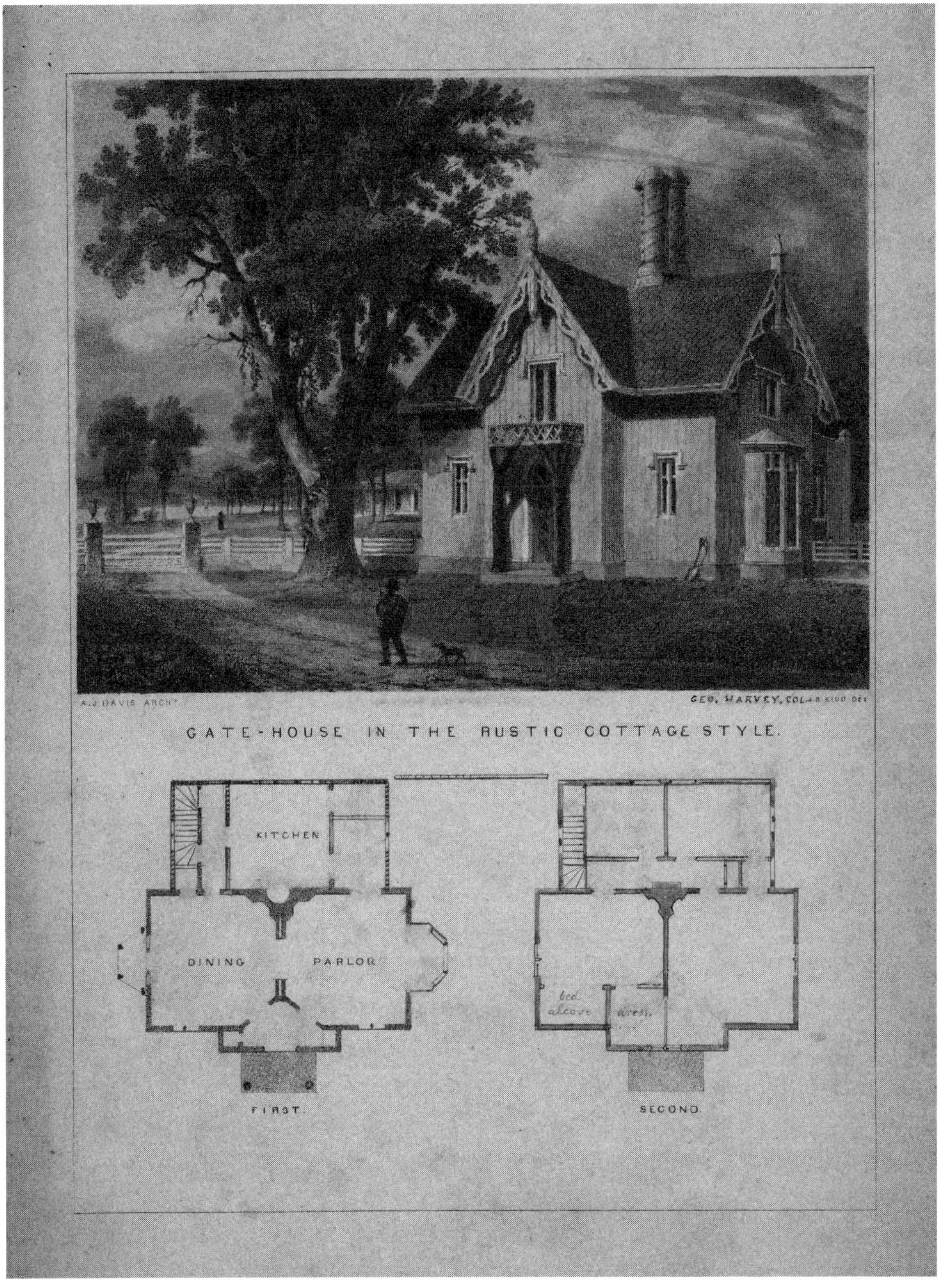

FIG I.1 "Gate-house in the Rustic Cottage Style." From A. J. Davis, *Rural Residences* (1837).

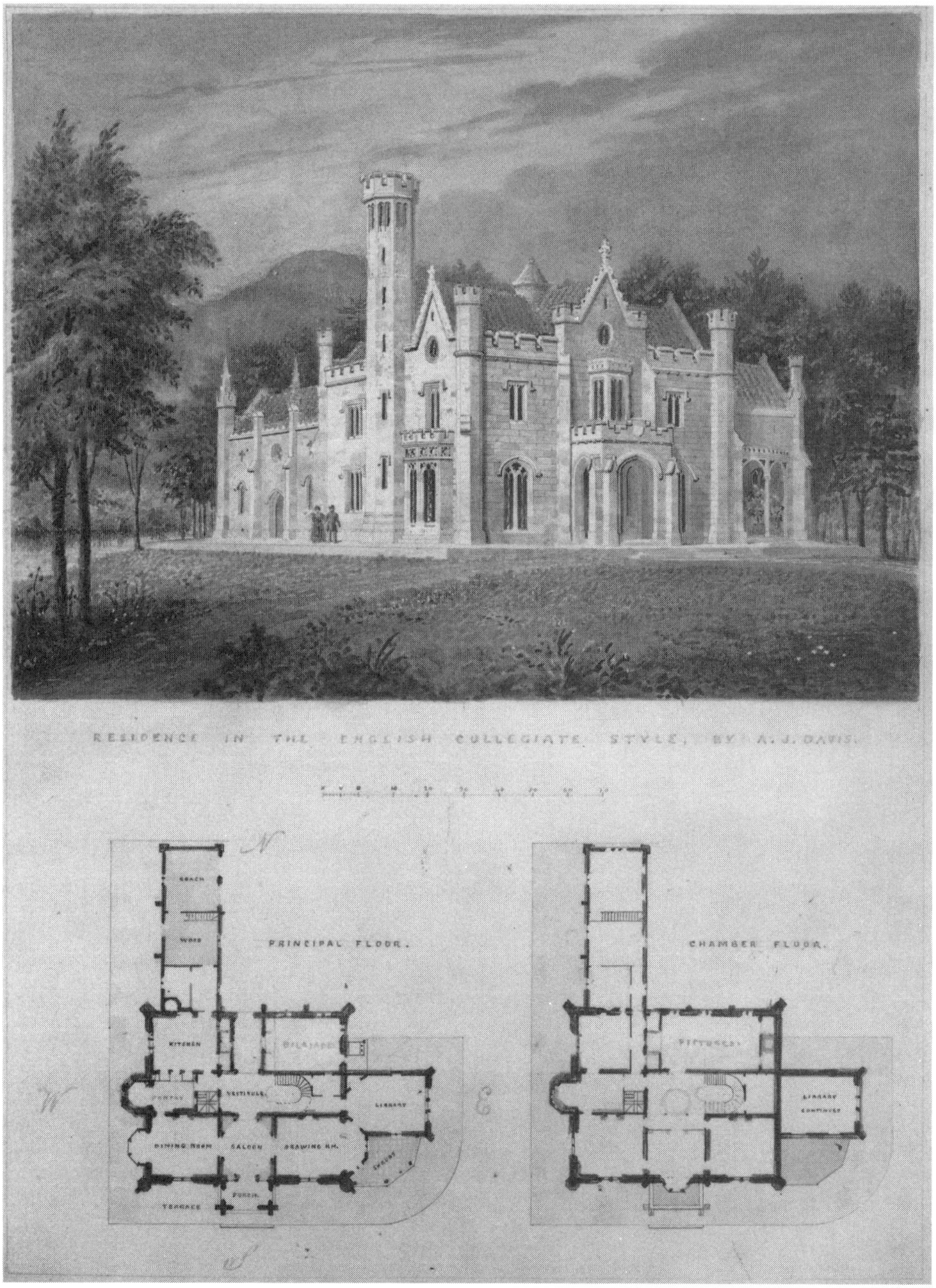

FIG I.2 A. J. Davis, Villa for Robert Donaldson, Fishkill Landing, N.Y., 1834 (project). Watercolor, ink, and graphite on paper, The Metropolitan Museum of Art.

noted Davis's advocacy of the newly fashionable Gothic Revival style and his careful attention to the landscape setting of these buildings in the Hudson River Valley. The studied asymmetry and Gothic detailing of the main house reflects a historically informed view of architecture, whereas the board-and-batten walls and steeply pitched gables of the gatehouse anticipate the cottages and farmhouses that Downing was to recommend for readers of more moderate means than Donaldson.[3]

Yet Downing's circle did not consist only of elites and those who aspired to the elite. He also maintained a collegial relation with important American scientists such as John Torrey, professor of natural history at the University of the City of New York. Torrey was president of the Lyceum of Natural History in New York City, and in 1835 he had discussed with A. J. Davis the idea of a building for the lyceum. Indeed, Torrey may also have been the first to make Downing aware of Davis. He was also one of the earliest admirers of Downing's architectural efforts. In 1839, well before the start of Downing's publishing career, Torrey was thinking of building a house for himself. Though he had known A. J. Davis for several years, he decided to turn not to the professional architect Davis but to the young amateur Downing, who had just finished his own house on the grounds of his botanical garden in Newburgh (figure 1.3). "When I saw it last summer," Torrey wrote to

FIG 1.3 A. J. Downing House, Newburgh, N.Y., 1838–39. From Downing, *A Treatise on the Theory and Practice of Landscape Gardening* (2nd ed., 1844).

his fellow scientist Joseph Henry, "it suited my notions entirely, and now that it is done, I think I shall not change my opinion. I should like to copy the plan very nearly, and shall borrow Mr. D's drawings." Though Torrey did not build a house, his letter is telling on several accounts—that Torrey had visited Downing's house, that it had appealed to him, that he desired to copy it, and, most intriguingly, that Downing had done his own drawings for it.[4]

Torrey also encouraged Downing in his career as a naturalist and landscape gardener and as an author on those subjects. In November 1837 the twenty-two-year-old Downing wrote to Torrey that he was planning a volume on "landscape gardening and the improvement of country residences. There is a great want of something in this way felt in this country, and great groping in the dark in the absence of it." He requested that if Torrey saw "anything in the way of books calculated to assist me, pray oblige me by laying violent hands on it." Downing observed that he could not "find a copy of Loudon's *Arboretum Brittanicum* in this country." This letter not only shows that Downing was planning a work on landscape gardening and architecture more than a year before his oft-quoted letter to Davis but also shows the importance of books to Downing's literary enterprise. Moreover, Downing was already well aware of the works of John Claudius Loudon, the Scottish-born gardener, author, and editor. Indeed, Torrey had encouraged Downing to correspond with European naturalists such as Loudon and John Lindley.[5]

Almost all recent scholarship acknowledges the formal influence of Loudon upon Downing—that is, the specific pattern book plans and the general mode of presentation—but fails to consider the philosophical impact of Loudon. The Downing-Loudon connection is critical, as it was through Loudon's works that Downing was introduced to the aesthetic philosophy of Archibald Alison and other Enlightenment philosophers. Alison, like earliest Enlightenment philosophers such as Francis Hutcheson, David Hume, and Henry Home (known as Lord Kames), described two categories of beauty; absolute (or intrinsic) beauty, which is formal and perceived by an innate sense of beauty, and relative beauty, which is comparative and requires use of the rational faculty. Alison added a third category, however: associations, which earlier philosophers would have considered under relative beauty. Alison argued that random images or ideas could inspire a train of related ideas. Earlier, David Hume had suggested that associations were the organizing principle of consciousness, the "cement of the universe," but Alison linked associations with the imagination and with the creative impulse. At the same time, he insisted that associations were only a tertiary form of beauty, and that they might actually distract from the more fundamental categories.[6]

Alison, like Hutcheson, Hume, and Kames, had no practical experience in architecture or the other arts. But John Claudius Loudon blended Alison's philosophy with the picturesque principles of Sir Uvedale Price, author of *Essay on the Picturesque* (1794). Loudon had apprenticed to an Edinburgh landscape gardener at age fifteen but also took classes at the university, thus blending the practical and the intellectual in a way that was to be reflected in his books. Loudon's most influential book was the *Encyclopaedia of Cottage, Farm and Villa Architecture*, but his *Architectural Magazine*, founded in 1834, also found its way to American readers. Loudon took the sometimes diffuse ideas of Alison and distilled them into three principles: fitness, expression of the end in view, and expression of some particular architectural style. The principle of fitness covered the gamut of functional issues, from solidity of construction to the arrangement of interior spaces. The expression of the end in view meant that a building should not hide the nature of the construction and should express its particular use, its purpose. The expression of style dealt with two types of beauty: "universal and inherent," which were present in all styles, and "historical or accidental," which varied from style to style and included the associations of a style. Such a theory had no bias toward any particular architectural style, but the designs that Loudon published made clear that he admired the beauties of the Gothic style (figure 1.4). Loudon also had a strong egalitarian impulse; taking seriously the notion that all people deserved a house that was neat and decent, he published designs for smaller houses as well as for elaborate town houses and country estates (figure 1.5).[7]

The principles of Alison and Loudon informed Downing's *Treatise on the Theory and Practice of Landscape Gardening*. No more than five pages into the *Treatise*, Downing was quoting Archibald Alison to the effect that in formal gardens men perceive the beauty of form and human design, whereas natural gardens avoid evidence of human designs in order to create the higher beauty of expression. Moreover, the chapter on "Rural Architecture" was clearly indebted to Loudon, although Downing dealt less extensively with fitness than did Loudon, stating simply that fitness related to the "comfort and convenience" of a home. Nor was his discussion of "expression of purpose" as complicated as Loudon's, for which American readers could be grateful. Ignoring the Scot's precepts about expressing structure and interior spaces, Downing contended that the "architectural character" of a building should distinctly point out "the particular use or destination for which the edifice

FIG 1.4 Ebenezer Trotman, "A Villa in the Latest Style of Pointed Architecture." From John Claudius Loudon, *Encyclopaedia of Cottage, Farm and Villa Architecture* (1833).

is intended." With regard to the expression of architectural style, Downing wrote that a rural style should be evaluated on the basis of its intrinsic beauty, its associations, its fitness for country life, and its suitability to its site. The first two categories relate to Loudon's "intrinsic" and "historical" beauties, but Downing went beyond Loudon in insisting on a style suited to country life and to the particularities of its natural setting. Having said this, Downing provided no further explanation of any of the categories but quickly moved on to discuss the relative merits of "classic" versus "romantic" or "picturesque" styles. Even though the quotation from Alison and a brief history of natural gardens were trimmed from later editions—helping to obscure this important source for Downing—Loudon and Alison had been formative influences on the young author.[8]

Downing returned to the subject and made some refinements to his thinking in *Cottage Residences*. He explained that fitness and expression of purpose appeal to the reason, and that expression of style appeals to the imagination. Intrinsic beauty, he noted, derives from beauty of form, and associations from "the sentiment associated with certain modes of building long prevalent in any age or country." Among the intrinsic characteristics of beauty were "Unity," which was essentially unity of style, and "Uniformity" and "Symmetry," one referring to "artistical regularity"

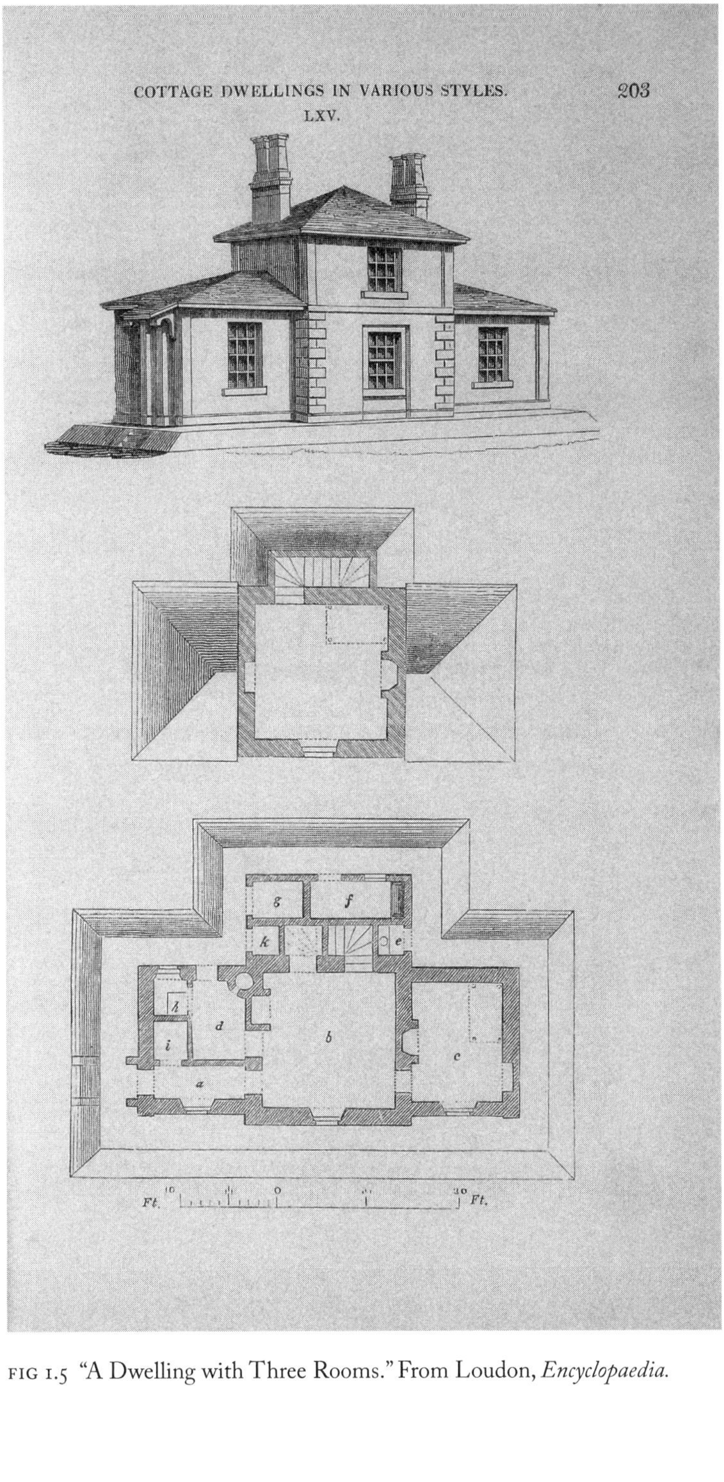

FIG 1.5 "A Dwelling with Three Rooms." From Loudon, *Encyclopaedia.*

and the other to "artistical irregularity." While symmetry might not seem to be described by "artistical irregularity," Downing was attempting to place informal, romantic houses and gardens on a footing equal to classical houses and gardens. This was analogous to his argument in the *Treatise* that formal gardens reveal the design of men, while natural gardens hide the hand of man to achieve greater expressiveness. Associations he again linked to "the *sentiment* of architecture": that is, the emotive and the imaginative.[9]

Downing was by no means the first American to embrace Enlightenment aesthetic principles; indeed, his significance may be said to be that he was one of the last to embrace them. Among his most notable forerunners in American aesthetic thinking informed by Enlightenment principles was Thomas Jefferson. William H. Pierson Jr. drew a parallel between Jefferson and Downing, based upon their mutual love of the American landscape, love of country life, and disdain for cities and industrialization. While all these parallels are true, they have little to do with how one would design a building or evaluate its beauty. Rather more fundamental to Jefferson's philosophy of design was his belief that all men were endowed by their creator with an innate sense of beauty and that anyone, regardless of the sharpness of his or her reasoning skills, had the capacity to detect a building that was poorly proportioned or had too little or too much ornament. At the same time, Jefferson acknowledged that other aspects of architectural criticism—particularly with regard to planning and structure—did require the use of the rational faculty. Downing's nod to intrinsic beauty, based as it was on uniformity and symmetry, was the philosophical principle that allied him most closely to Jefferson.[10]

The points where Loudon and Downing diverged from Jefferson were the expression of fitness and the importance of associations. Jefferson certainly approved of fitness as an aesthetic criterion, and Loudon's "universal and inherent" beauty was simply a recasting of absolute beauty as promoted by Kames and a variety of other Scottish philosophers. But Jefferson embraced the expression of fitness only to the degree that it reflected structural integrity and spatial rationality—not to the point where chimneys express comfort and domesticity or the Gothic style the presence of an idealistic owner. Jefferson was an admirer of Francis Hutcheson and especially of Lord Kames, but he never owned a copy of Alison's *Essays* and had little use for the concept of associationism as a design tool or as a tool of criticism.

The point here is not that Downing was directly influenced by Jefferson's aesthetic thought but that the two men shared certain aesthetic beliefs typical of the Enlightenment. Nor should one use evidence of agreement in aesthetic philosophy to assume that there was a similar concord in political philosophy: Enlightenment aesthetic principles also informed the thought of Timothy Dwight, president of Yale College and a rock-ribbed Federalist. In describing the stone walls that bounded many New England farms, Dwight flatly stated that "a great deal of what we call beauty arises from the fitness of means to their end. This relative beauty these enclosures certainly possess, for they are effectual, strong, and durable." He found such walls "neat and agreeable," presenting to the mind "the image of tidy, skillful, profitable agriculture, and promis[ing] to me within doors the still more agreeable prospect of plenty and prosperity."[11]

The opposite of neat and tidy farmsteads Dwight saw as evidence of a lack of industry, and this criticism Downing approvingly quoted in "The Moral Influence of Good Houses," published in *The Horticulturist* in February 1848. Dwight had suggested that "uncouth, mean, ragged, dirty houses constituting the body of any town will regularly be accompanied by coarse, groveling manners. The dress, the furniture, the mode of living, and the manners will all correspond with the appearance of the buildings and will universally be in every such case of a vulgar and debased nature." A straightforward political reading of Downing's use of Dwight would be that the snobbish Downing was endorsing the ideas of a conservative social critic. Dwight was enough of a democrat, however, to believe that exposure to neat and beautiful houses would inspire imitation and ultimately improve the manners and the mode of living of all people. Indeed, Dwight was praised by no less a progressive than J. C. Loudon himself: the Scot approved the "masterly manner" with which Dwight demonstrated "the influence of architecture on taste and morals." Downing may well have been introduced to Dwight via Loudon.[12]

Between the publication of *Cottage Residences* in 1842 and *The Architecture of Country Houses* in 1850, there was a distinct shift in Downing's aesthetic philosophy. William H. Pierson Jr. has suggested that this shift was the result of his reading of Ralph Waldo Emerson. And, indeed, we have the testimony of Fredrika Bremer that when she visited Downing and his wife Caroline in October 1849, they introduced her to the writings of Emerson, with which she was "charmed and elated." Pierson found several points of connection between Downing and Emerson: a mutual interest in the relationship between nature and beauty; a shared view that nature is a reflection of a higher—that is, a divine—beauty; an emphasis on self-reliance and the sanctity of the individual; and a high moral tone.[13]

Moreover, there is at least one parallel phrasing between Emerson's seminal essay "Nature" and Downing's *Architecture of Country Houses*. Where Emerson proclaimed that "particular natural facts are symbols of particular spiritual facts," Downing, in the midst of a discussion of twisted pillars, stated that "every outward material form is a symbol or expression of something which is not matter, and which, rightly understood, gives us the key to the power with which that form, immediately and without reflection, acts upon the sense of beauty." Neither as concise as Emerson nor as categorical, Downing was nevertheless flirting with Emersonian dualism, though he linked the more familiar term "expression" with the transcendental term "symbol" and did not name that which matter symbolizes: spirit.[14]

Yet Pierson's parallel, based on self-reliance, does not stand up to a close scrutiny of his own evidence. He quoted Emerson's desire that American artists—by which he meant architects—should study their own climate, and the needs and manners of the American people, to create a house fitted for this country. Downing, however, was on a completely different tack, insisting that a house should be adapted to the climate of a particular region (he specified the eastern and northern states as opposed to the mid-Atlantic and southern states) as well as to the expression of individual character. Emerson the individualist was here promoting the idea of an American national style; Downing the pragmatist was promoting regionalism and individualism.

Another, more likely source for this shift in Downing's philosophy may have been his exposure to the works of John Ruskin, whose first writings on aesthetic philosophy were published in Loudon's *Architectural Magazine*. In the 1849 edition of the *Treatise*, Downing cited Ruskin, noting that Hogarth considered a curving line to be the line of beauty but that Ruskin had suggested in *Modern Painters* that the curving line represented the infinite. Moreover, in the first chapter of *The Architecture of Country Houses,* Downing quoted Ruskin's definition of proportion as "the sensible relation of quantities" and symmetry as the symbol of abstract justice.[15]

Downing's introductory essay in *The Architecture of Country Houses*, "The Real Meaning of Architecture," devoted nine pages to "The True in Architecture." He wrote, "Although Beauty and Truth are not synonymous in art, all beauty, to be satisfactory, must be based on Truth." Downing's Truths boiled down to three sorts of expression: a residence should express that it is a house; it should express whether it is for town or country; and it should express that it is a house of a specific size, whether cottage, farmhouse, or villa.[16]

Downing also paid lip service to Ruskin in speaking of the truthful expression of materials. In *The Architecture of Country Houses* he stated that "when we employ stone as a building material, let it be clearly expressed; when we employ wood, there should be no less frankness in avowing the material." Yet as David Schuyler has recently pointed out, Downing lived in a frame house that was stuccoed to resemble stone (figure 1.3), and even in his later writings he prescribed the staining of cheaper wood to look like oak and the use of nonstructural ceiling ribs for stylish effect, to "convey the idea of vertical support" (figure 1.6). Downing also approved of the use of wallpapers known as fresco-papers, which made the walls seem to be divided into compartments or panels, each complete with a suitable cornice. Indeed, truth to materials was never high on his list of things to be expressed.[17]

Ultimately, for Downing, an endorsement of truthfulness did not translate into an endorsement of utilitarianism, as it did for the American sculptor and theorist Horatio Greenough. For Greenough, "Beauty is the promise of Function," and he

FIG 1.6 "Interior in a simple Gothic style." From A. J. Downing, *The Architecture of Country Houses* (1850).

praised the beauty of sailing ships for their "majestic form," devoid of applied ornamentation. Downing, however, believed that such thinking confused the useful and the beautiful: "A head of grain, one of the most useful of vegetable forms, is not so beautiful as a rose; an ass, one of the most useful of animals, is not so beautiful as a gazelle; a cotton-mill, one of the most useful of modern structures, is not so beautiful as the temple of Vesta; yet no one thinks of comparing them for utility." Clearly, Downing found it difficult to subscribe to the idealistic notions of Emerson and Greenough and offered a definition of architectural truth moored in the commonsense realism of Loudon and earlier Enlightenment philosophers.[18]

* * *

The one scholar who has explored the implications of Downing's admiration for Loudon is Dell Upton, in his *Winterthur Portfolio* article "Pattern Books and Professionalism." Upton, following George Hersey, linked Downing not only to Loudon but to Loudon's key influence, Archibald Alison. Upton's desire for a political reading of pattern books, however, forced him to attempt to dissociate Downing from Loudon, suggesting that Loudon was a radical and a nineteenth-century liberal and that Downing "reversed Loudon's technical aesthetic theory and its social implications." Upton offered two types of evidence in support of this assertion: from Downing's own writings, and from Downing's contemporaries.[19]

Upton began by comparing Downing's philosophy with that of Loudon. He observed that Downing postulated similar principles but "reversed Loudon's whole meaning" by claiming that formal beauty could be appreciated by the many, historical style only by the few. Upton conflated Downing's earliest books however—the *Treatise* and *Cottage Residences*—with *The Architecture of Country Houses*, which was published eight years after *Cottage Residences*. It contains the passages which Upton deemed to be a conservative reading of what he called "the social structure of taste."[20]

What Upton described, though, is not a politically based rejection of Loudon's aesthetic philosophy but a shift that reflected Downing's familiarity with earlier versions of Enlightenment aesthetic philosophy. To be sure, this shift could be given a political reading as well: it could be argued that Downing abandoned the progressive philosophy of Loudon to identify with a more aristocratic view of taste. Upton had suggested earlier that in eighteenth-century thought, "taste was inherent in the upper social classes, and whatever those people preferred was by definition good taste." Although it is probable that this belief *was* prevalent among the members of the upper class, it is the case that such notions cannot be found in eighteenth-century aesthetic philosophy. It is not surprising that Upton did not provide an eighteenth-century source for this particular definition of taste.[21]

The difficulty with Upton's thesis is that aesthetic philosophy in the eighteenth and nineteenth centuries was not politically driven. This is not to say that aesthetics could not be given a political spin in either a democratic or an elitist direction, but it was not inherent in the philosophy. Though an aristocrat himself, Anthony Ashley Cooper, Third Earl of Shaftesbury, was also a Whig and a supporter of Parliamentary prerogative and limitations on the monarchy. Shaftesbury claimed that a poor shepherd had as much possession of the beauty of a landscape as its wealthy owner. His insistence that a sense of beauty was innate in everyone set the stage for most British aesthetic philosophy for the next century and found continental admirers as well, notably Diderot and Rousseau. The philosophy of Hutcheson, Hume, and Lord Kames was egalitarian, because they contended that almost all people were born with a sense of beauty—although a lack of exposure to beauty, a lack of leisure time, or a lack of education would inhibit the development of the sense of beauty. Such lacks would apply particularly to the lower classes, but it must also be noted that all these philosophers agreed that a lifestyle of wantonness and opulence could just as easily warp the sense of beauty. They took great pains to insist that beauty was not a prerogative solely of the upper classes.[22]

Downing was quite clear that not all Americans were likely to build their own villas, nor did he think that the working classes should try to build large and impressive houses. He suggested instead that poorer Americans should build cottages, which could partake of absolute beauty, even if lack of ornament lessened their relative beauty. Upton argued that Downing thus handed the working and farming classes the short end of the stick, because relative beauty was where the aesthetic action was: "It was to the villas of the rich that Downing applied his elaborate exegeses of personal character; it was their prominence, their wealth, and their long family histories that entitled them to use those styles."

Upton's argument is problematic on several fronts. First, Downing was shifting over the course of the 1840s to emphasize associations and relative beauty less, and sensibility and absolute beauty more. As did Americans of such diverse political philosophies as Thomas Jefferson and Timothy Dwight, Downing believed that all people were endowed with a sense of beauty. His was by no means an acknowledgment or defense of an architecture based on social class.[23] Second, on the very page that Upton referenced, Downing asserted that the predominant character of a cottage must be simplicity: "There should be a convenient simplicity of arrangement, to facilitate the simple manner of living; an economical simplicity of construction, to suit the moderate means of the builder or owner; and a tasteful simplicity of decoration, to harmonize with the character of the dwelling and its occupants." Many Enlightenment philosophers, such as Lord Kames, had seen simplicity as a fundamental source of absolute beauty. Such thoughts were appealing to Thomas Jefferson, who, in lamenting the large and expensive houses erected by his fellow Virginians, wrote that "to give these symmetry and taste would not increase their cost. It would only change the arrangement of the materials, the form and combination of the members." Downing was doing nothing more than suggesting that all Americans deserved a modicum of convenience and economy and tasteful decoration.[24]

Moreover, while criticizing Downing's "elaborate exegeses of personal character," Upton ignored Downing's belief that architectural expressions could be negative as well as positive and his sharp criticism of architectural ostentation. Downing noted that "vices may be expressed in architecture as well as virtues; the worst part of our natures as well as the best." He specified that "a residence marked by gaudy and garish apartments, intended only to dazzle and impress others with the wealth or importance of the proprietor, will express pride and vanity instead of a real love of what is beautiful for its own sake." There was even an implicit criticism of reserving best rooms—such as a parlor—for purposes of show: "To delude others into the belief of dignity and grace on our part, while our actual life is one in mean apartments, expresses anything but honest sincerity of character."[25]

Finally, it is a misreading to suggest, as Upton did, that relative beauty is created only by ornament or by historical references. Lord Kames made very clear in his *Elements of Criticism* that the expression of fitness was a cause of relative beauty. This should remind us that relative beauty was an extremely broad category, covering any aspect of beauty that could be grasped by the rational faculty rather than by the sense of beauty.

Upton claimed that Downing's contemporaries recognized "the implications of his theory, and lampooned him mercilessly, even as they took over his designs and sometimes his aesthetic principles." As proof, Upton offers quotations from Solon Robinson, an agricultural journalist who became a rival of Downing's, and William Ranlett, the author of another pattern book. Although it is absolutely true that Robinson and Ranlett criticized Downing and claimed that he wrote for the few rather than the many, it is surprising that Upton did not recognize that Downing's critics were pursuing the "professional project" he had just described a few pages earlier. That is, they were asserting their professional abilities to design and to build, based on their philosophical and scientific knowledge, and denouncing Downing as a dilettante. Downing, after all, did not fit Upton's paradigm of builders defining themselves as professional architects through the pattern books they produced, for Downing was neither an architect nor a builder when he began to write his volumes; like his role model, Loudon, he was a gardener who became an author on landscape gardening and architecture.[26]

Perhaps even more surprising is Upton's unstated implication that Robinson and Ranlett were criticizing the conservative Downing but not the progressive Loudon. Indeed, their criticism of the theory of the expression of fitness and of style applies equally well to Loudon as to Downing and in fact provides confirmation that *they* read Downing to be emphasizing relative beauty, not absolute beauty as Upton suggested. They were thus criticizing Downing for the very position that Upton claimed he did not hold! Indeed, one could just as easily give this a politicized reading in which Robinson and Ranlett are the conservatives criticizing Downing for his association with the radical Loudon.

It seems clear that the self-interested criticism of competitors has only limited usefulness as historical evidence, yet the question of the precise extent of Downing's influence upon the vernacular landscape remains an open one. William Pierson attempted to assess Downing's influence by discussing a number of extant houses that are clearly drawn from the pages of Downing. This was certainly valid to the extent that it demonstrated direct influence on a limited number of examples, but it did not go very far in demonstrating that his influence was broad-based. Upton suggested that few of Downing's designs were copied literally and that "it is just a small exaggeration to say that the favorite examples are almost the only examples." The issue is somewhat confused by the fact that many of the most prominent examples of the Gothic Revival and other Picturesque styles were not drawn from Downing's works but illustrated in them: he featured houses by such well-known architects as A. J. Davis, John Notman, and Richard Upjohn, and his works were certainly seen by these architects as a useful form of promotion. For example, Upjohn's 1845 residence for Edward King of Newport was illustrated in *The Architecture of Country Houses* as "a Villa in the Italian Style" (figure 1.7). Downing's close association with professional architects, however, is hardly evidence that he was unread by the masses. He may have sought to upgrade the homes of all, but the immense popularity of his works may have subverted this aspect of his mission. Downing wanted to recognize and praise elite patrons who built in a manner of which he approved. As a result, he began to attract elite clients who wanted him

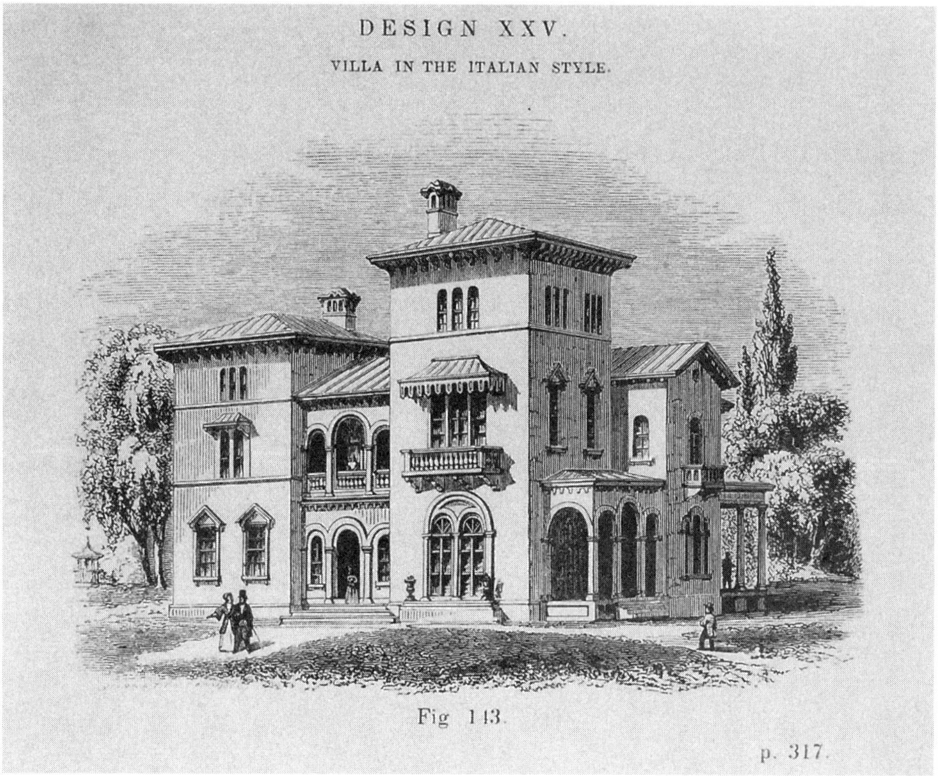

FIG 1.7 Richard Upjohn, Edward King residence ("Villa in the Italian Style"), Newport, R.I., 1845. From Downing, *The Architecture of Country Houses.*

to design their grounds and houses, a phenomenon that led him to associate with Calvert Vaux and open his own architectural practice. Without necessarily having planned it, he fulfilled the professional project that many architects had hoped for but only partially achieved.

* * *

Upton has made the strongest case that the influence of Downing's and other pattern books was sharply limited. He claimed that vernacular builders subverted Downing's advice by selecting only the particular motifs that either made a novel stylistic statement or accorded with previously held vernacular patterns. He compared Design I in *The Architecture of Country Houses* (figure 1.8) to a board-and-batten cottage in Kingston, New York, noting that the builder of the Kingston house followed Downing's floor plan closely but created a stripped-down version of the exterior by omitting the overhanging eaves, rafter brackets, and door and

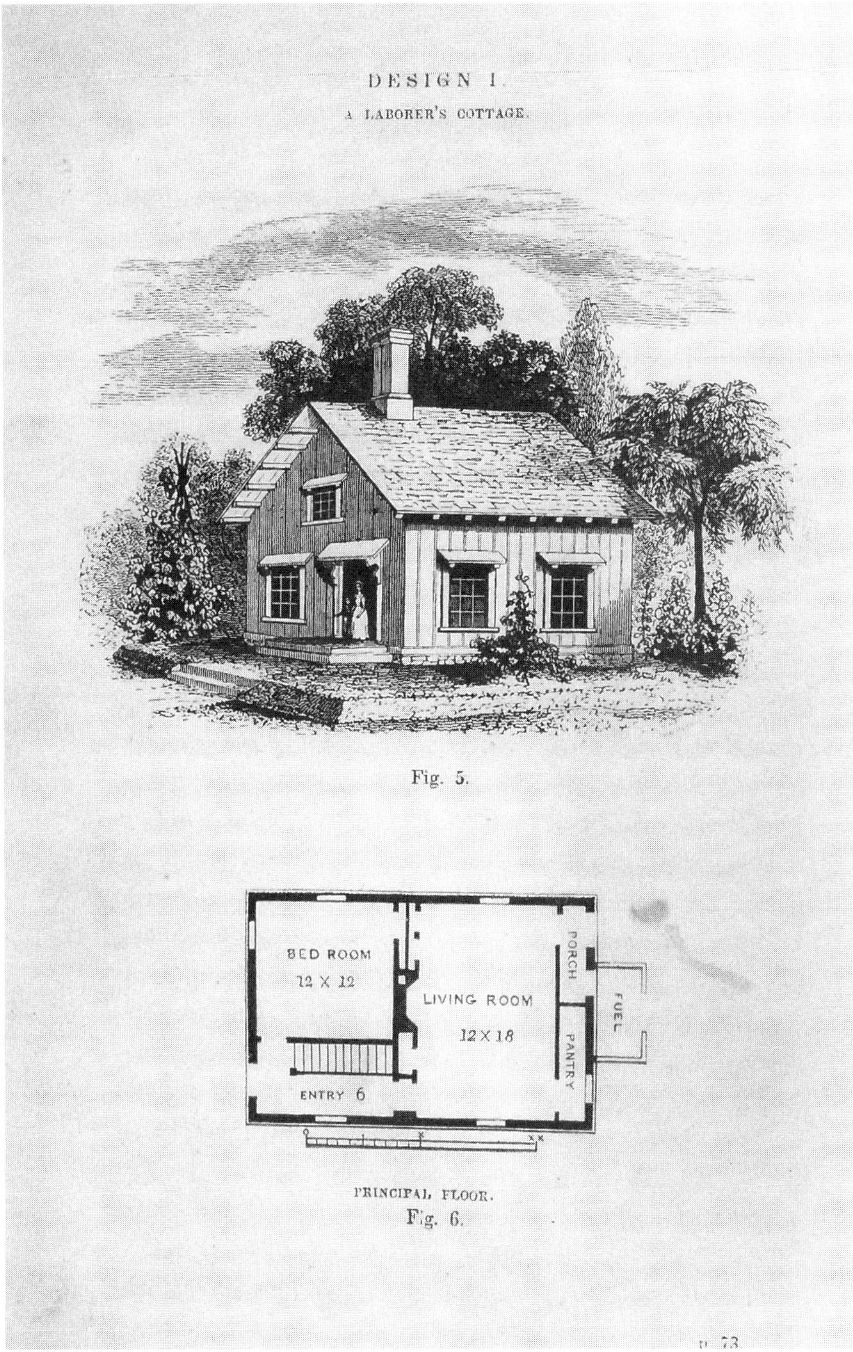

FIG 1.8 A. J. Downing, "A Laborer's Cottage," design 1. From *The Architecture of Country Houses.*

window frames. It is true that there is no expression of the roof structure and only rudimentary window frames, but Upton neglected to note the bracketed hood over the front door and that the vernacular builder embraced board-and-batten construction, which, in Downing's view, clearly expressed "the picturesqueness of wood." It is clear that the builder modified Downing's scheme, but his changes hardly represent a rejection of Downing's advice.[27]

To support his assertion that Downing's influence at the vernacular level was limited, Upton cited Susan Fenimore Cooper (daughter of the novelist James Fenimore Cooper) as writing that the rural Gothic and Elizabethan styles had failed to penetrate the New York countryside to any significant degree. Cooper's commentary about the architecture of Otsego County, New York, is actually far more nuanced than Upton suggested, and can serve as a critique not only of Upton's vernacular reading of Downing but also of Pierson's high-style, art-historical reading.

First, it must be noted that Upton failed to capture the precise meaning of Cooper's passage. She did not state that the Gothic style had failed to penetrate at all; she wrote that there were only a few examples. Nor did Upton mention that she was writing from one of them, Otsego Hall, an early house that had been Gothicized by her father, with the help of Samuel F. B. Morse, in 1834 and which therefore predated Downing. (figure 1.9). And, indeed, when Otsego Hall burned in 1852, Miss Cooper built a new and more fashionable house in the Gothic style which she named Byberry Cottage (figure 1.10). And Upton did not mention that her discussion of such houses was at the end of a brief history of the architecture of Otsego County, which was in fact a brief history of the *vernacular* architecture of Otsego County. She could write such a history because her book, *Rural Hours*, was not a travel book consisting of observations made on the fly but a sort of natural history of Otsego County, written by a resident.[28]

It was a county that had been settled by Anglo-Americans only a few decades earlier. Cooper noted that the Indian wigwam had become "only a tradition" and that the earliest Anglo settlers had built log cabins, which could range from miserable hovels to snug and cozy cottages. These, however, had been largely supplanted by houses of frame construction. She described a house with two second-story rooms over two on the first floor. Modern-day vernacularists would call this an I-house; she called it "the *shallow* order," which she characterized as a "lank and lean style." More ambitious locals would augment this basic form with an approximation of a Grecian portico, which she termed "the *shallow-ornate*." Next came a full-blown four-over-four, which she termed "the plain, straightforward style."

The most recent style was indeed the rural Gothic, of which she wrote: "The 'rural Gothic' and 'Elizabethan,' which have grown rapidly into favor about the suburbs of large towns, have scarcely as yet made any impression here. There are, probably, not more than half a dozen houses of the kind in the whole county." Her history allowed for the fact that some families were more traditional in taste and also for the fact that not every family rebuilt its house in every generation.[29]

At the same time, Cooper confirmed Upton's point that mid-nineteenth-century homeowners did tend to make additions to their houses. She observed that many houses in the plain, straightforward style "have a wing, sometimes two, but more frequently the addition is put up with an eye to convenience rather than symmetry, and a long, low building, containing the kitchen, wood-shed, &c., &c., projects from the rear." Upton correctly pointed out that such additions were not consistent with the Gothic style, but it must be further noted that they were not consistent with any formal style.[30]

Cooper's architectural history of Otsego County provides only limited support for Upton's point, but it is positively problematic for those trying to maintain a

FIG 1.9 Otsego Hall, the home of James Fenimore Cooper, Cooperstown, N.Y. Remodeled in the Gothic style in 1834. From *Memorial of James Fenimore Cooper* (1852).

FIG 1.10 Byberry Cottage, the home of Susan Fenimore Cooper, Cooperstown, N.Y., 1852. Photo ca. 1958. Historic American Buildings Survey, Library of Congress.

high-style reading of Downing's influence. In Susan Cooper's county, the works of Downing were competing not against the recent pattern books of Asher Benjamin and Minard Lafever—that is, against fairly sophisticated interpretations of the international Greek Revival style—but against vernacular options that had their roots in permutations of the Georgian house: bilaterally symmetrical, with a central passage, either two rooms over two or four rooms over four. Such vernacular houses had little to do with the recently fashionable Greek Revival, though the Grecian house usually shared with earlier Georgian houses the central passage plan or the related side-passage, two-thirds Georgian plan, in which the stair hall is to one side and provides access to rooms of living to just one side and often to the rear. Cooper may have been implying that Otsego County was just arriving at the point where the vernacular gives way to the high style, but she also showed respect for the traditional forms that had served earlier generations well.

Cooper's history also puts Downing in a different light from that of any other architectural writer or historian. It is clear that Downing was less concerned about the vernacular house in which his grandfather had lived than he was about the high-style house in which a grandson might live. His own history of American architecture was not strongly developed, as he preferred to base his designs less in recent history than in recent philosophy. To the degree that he had an architectural history, it was the architectural history of Europe, and it was a history more interested in regional styles than in subtle chronological distinctions. Cooper's history, however, reminds us as well that Downing was very much a creature of the eastern cities and suburbs. This is not to say that he did not think his advice relevant to those living well beyond the Hudson, but it is to say that the Hudson River Valley was his home turf and that his America was centered in the area between Boston and Washington, D.C.

The vernacular builder was probably almost never confronted with a stark choice between Greek and Gothic or, more broadly put, between classical and medieval styles; this is the weakness of the high-style view of Downing's influence. Paradoxically, the weakness of the Uptonian vernacular view of Downing's influence is Upton's implication that literal copies of Downing were the only test of that influence. In this regard, Upton remained too close to the high-style position, where the closeness of an imitation was often taken to be evidence of whether Downing was the source: the closer the imitation, the stronger the influence. But a more commonsense view has to be that there are many degrees of influence: copying ornamentation is probably the easiest and also the most superficial; copying the general form of a design is more difficult and also more fundamental; and copying a floor plan is more fundamental still and probably most expressive of the degree to which a Downing plan seemed to meet the needs of Americans in the mid-nineteenth century.

* * *

Downing himself believed that his books had achieved a broad influence, far more influence than he had initially hoped. He wrote to the botanist B. V. Darlington in 1846, "My different works have indeed been most kindly received by my country men—and I have in various parts of the country had the satisfaction of seeing what I believe few authors do see—my hints carried at once into execution." This statement appeared not in a public forum where it could serve as advertising but in a private letter to a colleague. A related form of influence documented by Upton was the degree to which Downing's plans and ideas were cribbed by his pattern book competitors. Upton found them copying not only stylish novelties such as cross gables and Gothic trim but even Downing's variations on the traditional New England central chimney plan. He further paired Gervase Wheeler's "Plain Timber Cottage Villa" in *The Architecture of Country Houses* with Lewis F. Joy's "Timber Villa in the Gothic Style," published just two years later. Downing's influence did not end with those who read only his books but often carried over to those who were reading the works of his imitators.[31]

In his recent biography of Downing, David Schuyler has offered other kinds of evidence of Downing's impact. One was the success of *The Horticulturist*, the journal that Downing published from 1846 until his death in 1852. In the first year of publication it had 2,000 paid subscribers, a number that certainly increased over the next six years. In those years Downing wrote thirty-three articles on architecture, of which twenty-seven discussed designs for residences. He also printed correspondence from admirers throughout the country.[32]

Other journals provide further evidence of Downing's impact. In 1846 *The Cultivator*, edited by Solon Robinson, published the Gothic cottage of Thomas H. Hyatt in Mount Hope, New York (figure 1.11). Hyatt reported that he had read and reread Downing's *Treatise on Landscape Gardening* and *Cottage Residences* "with so much interest and delight, and I trust with no little profit also." David Schuyler has pointed out that Hyatt paid particular attention to Design II from *Cottage Residences* (figure 1.12), but Hyatt's architect, Merwin Austin, also incorporated a kitchen ell that projected from one side of the house. Similarly, in 1848 the New York State Agricultural Society sponsored a competition for the design of a farm cottage; the winner, Mrs. Matilda Howard of Zanesville, Ohio, borrowed freely from Design V in *Cottage Residences*. Schuyler notes that Mrs. Howard reorganized the interior for practical reasons and added an extension, but he does not specify that it is a single side wing, a traditional way of expanding a rectangular block in the Northeast but also incorporated in designs for new houses in the mid-nineteenth century. Upton saw the use of such a side wing as a rejection of Downing's principles, and it certainly is a solution to housing utilitarian spaces that he never recommended. Yet this glass is more than half full: the main block of the house is perfectly Downingesque, and is clear evidence that Downing's designs could be (and were) integrated into a more vernacular mind-set.[33]

The most significant variance between Mrs. Howard and Downing—not noted by Schuyler—was in the plan (figure 1.13): Mrs. Howard liberated the kitchen, laundry, and storeroom from the basement, all rooms that Downing lit with windows that were little more than horizontal slits. Mrs. Howard shrank the width of the house from 45 feet to 40 feet but extended it to the rear. By so doing—and by reducing the size of the parlor, dining room, and library—she was able to fit a bedroom and a kitchen into the main block of the first floor. Where Downing had a single veranda wrapping around the room containing the library, Mrs. Howard had a 10-by-18 piazza opening off the library but another 6-by-20 piazza fronting the ell for more work-a-day purposes. Her dream kitchen included a bake oven, a dry sink, and a spacious pantry—all unthought-of by Downing—and within the ell she placed the washroom, bathroom (set aside specifically for bathing), dairy, ice

FIG 1.11 Merwin Austin, Elm-Wood Cottage (Thomas H. Hyatt, owner), Mount Hope, N.Y., 1845. From *The Cultivator*, n.s. 3 (1846).

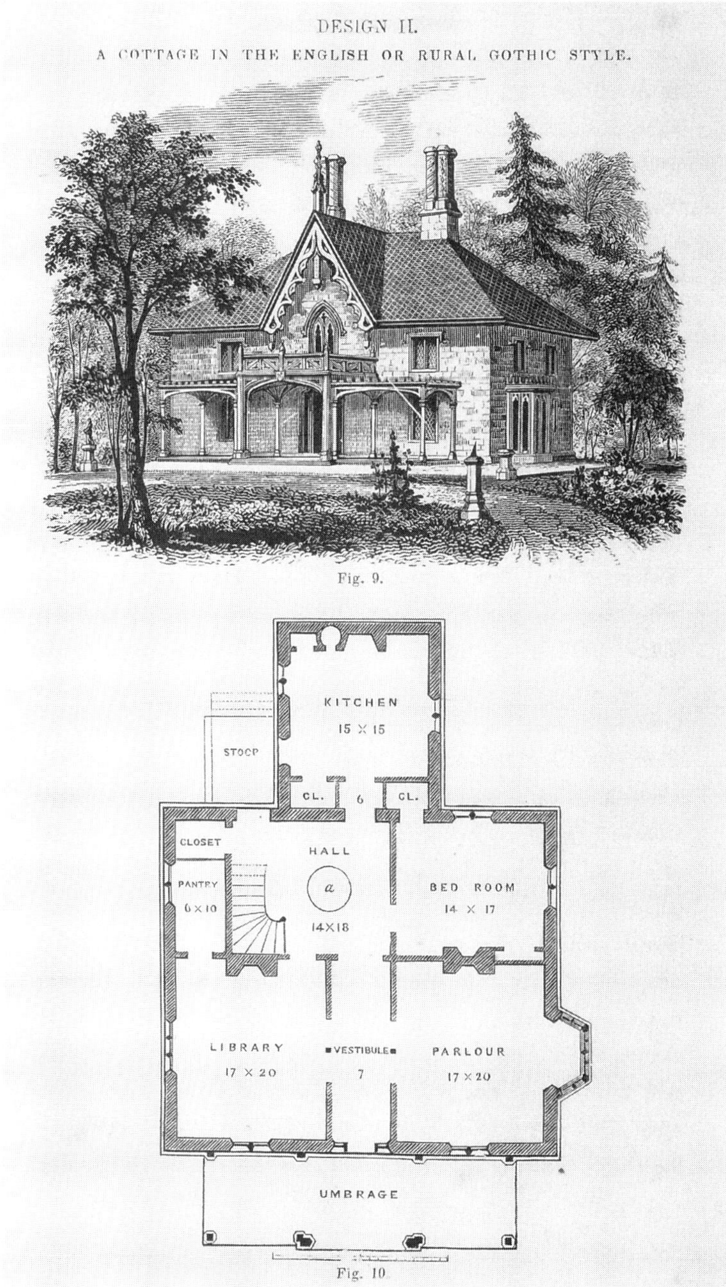

FIG 1.12 "A Cottage in the English or Rural Gothic Style," design 2. From A. J. Downing, *Cottage Residences* (1842).

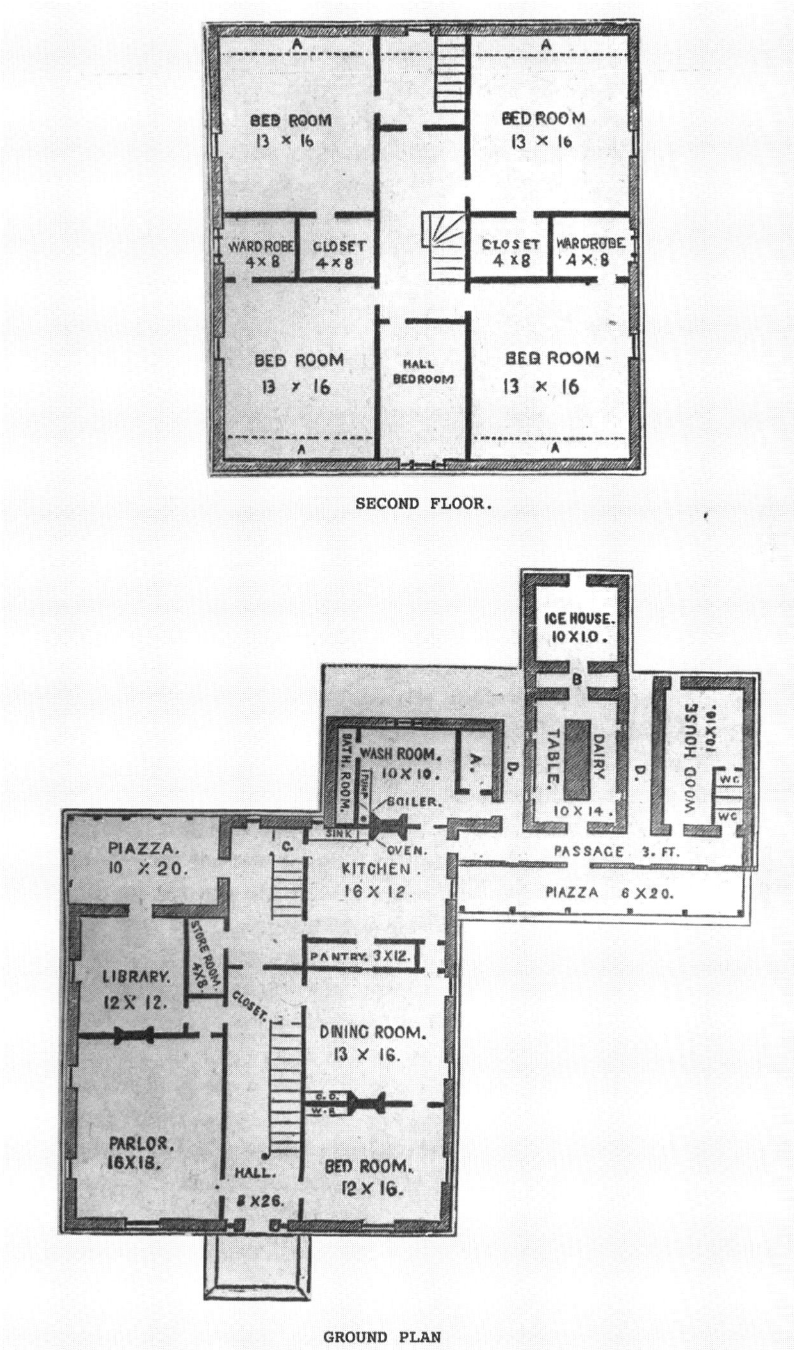

FIG 1.13 Mrs. Matilda S. Howard, plan of a farm cottage. New York State Agricultural Society, *Transactions* 7 (1848).

house, wood house, and two water closets replacing the traditional outhouse. Her expanded main block allowed not only for four sizable bedrooms upstairs but also for closets in each of them, a reflection of the ability of Americans by then to buy more clothes cheaply made in American mills.[34] Mrs. Howard's practical experience in running a household resulted in a house perfectly dependent on Downing for style but with a range of features undreamed of in Downing's philosophy.

* * *

Though the precise extent of Downing's influence may never be known, it was certainly substantial. But did his readers care whether he was attempting to be a democratic tastemaker, or would they have been as receptive to a Downing who was frankly aristocratic and who was simply showing Americans a style of life that most of them could never afford? It seems most likely that the style Downing promoted was more compelling to his readers than the theory. Images, after all, have a life of their own and need no theory to justify them. Yet those images and the words that accompanied them had to have some connection, some relevance to the life that Americans were then living; otherwise, Downing would not have succeeded as he did. Americans of the 1840s and 1850s did not necessarily wish to live inside a high-style architectural masterpiece, but they did hope that the styles and the principles that Downing espoused could be fitted into their own lifestyle. And Downing firmly believed—as had Loudon and Alison and Jefferson and Kames before him—that all persons had some sense of the beautiful inside them, and at least some of the reasoning ability needed to build with an eye toward fitness and an appreciation of the landscape in which they lived.

NOTES

1. George B. Tatum, "Andrew Jackson Downing, Arbiter of American Taste, 1815–1852" (Ph.D. diss., Princeton University, 1950); William H. Pierson Jr., *American Buildings and Their Architects*, vol. 2, *Technology and the Picturesque* (Garden City, N.Y.: Doubleday, 1976); Jane B. Davies, "Davis and Downing: Collaborators in the Picturesque," in *Prophet with Honor: The Career of Andrew Jackson Downing, 1815–1852*, ed. George B. Tatum and Elisabeth B. MacDougall (Philadelphia: Athenaeum of Philadelphia, Washington, D.C.: Dumbarton Oaks Research Library and Collection, 1989); and David Schuyler, *Apostle of Taste: Andrew Jackson Downing, 1815–1852* (Baltimore: Johns Hopkins University Press, 1996).

2. This letter of A. J. Downing to A. J. Davis, December 12, 1838, was long in the collection of Anthony N. B. Garvan, and has been quoted in Tatum, "Andrew Jackson Downing," 53–54; Pierson,

American Buildings and Their Architects, 2A: 351; Davies, "Davis and Downing," 81; and Schuyler, *Apostle of Taste*, 50–51.

3. On the Donaldson estate, often known as Blithewood, see Jane B. Davies, "Alexander J. Davis: Creative American Architect," in *Alexander Jackson Davis: American Architect 1803–1892*, ed. Amelia Peck (New York: Metropolitan Museum of Art/Rizzoli, 1992) 15–16; Pierson, *American Buildings and Their Architects* 2:298–307.

4. Joseph Torrey to Joseph Henry, 18 September 1839, Joseph Henry Private Papers, Smithsonian Institution Archives.

5. I have discovered a group of thirty-six letters from A. J. Downing to John Torrey in the Torrey Papers, New York Botanical Garden Library. Quoted in this paragraph is the letter of 9 November 1837. See also the letters of 28 August 1833, 11 March 1834, 21 April 1834, 28 July 1834, and 29 December 1834. On the Lyceum proposal, see Richard G. Carrott, *The Egyptian Revival: Its Sources, Monuments, and Meaning, 1808–1858* (Berkeley: University of California Press, 1978), 69–70 and plate 99; and Peck, *Alexander Jackson Davis*, 52–53.

6. Archibald Alison, *Essays on the Nature and Principles of Taste* (London, 1790).

7. John Claudius Loudon, *Encyclopaedia of Cottage, Farm, and Villa Architecture* (London: Longman et al., 1833), 1106–15. On Alison and Loudon, see George L. Hersey, *High Victorian Gothic: A Study in Associationism* (Baltimore: Johns Hopkins University Press, 1972), 10–22. A more recent study notes that Loudon was also influenced by Lord Kames and David Hartley: see Melanie Louise Simo, *Loudon and the Landscape: From Country Seat to Metropolis, 1783–1843* (New Haven: Yale University Press, 1988), 25–26, 42, 101, 103, 114, 131.

8. A. J. Downing, *A Treatise on the Theory and Practice of Landscape Gardening* (New York: Wiley & Putnam, 1841), 13, 300–301.

9. A. J. Downing, *Cottage Residences* (New York: Wiley & Putnam, 1842), 19–33.

10. Pierson, *American Buildings and Their Architects*, 2:355–57; Kenneth Hafertepe, "An Inquiry into Thomas Jefferson's Ideas of Beauty," *Journal of the Society of Architectural Historians* 59 (June 2000): 216–31.

11. Timothy Dwight, *Travels in New England and New York* (1822; Cambridge, Mass.: Belknap Press of Harvard University Press, 1969), 1:272–73.

12. A. J. Downing, "The Moral Influence of Good Houses," *The Horticulturist* 2 (February 1848): 546; Dwight, *Travels*, 2:346–47; Loudon, *Encyclopaedia*, 1122. On Downing and Dwight, see Schuyler, *Apostle of Taste*, 92.

13. Pierson, *American Buildings and Their Architects*, 2:358–59; Fredrika Bremer to A. J. Downing, December 1849, in "Fredrika Bremer's Unpublished Letters to the Downings," ed. Adolph B. Benson, *Scandinavian Studies and Notes* 11 (1930–31): 52; Signe Alice Rooth, *Seeress of the Northland: Fredrika Bremer's American Journey, 1849–1851* (Philadelphia: American Swedish Historical Foundation, 1955), 59.

14. Stephen E. Whicher, ed., *Selections from Ralph Waldo Emerson* (Boston, 1957), 31; A. J. Downing, *The Architecture of Country Houses* (New York: D. Appleton, 1850), 346.

15. A. J. Downing, *A Treatise on the Theory and Practice of Landscape Gardening*, 2d ed. (New York, 1859), 54; Downing, *Architecture of Country Houses*, 10, 14; see also Roger B. Stein, *John Ruskin and Aesthetic Thought in America, 1840–1900* (Cambridge, Mass.: Harvard University Press, 1967), 51–53.

16. Downing, *Architecture of Country Houses*, 31.

17. Ibid., 35–36, 109, 183, 367, 383–84, 398; Schuyler, *Apostle of Taste*, 136–37.

18. Horatio Greenough, "American Architecture," *United States Magazine, and Democratic Review* 13 (August 1843): 206–10; Downing, *Architecture of Country Houses*, 8.

19. Dell Upton, "Pattern Books and Professionalism: Aspects of the Transformation of Domestic Architecture in America, 1800–1860," *Winterthur Portfolio* 19 (Summer/Autumn 1984): 126.

20. Ibid., 125.

21. Ibid., 120.

22. For a recent edition of Shaftesbury, see *Characteristics of Men, Manners, Opinions, Times*, ed. Lawrence E. Klein (Cambridge: Cambridge University Press, 1999). Kenneth Hafertepe, "The Enlightened Sensibility: Scottish Philosophy in American Art and Architecture" (Ph.D. diss., University of Texas, 1986), 1–75; and Hafertepe, "Inquiry into Thomas Jefferson's Ideas of Beauty," 216–31, esp. 217–19.

23. Upton, "Pattern Books and Professionalism," 126–27, citing Downing, *Architecture of Country Houses*, 43, 25.

24. Downing, *Architecture of Country Houses*, 43; Thomas Jefferson, *Notes on the State of Virginia* (Chapel Hill: Published for the Institute of Early American History and Culture, Williamsburg, Va., by the University of North Carolina Press, 1955), 152–53; Hafertepe, "Inquiry into Thomas Jefferson's Ideas of Beauty," 220.

25. Downing, *Architecture of Country Houses*, 24–25.

26. Upton, "Pattern Books and Professionalism," 127, 112–20.

27. Ibid., 141.

28. Ibid.; Susan Fenimore Cooper, *Rural Hours, by A Lady* (New York: G. P. Putnam, 1850) 384–85. Almost four decades later Cooper published a revised edition of *Rural Hours* (Boston: Houghton, Mifflin, 1887). Perhaps because Otsego County had moved far beyond the pioneer phase, she deleted her analysis of the county's architectural history. It is this edition that has been given a modern reprint (Syracuse, N.Y.: Syracuse University Press, 1968), so scholars seeking her architectural commentary must find an earlier edition. On Otsego Hall, see Ralph Birdsall, *The Story of Cooperstown* (Cooperstown, N.Y.: Arthur H. Crist, 1917), 234–36; for Byberry Cottage, see 304–5, 398–99. Cf. figures 4.8 and 4.9.

29. Cooper, *Rural Hours*, 380–85.

30. Ibid., 383; Upton, "Pattern Books and Professionalism," 133, 136.

31. A. J. Downing to B. V. Darlington, 12 October 1846, in Darlington Papers, New-York Historical Society; Upton, "Pattern Books and Professionalism," 117–18, 133–34.

32. Schuyler, *Apostle of Taste*, 107–9 and 130–34.

33. Ibid., 114–16.

34. On Matilda Howard, see Sally McMurry, *Families & Farmhouses in 19th Century America* (New York: Oxford University Press, 1988), 67–71, which places Mrs. Howard in the context of houses designed by progressive farmers.

11

OLIVER SMITH, HOUSEWRIGHT AND ITINERANT ARCHITECT

Ted Cavanagh

Historians of architectural practice emphasize two paths to becoming an architect in the United States of the nineteenth century: the "English" method of apprenticeship, and the "French" method of education.[1] There was a third source—the indigenous carpenter-builders. Without exaggeration, they made up the majority of the best-trained architects in the Antebellum period.[2]

Many carpenters taught themselves architecture. This remained an important route to becoming an architect throughout the nineteenth century, in fact, several master builders were early proponents of professionalism in architecture. But the "rise " to professional status is not the entire story.[3] Though historians often dismiss their declarations as arbitrary self-promotion, many biographies describe young men learning the building trade as carpenters before they decided to call themselves architects.[4] Yet many carpenters were cautious about claiming the latter title and showed consciousness of a considerable boundary.[5] And although it is true that carpenter-architects continued to operate as effective boundary crossers—partly because qualifications in building science were an essential and egalitarian entry into the newly established profession of architecture—the orientation was not all in the direction of "upward" mobility into the architectural profession. Especially on the frontier, the carpenter-architect's combined attributes of designer, draughtsman, and builder were essential. Still, they were effective architects by any measure of the time and, in this beginning period of national and architectural awareness, did much to advance a culture indigenous to the United States.

On the frontier, carpenter-architects were an integral part of a wide socio-economic record. Many historians regard the largely rural population of two hundred years ago as a unique incubator for capitalism.[6] Throughout the nineteenth century, rural people had an aptitude for organizing a mixed productive household economy and establishing networks of trade relations; these, in turn, were supported by itinerant tradesmen and peddlers who established patterns of commerce in the countryside. Gradually, and with increasing frequency in the 1850s, these networks of rural trade were co-opted by urban merchants (and architects), and the era of the city-based entrepreneur began.[7] Oliver Smith and his family were part of this trend, first as agricultural pioneers and house builders; then, at midcentury, Oliver and his brother Sheldon became itinerant architects on the rural frontier.

The writings of Asher Benjamin, Andrew Jackson Downing, Oliver Smith, and George Woodward demonstrate the rural basis for architecture in successive decades from the 1830s to the 1860s. In the preface to his *Practice of Architecture*, published in 1833, Asher Benjamin speaks plainly about his anticipated audience: "Those carpenters in country villages who aspire to eminence in their business, having no Architect to consult, are under the necessity of studying the science thoroughly and without a master."[8] The carpenter-architect Oliver P. Smith aspired to such eminence in unique and interesting ways. His career illustrates the architectural implications of working on the rural frontier: his own experiments in simplifying building construction are astonishingly inventive, and his record of the techniques of the radical vernacular being built around him is unusual if not unique among architectural books of his century.

An overview of books written before 1860 in Henry-Russell Hitchcock's bibliography, *American Architectural Books*, shows that roughly 30 percent of the titles deal with rural situations and subjects (very few with the urban or suburban).[9] Perhaps indirectly, the rural basis of architecture has been recognized in historical studies about the work of Andrew Jackson Downing and his campaign for the improvement of cottages and country houses.[10] In addition to Downing and his re-visioning of composition, form, and landscape, many other authors of building guides, pattern books, and farm journals introduced a progressive wave of scientific thinking into house organization and house construction.

In his book of 1865, George Woodward recognized the beginning of an urban focus to domestic architecture and argued that it represented a significant shift away from the architectural preoccupations of the early nineteenth century. He heralded the end of the concern for "rural art" and repositioned its values to apply to housing in suburban situations for the urban-based architect. A generation after Andrew Downing had initiated the project of improving the domestic architecture of the United States, George Woodward declared that the case had been made and the situation was improving. He recognized the existence of an established entrepreneurial and domestic architecture based in the rural United States on the very first page of *Woodward's Country Homes*: "Among the permanent dwellers in the country this spirit of improvement, fostered as it is by the diffusion of publications in the various departments of Rural Art, and by a wider and more genial general culture as the means of intercommunication and education are increased, is becoming more manifest every year."[11] The statement reflected the increased application of principles of domestic architecture laid out by Downing, the increase of available knowledge in books and journals, the increased interest in Downing's trade of horticulture, and the evident advances of agricultural science.[12] It appears that Woodward's orientation to building science and engineering sprang from his earlier practice in the rural situations and railroad offices of the West, showing that rural environments were as likely to produce innovations in architecture as urban ones, perhaps more so.

The Smith Brothers

Oliver P. Smith was a progressive carpenter-architect roughly twenty years senior to Woodward. He was born in 1806 near Utica, the first of seven children, and, at the age of ten, moved with his parents to be among the first settlers in far western New York state.[13] Throughout his career, he stayed on the rural frontier and never moved to the growing architectural centers on the Atlantic coast. At the beginning of his career, 93 percent of the country's population was rural.[14] This period has been identified as a time of household manufactures—a period of incipient industrial production ranging from "kitchen" production of surplus goods for "pin money" to small-cottage manufactures in domestic settings. Over the time span of Smith's working life, he was educated as an architect, designed and built houses in his country village, and moved his practice to the frontier city of Buffalo. After a few years in Buffalo, he moved farther west, demonstrating an orientation to frontier architectural practice rather than to the urbanizing centers of the Atlantic coast. His writing and lecturing demonstrated an impressive command of both architectural history and carpentry practice—knowledge necessary to the rural architect of the early nineteenth-century economy and skills common to itinerant tradesmen and peddlers; in fact, Smith may be an exemplar of a significant number of itinerant architect-builders.

Histories identify the nineteenth century as the beginning of the period of national and architectural awareness of a culture indigenous to the United States. In many ways, Oliver Smith was an early contributor, particularly as he not only built but chronicled innovative methods of indigenous architecture. Smith and his younger architect brother, Sheldon, grew up on the family farm, like most children in the United States at that time. His Uncle Sheldon was an influential lawyer in nearby Jamestown, New York, and later in Buffalo, where he was so prominent and popular an orator that he gave the address at the opening of the western terminus of the Erie Canal. Oliver's father was elected school commissioner and was an important organizer in the abolitionist movement and Underground Railroad. Oliver's brother Harvey was both a lawyer and an active abolitionist who started many newspapers in upper New York state—the *Liberty Star,* the *Northern Citizen,* and the *Undercurrent* (an abolitionist paper)—and one in Ohio, the *Medina Tribute.* Harvey was probably a major influence on Oliver's public career as lecturer and author.[15]

Oliver and three of his brothers were all in the building trades. Ransom was a carpenter-joiner and inherited the family farm in Busti. The youngest brother, Jewett, followed a path very similar to Ransom's. Sheldon, twelve years Oliver's junior, identified himself as an architect early in his career; he must have learned architectural practice and his teaching orientation from Oliver. He moved west, stopping in places such as Oberlin and Sandusky, Ohio, where he practiced and set up teaching studios, and soon thereafter became an important architect in Detroit.[16] The scale of Sheldon's practice in Sandusky and Detroit was impressive; the family firm of Smith, Hinchman & Grylls—or SmithGroup—is now one of the world's largest architectural firms.

Even though he was the traditional heir to the farm, Oliver turned his energies to building houses in Jamestown, the nearest town. He advertised in the local newspapers to promote classes in architectural theory and drawing at an academy he founded. His published 1843 lecture demonstrated a detailed knowledge of the classical orders, their positioning and derivation, and described a series of steps to becoming an architect, although how he himself was educated is unclear.[17] In the talk he quoted a lecture given by a Mr. Todd on the "ancient Egyptians before the Mercantile Library Society in Philadelphia" and cited "Mr. Elms, an eminent

English Architect and scholar" who credited the Greeks with a deep investigation into first principles.[18] "Yet our modern architects are in some measure thrown upon their own resources for the construction of private buildings, as time has swept from us every vestige of their private dwellings, and it is impossible to ascertain at the present day, whether the Grecian architects gave the same proportions to the orders when used in their private houses as when used in their temples." In other words, though "nothing remains to be added" when designing public buildings, private dwellings are open to interpretation.

The lecture concluded with a condemnation of contemporary values that put the experienced and inexperienced house builder in competition, with low price being the only measure. (Apparently, during lulls in his trade, Smith earned his way as a logger.) He emphasized the range of architects' skills: "The student should be master of his native language—know something of ancient and modern history; be well-skilled in mathematics and geometry, and a tolerable knowledge of perspective drawing. These qualifications in addition to an inventive mind, lively imagination and good taste, (for taste gives the polishing stroke to art) and never fails to inspire with intellectual delight, every man of good sense and refined appreciation."

Oliver remained a builder-architect in the Jamestown area for perhaps as long as twenty-five years.[19] As in the household mode of production, his practice involved local trading relations influenced by genealogical and acquaintance networks. He probably built a number of houses with a "Smith" connection, such as the Smith Bly House in Ashville, New York, and a house in Sinclairville that was first owned by a Smith—though neither Smith is identifiable as a family relation.

The Smith Bly House is a surprisingly refined version of Grecian style building (figure 2.1).[20] Though the architect is unknown, historians describe a Pennsylvanian influence: woodcarving by "workmen from Philadelphia" and carpentry based on books "by Minard Lafever and others."[21] At twenty-nine, Smith was capable of a house design of this quality. His own book, written when he was in his late forties, is evidence of a sophisticated knowledge of construction and architectural detail. In a public lecture at the age of forty-two he spoke knowledgably of architectural issues grounded in history and based on contemporary theory. He had a foot in the traditions of European architecture and a set of attitudes and experiences based in rural, upstate New York. Smith improved his knowledge by attending lectures such as the one given in Philadelphia by Todd at the Mercantile Library (a library for mechanics or artisans), and with help from Philadelphia builders and other skillful carpenters building in upstate New York at the time.[22]

FIG 2.1 Attributed to Oliver Smith, Smith Bly House, Ashville, N.Y. Photo by Jack Boucher, 1965, Historic American Buildings Survey, Library of Congress.

Oliver Smith was the architect of the Allen Tavern (1846), William Hall Mansion (1845), and Arthur Wade House (1848). In the *Jamestown Journal* of 23 July 1847, William Hall, a satisfied client, described Smith's Allen Tavern as "decidedly the finest building in the county." Further, Smith introduced the town to the "importance to arranging and drawing designs and plans for buildings," suggesting an influence on other local carpenter-builders, and he was a conspicuous and innovative practitioner.[23] Also in Jamestown, Jewel Conover identifies the Nathan Breed Mansion of 1848 as definitely built by Smith.[24] Other buildings generally attributed to him are in Ashville, Sinclairville, and Panama, New York.[25]

In a recent book by Daniel Reiff, two houses are credited to Smith as similar to plate 41 in *The Domestic Architect* (figure 2.2). "Not only is the general outline [of the house in Cassadaga, N.Y.] just like Smith's plate, but the details too are drawn from his book: The bargeboards of the front gable copy those of plate 10; the front

PL. XLI.

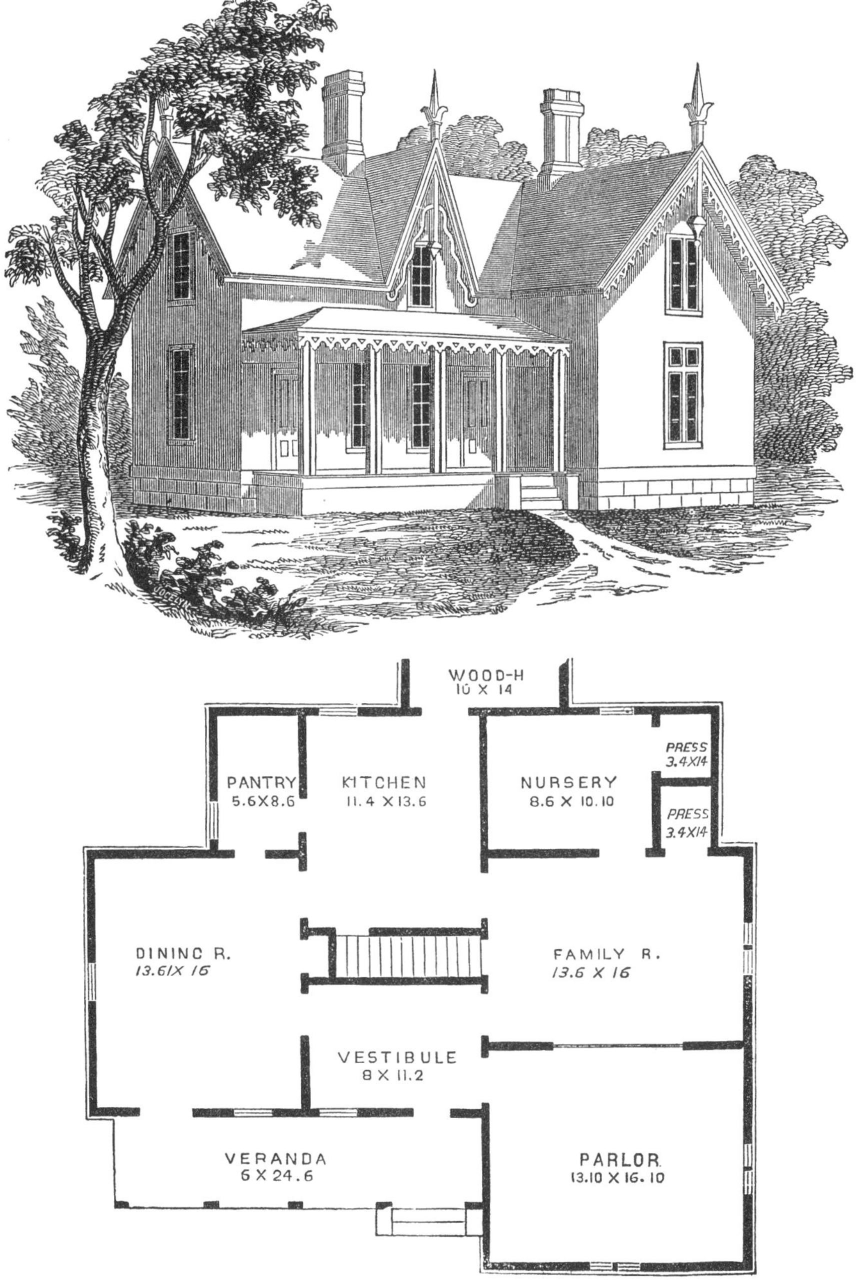

FIG 2.2 Cottage in the Rural Gothic style. From Oliver Smith, *The Domestic Architect* (1852), plate 41.

finial copies that in plate 32, figure 4; and the bay windows, with panels below the sash, are quite close to plate 32, figure 1."[26] One house in Stockton has intricate and unusual woodwork lining the eave that is replicated from Smith's book (figures 2.3 and 2.4):

> Those of the main façade gable are copied from plate 10, figure 1; those in the end gable are based closely on those in plate 27, figure 4; and while there is no plate for the bargeboards in the dormer, they are generally like the serpentine ones visible in both plate 41 and as a dormer on a more complex gothic cottage depicted in Smith's plate 31. Even smaller details can be traced to plates in this volume. The finial in the façade gable copies that in plate 32, figure 4; the apex of the finial in the dormer duplicates the design of plate 24, figure 4, while the boxed rosette at the base of this finial is taken from plate 10, figure 2. The use of arched windows with a leaf pattern in the spandrel above, comes from plate 31 (and the leaf detail shown enlarged in plate 24, fig. 4).[27]

In 1854, Smith lamented the death of Downing, and Reiff suggests a direct influence in Smith's design shown in plate 41, "most likely inspired by Downing's design 11, published in the fourth edition (1852) of *Cottage Residences,* after first appearing in *The Horticulturalist.*"[28] He characterizes Smith's uptake of Downing's model as immediate, albeit an enriched adaptation, which "signals the authority and popularity of Downing's models." Undoubtedly, but in this case the chronology isn't so clear. Smith published his first edition in 1852. Add to this the possibility that Smith had built the L-shaped cottage before he published it and that he had moved to Buffalo by 1852. The chronology of influence suggested by Reiff is now much more compressed, suggesting almost instantaneous connections between the published and built work or interesting reversals of influence and book to building sequence.

The writing and, indeed, the reading of pattern books and building guides influenced the direction of domestic building. In the first and only issue of *The Modern Architect* (figure 2.5), Oliver Smith and his son described a reader's reaction to architectural books:

> It is too common a practice among builders, when an architectural work falls into their hands, to examine the plates, and then decide on the merits of the work, with scarcely a passing notice of the suggestions, directions, explanations, and opinions of the author ... [and thus] they will not readily understand the lines, or even the intent and purpose

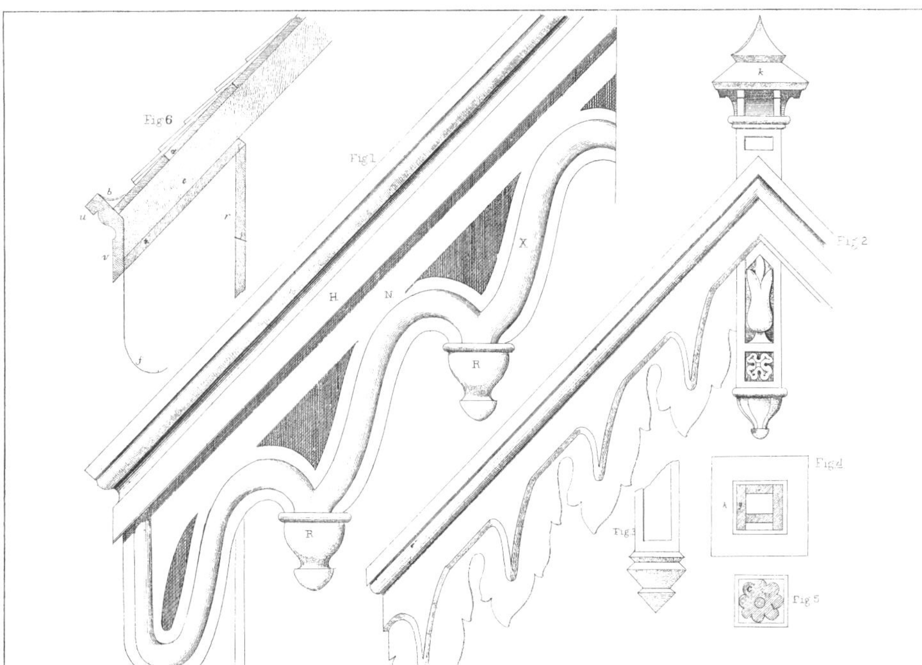

FIG 2.3 Attributed to Oliver Smith, house at Stockton, N.Y. Photo by the author.

FIG 2.4 Gable cornice. From Oliver Smith, *The Domestic Architect,* plate 10.

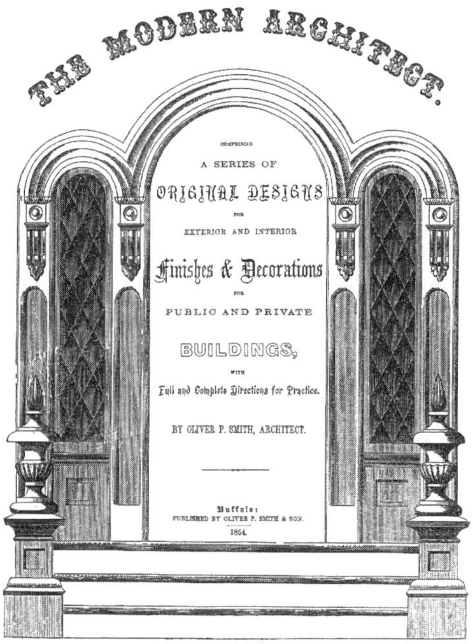

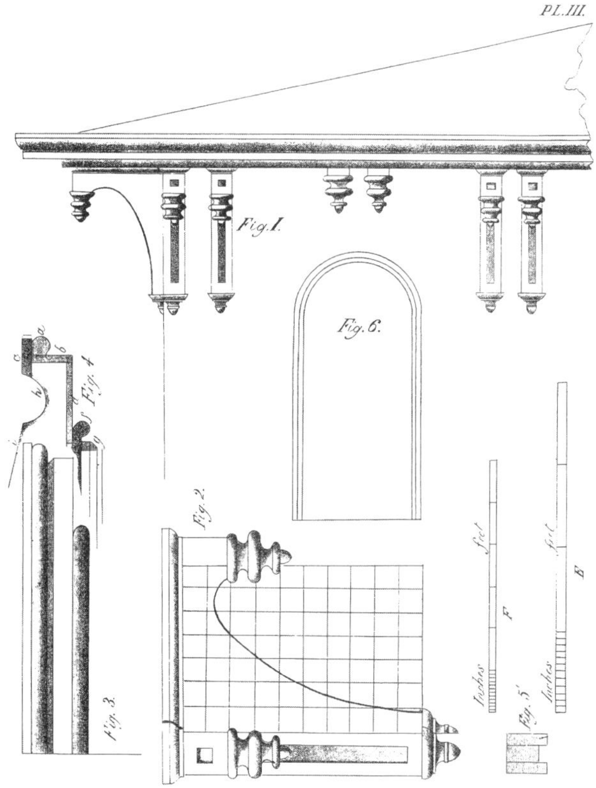

FIG 2.5 *The Modern Architect* (1854), front cover of vol. 1, no. 1.

FIG 2.6 Brackets with construction template. From Smith, *The Domestic Architect*, plate 3.

> of the author, in many simple figures they now believe themselves to be very stupid, or consider the work to be an intricate and blind treatise on the very subject they are most anxious to have knowledge of, and, therefore, close the book, disappointed and discouraged.[29]

In response, Smith found himself apologizing for the "prolixity of my directions for enlarging tracery."[30] He was entering into a strategy often repeated during the middle to late nineteenth century—the author refiguring his audience and publishing for a new set of people. *The Modern Architect* combined an article on the choice of styles ("to be continued") appropriate to house appearance in which he surveyed the recent history of the Grecian, Gothic, Rural Gothic, Italian, and Romanesque, and proposed the bracketed Norman style modified by deeper cornices. There followed detailed instructions for brackets that could be made by the reader, including instructions for translating drawings by grid enlargement to a wooden template (figure 2.6). The audience he was attempting to interest was concerned about exterior appearance and the exact composition and detailing of the bracketed trim. Smith was particularly good at explaining things fully, though he anticipated an accumulation of knowledge throughout the text. He was clearly a teacher (he ran "academies" in Jamestown and Buffalo, as did his brother, and possible pupil, Sheldon in Oberlin, Sandusky, and Detroit). This clarity was in no way an innate quality of nineteenth-century instructive literature.[31]

In social histories of the United States, the time before 1850 is identified with a form of capitalism based in rural areas, gradually changing into mixed modes of production—both household and capitalist. The Smiths were a successful rural family, especially so when one considers that upstate New York was relatively unsettled in the 1810s and 1820s. Their household production exemplifies the rural basis of the economic and technological development of U.S. society in the 1830s and 1840s. Before Oliver and Sheldon migrated to the rapidly growing cities of Buffalo and Detroit around 1850 (and economic and technological development was shifting to urban centers as well) farm households became the center of the manufacture, in its simplest form, of simple commodities such as textiles and nails: "Most of the nails for domestic use were made either by the user or by local cottage industries, while commercial naileries specialized in making nails for ship-building."[32] At the same time, the agrarian economy underwent a transition from subsistence to surplus farming. Networks of transportation were essential to this transition. Construction, particularly building materials and manufactured building components, were part of this increase of market exchange.

Oliver and his siblings were thus representative of their time. The early nineteenth century was a period of manufacture at home, and throughout most of Oliver's lifetime, entrepreneurial activity was rural. For the Smith household, farming and construction were their mix; they established a network of trade relations and an aptitude for organizing a mixed, productive household economy.

Oliver Smith's Writings

Oliver Smith's published work includes a book that is both building guide and pattern book—*The Domestic Architect.* There is also the text of a lecture published in the *Jamestown Journal*, and the magazine he initiated called *The Modern Architect*, of which apparently just one issue was published. In the historical record of architects and builders of the nineteenth century, few others published in a frontier location. Smith's public explanations of contemporary architectural theory, his apparent interest in education, and his evident ability to draw were all remarkable for their time.

The long title of his book is (entry 1221 in Hitchcock) *The Domestic Architect: comprising a series of Original Designs for Rural and Ornamental Cottages, with full and complete explanations and Directions to the Builder, embracing the elementary principles of the Grecian and Cottage Styles, with Primary Rules for Drawing and Shading, and the Rudiments of Linear Perspective, Illustrated by over Two Hundred Engravings* (Buffalo: Derby & Co., 1852). It contains 125 pages with 43 full-page plates, of which 35 are lithographs and 8 are large wood engravings. These plates are unusual, as almost all the builder's guides of the period were illustrated with copper engravings. A contemporary catalogue describes its copy as an interesting provincial imprint of some quality in a splendid binding of "dyed red full sheep, blind stamped with the title and an emblematic gothic window in gold blocking on the upper cover. . . . A particularly important work for illustrating the history of architectural book making. . . . Edges of covers rubbed; neatly rebacked in matching dyed sheep."[33]

One possible explanation for the unusual plates is that some portions of the book were published before 1852—in fact, the lithographic signatures of some of the plates suggest that they might have appeared a few years earlier, perhaps for individual sale in Buffalo as emigrants moved up the Erie Canal to points west. The lithographic firm of Hall and Mooney went through several different partnerships in the 1840s and 1850s, perhaps leading to different signatures. In *The Domestic Architect*, some plates are definitely more painterly than others, perhaps in a different hand. Few of the plates are signed, though in several cases F. R. Smith, possibly Oliver's son, was the delineator of the perspective.

The Domestic Architect was published in 1852 in Buffalo and concurrently in Chicago. These cities were unusual locations for the publication of building guides and pattern books; possibly C. W. Elliot's *Cottages and Cottage Life*, published in Cincinnati and New York in 1848, was the only one that predated Smith's west of the Appalachians. In another way, however, the publishing location does make sense: Buffalo was one of the major centers of western migration and had strong connections to Chicago. It is reasonable to assess the content of *The Domestic Architect* within this context.

By 1854, it had sold well enough to be republished—this second impression by Phinney & Co. in Buffalo and by Ivison & Phinney in New York City—again bound in leather and gilt-stamped. Phinney was a well-known press that published histories, Bibles, and almanacs. Established in Cooperstown, New York, in 1795, the press had moved to Buffalo in 1849. In Cooperstown, young James Fenimore Cooper had set type in the printing office; later the firm published several of Cooper's books (*Chronicles of Cooperstown*, *The American Democrat*, *History of the Navy*).[34] Another contemporary, Erastus F. Beadle, served his printing apprenticeship at H. & E. Phinney in Cooperstown, moved to Buffalo, and used Phinney & Co. to print the first of his magazines and dime novels. *The Domestic Architect* had found a strong, populist publishing house for its second printing—surely a sign of success.

Nevertheless, Smith's book did not have the popularity of those by Asher Benjamin and Peter Nicholson, or initiate a career as did Minard Lafever's, or document a successful practice as did John Haviland's. There is, however, something surprisingly modern about the book: it engages the reader, anticipates its use, and has a "textbook" clarity of instruction. It tries to make the content and the explanations explicit, avoiding the many assumptions of conventional practice left unexplained in other books. It has a compelling quality; it exudes experience. Smith's culturally peripheral location in Buffalo and his lucid descriptions of mundane building techniques are unique, revealing a well-trained architect precisely delineating simple wood-building practices. And its content is original.

The book reads as if Smith anticipated a future that never did happen—an extension of the trade of housewright, a skilled and innovative practitioner suitable to the burgeoning housing needs of the late nineteenth century. This was clearly one of the possible futures of his time; in fact, many of the books written by or for carpenters or "mechanics" are introduced with just such professional aspirations in mind. Typically, most other authors imagined idealized techniques or prescribed accepted ones. Smith wrote a practical manual as a commercial venture suitable for popular consumption, but what was unique about his book and, indeed, his practice was that he was also acting in an anthropological manner, recording indigenous techniques. Oliver acted as a recorder of frontier building practices. Historically, these practices were radically pragmatic and quite diverse. Through the very act of recording, he rationalized and prescribed these frontier building techniques. In the process, he kept their radical simplicity and verified their efficacy through application.

Despite its evident success, *The Domestic Architect* has not been acknowledged as part of the mainstream tendencies in architectural writing in America. It fits uneasily into existing historical studies that describe the increase of pattern books and the decrease of building guides at midcentury.[35] Following Hitchcock, Reiff comments that the book illustrates this "period of transition in architectural publications." Further, the "artlessness of [Smith's] illustrations suggest that these were copied directly from his own drawings," which I suggest is a positive rather than a negative criticism, since it was "oriented to 'the country builder' who is in need of 'the plainest and easiest rules in the rudiments' of architecture."[36] This perceived transition has an implied association with the increased professionalization, urbanization, and commericialization of architecture, linking pattern books to a new way of describing and prescribing building. In my view, it also represents the dismissal of carpentry practice as part of architectural practice in the histories of the nineteenth century, not necessarily reflecting an actual tendency of the time.

Smith's book was unusual among builder's guides and pattern books in another way as well. Like most of them, his represented the designs that he had completed, or perhaps proposed, for building in his Chautauqua County home and in the early 1850s in Buffalo. But unlike most authors, he observed the rural situation—the locus of the construction innovations he proposed—and recorded his observations. Smith was an active agent, documenting and analyzing his contemporary building situation. He was operating at a time of increasing variety, and he built houses with varied appearances and methods of construction. He appeared to be unconcerned about such variation in construction technique and confident in his own abilities. Doubtless, he had tried all the different techniques explained in the book, since the instructions work well in conjunction with his drawings. Essential sequences are labeled and explained far better than in the drawings and explanations in most other building guides and pattern books.

Oliver Smith's Frontier Constructions

Smith's practices extended to recording and documenting multiple varieties of simple indigenous construction methods. *The Domestic Architect* can be seen as a catalogue of construction methods that Smith, by the very act of recording them, helped to legitimate. Collecting an (oral) artisanal culture of construction, he clarified, created routines, and simplified the various methods.[37] He documented traditions of construction and showed them interrelating or adapting to the environment, becoming conventionalized and more homogeneous. In written and self-conscious form Smith might have been mirroring what had happened as technology entered construction practice. He refined technique, thus beginning the cycle of improved production of building and anticipating the light-wood frame.

As an instructional text, his book explains things in drawings and in terms that can be built from, and it supplies reasons that an experienced builder would have understood. For instance, the two-page description of plate 7, his simplest design, says "Frame—The posts should be 5 by 8 inches, and the studding 2 by 5, obviating the necessity of having corners of posts in the angles of rooms." These visible corner posts were common in the interiors of heavy-timber-frame construction. In the 1840s, however, these posts characteristically became thinner and started to recede behind the plaster surface of the wall.[38]

At the end of the paragraph on the frame, Smith suggests putting in some of the studs in the interior bearing partition before putting on the roof to prevent the "tendency to spread the plates. It would also be desirable to mark the place for the collar-beams, on the rafters, when framed, and nail on the collar-beams at the time the rafters are raised." There are two very practical hints here—the suggestion to create a roof truss with collars and rafters prior to lifting the roof structure into place, and the coordination of the 5-inch stud with the 5-inch corner post to prevent the usual protrusion of a square post into a room or the necessity of chiseling out the corner by hand. Such practical advice creates economies of labor—an important role of the modern designer. There are also indications of the balloon-frame method of construction with the advice to extend the studding from sill to plate—in this design a distance of one and a half stories: "The studding on the side may extend from the sill to the plate, then spike the first joists to every stud, in place of employing girders."[39] Here a basic principle of the balloon frame, the continuous stud, forms part of Smith's advice, and the spiking of every joist to these studs shows the use of nails as a basic structural connection. If "first joist" means first-floor joist, as it probably does, then the connection by nails of the first-floor joists to these studs has everything, except a ribbon support, to match the balloon frame.

Plates 22 (figure 2.7), 25 (figure 2.8), and 31 generate a set of interrelated details and framing elevations represented in some of the intermediate plates and explanations. They suggest optional arrangements and even methods of construction for the same design, and frequently these mention the choice between horizontal and vertical siding. Two methods of framing are detailed for vertical plank and batten (figures 2.9 and 2.10, bottom half). Several framing elevations are drawn; some specify "common siding" (probably horizontal clapboard).

Smith draws the frame either in elevation or in a detail plan of the wall at the ground floor (there are small details of rafters meeting the top of wall plates). Here

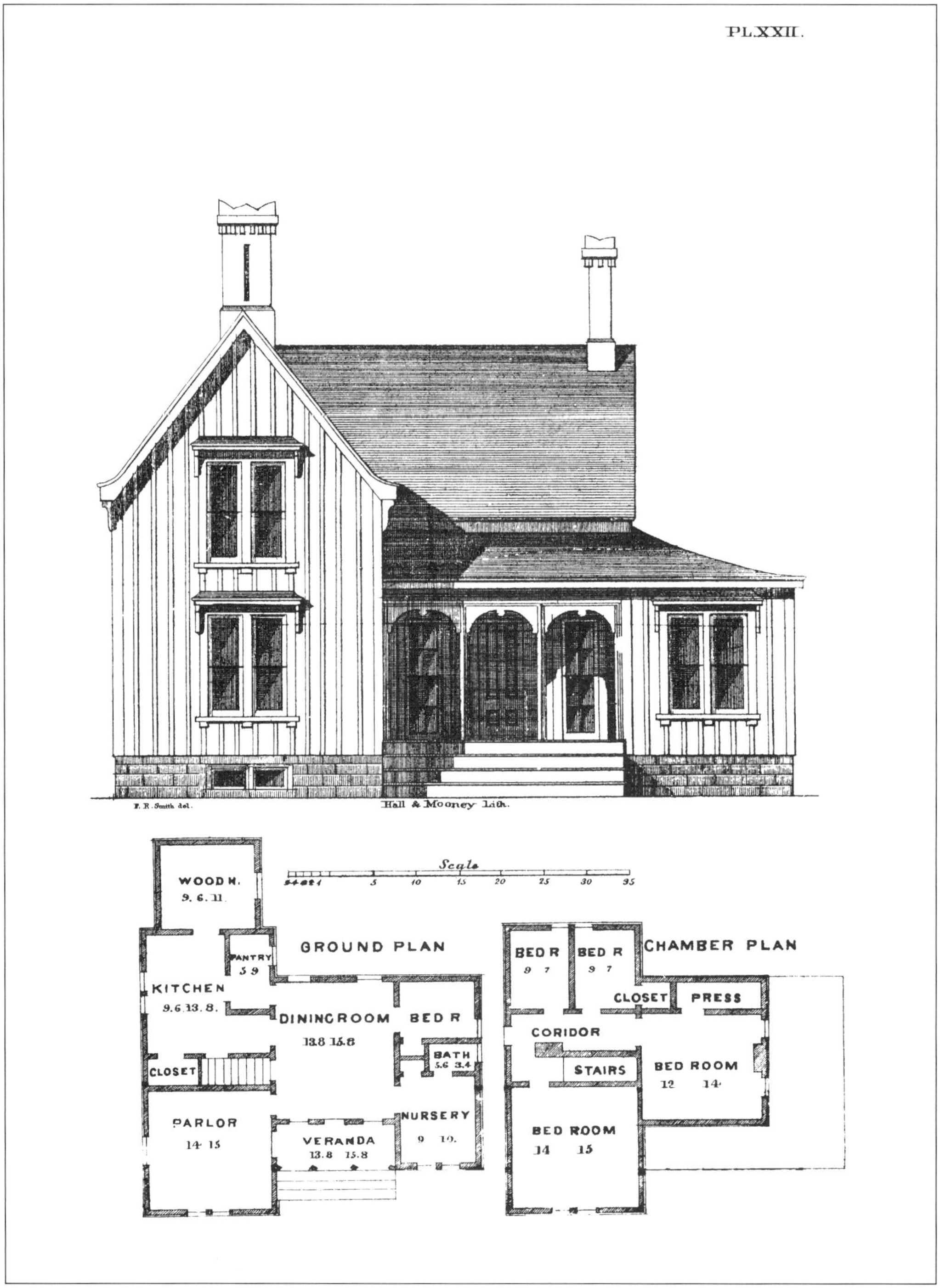

FIG 2.7 Cottage design. From Smith, *The Domestic Architect*, plate 22.

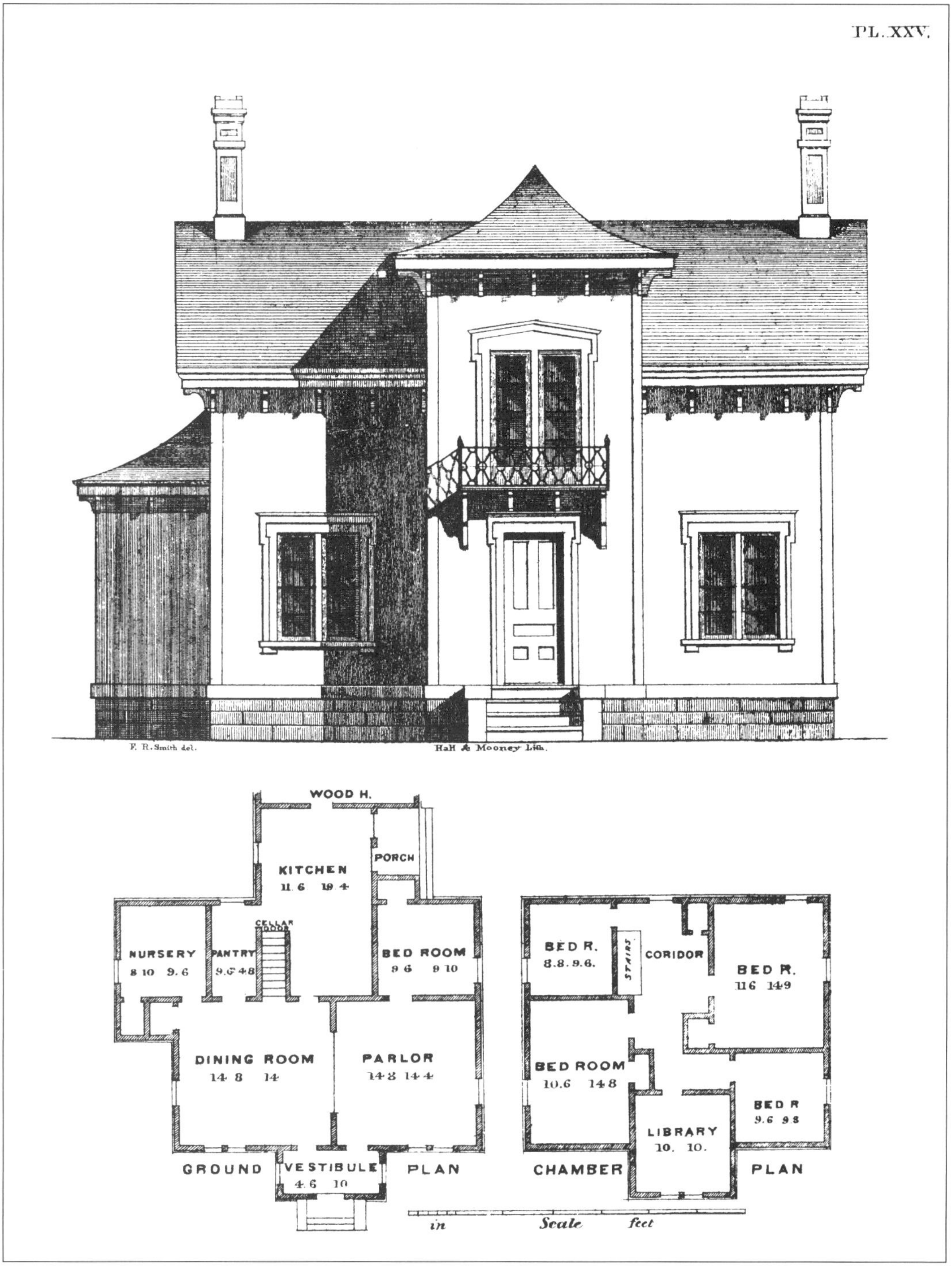

FIG 2.8 Cottage in the bracketed style. From Smith, *The Domestic Architect*, plate 25. The description refers to framing according to plate 23, fig. 4 (see figure 2.10). The (balloon) frame is covered with common siding (clapboard). "Farther explanation is not needed."

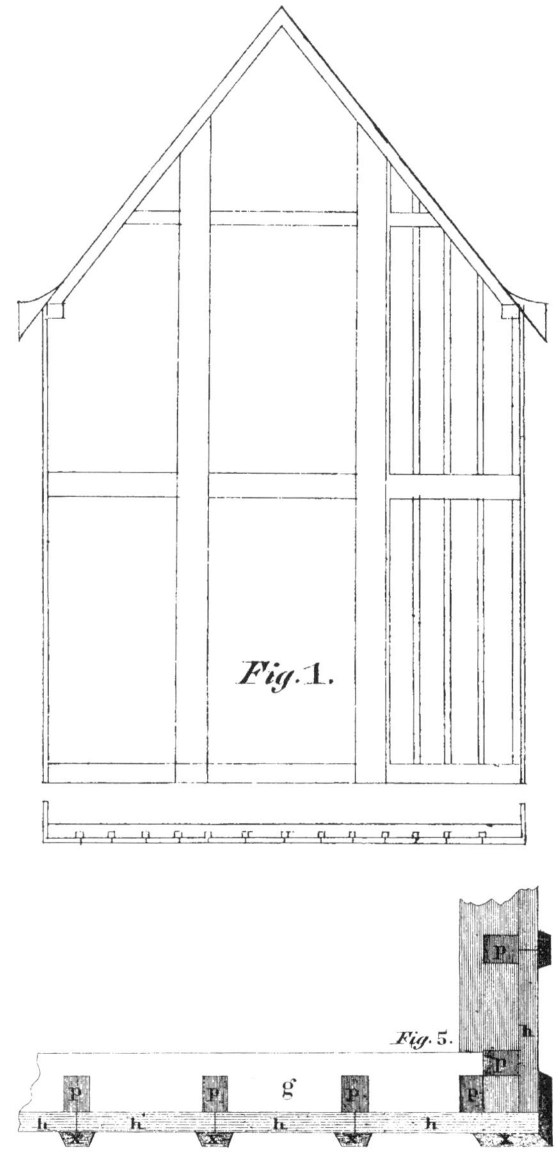

FIG 2.9 Construction framing. From Smith, *The Domestic Architect*, plate 24, figs. 1 (elevation) and 5 (enlarged horizontal section), for the cottage design in plate 22 (see figure 2.7). Notice the vertical planks each side of the window.

FIG 2.10 (Top facing page) Framing. From Smith, *The Domestic Architect*, plate 23. Fig. 4 likely shows balloon framing, and, if so, this would be the earliest known drawing of the method. Other ways of light-wood framing are shown in the other figures of this plate.

FIG 2.11 (Bottom facing page) Window casing and sash. From Smith, *The Domestic Architect*, plate 28, figs. 4 (plan) and 6 (detail).

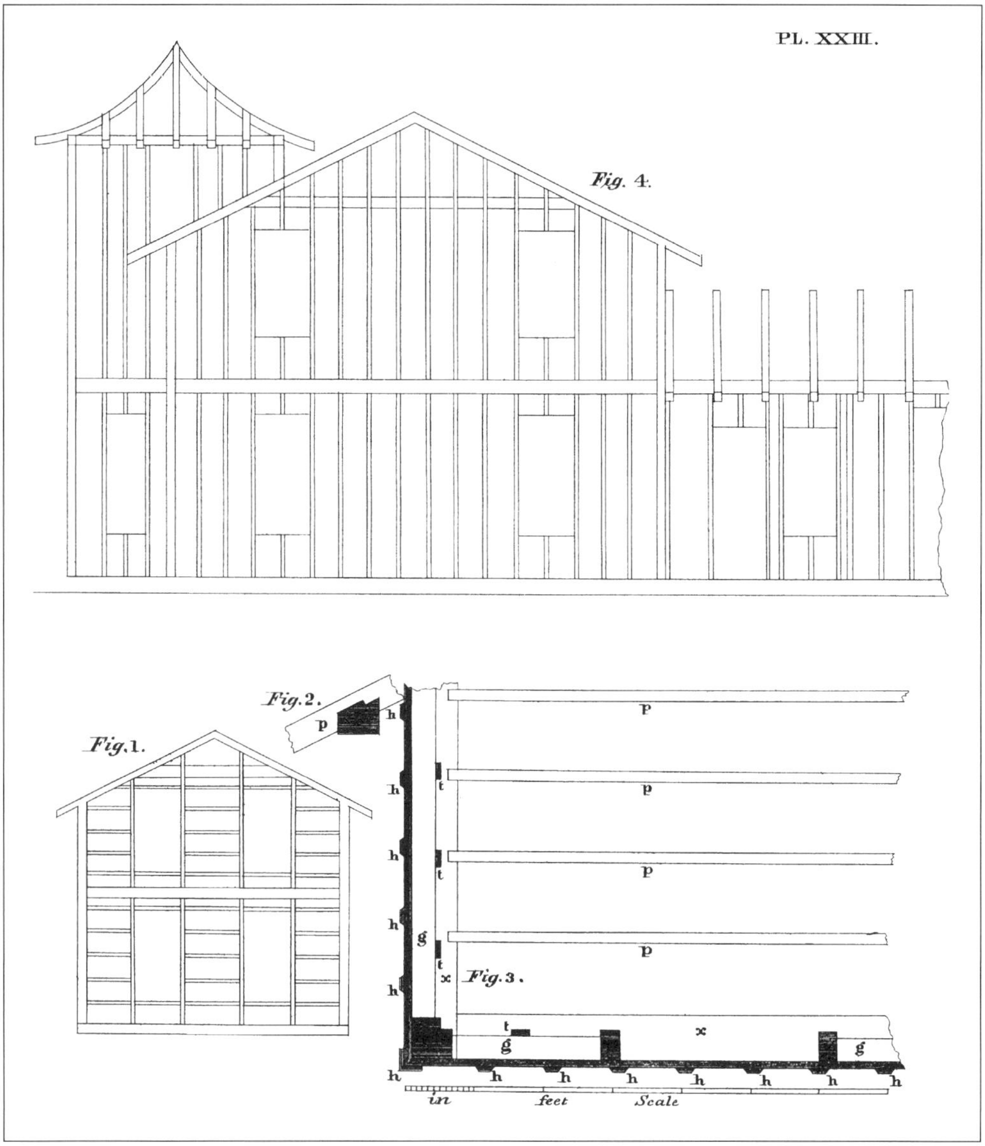
PL. XXIII.
Fig. 4.
Fig. 2.
Fig. 1.
Fig. 3.
p
h
t
g
x
in
feet
Scale

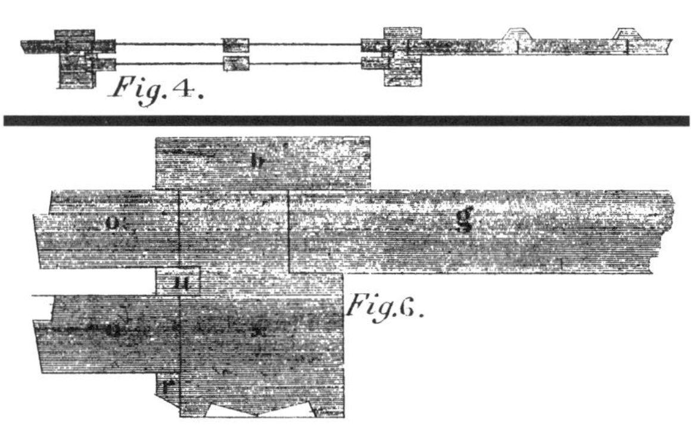
Fig. 4.
Fig. 6.
b
g
u
r

again, the studs are continuous from foundation to roof, according to an interpretation of the drawings and a comment by Smith. There are indications of a let-in ribbon in some designs. Some elevation drawings show horizontals at the upper floor and the ceiling level. These horizontals must be flush with the outside face of the studs to allow for sheathing or clapboarding, so they must be let into the studs, much like the ribbon or ledger in a balloon frame, albeit on the outside rather than the inside face.

Smith's interest in building construction is evident in the variety and range of methods that he explains. His orientation to efficient and material-saving methodologies is apparent in a description of a method that crosses the plank frame with an idea for a window frame involving carpentry and an understanding of structure. Plate 28 depicts a method of "peculiar construction" that involves vertical boards finished with battens (figure 2.11). Unfortunately, Smith is uncharacteristically brief in his description of the "peculiar construction" method, entering it through the detailing of a window. "It is therefore, necessary, first to notice the construction of the house before entering upon a description of the window casing. The casing was designed to be employed on a house, the outer walls of which are boards, dressed on both sides and matched." These boards form the inside and outside "finish of the wall, its entire thickness." This construction practice might be the plank frame, but Smith does distinguish it as "peculiar," and he does describe what is probably the plank frame in other designs such as those previously mentioned. Throughout the book, wherever drawings or instructions repeat, he refers back to the first description rather than detail its construction again. Smith continues:

> The frame, or timbers, supporting the floor, joists, or ceiling, to be of scantling, 4 by 4 inches, to which timbers the boards are nailed. The joists are placed on top of the scantling, and the ceiling to be plastered; or, the joists may be 3 by 7, and dressed, in which case, the outside timbers should be also 3 by 7. The edges of the joists should be flush with the edges of the timbers. Then dress both sides of the floor boards, as the joists and floor will constitute the ceiling. The plate will also be of scantling, and supported by nails through the upper ends of the perpendicular boards which constitute the outside wall.

The description is supported only by a detail plan of the window construction. "It will be seen that, in this building, posts, studs, braces and even lath and plaster on the walls, are entirely dispensed with. But, to give greater security to the joist timbers, the peculiar window casing . . . has been designed." The vertical on each side of the window runs the full height of the building and is 3 by 4 inches rabbeted to accept 1.5-inch boards. According to the description, these are the only verticals; no studs and no corner posts are mentioned. Supporting the floor construction on sills and plates that are nailed to the boards must have required the builder to assemble the walls flat (boards, sills, and plates), then tilt them up and nail the joists in place.

In one design there is a description and drawing of plank-frame construction with some clear if unusual details. This version describes the studs as "strengthening the joints of the vertical planking" (figure 2.7).[40] Again, there are no corner posts; rather, two small studs are located near the corner, suggesting an intentional, almost perverse, lack of perimeter frame. The other framing elevation employed in a number of the designs appears to be a perimeter frame of heavy plates, sills, and posts with the remaining studs in light-dimension lumber (figure 2.8, bottom half).[41] The drawing is unclear about the horizontal members around windows and at the base of the walls, and one can't be sure whether Smith means "frame" in the sense of the rectangular perimeter of a wall (using Charles E. Peterson's distinction of "frame" as the perimeter rectangle formed by plate, sill, and corner post).[42]

Smith's descriptions of everything—from brackets to window casings—are the details of a skilled carpenter, mentioning screws and nails where required. For example, he explains how to lay out the length, bevel, and required miter angles of all roof framing members. He was an architect who understood carpentry technique and had an ability to translate it into architectural detail in support of any contemporary style or appearance. In the literature of the mid-nineteenth century, Smith stands out as a carpenter-architect who wrote about the connection between architectural detail and carpentry practice. One of the few authors who collected frontier innovations, he recorded these innovations and related them to the practices of both carpentry and architecture.

Buffalo and the Balloon Frame

The set of framing methods is remarkable as much for those methods left unsaid—there are no versions of the heavy-timber tradition, for instance; there are no joints like mortises mentioned or drawn; there is no diagonal bracing, and there are no angled corner braces. Apparently, there are butt and nailed joints throughout the roof, though there is sometimes a complex bird's mouth at the connection between the rafter and plate. The lack of angled braces shows a surprising independence from the traditions of the East Coast. The absence of timber joints and the omission of timber frame might have been truly representative of the construction practices of the frontier.

As a byproduct of his writing and practice, Smith refined some of the "parent" techniques that evolved into the quintessentially North American building method—the light-wood frame. If indeed his framing illustrations are of the balloon frame, then this is the earliest publication of it in drawing form. To situate it more precisely: the first verbal description was in 1847 by Solon Robinson, a farm journalist and champion of the balloon frame. Occasionally, a drawing by Edward Shaw in his *Modern Architect* of 1854 has been called the earliest drawing of the balloon frame.[43] This is essentially incorrect. Shaw's vignette shows carpenters and architect in very proper attire in front of a partially constructed building made up of heavy timbers and the diagonals of braced frame. Probably, this drawing shows the state of construction on the Atlantic coast. Smith, in contrast, did not explain either heavy-timber frame or braced frame. Was this representative of the Buffalo frontier? The first known drawing accompanying a precise verbal instruction was in an 1858 builder's guide by William Bell. Bell, born in Virginia, was trained as a carpenter in Ohio and in a shop of thirty men in Michigan City, Indiana. He worked for the Rock Island and Northwestern Railroad, building "many of their bridges and shops." According to the *Ottawa* [Illinois] *Directory* of 1866, he was partner in a lumberyard and had "been engaged for the past thirty years as Carpenter and Bridge Builder." Bell mentions in his book that he had been building balloon-frame houses for fifteen years before publishing a guide to its assembly. His version of the balloon frame, however, had heavy timber sills and corner posts, and mortises.[44] Smith's does not. It might even be a lighter version in some other areas: for instance, the corner details probably follow Smith's detail discussed above.

Buffalo, an important center of popular publishing, was home to Smith and another important architectural writer, Charles Dwyer. Dwyer brought an immigrant's interest to frontier construction and published a number of important books.[45] In *The Economic Cottage Builder* (1855), Dwyer refers to a different framing system as "PLANK, OR BALLOON. . . . The requirements are, a moderately heavy cap and sill, and sides of plank nailed to both."[46] He is describing the plank frame; for him, "plank" and "balloon" are apparently interchangeable.

It is interesting to compare Smith with Charles Dwyer, who published shortly after Smith and was a Buffalo collector of frontier building practices as well. As architects, their interest in the ordinary was rather extraordinary. It might have had something to do with their frontier location, because their backgrounds were quite different. Dwyer emigrated from Ireland and arrived in Buffalo after spending some time in Ontario. He was a reporter for the *Buffalo Republic* in 1850 and 1851 and wrote at least one volume of a promised nine-volume *History of Buffalo* in 1852. He produced three builder's guides, two in the mid-1850s during his time in Buffalo. In 1860 he also wrote a *Memoir of Commodore O. H. Perry*, published in Cleveland. Despite the fact that he sold life insurance for a time, Dwyer was clearly qualified to write about architecture and continued to do so later in Philadelphia when, according to Roger Moss, "he lists himself as an editor of Samuel Sloan's short-lived *Architectural Review and Builders' Journal*." Dwyer had written two articles on foundations in 1868, and "for the following decade, Dwyer is variously listed in the Philadelphia city directories as a civil engineer, professor of architecture, and as an architect."[47]

Dwyer, like most authors, prescribed idealized techniques, whereas Smith collected actual techniques and analyzed what he collected, probably because he was a builder before he was an author.[48] Dwyer's description of the plank frame that he (mis)labels as the balloon frame might be a clue to practices of the time. Either way it can be used as a stimulus for analysis. "From a purely architectural point of view," says Charles Wood, "Dwyer's designs are among the most interesting of all those published during the 19th century in America—they have about them a sense of the rationalism of the French architects of the same period as well as obvious references to English pattern book designs. Dwyer must have owned or had access to a good architectural library."[49]

The Itinerant Architect

Historically, North American construction has involved many builders on the move, and it is evident that they moved with far more frequency than the settled farming population. For example, during the 1790s, Isaac Byington was clearly an itinerant worker but also an artisan taking care to record those items important to his trade. He spent time framing pictures and sawing lumber in South Carolina and Georgia after he left Bristol, Connecticut. In his travels he recorded comments on carpentry work, sawmills, and indigo production, and he described his own business ventures.[50] As an itinerant artisan, he was an early example of a widespread phenomenon, an educated tradesman loyal to his family yet finding it necessary to travel to extend his possibilities. His observant nature led him to record his travels but also to include useful findings having to do with his trade. Traveling as an artisan and writing about the trade often occurred together.

In the colonial period in Maryland, there were early indications of a frequent occurrence in North America: when skilled craftsmen came to a new settlement, insufficient demand for their services often led them to leave or change occupation.[51] The combination of rural manufacture and itinerant tradesmen became widespread within a context of expanding settlement after the War of Independence.[52] Samuel Partridge of Wethersfield, Connecticut, was a traveling joiner who by prearrangement boarded with his clients to build doorway facades and furnish other decorative woodwork.[53] By 1800, reports Bernard Herman, among Delaware carpenters "there were established families working over a period of years in various construction trades, [but] the majority of the carpenters, masons, and other builders were itinerants or short term residents."[54]

In the early nineteenth century, itinerancy—whether peddling or mobile artisanship—was an effective response to general social change. There was the prevailing sense that although agriculture was stable, it was an ineffective way to financial improvement, a situation often exacerbated by the problem of primogenesis. "For displaced farm boys, peddling could also serve as a means of social mobility, a way out of the demographic and social stresses of northern agrarian economy and into the newer opportunities of the region's emerging commercial villages."[55] Mobile artisans established networks of trade that contributed to the establishment of the rural itinerant and the new capitalist economy. Construction was an example of both.[56]

These commercial and cultural activities allowed the rising rural generation born after the War for Independence to fashion new careers and identities. Itinerancy, occupational and social, facilitated the move from the constricted opportunities of northern farms to the new developments under way in commercial and industrial villages. And peddler and consumer both shared in the activity of self-fashioning through the exchange of goods that facilitated the democratization of gentility and fluidity of social identity.[57]

Oliver Smith, after practicing in Jamestown for a number of years, in the late 1840s became more visible, leaving a few public records. In 1848 his lecture on architecture at the Jamestown Academy was subsequently published in the *Jamestown Journal.* For an entire year thereafter he published this advertisement:

> O. P. SMITH—Architect, and teacher of Architectural Drawing. Plans and specifications for buildings drawn with special reference to convenience, economy, taste, and

> durability. Gentlemen who are concerned in erecting either public or private buildings will find it to their advantage to consult an architect, as it is important to expend all money in a building to the best possible advantage. He will also teach builders the principles of architecture, and the rules of architectural drawing and shading. Jamestown, Chautauqua County, N.Y.

It appeared in the *Jamestown Journal* and headed the column titled "Business Cards." Advertising, "by turns inflated, formulaic, and obsequious, was the mainspring of itinerant careers in widely differing fields."

But Smith had never advertised in the *Journal* before—something had changed. The sudden increase in publicity (advertisement, lecture, and testimonial from a client for whom he built the Allen Tavern and a house) perhaps implies a reorientation of his practice, substituting market exchange for the earlier concentration on domestic exchange.[58] Smith developed a public profile through publicity. He identified himself as an architect on the basis of his understanding of the "principles of architecture" and his ability to draw according to the "rules of architectural drawing." He reinforced his public profile by describing himself as a "teacher of Architectural Drawing" and differentiated himself from builders by offering to teach his students about architecture. In a similar way, his brother Sheldon established schools of architecture during his period of itinerancy as he traveled west through Ohio to Michigan.

Oliver Smith's emphasis on "convenience, economy, taste, and durability" suggested that architects were able to design improved value into buildings. On the basis of utilitarian values, he critically assessed economic frontier building technologies for durability and plan organizations for convenience. He connected his experience and these particular utilitarian values to architectural principles through the medium of taste. This connection is evident in his essay on the carpentry details for the exterior of buildings in the Romanesque and bracketed styles of architecture—a major component of the extant number of his journal, *The Modern Architect*, of 1854. His argument established his connection to his market by associating his values with those around him; as a "progressive" builder, his practice involved cultural mediation.

He was clearly oriented to the construction of modest houses on the frontier and to the everyday practice of architecture. His background in cultural mediation was common on the frontier, where carpentry and architecture were associated rather than differentiated. What was uncommon, I think, was Smith's interest in simplifying both carpentry and architectural practice. He foreshadowed the innovation of simplified technique important to the establishment of the new capitalist economy. His lack of recognition by the public of the day had much to do with the unresolved relationship of writing to the practice of architecture in the 1850s, perhaps, too "progressive" for an audience that was no longer the rural carpenter identified by Benjamin and not yet the suburban contractor identified by Woodward.

Settlement and Itinerancy

While his brother Sheldon was establishing himself in Detroit, Oliver Smith was attempting to do the same in Buffalo. It is unclear why the brothers moved from Jamestown at approximately the same time. Starting in the 1820s, however, there was a general migration westward or to urban centers in search of new opportunities for children of large farm families. Itinerant artisans such as Oliver, Sheldon, and Harvey Smith were part of this changing economy, and they all moved away to further their chosen careers.

Oliver Smith was apparently in the process of reorienting his career in the late 1840s, and he refocused on the close, fast-growing urban center of Buffalo. He took his skills, his aptitude for innovation, and his simplification of construction method and opened an office in the central post office building. His name appears in the city directory for the years 1852 and 1853. Smith closed his Buffalo office in 1854, even after the apparently successful publication of *The Domestic Architect* and just one issue of *The Modern Architect.* Next, there are indications that he moved to rural Michigan, and joined the westward expansion of the United States that included both the agricultural settler and the itinerant artisan.

Like Oliver Smith, many who declared themselves architects, by training or by the scale of their practice, were on the move in the 1840s and 1850s. Despite the placebound nature of dwellings, artisans had little choice but to travel in order to ply their trade when local building slowed or became overly competitive. Mobile artisanship was an effective response to general social change, since agriculture, though stable, was not lucrative. In the mid-nineteenth century, however, some artisans landed lucky and were not forced to relocate to continue working at their trade. Chicago, for example, became a big city within a lifetime. As W. W. Boyington relates:

> When I came to Chicago [in 1853] I found the architects then in practice were recent master builders or contractors. . . . At that time the structures were but simple buildings,

> but the builders soon found that it would be better for them to have plans made rather than to spend their time in making plans, so they clubbed together, and induced one of them most apt in drawing plans to give up his contracting and devote his whole time to architecture, and guaranteed him a compensation of $2 per day, which should be paid to him if he did not get business enough to aggregate that amount.[59]

No matter where artisans chose to settle, the future of the settlement and the relative time of arrival were critical. "As early comers to the county," explains John Cordulack, "they could buy land cheaper than later artisans. The shift [from tradesman] to farming did not constitute a wrenching decision. . . . But farming claimed them once they saw the opportunity to own land." In fact, a study of Bureau County, Illinois, shows that artisans arriving in the Midwest in the forefront of settlement often abandoned their trade in favor of becoming landowners. This contrasted with later arrivals, when land had become more expensive. This second wave of artisans was more likely to move on. In Bureau County, however, there is evidence of persistence in the building trades in 1860 and after: "The building trades remained strong because they did not encounter the same competition from outside manufacturers: houses were not imported but made to order. . . . In a time when many artisans' sons were entering other occupations, the building trades offered opportunities. About 40% of the sons who remained artisans entered the building trades."[60]

So mobility was fashioned in at least two ways: carpenter-architects who arrived in the first wave of midwestern settlement often moved from their trade to what became the more lucrative area of farming and landowning; second, carpenter-architects unable to take advantage of doing so either continued with their itinerant practices or moved to urban centers.

In the Midwest, perhaps to state the obvious, it is important to remember that in the beginning, all artisans and all members of the building trades were itinerant. Sheldon Smith settled in Detroit to become recognized as one of the founding architects of the city. Oliver, on the other hand, tried the urbanizing center of Buffalo and then may have settled in rural Michigan. He had come full circle, replicating his father's experience of settling in upstate New York. Oliver nevertheless deserves recognition. Among his many qualities, he appears flexible and responsive, willing to deploy whatever strategies, methods, or empirical materials were at hand, to get the job done even "if new tools [had] to be invented, or pieced together," as Norman Denzin and Yvonne Lincoln put it. He was technically curious and multicompetent, skilled at using different methods (interviews, observation, personal experimentation) and intellectually informed; he read widely and was knowledgeable about different methods. He was reflexive; he understood that research is "an interactive process shaped by . . . personal history, biography, gender, social class, race, ethnicity." He wrote well—he was capable of producing a "complex, dense, reflexive, collage-like creation."[61]

Perhaps, today, we are returning to the carpenter-architect with renewed emphasis on design-and-build. For historians, the rural and building-trade roots of architecture warrant more attention.

BIBLIOGRAPHY OF THE WRITINGS OF OLIVER PERRY SMITH

The Domestic Architect: comprising a series of Original Designs for Rural and Ornamental Cottages, with full and complete explanations and Directions to the Builder, embracing the elementary principles of the Grecian and Cottage Styles, with Primary Rules for Drawing and Shading, and the Rudiments of Linear Perspective, Illustrated by over Two Hundred Engravings. First edition, first imprint. Buffalo and Chicago: Derby & Co., 1852.

The Domestic Architect: comprising a series of Original Designs for Rural and Ornamental Cottages, with full and complete explanations and Directions to the Builder, embracing the elementary principles of the Grecian and Cottage Styles, with Primary Rules for Drawing and Shading, and the Rudiments of Linear Perspective, Illustrated by over Two Hundred Engravings. First edition, second imprint. Buffalo: Phinney & Co.; New York: Ivison & Phinney, 1854.

The Domestic Architect. Facsimile of 1854 edition, renamed *Victorian Domestic Architect.* Watkins Glen, N.Y.: American Life Foundation Library of Victorian Culture, 1978.

The Modern Architect. Buffalo: Oliver P. Smith & Son, 1854.

NOTES

1. Apprenticeship is emphasized in James Wollon, "History of the Historic Architects' Roundtable," Baltimore Architecture Foundation, [10 March 2006], http://baltimorearchitecture.org/das.html. Bernard Boyle emphasized two paths in "Architectural Practice in America, 1865–1965—Ideal and Reality," in *The Architect: Chapters in the History of a Profession*, ed. Spiro Kostof (New York: Oxford University Press, 1977), 309–10.

2. See Mary Woods, *From Craft to Profession: The Practice of Architecture in Nineteenth-Century America* (Berkeley: University of California Press, 1999). Woods describes professionalism as a novel social strategy to overcome the artisan/amateur dichotomy in architecture.

3. Ibid., 31. Woods makes much of builders leaving their artisanal orientation behind; I concentrate on the implications of remaining associated with building.

4. Dell Upton concentrates on this transition in Asher Benjamin's career in "Pattern Books and Professionalism: Aspects of the Transformation of Domestic Architecture in America, 1800–1860," *Winterthur Portfolio* 19 (1984): 107–50. For Minard Lafever, see Jacob Landy, *The Architecture of Minard Lafever* (New York: Columbia University Press, 1970).

5. For most of the 1800s, carpentry was the most populous occupation after the four categories of the working population in agriculture. In the 1870 census there were 344,596 carpenters (3 percent of the total) the fifth largest occupation. Margo Conk, *The United States Census and Labor Force Change* (Ann Arbor, Mich.: UMI, 1988), 57. The 1860 *Michigan State Gazetteer and Business Directory* lists 600 names under the category "architect, carpenter, and builder," identifying forty-seven architects (8 percent of the total). Only five were located in Detroit.

6. Most factories were rural. Franklin Mendels finds early capitalist development in the spare capacity of agrarian economies; see Sheleigh Ogilvie and Markus Cerman, *European Proto-Industrialization* (Cambridge: Cambridge University Press, 1996). For North America, see Bernard Bailyn, *The Peopling of British North America: An Introduction* (New York: Knopf, 1986); and Carole Shammas, *The Pre-industrial Consumer in England and America* (Oxford: Clarendon Press, 1990). See also Charles Orser, "Historical Archaeology and the Capitalist Transformation of the Illinois Countryside" in *Landscape, Architecture, and Artifacts: Historical Archaeology of Nineteenth Century Illinois*, ed. Erich Schroeder (Springfield: Illinois Historic Preservation Agency, 1991), 14–21; and Margaret Purser, "Ex Occidente Lux? An Archaeology of Later Capitalism in the Nineteenth Century West," in *Historical Archaeologies of Capitalism*, ed. Mark Leone and Parker Potter (New York: Plenum Press, 1999).

7. See David Jaffee, "Peddlers of Progress and the Transformation of the Rural North," *Journal of American History* (September 1991): 511–35; Peter Benes and Jane Montague Benes, editors' introduction in *Itinerancy in New England and New York* (Concord, Mass.: Boston University, 1986); Christopher Clark, "Rural America and the Transition to Capitalism," *Journal of the Early Republic* 16 (Summer 1996): 223–36; and Timothy Spears, *100 Years on the Road: The Traveling Salesman in American Culture* (New Haven: Yale University Press, 1995).

8. Asher Benjamin, *Practice of Architecture* (Boston: Carter Hendee & Co., 1833), iii.

9. Based on a count of titles in Henry-Russell Hitchcock, *American Architectural Books: A List of Books, Portfolios, and Pamphlets on Architecture and Related Subjects Published in America before 1895* (1946; expanded ed., New York: Da Capo Press, 1976).

10. See, for example, Arthur Downs, *Downing and the American House* (Newton Square, Pa.: Downing and Vaux Society, 1988); George B. Tatum and Elizabeth B. MacDougall, eds., *Prophet with Honor: The Career of Andrew Jackson Downing, 1815–1852* (Philadelphia: Athenaeum of Philadelphia; Washington, D.C.: Dumbarton Oaks Research Library and Collection, 1989); and David Schuyler, *Apostle of Taste: Andrew Jackson Downing, 1815–1852* (Baltimore: Johns Hopkins University Press, 1996).

11. George Woodward, *Woodward's Country Homes* (New York: Geo. E. & F. W. Woodward, 1865), 7–8. His views represent a new, urban-centered market economy reassessing its rural surroundings. Though he was "progressive" in his writing for agricultural journals, Woodward in his books and practice did not apply the construction innovations that he championed.

12. See Sally McMurry, *Families and Farmhouses in Nineteenth-Century America: Vernacular Design and Social Change* (New York: Oxford University Press, 1988).

13. In addition to my other citations, the story of Oliver Smith and his family has been compiled from Samuel A. Brown, *History of Ellicott* (N.p., n.d.); Buffalo City Directory 1853 and 1854; *Buffalo Patriot*, obituary, Sheldon Smith, 10 June 1835; grave headstones, Lakeview Cemetery, Jamestown; Obed Edson, *History of Chautauqua County, New York* (Boston: W. A. Fergusson, 1894); Crisfield Johnson, *Centennial History of Erie County, New York: Being its annals from the earliest recorded events to the hundredth year of American independence* (Buffalo, N.Y.: Print. House of Matthews & Warren, 1876); Edna Ingham, notes, Fenton Historical Society, Jamestown, N.Y.; *Jamestown Journal*, list of contributors, 27 November 1846; marriage, Julius C. Smith and Mary Robertson, 28 May 1835;

marriage, Ransom Smith and Lucinda Davis, 23 January 1839; marriage, Ransom Smith and Smith Agnes Baxter, June 1889; obituary, Clark Smith, 29 July 1864; Land Transfer Index of Holland Land Company 1815–25 and 1825–35; newspaper originals based on the Marriages Index Fredonia Censor, Collection SUNY Fredonia; New York State Census, 1845 and 1855; *Post-Journal,* 29 March 1969, notice of grave relocations; C. B. Sampson, notes, Fenton Historical Society, Jamestown, N.Y.; James Anderson, *The Conquest of Chautauqua: Jamestown and Vicinity in the Pioneer and Later Periods as told by Pioneer Newspapers and Persons* (Jamestown, N.Y.: Journal Press, 1932); and the United States Census, 1810, 1820, 1830, 1840, and 1850.

14. Despite explosive urban growth, as late as 1870, three out of four still lived in rural areas, though "city households generally spent three times as much as rural households. Also, home manufactures—from butter to clothes—were much less common in larger cities." See David Goldfield and Blaine Brownell, *Urban America: A History* (Boston: Houghton Mifflin, 1990), 87.

15. Harvey might be the "H. A. Smith" in the credits of Oliver's book of 1852. He died of camp fever in Missouri while serving as a major in the Union army during the Civil War.

16. Thomas Holleman and James Gallagher, *Smith, Hinchman & Grylls: 125 Years of Architecture and Engineering, 1853–1978* (Detroit: Wayne State University Press, 1978), 19–20.

17. Oliver Smith, "Science and Progress of Civil Architecture," "extract" of a lecture delivered at the Jamestown Academy, *Jamestown Journal,* 19 and 26 October 1848.

18. James Elmes (1782–1862), a prominent English architect and prison reformer, trained John Haviland, who taught at the Franklin Institute and in his own academy; Smith might have attended either. Elmes wrote *Sir Christopher Wren and His Times* (1823); *Lectures on Architecture* (1823); *The Arts and Artists* (1825); *General and Biographical Dictionary of the Fine Arts* (1826); *Treatise on Architectural Jurisprudence* (1827); and *Thomas Clarkson: A Monograph* (1854).

19. Accounts suggest that Oliver moved to Jamestown in the 1830s for at least fifteen years. He was listed as a resident there in the 1840 and the 1845 census.

20. Smith Bly house, Ashville, New York. Historic American Building Survey, HABS, NY, 7-ASH.V,2.

21. Details of this 1835 house match plate 48 in Minard Lafever, *The Modern Builder's Guide* (1833).

22. Jewel Conover, *Nineteenth Century Architecture in Western New York* (Albany: State University of New York Press, 1966), 131; David G. Smith quoted in the foreword to the 1978 reprint of *The Domestic Architect.* For examples of Greek Revival houses from a nearby town, see Daniel Reiff, *Architecture in Fredonia, New York, 1811–1997* (Fredonia, N.Y.: White Pine Press, 1997).

23. William Hall, *Jamestown Journal,* 23 July 1847.

24. Conover, *Nineteenth Century Architecture,* 142.

25. In a 1978 reprint of *The Domestic Architect,* David G. Smith credits Oliver Smith with "many of the fine Greek revival houses" in the Ashville and Panama area. According to William J. Doty, *The Historic Annals of Southwestern New York* (1940), 3:562, Smith designed some "finer houses on classic lines in Jamestown, Panama and the surrounding region, some of which he probably built," and specifically the Breed and Hall Mansions.

26. Daniel D. Reiff, *Houses from Books: Treatises, Pattern Books, and Catalogs in American Architecture, 1738–1950, a History and Guide* (University Park: Pennsylvania State University Press, 2000), 67. The house in Cassadaga is also in Conover, *Nineteenth Century Architecture,* 81.

27. Reiff, *Houses from Books,* 67. Also see *Jamestown Post-Journal,* 20 January 1990.

28. Reiff, *Houses from Books,* 67.

29. Smith, *Modern Architect,* viii. See also Jean-Christophe Agnew, *Worlds Apart: the Market and the Theatre in Anglo-American Thought, 1550–1750* (New York: Cambridge University Press, 1986), 69.

The author's "very effort to transport the reader behind the . . . rhetoric of mutuality and through his or her logic of instrumentalism merely reenacted, where they did not in fact deepen, the reader's sense of estrangement—of distance."

30. Smith, *Modern Architect*, 14.

31. Joseph Corn, "Textualizing Technics: Owner's Manuals and the Reading of Objects," in *American Material Culture: The Shape of the Field*, ed. Ann Smart Martin and J. Ritchie Garrison (Knoxville: Henry Francis du Pont Winterthur Museum, University of Tennessee Press, 1997), 177.

32. Amos Loveday Jr., *The Rise and Decline of the American Cut Nail Industry* (Westport, Conn.: Greenwood Press, 1983), 5 n. 8, from *Abridgments of the Debates of Congress from 1789 to 1856* (New York: D. Appleton, 1857), 1:38. See also David Thomas, *Travels through the Western Country in the Summer of 1816*, facsimile of the 1819 edition (Darien, Conn.: Hafner, 1970), 54.

33. Charles B. Wood, book catalogue, http://www.cbwoodbooks.com/american_architecture7.htm.

34. Milton W. Hamilton, *The Country Printer, New York State, 1785–1830* (New York: Columbia University Press, 1936).

35. First mentioned in Hitchcock, *American Architectural Books*.

36. Reiff, *Houses from Books*, 66–67.

37. Analogously, the Grimm brothers wrote their fairy tales in a common language, using German from the oral tradition and routine structures such as "once upon a time" and "happily ever after").

38. Wayde Brown, personal communication, regarding houses in Nova Scotia.

39. Smith, *Domestic Architect*, 61.

40. Ibid., plate 24, figs. 1, 5.

41. Ibid., plate 23.

42. Charles E. Peterson, *Colonial St. Louis: Building a Creole Capital* (St. Louis: Missouri Historical Society, 1949).

43. Solon Robinson, "A Cheap Farm-House," *American Agriculturalist* 6 (July 1847): 218; Edward Shaw, *The Modern Architect; or, Every Carpenter His Own Master* (Boston: Dayton & Wentworth, 1854), frontispiece. See, e.g., Spiro Kostof, *America by Design* (New York: Oxford University Press, 1994), 25, for attribution.

44. William E. Bell, *Carpentry Made Easy* (Philadelphia: J. Challen, 1858), 53. Bell lived in Ottawa, Illinois; see *History of LaSalle County Illinois* (Chicago: Interstate Publishing, 1886), 508–9.

45. Charles Dwyer, *The Economic Cottage Builder; or, Cottages for Men of Small Means* (Buffalo: Wanzer, McKim, 1855), 33; Charles Dwyer, *Economy of Church, Parsonage, and School Architecture* (Buffalo: Phinney & Company, 1856); Charles Dwyer, *Immigrant Builder; or, Practical Hints to Handymen Showing Clearly How to Plan and Construct Dwellings in the Bush, on the Prairie, or Elsewhere, Cheaply and Well, with Wood, Earth, or Gravel.* (Philadelphia: Claxton, Remsen & Hafflefinger, 1872).

46. Dwyer, *Economic Cottage Builder*, 33. The instructions continue: "The joints throughout these plank walls are to be covered with slips, three inches wide each. It is usual to apply flooring boarding, tongued and grooved, to the purpose of forming these plank walls; but much the better plan is to use two-inch undressed hemlock, and sheet the outside of it with inch dressed boards, laid on horizontally."

47. Roger W. Moss MS, Athenaeum of Philadelphia, Philadelphia Architects and Buildings Project; also, http://www.philadelphiabuildings.org/pab/app/ar_display.cfm/22834.

48. Upton makes this point about Dwyer but suggests that it is true of his 1870 book and not his 1856 one. See Dell Upton, "The Traditional House and Its Enemies," *Traditional Dwellings and Settlements Review* 1 (1990): 73.

49. Wood, book catalogue.

50. Isaac Byington, diary, collection of the Winterthur Library, doc. no. 531.

51. Shammas, *Pre-industrial Consumer*, 169.

52. Clark, "Rural America and the Transition to Capitalism," 227–28.

53. Benes and Montague Benes, *Itinerancy*, 7.

54. Bernard Herman, *Architecture and Rural Life in Central Delaware, 1790–1900* (Knoxville: University of Tennessee Press, 1987), 130–31: "While farmers and landholders may have been designers using popular and easily accessible architectural guides as sources for inspiration, they were not builders."

55. Jaffee, "Peddlers of Progress," 513.

56. Itinerants resembled vagabonds and hobos: "Only the faintest of lines separated the multiple by-employments of the rural outworker from the multiple impostures of the professional rogue" (Agnew, *Worlds Apart*, 66).

57. Jaffee, "Peddlers of Progress," 535. Self-fashioning was a controversial activity: "Bulwer concluded that man's presumptuous self-fashioning had already left him 'shoared upon the Continent of Change and confusion, where the inconstancy of his actions, and the various shapes he entertained, by the new modeling of his person, justly brought upon him the judgment of dereliction" (Agnew, *Worlds Apart*, 96).

58. Benes and Montague-Benes, *Itinerancy*, 11. See also Jaffee, "Peddlers of Progress," 521.

59. W. W. Boyington, "Architecture at the Present Time as Compared to That of Fifty Years Ago," *American Architect and Building News*, 29 October 1887, 205.

60. John Cordulack, "The Artisan Confronts the Machine Age: Bureau County Illinois, 1850–1880" (Ph.D. diss., University of Illinois–Urbana, 1975), 78, 85, 148–49.

61. This list is based on the *bricoleur* described in Norman Denzin and Yvonna Lincoln, eds., *Handbook of Qualitative Research* (Thousand Oaks, Calif.: Sage, 1994), 2–5.

III

"VAST AVENUES TO KNOWLEDGE"

Thomas Ustick Walter's Books

Jhennifer A. Amundson

Early in his career Thomas Ustick Walter (figure 3.1) acquired a self-described "strong disposition to indulge in books" that lasted through the fluctuations of his frequently successful, and occasionally tragic, life (1804–87).[1] The expansion and contraction of his library across his six-decade career indicates the ebb and flow of his professional fortunes as clearly as any office ledger could. Even as its size changed, the library's content remained remarkably consistent. From the start of his career during the historically derived stylistic revivals of the 1820s to its culmination in the aesthetically indeterminate 1880s, Walter maintained a preference for certain architectural texts published prior to midcentury. The consistency of his bibliophilia can be traced through several sources, including notebooks from the early 1830s, lectures written at midcentury, and the library inventory taken upon his death in 1887. Although such uniformity would seem to indicate at first that Walter's approach was stagnant, or at least conservative, the view through Walter's own theoretical lens reveals not obsolescence so much as his particular understanding of modernity, which differed from the common one in the postbellum period. Such an examination also reveals the centrality of books to Walter's definition of modern architectural practice. A self-consciously progressive architect, Walter delighted in the nineteenth century's explosion of architectural publications, which, despite the allegations of others, he believed to be neither design props nor guides to outmoded

FIG 3.1 Portrait of Thomas U. Walter by Albert Newsam (after John Neagle), ca. 1835. Thomas U. Walter Collection, Athenaeum of Philadelphia.

fashions; they were instead a means by which to define the century's modernity and to bolster the architect's rising professionalism.

Becoming an Architect

Walter set his sights on practicing architecture in his youth, as an apprentice brick mason learning the family trade from his father. Tradition could have led the ambitious young mason to label himself "architect" after a length of this training and then to seek design opportunities on building sites. But a novel opportunity presented itself as father and son worked side by side laying the brick foundation of the Second National Bank (1818–24) in their hometown of Philadelphia, when the sixteen-year-old arranged to work in the office of its architect, William Strickland. Later, Walter would describe the periods he spent in Strickland's office (1819–ca. 1821 and 1828–30) as the laboratory in which he both developed his drawing skills and learned "a general knowledge of the professional practice of architects" from this leading protagonist in the efforts to establish architecture among the learned professions in America.[2] Strickland introduced Walter to a bookish approach to architectural design and such works as the *Antiquities of Athens* by James Stuart and Nicholas Revett (London, 1762), the starting point for some of Strickland's best-known works, such as the elevation of the Second Bank, drawn from an engraving of the Parthenon. Through such projects, Strickland taught Walter his own approach to selecting approved and noble images to fulfill the requirements of contemporary building types. Strickland also exercised his own literary bent by writing books and articles, publishing several works on architecture and engineering, and by presenting public lectures on the topic.[3] In addition to thus demonstrating his use of books to Walter, Strickland shared his own fine library with his talented pupil.

Such practical office experience was rare among building designers in America; its availability to Walter was an aspect of the providential circumstance of his living in Philadelphia, where opportunities arose to fulfill the desires of his considerable ambition. His early office training with Strickland was enhanced through an academic relationship he established with émigré architect John Haviland. Starting in 1824, Walter augmented his office and job-site training with architectural lessons at the Franklin Institute of the State of Pennsylvania for the Promotion of the Mechanic Arts (figure 3.2). The institute's very building, completed by Haviland in 1825, paid homage to the importance of books to architectural design: like Strickland's Second Bank, its elevation depends upon a plate from the *Antiquities of Athens*, representing the Choragic Monument of Thrasyllus (figure 3.3).

As one of the first students to matriculate into the newly founded program, Walter could attend a series of lectures presented by Strickland, who held the post of professor of architecture, and also study with Haviland, the Franklin Institute's professor of drawing. Haviland, who would also encourage Walter's growing relationship with books, had himself embellished the academic reputation of architects by adding to the growing stream of architectural publications. Before reissuing the highly influential *Young Carpenter's Assistant* by Owen Biddle, he published his own *The Builder's Assistant* (Philadelphia, 1818), noteworthy as the first American book on architecture to portray the Greek orders. In addition to making use of

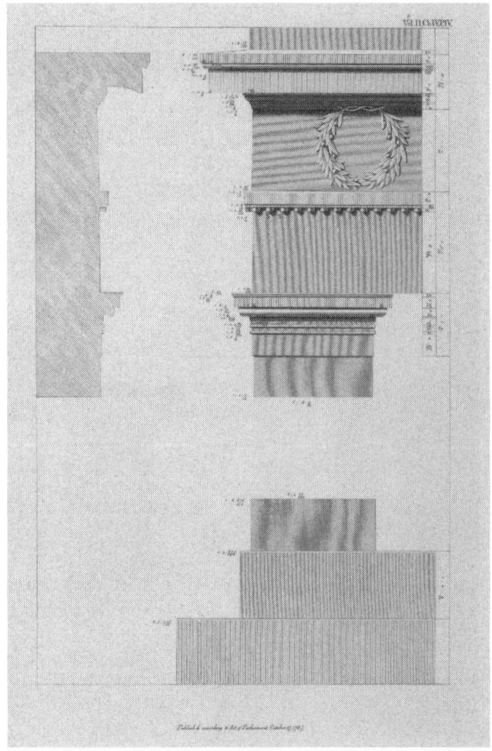

FIG 3.2 John Haviland, The Franklin Institute, Philadelphia, 1825. Karl Lutz Collection, Athenaeum of Philadelphia.

FIG 3.3 The Monument of Thrasyllus. From James Stuart and Nicholas Revett, *The Antiquities of Athens* (1762), vol. 2, plate 4. Athenaeum of Philadelphia.

this book, Walter purchased several other volumes that appeared in Haviland's library.[4] Comparisons between the contents of Haviland's and Walter's libraries reveal striking similarities, which may be either the result of similar reading tastes or a more direct influence from Haviland on Walter's early purchases.

Together, Strickland and Haviland instructed and influenced Walter through their personal contact and their building designs, the latter of which remained potent symbols for him after the death of his mentors. Having risen in Philadelphia during Walter's formative professional years, both the Second Bank and the Franklin Institute revealed to him the importance of books in architectural design. Although the two buildings shared a common source in *The Antiquities of Athens*, their characters and architects' approaches were widely different. Strickland's freestanding civic building recalls the most chaste and iconic specimen of Classical

Greek architecture. On a much less prominent site on Seventh Street, Haviland accommodated an institute that aimed to elevate mechanics, inventors, and scientists, as well as offer scientific education to the general public. The lesser-known Monument of Thrasyllus offered a Greek pedigree, while the highly unusual design of its facade suggested the inventive nature of the institution that would be housed in Haviland's building. These two projects manifest the lessons Walter learned from his mentors concerning the centrality and use of books in architectural practice, as well as the flexibility of Greek architecture and its symbolic potential for a variety of building types. His understanding of the architects, their buildings, and the books they shared secured a primary notion that would guide his practice for some six decades: books could help the modern architect solve a host of contemporary building problems within a style that was accepted as the highest level of artistic achievement.

Collecting Books

Throughout the 1820s, Walter worked intermittently with Strickland, attended lectures and lessons at the Franklin Institute and pursued his own course of study in the libraries open to him. His reading was directed toward greater than professional ends alone. Like many Americans in the first decades of the nineteenth century, Walter believed literature to be a method of personal enrichment and a respectable response to the waves of social reform that had followed the Great Awakenings, which called on Americans to enhance their personal ethical vigor through various moral activities exercised on the public stage. Books paved the road to such improvement, because literature—of the proper sort—played a strong role in communicating ideals of spirituality, patriotism, morality, and honor.

A devout member of the Baptist Church and a Sunday School teacher throughout his adult life, Walter was part of a religious community that encouraged education as a means to bolster belief and strengthen evangelistic efforts. In addition to the Bible and church-generated tracts, allegorical literature along the lines of John Bunyan's classic of 1678, *Pilgrim's Progress*, was encouraged by and for members of the church. Even a recent work of fiction such as Sir Walter Scott's *Ivanhoe* (1819) was said by the conservative editor of the *Port Folio*, Nicholas Biddle, to foster "the principle of individual honour" and to serve as "a sort of school of moral discipline."[5] Although moral leaders denounced literature and poetry that aimed no higher than mere entertainment, they acknowledged that those works with moral and historical foundations had found a place in the homes of "even religious families," like Walter's.[6]

In addition to regular reading of the Bible with his family, Walter examined patriotic poetry and moralistic novels. Sir Walter Scott, Felicia Hemans, Washington Irving, John Bunyan, and John Milton complemented Holy Scripture in Walter's socially minded spiritual development. He exercised his faith every day of the week both privately and professionally, as evidenced in the very makeup of his library. As it grew, architectural treatises, collections of poetry, archaeological publications, engineering manuals, and historical fictions intermingled with Christian tracts on its shelves. Walter summarized his approach to building his library: "I buy nothing for *ornament*,—nothing with the mere idea of increasing my library; but anything that will make me a better *Architect*, a better *Christian*, or a better *Citizen* I am always ready to go in for."[7] These three identities, interwoven in Walter's theory and practice, were expressed through the titles that filled the shelves in both his home and his office in Philadelphia.

Walter was indoctrinated from the start of his adult life with the notion that books could provide the key to both improving society (as his church encouraged) and enhancing architectural practice (as his mentors demonstrated). The hours he spent poring over books as part of his self-determined course of study marked both a personal and a professional advance beyond the custom of manual employment practiced by both his father and grandfather. Walter consumed dozens of books, directing and dedicating himself to a demanding program that included developing professional literacy as an essential part of his course of architectural study. Probably because of Haviland's and Strickland's combined influence, he considered conversance with such canonical authors as Stuart and Revett, as well as with new titles from the fields of engineering and archaeology, as an essential part of the training that separated architects from mechanics. They were tools that recorded images and an ever increasing body of knowledge, the mastery of which Walter believed would differentiate "real" architects from mechanics who had taken part in the custom of exchanging trowel and chisel for divider and pencil without indulging in the "liberal" education that he himself had undertaken[8]—those he called "assuming pretenders" and "brainless bunglers."[9] He believed strongly that only persons versed in the intellectual aspect of the profession should be recognized as architects and trusted with the design of buildings.

Walter's own journey from mechanic to architect is chronicled in two surviving pocket notebooks in which he began writing when he was still listed as "bricklayer" in city directories.[10] Dating to the early 1830s, several years after his introduction to Strickland and Haviland, they are the earliest physical documentation of his book-based architectural studies. As an architectural assistant with a growing family, and little money to spend on his own books, Walter visited the libraries of such Philadelphia institutions as the Franklin Institute and the Philosophical Society, as well as the private collections of his mentors, copying excerpts of all kinds into these miniature digests of essential readings. From sweeping, multivolume architectural dictionaries to highly specialized titles, Walter recorded kernels of learning both practical and theoretical. He studied new key works in the scientific aspects of architecture, including structural statics and environmental comfort. He copied detailed drawings, charts, and text passages, noting elements of truss construction from Charles Frederick Partington's *Builder's Complete Guide* (London, 1825); passages from Thomas Tredgold's *On the Principles and Practice of Warming and Ventilating Buildings* (Edinburgh, 1825); the characteristics of structural cast iron both from Tredgold's *Practical Essay on the Strength of Cast Iron, and Other Metals* (2nd ed., London, 1824) and from *Treatise on the Strength of Timber, Cast and Malleable Iron*, written by Peter Barlow in 1817. In several places his detailed transcriptions are illustrated with very fine ink drawings and diagrams (figure 3.4).

Walter interleaved these practical building notes with matters of theory and design. His commentaries on the Classical orders are illustrated with esteemed examples reproduced from canonical sources. The elevation of a Tuscan temple accompanies observations from an 1812 edition of Vitruvius edited by William Wilkins; an ink-wash study illustrates Andrea Palladio's directions for drawing an Ionic column capital (figure 3.5). In this early stage of his career, the practical bent of the mason is evident in the eclipsing of these few theoretical notations by the lengthier ones on building technology which take up the greater part of the notebooks.[11] With these small, comprehensive compendiums assembled from those books that he could access (see Appendix A), Walter built his early practice.

If these notebooks perfectly represent Walter's earliest studies in architecture, they reveal an early dedication to the pragmatic and practical concerns that he would view as elemental to the architect's responsibilities for his entire career. Although theoretical commentary is relatively spare in these early notebooks, the appearance of aesthetic considerations in them points to the creative and inventive aspect of his work, and his dedication to practicing architecture as more than preparation for construction. The mason's son would be concerned perpetually with

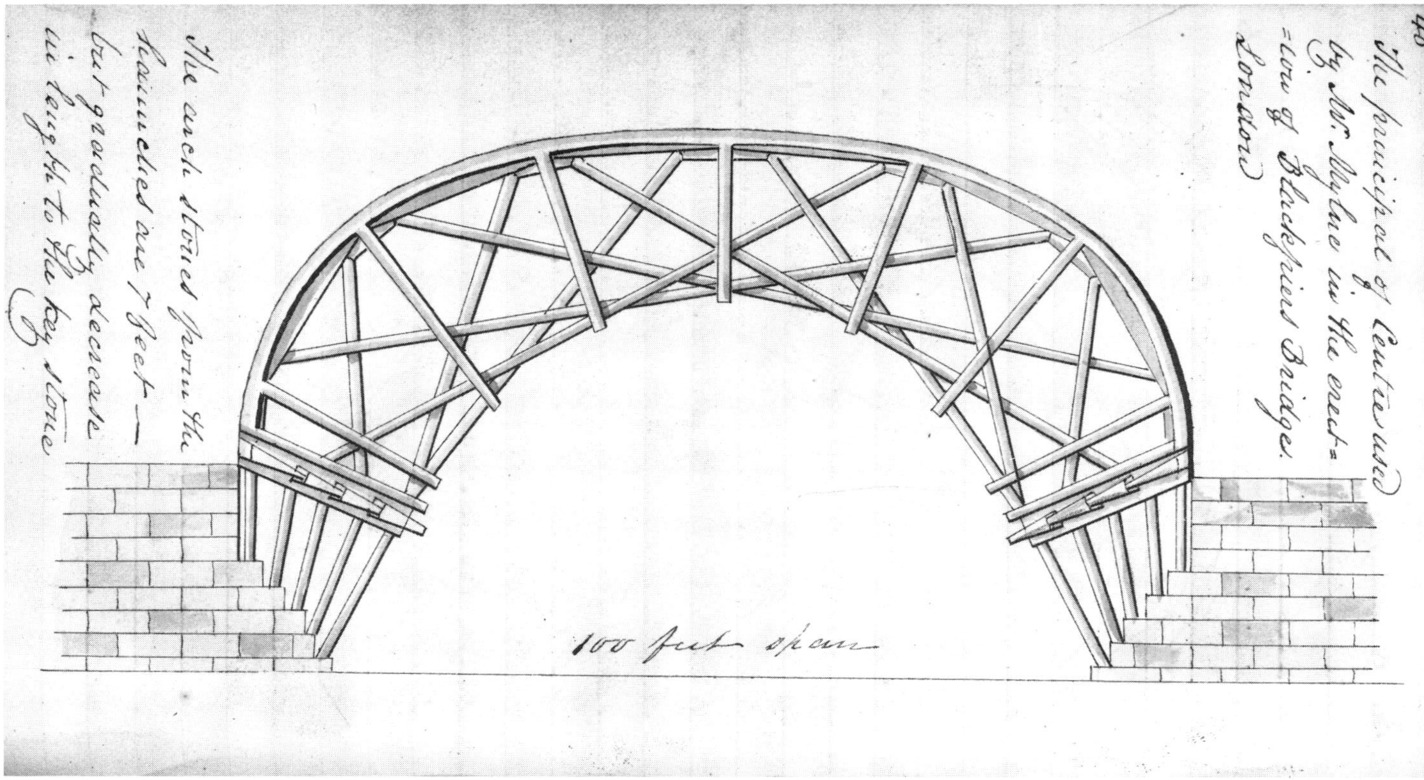

FIG 3.4 Thomas U. Walter, “The prinicpal of Centre used by Mr. Mylne in the erection of the Blackfriars Bridge, London.” From his “Architectural Notebook” (ca. 1830), p. 48. Thomas U. Walter Collection, Athenaeum of Philadelphia.

both the grounded necessities of building and the elevated nature of his profession as an art.

With the rising success of his practice in the mid-1830s, Walter enjoyed the friendship of a number of prominent American architects including Ithiel Town, renowned for his colossal library and appropriately memorialized, lounging on a stack of divan-sized folios, in Thomas Cole's 1840 painting *The Architect's Dream*. Walter's portrait could easily substitute for Town's in the painting, for in

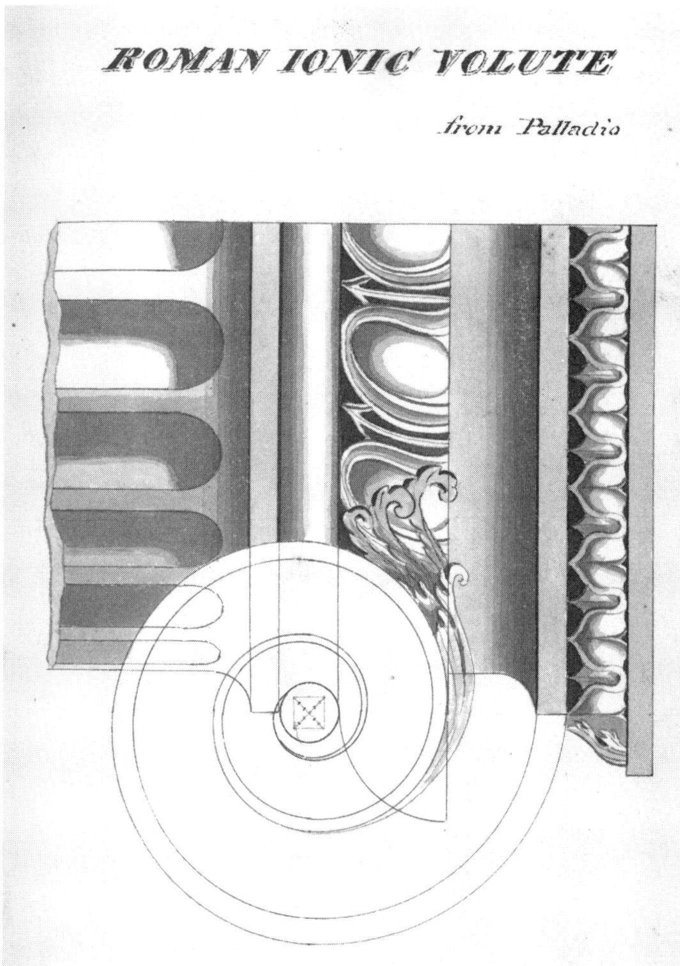

FIG 3.5 Thomas U. Walter, "Roman Ionic Volute from Palladio." From his "Architectural Notebook" (ca. 1830), p. 19. Thomas U. Walter Collection, Athenaeum of Philadelphia.

his growing inclination and proclivity for collecting books he was overshadowed by probably very few architects other than Town, whose famously large library in New York Walter visited as early as 1835.[12] Walter's experience, new wealth, and association with Town—and no doubt his covetous relationship with Town's library—spurred his collecting in the second half of the 1830s. Receipts and diary entries reveal extraordinary spending patterns in bookshops in Philadelphia, New York, and London: about $200 per year during his most prosperous days.[13] After a bankruptcy in 1841 forced him to sell much of the collection, Walter rebuilt it; by midcentury its volumes numbered in the hundreds. In 1861, as Walter began planning for his retirement to Germantown, Pennsylvania, he regretted having dedicated only 400 square feet of his large new villa to his books. He complained of the library room, "It wont hold all my books now, and [in short time] I shall have to use, in addition to it, one of the chambers: if I could afford it I would have my Library as large as the whole house."[14]

At its peak, the collection likely numbered one thousand titles. Even after reduced circumstances forced him out of retirement and back to the drawing board in the early 1870s, Walter owned more than seven hundred books.[15] Following a string of family tragedies and unfortunate investments, however, the number would continue to dwindle through his remaining years. Yet the presence of seventy-four volumes at the time of his death confirms the unceasing importance of books in his life. For Walter, books were not just a means of spending leisure time or of ornamenting a salon but, instead, the substance of his productions in architecture. Increasingly toward midcentury he had defined such efforts not only with buildings but also through written work.

Reading and Writing

Although Walter consumed architecture books voraciously early in his career, he revealed little inclination then to produce them himself. In his opinion, the increased production of such books did not necessarily guarantee an increase in their quality; too many of them simplified the principles and poetry of architecture in a way that made only a reduced vision of beauty achievable by otherwise unskilled builders. An application of his lifelong struggle to see architecture recognized as the jurisdiction of specifically trained specialists was his condemnation of builder's guides that usurped the architect's functions by making design details and even whole building plans available to "mechanics." Walter disparaged architects who took part in the production of books that hindered the profession; he dismissed the shoddy scholarship of those who included long historical excerpts from earlier works and rebuked those who too freely divulged their own creative productions. In a diary entry of 1835, Walter recorded his reaction to a recent book by his colleague Minard Lafever: "[I don't] like bookmaking while we have so many more good books than we read—don't think I'll ever make a book, was I ever to attempt it I might give every man an opportunity of buying for a few dollars, all the brains I've got."[16] These words, however, were written by a young architect enjoying a quickly expanding practice in the mid-1830s. Within the following decade the country experienced the significant financial turmoil that led to Walter's own first bankruptcy. In 1846 he succumbed to the fiscal lure of publishing by coauthoring two rather unremarkable albums, *A Guide to Workers in Metals and Stone*, and *Cottage and Villa Architecture: Two Hundred Designs* (figure 3.6). Neither book offers more than scant written commentary, and the meager quality of the illustrations suffers in comparison with the usually fine hand displayed in virtually all the hundreds of Walter's original drawings. The books present only uninspired assemblages of handrail details, candelabras, and cottage designs. Walter clearly did not run the risk of giving away "all his brains" for the price of these volumes.

Still, his hopes for architectural publishing paralleled his expectations for the profession itself: both were to increase in quality and academic character. He embraced publishing opportunities that could fortify architectural practice. Directed to an audience of peers in architecture and other scientific professions, his seven articles for the *Journal of the Franklin Institute*, appearing in 1840–41, offered his findings on a variety of subjects—including contemporary prison design and the history of glass in buildings—and his observations on architectural "chromatics," as he described the "scientific" use of color in buildings (see Appendix B). Such carefully researched articles were intended to raise the intellectual approach of architects and thus strengthen, rather than challenge, their professional authority.

While promoting the status of architects through such focused studies, Walter also cultivated public awareness of architecture by means of a different and more popular kind of literature: the public lecture. He completed the first draft of his six-part "Lectures on the History and Philosophy of Architecture" in 1841 for the Franklin Institute in Philadelphia, revising them in 1853 and again in the 1860s for audiences in Washington, D.C.[17] The board of the Franklin Institute had requested only a course of lectures on architecture, without specifying the character or content. As his earlier *Journal* essays show, Walter was capable of a wide variety of

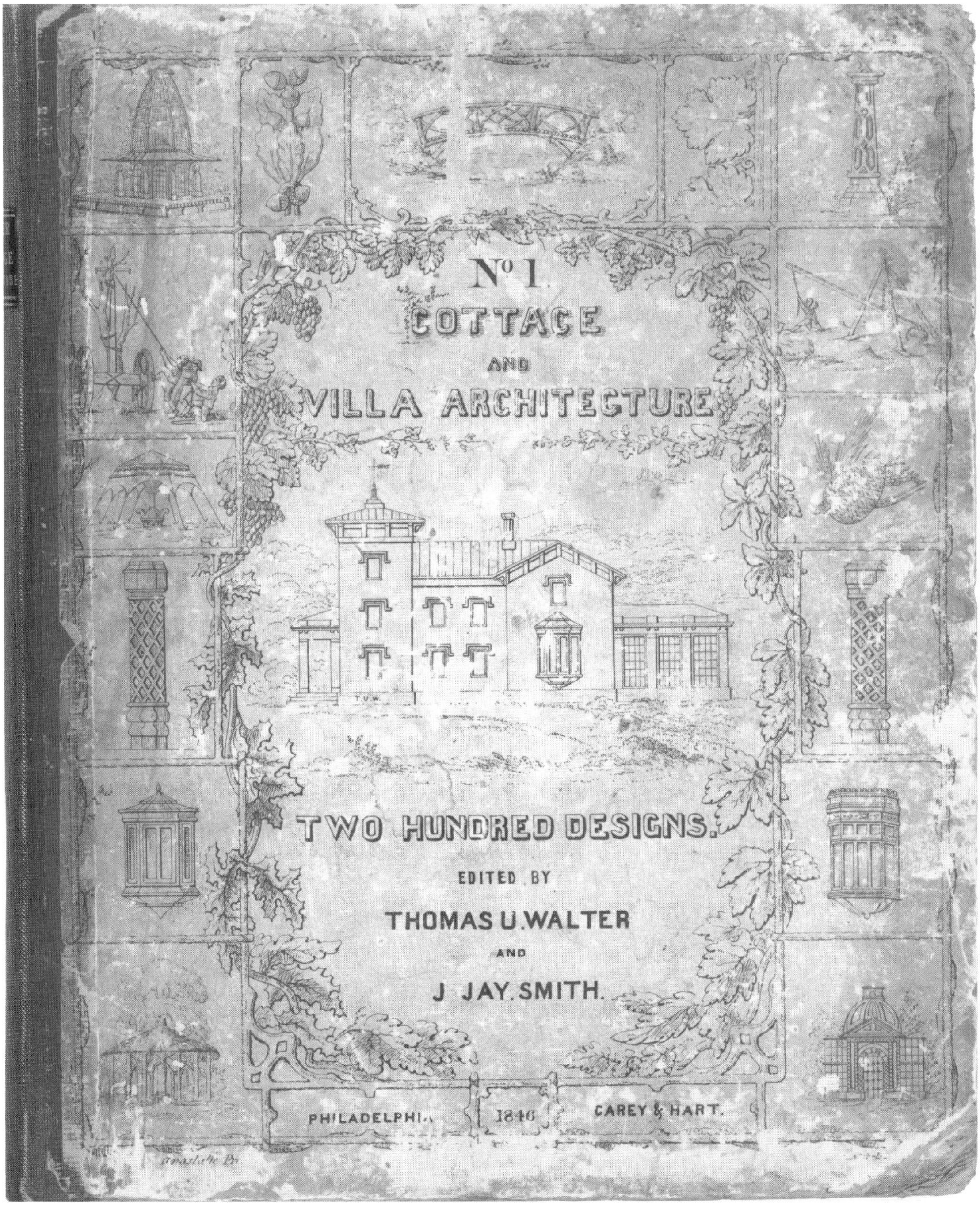

FIG 3.6 Thomas U. Walter (with J. Jay Smith), *Cottage and Villa Architecture: Two Hundred Designs* (1846). Athenaeum of Philadelphia.

topics of interest to professionals and students, including theory, technology, building type, and urban design; his notebooks from the 1830s also testify to his grasp of such specialized subjects. And yet Walter conceived of the oral presentations as dealing with none of these professionally focused topics; instead, he adopted a genre of writing that was unprecedented in his own experience. Open to the public, his lectures would be cast as a history of architecture. As a kind of literature that was of great interest and popularity among American readers, history would serve his intent to persuade his listeners of architecture's importance to civilization. Walter broke from the time-honored tradition of Asher Benjamin, Minard Lafever, even the otherwise inspirational John Haviland, and others who borrowed heavily from previous authors in compiling their own historical summaries. Walter actually wrote his own architectural history based on a thorough course of research.

Walter's considerable reading program included ancient history, scripture, Renaissance treatises, modern travel guides, recent archaeological investigations, recent aesthetic theory, contemporary travel literature, classical mythology, and modern fiction. The character of these presentations were in marked contrast to the professionally focused articles and addresses he had previously written. By assimilating such diverse sources, Walter's lectures reached beyond the pragmatic minutia of tasteful design which had been the focus of his pattern-book-publishing forebears (and even Strickland's own lectures at the Franklin Institute some fifteen years earlier). Walter's commentary was more appropriate to the public audiences he addressed at the Franklin Institute, Smithsonian Institution, Columbian College, and various social clubs and improvement societies in and around Philadelphia and Washington.

Of the eighty bibliographic sources noted by Walter in the lecture manuscripts, the vast majority are histories. Walter's reading list reflects those books which he accepted as classics and reveals the increase, in both depth and breadth, of his century's historical knowledge, a result of increased travel, trade, and publications which by the early 1840s had expanded the Eurocentric concept of civilization prevalent among earlier Americans. He could avail himself of new, specialized histories of architecture by James Elmes (1823) and Thomas Hope (1835), along with such rare earlier works as an English translation of Giorgio Vasari's *Le vite de' più eccellenti pittori, scultori, e architettori* (Florence, 1550).[18] Having been introduced to them in his earliest days, Walter had collected, and still used, canonical titles on classical antiquity, including those of Vitruvius and Palladio, as well as eighteenth-century works by William Chambers (*Treatise on the Decorative Part of*

Civil Architecture, 1759; expanded and reissued 1791) and Richard Chandler (*Ionian Antiquities*, London, 1769).[19] The four-volume *Antiquities of Athens* (London, 1762–1818) by James Stuart and Nicholas Revett remained his most frequent reference. In Walter's view these authors had set the standard for clarity, competence, and fine drawing. Their books were model depictions of ideal architecture, providing reliable and clear descriptions from which Walter could draw his own oral descriptions of landmarks, and also images that he could direct local artists to copy in the production of the large watercolor renderings that accompanied his lectures.

The historical context that Walter was able to study expanded significantly in his lifetime. Beyond the established works dedicated to the renowned cultures of classical antiquity, new attention to other antique lands accompanied the expanded travel possible in the nineteenth century. Walter depended for his lectures' text and accompanying images on such volumes as Vivant Denon's 1803 landmark folio *Voyages dans la Basse et la Haute Egypte* (*Travels in Upper and Lower Egypt*; see figures 3.7, 3.8) and studies by premiere Egyptologist Sir John Gardner Wilkinson, plus many other early nineteenth-century titles on Nubia and Ethiopia by Giovanni Belzoni, George Hoskins, and Charles Rollin.[20] Such works included the richly illustrated mid-eighteenth-century folio *Ruins of Palmyra* by Robert Wood; the two-volume *Travels in Georgia, Persia, Armenia, Ancient Babylonia, &c.* by Robert Ker Porter (London, 1821–22); Alphonse de Lamartine's popular *Pilgrimage to the Holy Land/Voyages en Orient* (1833, 1835); and one of the newest books in Walter's lecture bibliography, Sir Austen Henry Layard's *Nineveh and Its Remains* (London, 1849). New fields of study included the ancient Americas, for which Walter relied on *Description of the Ruins of an Ancient City Discovered near Palenque* (London, 1794) by Antonio Del Rio; John Lloyd Stephens's *Incidents of Travel in Central America, Chiapas, and Yucatàn,* (London, 1841); and the voluminous writings of Baron Alexander von Humboldt. These authors opened the field of ancient American architecture to Walter. He was able to consider China through the availability of such books as Dr. Clarke Abel's *Narrative of a Journey in the Interior of China* (London, 1819) and Sir John Barrow's *Travels in China* (London, 1806); the journal *Asiatick Researches* (published 1788–1839 by the Asiatic Society of Bengal) also offered new insights to that otherwise closed culture.

Although the Middle Ages had held literary interest since the mid-eighteenth century, Walter was not drawn to the "gothick" of Horace Walpole as much as to the more archaeological catalogues of Gothic architecture made in the early nineteenth century. In all, he consulted over a half-dozen titles published in the 1830s

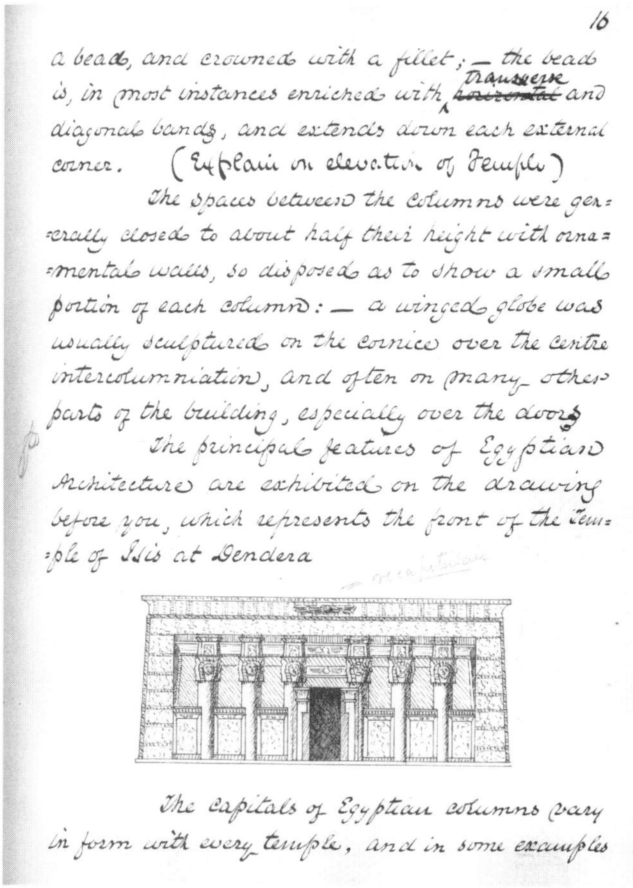

16

a bead, and crowned with a fillet; — the bead is, in most instances enriched with [transverse] ~~horizontal~~ and diagonal bands, and extends down each external corner. (Explain on elevation of Temple)

The spaces between the columns were generally closed to about half their height with ornamental walls, so disposed as to show a small portion of each column: — a winged globe was usually sculptured on the cornice over the centre intercolumniation, and often on many other parts of the building, especially over the doors

The principal features of Egyptian Architecture are exhibited on the drawing before you, which represents the front of the Temple of Isis at Dendera

The capitals of Egyptian columns vary in form with every temple, and in some examples

FIG 3.7 Elevation of the portico of the Great Temple of Tentyra (Dendera). From Vivant Denon, *Travels in Upper and Lower Egypt* (1803), plate 20. Athenaeum of Philadelphia.

FIG 3.8 Thomas U. Walter, The Temple of Isis at Dendera. From "Lecture 1st: On Ancient Architecture" (1841), p. 16. Thomas U. Walter Collection. Athenaeum of Philadelphia.

and 1840s on English medieval architecture, including several of John Britton's famous works—in particular, the five-volume *Architectural Antiquities of Great Britain* (London, 1807–26). Again, having expanded his studies to include material excluded from most other architectural histories, Walter integrated works which focused on that culture where the "the torch of literature was kept alive" during the Dark Ages: Arabia and the Muslim establishments in Europe.[21] For these, he reviewed Henry Swinburne's *Travels through Spain in the Years 1775–76* and Comte de Alexandre Laborde's *Voyage Pittoresque et Historique de l'Espagne*, 2 volumes (Paris, 1806–20), among other titles.

In addition to historians and archaeologists, Walter was familiar with modern theoreticians, whose ideas may have become familiar to him through either their own publications or the excerpts and reviews of philosophical books included in the first regular publication on architecture, the *Architectural Magazine*, to which Walter subscribed during its run between 1834 and 1839. His favored translation of Vitruvius (*The Civil Architecture of Vitruvius*) was edited by William Wilkins in 1809 with a lengthy introductory essay including theoretical commentary on ancients (Aristotle, Pliny, and Thucydides) and moderns (Edmund Burke, Richard Payne Knight, Uvedale Price). Walter's lectures reveal a familiarity also with the work of Sir Joshua Reynolds, André Félibien, and Antoine-Chrysostome Quatremère de Quincy, and the *Oration* presented by Benjamin Henry Latrobe before the Society of Artists in Philadelphia in 1811.

Both to entertain his audience members and to advance their understanding of the architect as a cultured intellectual, Walter ornamented his lectures with vignettes drawn from classical myth, classic drama, and popular literature. By both direct quotation and passing reference, he included selections from Lord Byron, William Wordsworth, John Dyer, Felicia Hemans, Edward Bulwer-Lytton, Washington Irving, John Milton, and William Shakespeare.[22] These additions significantly enriched the character of his writings. Using recent archaeological sources, Walter could begin by describing a particular building as a lifeless mass. For example, he explained that the Colosseum was built by Vespasian and Titus beginning around 79 A.D.; that its elliptical plan measures 620 by 513 feet; and that the building reaches 157 feet in height with four stories of arcades decorated in Doric, Ionic, Corinthian, and Composite orders—such information allowed an audience to picture a building. But to place it in an atmosphere and context, Walter quoted from the poetry of Lord Byron:

And here, where buzzing nations choked the ways,
And roar'd or murmur'd like a mountain stream
Dashing or winding as its torrent strays.—
Here, where the Roman millions' blame or praise,
Was death or life, the playthings of a crowd.[23]

Likewise, verbal definitions and diagrams could position York Cathedral as an example of the Decorated Style of English Gothic architecture, but a passing reference to Sir Walter Scott's commentary on the building could quickly prompt the audience to consider the nobility, valor, and spirituality for which the best-selling Waverly novels were praised—values that could, by association, be accorded to the building.[24] The presence of playwrights, novelists, and poets among historical commentaries enhanced Walter's explanation of architecture in an evocative way, drawing in his audience and increasing their understanding of buildings as dimensions, materials, and forms could not do alone.

Reading and Practicing

More important even than the glow of erudition that books reflected on Walter's professional persona, and their effectiveness in evoking an emotional environment for historical structures, his use of historical, fictional, and archaeological publications was also an important part of the way that Walter worked. Practitioners in the popular revival styles of the nineteenth century depended on books to ensure the "accuracy" of their buildings as judged by historical models. In his lectures at midcentury, Walter highlighted the work of architects such as Minard Lafever and John Haviland, whose careful studies of historic architecture in library collections made possible the architectural correctness of their own designs. Although he disparaged some of Minard Lafever's work as an author, Walter praised him as an architect, calling his Dutch Reformed Church (New York, 1840) "the best example of Ecclesiastical Gothic" in the country; its "consistent" and "spirited" features were likely to promote "a correct taste in this particular species of building."[25]

Like Lafever, Walter produced hundreds of buildings in almost every conceivable style, always selecting carefully from traditions of the past. As an architect, he avoided "copying" old buildings in their entirety but judiciously used discrete elements of precedents in an approach that was similar to his work as an author:

FIG 3.9 The Corinthian order from the Choragic Monument of Lysicrates. From Stuart and Revett, *Antiquities of Athens*, vol. 2, plate 6. Athenaeum of Philadelphia.

FIG 3.10 Thomas U. Walter, The Corinthian order from the exterior colonnade of Founder's Hall, Girard College, Philadelphia, ca. 1841. Stephen Girard Collection, Girard College.

reading books by other writers and selectively quoting from them within an overall original lecture. Such was his approach in the colonnade of his most important early building, Girard College (Philadelphia, 1833–47), for which he made a careful study of the capitals from the Choragic Monument of Lysicrates, recreating the details of that Hellenistic monument on an unprecedented scale for the American campus (figures 3.9, 3.10).

For buildings of lesser stature, Walter allowed a greater latitude for invention and indeed found a precedent for invention in the same place where he found Girard's model: the pages of Stuart and Revett. In their volumes, Walter studied the general Greek approach to *practice* as well as its specific *products*. He regarded the variety of approaches to the Corinthian order recorded in the *Antiquities of Athens* as evidence of Greek creativity. Although they provided chaste details for study and imitation, the ancients also compelled contemporary architects (and justified their doing so) to vary, even invent, their own ornament within the system of the orders. A well-documented example is his portico for the Philadelphia Contributionship Insurance Office of 1835. One of his more ambitious students, John D. Jones, recorded Walter's graphic comparison of two specific examples of the Corinthian order: the capitals of the Choragic Monument and the Tower of the Winds as he studied them in Stuart and Revett. Walter described them as "two examples of the Corinthian order no more alike than a *rose* and a *lilac*; but these beautiful productions of nature are both flowers; so it is with these examples of the Corinthian order."[26] Jones includes in his parallel a third Corinthian, Walter's own design for this modern insurance office, which derives elements from both Greek columns and from the architect's own imagination (figure 3.11).

Walter's flexible reading of the folio images adopted them as both models for exacting details and validation for his own creative license. In a later Classical building Walter likewise depended on ancient principles for his choice to flute the exterior columns on the wing additions of the U.S. Capitol (figure 3.12). Breaking from the precedent set by William Thornton in the original building, Walter followed the lead of the ancients as their work was portrayed in his folios. The treatment of columns was based on their location: on the building exterior, fluted columns were more sculpturally modeled by the shifting sun rays and resultant cast shadows; interior columns, especially those of a dark stone, were left unfluted to make the most of their material's natural coloration, veining, and reflectivity. Walter explained that, while attuned to architectural tradition, he had never been afraid to think for himself: "Such I believe to have been the course of the Ancients, and I am much more desirous to think as they thought, than to do exactly as they did."[27] Thus Walter looked to his books not only for details to emulate but also for principles to direct his practice.

Reading and Understanding

In addition to assisting professionals, some books—historical studies in particular—offered to practitioner and public alike an evocative context: not only the *method of building* but also the *meaning of the building*. Like Walter's lectures, which

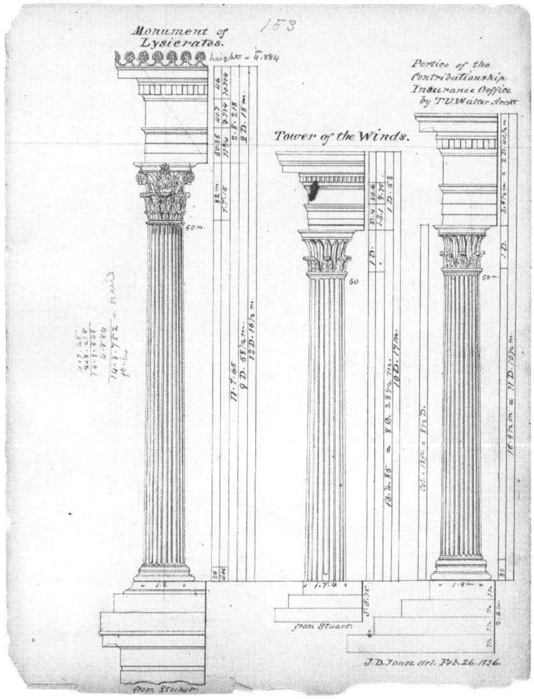

FIG 3.11 John D. Jones (completed under the direction of Thomas U. Walter), Comparison of the Corinthian orders of the Monument of Lysicrates ("from Stuart"), the Tower of the Winds, Athens ("from Stuart"), and Walter's Contributionship Insurance Office, Philadelphia, 1836. Thomas U. Walter Collection, Athenaeum of Philadelphia.

FIG 3.12 Thomas U. Walter, the United States Capitol dome and wings, 1855–65. Thomas U. Walter Collection, Athenaeum of Philadelphia.

he intended to publish so that they might reach a larger audience, such books could provide the reading public lessons and memories tied to historical architecture, which could be transferred to contemporary buildings in the historical styles. In this intellectual operation, called Associationism by Archibald Alison in *Essay on the Nature and Principles of Taste* (1790), ideas came from visual material such as architecture, which could communicate to those educated in its language. Like any language, that of architecture relied on two parties being familiar with its vocabulary. Architects could communicate with the public via buildings if both parties were aware of specific formal triggers, having either read the right books or attended the right lectures. The growing catalogue of architectural images, and information about them, made available through print sources promised to generate an improved civilization in which architecture would edify the population. The establishment of communally understood associations depended on a standardized canon of architectural imagery that architects and the public alike could comprehend. Books, which recorded architectural images and explained their buildings' associated cultural values, were essential to the process.

In Walter's view, the catalogue of books that could communicate these lessons was largely complete by midcentury, as is revealed in the inventory taken of his library at the time of his death (see Appendix D).[28] Of its seventy-three architectural titles, about three-quarters were published before 1850. Old favorites by Vitruvius (Wilkins's edition, 1812), architects William Chambers, Britton and Pugin, Stuart and Revett, historian James Elmes, and engineer Thomas Tredgold all date prior to 1825. The list's proportion of books from the next quarter-century, during which Walter's practice and reputation grew exponentially, is the largest. He maintained the full run of *The Architectural Magazine* (1834–39) and acquired several titles that served the practical needs of his practice, including books on topics related to civil engineering (roads, cements, arch construction, ventilation) and Peter Nicholson's *New Practical Builder* (1823). Compendiums by Robert Stuart (1830) and Thomas Hope (1835) balanced more thematic works by Quatremère de Quincy (1823) and A. J. Downing (1842).

Published near or after 1850, the most recent books in the list, although fewer in number, also balanced the practical and imaginative parts of the practice. On the one hand were several titles on strengths of materials, surveying, and additional engineering matters, and the *Civil Engineer and Architects' Journal* dating from the 1830s through the 1850s. On the other, Walter kept J. J. Jarves's *Art Hints* (1855), two books by John Ruskin (*Lectures on Architecture and Painting*, 1854; *The Seven Lamps of Architecture*, 1849), and one by Calvert Vaux (*Villas and Cottages*, 1857). Walter looked to the several engineering and surveying works for updated scientific, rather than stylistic, knowledge, whereas Ruskin and Vaux articulated themes similar to those in the pages of Walter's own lectures.

The consistency of Walter's reading mirrors that of his practice. For example, none of the books that he maintained to the end of his days, although he was still practicing until the time of his death, appear to have been dedicated to postbellum styles or modes of design. The absence of works concerning even the one new style to which he did subscribe after midcentury, the Second Empire (figure 3.13), is notable and suggests perhaps indifference toward this modern development on the long traditions of French architecture, as well as the harsh economic realities that put an end to his retirement and called him back to practice at the age of sixty-nine. Still more notable is the absence of anything related to the newer styles that would characterize the increasing stylistic inventiveness of the nineteenth century's later decades. Walter's aim for architectural communication demanded a consistency of aesthetic practice which placed him in an awkward position after the Civil War, when architectural expressions were diverging on paths marked by new styles free from clear historical traditions, such as Queen Anne, *néo-grec*, and Stick Style. Walter had patience for neither the license of architects in nontraditional styles nor their suggestion that truly "modern" architecture must break free from the tradition of using recognizable historical precedents.[29] He expressed his disillusionment with this kind of practice in 1880 when assailing the audience gathered for the annual meeting of the American Institute of Architects (AIA). He criticized those who designed buildings lacking in fundamental aesthetic principles, buildings that were merely, as he described them, "an aggregation of trivialities in the making up of details," largely because they exhibited "no trace whatever of paternity, ancient or modern."[30] Walter reviled such so-called creativity and invention because they made architectural communication impossible and expressed only self-indulgent caprice, personal taste, and individual fancy on the part of the architect.

Walter soundly rejected the notion, which would increase in popularity into the twentieth century, that for an architect to be modern he must design in an aesthetic with no ties to the past. Walter argued that his architecture was modern precisely for the opposite reason: because of the way it *could* draw from the past. It was the means by which he learned about historical architecture from other lands, since he could do so with greater ease than his professional forebears, that was modern. Walter measured modernity by the process as much as the product. Understanding

FIG 3.13 Thomas U. Walter, The Baptist Home, Philadelphia, 1872. Thomas U. Walter Collection, Athenaeum of Philadelphia.

how his architecture depended on knowledge unavailable to earlier generations, he wrote that the invention of printing had exercised "a greater influence on architecture than all the revolutions of antiquity"; engraving allowed the modern architect to broaden his horizons beyond the geographic constraints of the ancients and "to study and compare the works of every nation" in a way no previous architect could have imagined.[31]

In Walter's estimation the very use of such books, unparalleled in their breadth, depth, and number, defined contemporary architecture's modernity. Walter's books—whether on Persian, Gothic, Classical, Hindu, Egyptian, Meso-American, Chinese, or Islamic architecture—were for him not just a passport to other times and places but also guides to the future and a mark of modernity. Engraved images and printed books, which he referred to as "vast avenues to knowledge," were a result and fact of steam-powered modern life in the nineteenth century.[32]

The prudent contemporary architect would use them to communicate with an audience and contribute to the harmonious development of civilization. The irresponsible architect designed in a manner that would actually separate him from his public. He was not a more modern man; he was a more savage one.[33] The civilized, inventive modern architect would avail himself of books, indulging in the products of the past while creating the new.

* * *

From his earliest training, then, Walter understood books to hold an essential position in the architect's office. They were a means both of design inspiration and of communication with members of the profession and the public they served. During each phase of his long career, Walter championed those architectural styles and inherited traditions that members of the profession and the public could both learn about through books—like those which he prominently positioned when he sat for his first portrait as a professional architect (figure 3.1). Walter believed that architecture, like literature, was a tool to promote decent morals and good civic behavior, defined according to his faith and as part of the broad social goal of an improved civilization. Understanding a body of images chronicled in contemporary print media, professionals and public could communicate through architectural forms that spoke of the highest cultural endeavors and did so in a manner that would encourage contemporary society as well to aim toward such achievements.

APPENDIX A

Books as Referenced in Walter's Architectural Notebooks, ca. 1830

First Notebook

Haviland's Architecture
Newton's Vitruvius
Palladio's Architecture
Gregory, Dictionary of Arts and Sciences
William H. Hall, Royal Encylopaedia
Nicholson's Practical Builder
Wilkins's Vitruvius
Of the Construction of Prisons by the Prison Discipline Society of Boston, 1826
Tuscan Order, Sir William Chambers
Nicholson's Architectural Dictionary
C. F. Partington, The Builder's Complete Guide

Second Notebook

Smith's Philosophy
Tredgold on Cast Iron

Cited in lists

2. vol. Stuarts Athens
Hopes Furniture
Tremont house
Vallamys (?) Ornaments
Treadgold [*sic*] on Warming
Dunlap 2nd vol.
Davis Surveying
Barn Yard Architecture

1 Palladio's Architecture
1 Ionian Antiquities
2 Rome by Taylor & Cresse
1 Doric Order by Aiken
1 Erectheum by Inman
1 Vallamy's Ornaments
4 Stuarts Athens
1 Strickland's Reports
1 Orders of Architecture by Norman
1 Salisbury Cathedral
1 Unedited Antiquities of Attica
1 Art of Drawing the human fig., Smith
1 Designs for Lodges
1 Wilkins Vitruvius
1 Elsham's (?) Cottages
1 Norwich Cathedral
1 Architectural Plates
1 designs for cottages
1 Redclif (?) church

APPENDIX B

Articles Written by Walter for the *Journal of the Franklin Institute* (*JFI*)

"Architecture." *JFI* 1, no. 1 (January 1841): 11–12.
"A Description of the Eastern Penitentiary, of the State of Pennsylvania, designed and executed by John Haviland, Esq., Architect." *JFI* 2, no. 2 (August 1841): 118–20.
"A Description of the Philadelphia County Prison, and the Debtors' Apartment. Designed and Executed by Thomas U. Walter, Architect." *JFI* 2, no. 3 (September 1841): 189–91.
"On Chromatics as Pertaining to Architecture." *JFI* 2, no. 1 (July 1841): 32–37.
"On Glass as Applied to Architecture.—Extract from a Lecture on the Architecture of the Middle Ages, delivered before the Franklin Institute, by T. U. Walter, Professor of Architecture, December 10, 1840." *JFI* 1, no. 4 (May 1841): 266–67.
"The Orders." *JFI* 1, no. 3 (April 1841): 194–96.
"Street Architecture." *JFI* 1, no. 2 (February 1841): 90–91.

APPENDIX C

Sources Referenced in the Six-Part "Lectures on Architecture"

Authors and Titles

Abel, Dr. Clarke. *Narrative of a Journey in the Interior of China, and of a Voyage to and from that Country, 1816 and 1817.* London, 1819.
Asiatic Researches. Journal of the Asiatic Society of Bengal (Calcutta). [*Asiatick Researches* was published 1788–1839.]

Barrow, Sir John. *Travels in China: Containing descriptions, observations, and comparisons, made and collected in the course of a short residence at the Imperial Palace of Yuen-min-yuen; and on a subsequent journey through the country from Pekin to Canton.* London, 1806.

Bede, the Venerable. *The Ecclesiastical History of the English People.* [Walter read parts of this history within Henry Gally Knight's *Architectural Tour in Normandy.*]

Belzoni, Giovanni Battista. *Narrative of the Operations and Recent Discoveries within the Pyramids, Temples Tombs, and Excavations, in Egypt and Nubia.* 2 vols. London, 1820.

Benedict Biscopius, Abbot. [His introduction of glass art into Britain recorded in Knight, *Normandy.*]

Bentham, Rev. James. *Historical Remarks on the Saxon Churches.* [Reprinted as one of several articles in the compilation *Essays on Gothic Architecture* (London, 1808).]

The Bible

Britton, John. *The Architectural Antiquities of Great Britain.* 5 vols. London, 1807–26.

Bulwer-Lytton, Edward George Earle. *The Last Days of Pompeii.* London, 1834.

Byron, George Gordon, Lord. "Childe Harold's Pilgrimage," 1812–18; "The Giaour," 1813.

Chambers, Sir William. *Treatise on the Decorative Part of Civil Architecture.* 5th ed. Notes and essay by John B. Papworth. London, 1836.

Chandler, Richard. *Ionian Antiquities.* London, 1769. [Coauthored with Nicholas Revett and William Pars.]

Cressy, Edward, and George Ledwell Taylor. *Architectural Antiquities of Ancient Rome.* 2 vols. London, 1821–22.

Dallaway, Rev. James. *A Series of Discourses upon Architecture in England from the Norman Æra to the Close of the Reign of Queen Elizabeth.* London, 1833.

Del Rio, Capt. Antonio. *Description of the ruins of an ancient city discovered near Palenque, in the kingdom of Guatemala, in Spanish America.* London, 1794.

Denon, Vivant. *Voyage dans la Basse et la Haute Egypte.* Paris, 1803.

Dyer, John. "The Ruins of Rome." 1740.

Elmes, James. *Lectures on Architecture, Comprising the History of the Art from the Earliest Times to the Present Day.* London, 1823.

Félibien, André Sieur des Avaux et de Jàversy. *Principes de l'architecture, de la sculpture, de la peinture et des autres arts qui en dépendent.* [1676.] 3rd ed. Paris, 1699.

Field, George. *Chromatics, or an Essay on the Analogy and Harmony of Colours.* London, 1817.

Gunn, Rev. William. *Inquiry into the Origin and Influence of Gothic Architecture.* London, 1819.

Gwilt, Joseph. *A Cursory View of the Origin of Caryatides.* London, 1822.

Hakewill, James. *An Attempt to Determine the exact character of Elizabethan architecture, illustrated by parallels of Dorton House, Hatfield, Longleate, and Wollaton, in England; and the Palazzo della Cancellaria, at Rome.* London, 1835.

Hallam, Henry. *View of the State of Europe during Middle Ages.* Philadelphia, 1821.

Haydon, Benjamin Robert. *Lectures on Painting and Design.* 2 vols. London, 1844–46.

Hemans, Felicia. "Modern Greece." 1817.

Hooke, Nathaniel. *Roman History: From the Building of Rome to the Ruin of the Commonwealth.* London, 1738–71.

Hope, Thomas. *Historical Essay on Architecture.* 2 vols. London, 1835.

Hoskins, George Alexander. *Travels in Ethiopia . . . illustrating the antiquities, arts, and history of the ancient kingdom of Meroe.* London, 1835.

Irving, Washington. *The Alhambra: A series of tales and sketches of the Moors and Spaniards.* Philadelphia, 1832; *The Sketch Book of Geoffrey Crayon.* New-York, 1800.

Ker Porter, Robert. *Travels in Georgia, Persia, Armenia, Ancient Babylonia, &c. &c. during the Years 1817, 1818, 1819, 1820*. 2 vols. London, 1821–22.
Knight, Henry Gally. *An Architectural Tour in Normandy, with some Remarks on Norman Architecture*. 2nd ed. London, 1841.
La Comte, Louis-Daniel. *Memoirs and observations topographical, physical, mathematical, mechanical, natural, civil, and ecclesiastical: Made in a late journey through the empire of China*. London, 1667, 1668, 1669.
Laborde, Comte Alexandre de. *Voyage pittoresque et historique de l'Espagne*. 2 vols. Paris, 1806–1820.
Lamartine, Alphonse de. *Pilgrimage to the Holy Land/Voyages en Orient*. Philadelphia, 1833, 1835.
Latrobe, Benjamin Henry. *Anniversary Oration, Pronounced before the Society of Artists of the United States*. Philadelphia, 1811.
Layard, Sir Austen Henry. *Nineveh and Its Remains*. London, 1849; *The Monuments of Nineveh: From drawings made on the spot*. London, 1849; *Discoveries in the Ruins of Nineveh and Babylon*. London, 1853.
Le Brun, Cornelis de Bruijn. *Reizen van Cornelis de Bruyn, door de Vermaardste Deelen van Klein Asia* (1698); French trans. (1700): *Voyages au Levant;* English trans. (1702): *A Voyage to the Levant; or, Travels in the Principal Parts of Asia Minor*.
W. H. Leeds. "Design for a Villa Comprising Two Distinct Residences." *The Architectural Magazine* 5, no. 58 (December 1838): 554–64. [Ed. J. C. Loudon.]
Linschotten, John Huyghen van. *The Voyage of John Linschoten to the East Indies* (1579–1592); French trans. (1592); English trans. (1598).
Loudon, John Claudius. *The Architectural Magazine*. 1834–39.
Mason, William. *The English Garden*. 4 vols. London, 1772, 1782.
Milizia, Francesco. *Le vite de' più celebri architetti*. Rome, 1768; Eng. trans., *The Lives of Celebrated Architects, Ancient and Modern*. London, 1826.
Milner, Right Rev. John. *Treatise on the Ecclesiastical Architecture of England during the Middle Ages*. London, 1811. [Later ed. by J. Weale (1835) cross-references a number of Walter's sources, including Bede, Bentham, Dallaway, and Warton.]
Milton, John. *Paradise Lost*. 1667.
Niebuhr, Barthold Georg. *History of Rome*. 3 vols. 1811–32.
Niebuhr, Karsten [Carsten]. *Travels through Arabia and other Countries in the East*. 2 vols. Edinburgh, 1792.
North American Review. Boston, 1815–.
Palladio, Andrea. *I quattro libri dell'architettura*. Venice, 1570.
Papworth, John Buonarotti, pub. Chambers's *Decorative Part of Civil Architecture*. London, 1836.
Pocock, Rev. Richard. *Description of the East and Some Other Countries*. 2 vols. London, 1743 and 1745.
Priest, Josiah. *American Antiquities and Discoveries in the West*. Albany, 1834.
Quatremère de Quincy, Antoine-Chrysostome. *An Essay on the Nature, the End, and the Means of Imitation in the Fine Arts* (*Essai sur le nature, le but et les moyens de l'imitation dans les beaux-arts*. Paris, 1823. Eng. trans. J. C. Kent, London, 1837.
Ralph, James. *A Critical Review of the Publick Buildings, Statues, and Ornaments, in and about London and Westminster*. London, 1734.
Rennel, James. *Geographical System of Herodotus Examined and Explained*. 2 vols. London, 1830.
Reynolds, Sir Joshua. *Discourses on Art*. London, 1778.
Rich, Claudius James. *Narrative of a Journey to the Site of Babylon in 1811*. London, 1815.
Rollin, Charles. *Ancient History of the Egyptians, Carthaginians, Assyrians, Babylonians, Medes & Persians, Macedonians, and Grecians*. 8 vols. 1730–38; later ed. Philadelphia, 1805.

Scott, Sir Walter. *Ivanhoe*. 1819.
Shakespeare, William *Julius Caesar* (1599); *The Tempest* (1611).
Shee, Martin Archer. *Rhymes* (1805). Philadelphia, 1815.
Simond, Louis. *A Tour in Italy and Sicily*. London, 1828.
Sonnerat, Pierre. *A Voyage to the East-Indies and China performed by order of Lewis XV between the years 1774 and 1781*. 3 vols. Calcutta, 1788–89.
Spelman, Sir Henry. *Glossarium*. 1626.
Stephens, John Lloyd. *Incidents of Travel in Egypt, Arabia Petraea, and the Holy Land*. 2 vols. New York, 1837; *Incidents of Travel in Central America, Chiapas, and Yucatán*. London, 1841.
Stuart, James, and Nicholas Revett. *Antiquities of Athens*. 4 vols. London, 1762–1818.
Stuart, Robert. *Dictionary of Architecture*. 3 vols. London, 1830.
Swinburne, Henry. *Travels through Spain, in the years 1775 and 1776*. 2nd ed. London, 1787.
Thomson, James. "Liberty." 1735–36.
Vasari, Giorgio. *Vite de' piu eccellenti pittori, scultori e architetti* [*Lives of the most eminent painters, sculptors and architects*]. 1550.
Vitruvius. *De Architectura*. 17 B.C. or later.
Walpole, Horace *Walpoliana*. Europe and America, 1783–1820.
Wilkins, William. *The Antiquities of Magna Graecia*. Cambridge, 1807
Wilkinson, Sir John Gardner. *A Second Series of the Manners and Customs of the Ancient Egyptians including their Religion, Agriculture, &c.* 3 vols. London, 1841.
William of Malmesbury. *The History of the Kings of England*. 1125–42.
Wood, Robert. *The Ruins of Palmyra, otherwise Tedmor, in the Desart* [*sic*]. London, 1753.
Woods, Joseph. *Letters of an Architect, from France, Italy, and Greece*. 2 vols. London, 1828.
Wordsworth, William. "Ecclesiastical Sonnets." 1821–22.
Wren, Christopher. *Parentalia*. London, 1750.

Additional Authors

Anaxagorus
Democritus
Demosthenes
Dio Cassius
Diodorus of Sicily
Dionysius
Eschylus
Euclid
Euripides
Herodotus
Hesiod
Homer
Horace
Humboldt, Baron Alexander von
Jerome
John of Padua
Juvenal
Kirby, John Joshua
Livy
Lucian
Lucretius
McCartney, Lord George
Ovid
Pausanias
Philoponus, Johannes
Plato
Pliny
Pliny the Younger
Plutarch
Proclus
Procopius
Publius Victor
Pythagoras
Sallust
Seneca
Sextus Rufus
Socrates
Stephanus
Strabo
Theophrastus

Thucydides
Victor
Virgil
Warburton, Bishop William
Winckelmann, Johann Joachim
Xenophon

APPENDIX D

Inventory of Book Collection as taken upon Walter's Death in 1887

Antiquities of Athens	4 vols.
Architectural Illustrations of London	J. Britton & A. Pugin 2 vols.
Architecture of Normandy	2 vols.
Architectural Magazine	5 vols. 1834 to 1838
Art Hints—Architecture, Sculpture and Painting	J. J. Jarves
Architecture of France, Italy and Greece	2 vols.
Barlow on Timber	
Bernan's History of the Arts of Warming and Ventilation	2 vols.
Barton's Antiquities of Rome	
Britton's Dictionary of English Architecture	
Britton's Architectural Antiquities	5 vols.
Britton's Cathedral Antiquities	5 vols.
Chamber's [*sic*] Civil Architecture	
Civil Engineering	Sgarizin
Civil Engineering	
Callcott's History of Painting	
Civil Engineer and Architect's Journal	22 vols. 1837 to 1859
Civil Engineering	Mahan
Cottage and Villa Architecture	T. U. Walter & J. J. Smith
Cottage Residences & Cottage Grounds	Downing
Clark's Domestic Architecture	
Designs for Gates, Rails etc.	Cottingham Archt.
Domestic Architecture (Tudor Style)	P. F. Robinson
De Quincy on the Fine Arts	
Dictionary of Architecture	3 vols.
Davies' Surveying	
Dunlap's Art of Design	2 vols.
Dallaway's English Architecture	
Davy on Artificial Foundations	
Downing's Landscape Gardening and Rural Architecture	Sargent
Gwilt on Arches	
General Text Book for Architects and Engineers	Loudon Ed.
Hope's Architecture	2 vols.
Household Furniture and Interior Decoration	Thomas Hope
Historie des Architectes	2 vols.
Hydraulic Lime of Teil	Beckwith
Inman on Ventilation, Warming and Sound	
Knight's Normandy	

Knight's Vases and Ornaments	
Lectures on Architecture	James Elmes Archt
Laws of Colouring	Hay
Loudon's Encyclopedia, Arch., Gardening & Agriculture	3 vols.
Lectures on Architecture and Painting	Ruskin
Library of Fine Arts	4 vols.
Moses' Classical Ornaments, Vases, Candelabra etc.	
Music of the Eye	P. Legh M.A.
Manual of the Fine Arts	Huntington
New Practical Builder	3 vols.
Nicholson's Architectural Dictionary	4 vols.
Nicholson's Operative Mechanics	2 vols.
Ornamental Metal & Stone Work	T. U. Walter & J. Jay Smith
Pugin's Gothic Architecture	2 vols.
Practical Treatise on Ventilation	Wyman
Parnell on Roads	
Pasley on Cements	
Rapports Penitenciers des Etats Unis	
Richardson on Warming and Ventilation	
Ruttan on Ventilation and Warming	
Sloan's Architectural Review	Vol. I
Sketch of Civil Engineering	Stevenson
Seven Lamps of Architecture	Ruskin
Sacred Architecture	Brown
Transverse Strains	Hatfield
The Science of Beauty	Hay
Tredgold's Warming and Ventilation	
Treatise on Architecture	W. Hosking
The House—A Manual of Architecture	
Treatise on Roads	Bloodgood
Vitruvius' Architecture	
Vicat on Cements	
Villa and Cottage	Calvert Vaux
Views of Lancashire	
Views of Devonshire	

NOTES

1. T. U. Walter to Martin Harmistead, 14 November 1853, Walter Collection, Letterbooks. Athenæum of Philadelphia (hereafter AOP).

2. T. U. Walter, "Genealogical Sketches," AOP.

3. One book was the product of foreign travel at the behest of an American scientific society. See "A Chronologic, Bibliographic, and Descriptive Catalogue of the Architecture and Engineering Works of William Strickland," in Agnes Addison Gilchrist, *William Strickland, Architect and Engineer, 1788–1854* (New York: Da Capo Press, 1969), 45–118.

4. John Haviland (1792–1852), Papers, 1806–68, 26 vols., Ms. Coll. 176, University of Pennsylvania, Special Collections, Van Pelt Library. Documents are property of the Somerset Archaeological and Natural History Society, the Castle, Taunton, on indefinite loan to the university.

5. "Ivanhoe; a Romance," *Port Folio* 13 (1822): 493–94.

6. "The Pirate; by the Author of 'Waverly, Kenilworth, &c.,'" *Port Folio* 14 (1822): 237.

7. Walter to Martin Harmistead, 14 November 1856 (original emphasis), Letterbooks, AOP.

8. Walter described his own education as "liberal, though not collegiate" ("Genealogical Sketches," AOP).

9. Walter to John C. Loudon, 17 April 1838, *Architectural Magazine* 5 (July 1838): 327–28.

10. *Desilver's Philadelphia Directory* lists Walter as "bricklayer" for the years 1828–33.

11. This, at least, would appear to be the case; it is possible that dozens of such notebooks filled with theory have been lost and only the more "practical" survive.

12. Walter Diary, entry of 16 January 1835, AOP.

13. For a point of comparison, $200 represents roughly 13 percent of Walter's annual salary from Girard College in 1845.

14. Walter to John Skirving, 12 February 1861, Letterbooks, AOP.

15. Walter records moving 700 volumes into a new home one day; an undisclosed number were moved on a second day, and others were sent to an auction house. Walter Diary, 18 October and 10 December 1872, AOP.

16. Ibid., 16 January 1835, AOP.

17. These included the Smithsonian Institution and Columbian College (now George Washington University).

18. James Elmes, *Lectures on Architecture* (London, trans. and ed. Francesco Milizia, 1823); Thomas Hope, *Historical Essay on Architecture*, 2 vols. (London, 1835); Giorgio Vasari, *Lives of Celebrated Architects* (1768), trans. and ed. Francesco Milizia (London, 1826).

19. He owned an edition of Palladio's *I quattro libri*, and a recent edition of Vitruvius (*The Civil Architecture of Vitruvius*, ed. William Wilkins, 1813–17), though he preferred the 5th edition (London, 1836), to which John B. Papworth added notes and an essay.

20. Walter found special pleasure in new research in the Holy Land which he believed "when compared with the Scripture show a beautiful coincidence" with biblical authority: "20th Lesson: Exodus Chapters 1 and 2," dated 8 April 1855, Bible Lessons, AOP.

21. Walter, "Lectures on Architecture," 4:4, AOP.

22. Walter borrowed lines from the following poems: Lord Byron, "Childe Harold's Pilgrimage" (1812–18) and "The Giaour" (1813); William Wordsworth, "Ecclesiastical Sonnets" (1821–22); John Dyer, "The Ruins of Rome" (1740); Felicia Hemans, "Modern Greece: A Poem" (1817); and William Mason, *The English Garden* (1772–82). Other literary extracts came from Edward Bulwer-Lytton, *The Last Days of Pompeii* (1834); Washington Irving, *The Alhambra* (1832); John Milton, *Paradise Lost* (1667); and William Shakespeare, *Julius Caesar* (1599) and *The Tempest* (1611).

23. Walter, "Lectures on Architecture," 3:9, 37–38, AOP, quotes from Byron's poem "Childe Harold's Pilgrimage" (1812–18).

24. Written in 1820, Scott's *Ivanhoe* ranked in Walter's limited pantheon of fiction for the value with which it holds dignity, decorum, and spirituality; also, he found its historical accuracy valuable.

25. Walter, "Lectures on Architecture," 4:44–45, AOP.

26. Ibid., 2:27 (original emphasis), AOP.

27. Walter to Jonathan R. Niernsee, Washington, D.C., 7 December 1858, Letterbooks, AOP.

28. "Architectural Library of the late Thomas U. Walter," AOP.

29. As early as 1855 Walter had railed against "soi-dissant" architects like those who "completely infested the profession" in Chicago, where "all builders *call themselves* Architects [original emphasis], which has tended to mislead the public mind on the subject" (Walter to Edward Haviland, 24 December 1855, Letterbooks, AOP).

30. Quoted in William Sener Rusk, "William Thornton, Benjamin H. Latrobe, Thomas U. Walter and the Classical Influence in their Works" (Ph.D. diss., John Hopkins University, 1939), 161–62. Walter delivered this address before the AIA in 1880; it is recorded in the *AIA Proceedings* and also reprinted in William Sener Rusk, "Thomas U. Walter and His Works," *Americana* 33, no. 2 (1939): 161–62.

31. Walter, "Lectures on Architecture" 5:4, AOP.

32. Ibid.

33. Walter wrote, "It is only savages who disregard the past, and live and die without entertaining definite notions of lineage, of ancestry, or of the history of their progenitors" (Genealogical Sketches, 1871, AOP).

IV

SAMUEL SLOAN, PATTERN BOOKS, AND THE QUESTION OF PROFESSIONAL IDENTITY

Elspeth Cowell

In the preface to his first book, The Model Architect *(1852–53), Philadelphia architect* Samuel Sloan observed, referring to contemporary pattern books, that "a great number of handsomely engraved designs on fine paper have been presented to the public, threatening annihilation to the architect's bill." Sloan's book, rather than contributing to this "annihilation," would be "a 'matter of fact' business like book on cottages and country residences" which would "furnish valuable information to the experienced man and to the learner."[1] Underlying Sloan's intention of providing a practical guide to the reader was a less explicit aim of promoting the importance of the architect's role in the design and construction of buildings.

A close examination of *The Model Architect* (figure 4.1) offers a portrait of the vital but ambiguous role that architectural pattern books played in the emergence of the American architectural profession.[2] Professionalization in the pre–Civil War period was more a grassroots movement than an institutional one. Individual architects began to assert a role for themselves in the production of buildings and in the process, indirectly, promoted the broader aims of professionalization.[3] Without the formal mechanisms of education, institutionalization, and registration that would legitimize their role later in the nineteenth century, architects adopted other means to justify their function as a distinct and necessary part of erecting buildings. To gain acceptance as a viable profession, architects needed to establish a division between the designing of buildings and their construction, thereby defining the architectural profession as one dependent on mental ability and asserting the exclusivity of the architect's skills. Books were one means by which architects promoted their value.

As a pattern book, *The Model Architect* was not novel or innovative in its format and content but rather a refinement of existing trends, bringing into focus the

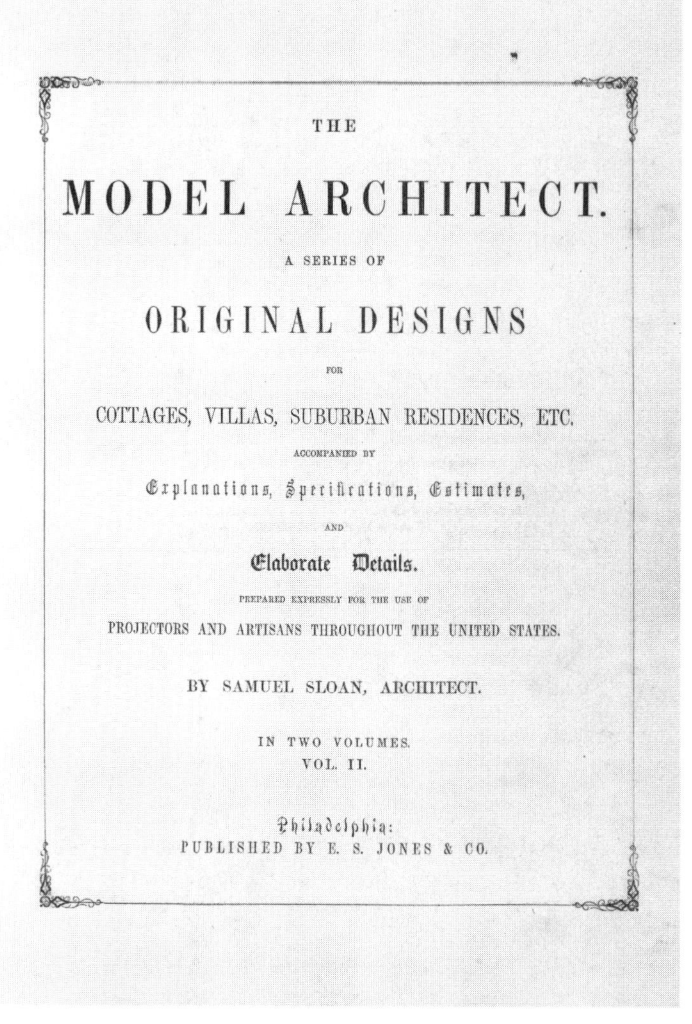

THE

MODEL ARCHITECT.

A SERIES OF

ORIGINAL DESIGNS

FOR

COTTAGES, VILLAS, SUBURBAN RESIDENCES, ETC.

ACCOMPANIED BY

Explanations, Specifications, Estimates,

AND

Elaborate Details.

PREPARED EXPRESSLY FOR THE USE OF

PROJECTORS AND ARTISANS THROUGHOUT THE UNITED STATES.

BY SAMUEL SLOAN, ARCHITECT.

IN TWO VOLUMES.
VOL. II.

Philadelphia:
PUBLISHED BY E. S. JONES & CO.

FIG 4.1 Title page of Samuel Sloan, *The Model Architect*, 1852–53. Courtesy of the Canadian Centre for Architecture.

role of the architect in relation to the contemporary market. Sloan was not the only pattern book author to promote the importance of architects, but *The Model Architect* was distinctive in successfully targeting a readership that was also a viable architectural clientele. Sloan was able to express the importance of hiring an architect to readers who were willing and financially able to do so. *The Model Architect* thus helped to define a client base for the emerging architectural professional. In a narrow sense, the book promoted Sloan's abilities as an architect in order to generate more clients for his Philadelphia practice. In a broader sense, it cultivated this clientele for all architects.

Pattern Books

To understand the context of *The Model Architect,* one must examine the genre of American pre–Civil War pattern books, paying specific attention to their intended readership in relation to the content and architectural designs included and their articulation of the role of the architect. The American-produced pattern book was in its infancy in the first half of the nineteenth century. From the 1837–38 publication of Alexander Jackson Davis's slender limited edition of *Rural Residences* to the start of the Civil War, fewer than thirty books were published which fall into the broad category of architectural pattern book.[4] These books reflect how the authors, mainly architects themselves, conceived of the profession's viability. Supporting the emerging sense of architectural professional identity, they positioned the architect ideally between the client and the builder as an arbiter of taste, conceiver of form, and bearer of technical knowledge. These books offered a key means by which the value of hiring an architect could be conveyed to potential clients. Yet architects' interests were not consistently expressed in the early pattern books, nor readers clearly defined as potential clients. Rather, these pattern books reflected the ambiguities of the emerging profession.

What exactly was their purpose, and who was their audience? Were they intended to promote the architectural profession? Were these books intended to offer complete, usable designs by architects to be constructed without further consultation? Were they intended to provide models for builders to use? Was their purpose to train amateurs to be their own architects? All these possibilities were suggested or implied by various pattern books in the pre–Civil War period.[5]

Following the publication of Davis's *Rural Residences,* one important intention—the desire to improve the quality of American domestic rural architecture—was stated and restated in some form by almost all subsequent pattern books. Davis's book and, in greater detail, those of Andrew Jackson Downing aimed to educate or, more accurately, *edify* the reader toward a better understanding of taste in architectural (and landscape) design. Following British precedents, these books established the emphasis on rural domestic architecture found in all early American pattern books. They promoted an idealized division of the urban sphere of work and a rural sphere of domesticity.[6] And although they discussed practical aspects of domestic design, they focused on aesthetic qualities—siting, form, style, and character. As Downing wrote in *Cottage Residences* (1842), "I am still more anxious to inspire in the minds of my readers and countrymen more lively perceptions of BEAUTIFUL, in everything that relates to our houses and grounds."[7] The designs in these books were intended to provide models of desirable rural architecture for readers contemplating building their own houses. In this respect, the audience of these books is clear: not builders or aspiring architects but a cultured, educated class of Americans with enough money to consider embracing Downing's ideal of moving to the country and building a rural home.

Downing's books urged his readers to hire architects. In the preface to *A Treatise on the Theory and Practice of Landscape Gardening* (1841), he commented on the infrequency with which professionals were consulted in matters of architecture and landscape; too often, potential homeowners thought themselves best able to design houses to fit their needs. In Downing's opinion, these amateurs' lack of necessary practical knowledge and understanding of design principles led not only to tasteless and inappropriate designs but also to the waste of much time and money.[8] In subsequent publications, he more explicitly expressed his views on the subject: first in a brief addendum to *Cottage Residences* titled "Employment of Architects and Professional Men"; then in a longer essay, "Hints to Persons about Building in the Country," published in the first American edition of George Wightwick's *Hints to Young Architects. Calculated to Facilitate Their Practical Operations* (1847). In both these essays Downing recommended hiring an "architect of talent and experience" for "buildings of importance," as this would lead to more tasteful and satisfactory results for the proprietor and save money as well. An architect would provide more complete and comprehensive drawings, estimates, specifications than a builder and, by overseeing the construction, would ensure that the design was carried out to the prescribed level of workmanship and without the countless changes that lead to additional costs.[9] Downing also emphasized that, given the benefit of *individuality* in the design, hiring an architect would add little to the overall cost of a house. He used the example of A. J. Davis's fee schedule to explain that it would add only 2 to 5 percent to the total cost.[10]

Given Downing's target audience of middle- and upper-class prospective homeowners, hiring an architect to design and supervise the construction of a new house was a feasible option. The content and format of his *Theory and Practice of Landscape Gardening* is consistent with the conception that pattern books were intended to improve readers' understanding of taste in architecture and landscape design and inspire them to hire professionals to design tasteful residences for them. This philosophical and practical guide to landscape gardening includes a section titled "Landscape or Rural Architecture," with illustrations depicting already-built houses as exemplars of the design principles he discusses, rather than designs for imitation. The houses included are primarily substantial rural villas.

In later books, however, Downing increased the focus on architectural design. His desire to improve all classes of dwellings, from worker's cottages to manor houses, led to a broadening of the range of designs shown. In his second book, *Cottage Residences,* the houses presented vary from small cottages and farmhouses costing as little as $800 to villas and mansions costing up to $15,000. The format is more typical of pattern books than is *A Treatise on the Theory and Practice of Landscape Gardening*: it provides a description, a perspective, plans, a few details, and a cost estimate for each design. *The Architecture of Country Houses* (1850) contains ten designs for cottages costing under $2,000 dollars (with several for less than $600) and five designs for farmhouses in a similar price range. These plans specify inexpensive material, simple and symmetrical forms, and the avoidance of unsuitable ornament. Downing discussed the need for *cheap* (i.e., affordable) cottage designs: "There are tens of thousands of working-men in this country, who now wish to give something of beauty and interest to the simple forms of cottage life; there are many of these who are desirous to have their homes of three rooms tasteful and expressive, no less than among those whose dwellings number thirty rooms."[11]

In broadening the range of designs, Downing introduced a dilemma that would reoccur in many subsequent pattern books. Could an egalitarian view of improved house design for all Americans be reconciled with promoting the need to hire architects, which was outside either the financial or geographical reach of many potential homeowners? Contemporary pattern books addressed this dilemma in one of two ways. Some authors, following Downing's lead, emphasized the importance of architects to domestic design in all sizes and budgets. Others suggested that architects were not necessary to the construction of inexpensive American houses and offered their books of designs as substitutes.

This latter direction was apparent in the production of inexpensive pattern books, often published in installments, consisting of illustrative plates, usually with brief descriptive texts. These books were publicized as accessible alternatives to foreign publications that were too expensive for many prospective homeowners. Influenced by Downing and British writers, they expressed an interest in promoting good taste in design but were more pragmatic in their emphasis on the utility and low cost of the designs presented. The texts used words and phases such as "useful," "novelty with utility," "practicality," "greatest economy of labour," and, of course, "cheap."[12]

A typical example of this trend was John Ritch's *The American Architect: Comprising Original Designs of Cheap Country and Village Residences* (1849–50). It was an inexpensive production sold in installments, twenty-five cents per monthly issue or $3.00 for a yearly subscription. Each issue consisted of one design, with perspectives, elevations, plans, woodwork details, a cost estimate, and carpenters' and masons' specifications; a brief text not only described the layout and construction of the design presented but also included short commentaries on the architectural theory, styles, and practical considerations of design.

In spite of being an architect himself, Ritch suggested that hiring an architect, besides being expensive, would not necessarily lead to a better or more tasteful house. In fact, his comments on architects were disparaging: "When furnished by Professional men from general ideas communicated by Proprietors, they are seldom satisfactory. *The American Architect,* by furnishing a collection of designs adapted to all tastes and means, will remove every difficulty in the choice, and save money expended on Plans of no use."[13] He implied that his book could actually replace the problems and expense of hiring a professional, since it supplied definite and complete plans with specifications which could be given to a builder to construct.

Ritch offered his "cheap dwellings" for the use of both the prospective homeowner and the country builder. Of the twenty-four designs included in his series, only two would cost more than $2,500, and the majority less than $2,000. In the introductory description of his fourth design, he explained his intentions: "To introduce a practical work on Architecture so as to be attractive and accessible to all, has seldom been attempted. . . . The subject of this number is illustrative of our intention to produce Designs, the cost of which shall come within the range of persons possessing small means, and who have a laudable desire to expend the fruits of their industry so as to enable them to be 'lords of their own castles.'"[14]

Ritch was not the only pattern book author to direct his attention to inexpensive rural houses for men of limited means. In the late 1840s and 1850s, books produced on this subject included T. Thomas's *The Working-man's Cottage Architecture* (1848), with cottages for $250; O. S. Fowler's *A Home for All or a new, cheap, convenient and superior mode of building* (1854); and Charles P. Dwyer's *The Economic Cottage Builder* (1855).[15] These books shared the common assumption that the potential homeowner would choose one of the published designs and have it constructed by a builder—or build it himself—without consulting an architect.

But other pattern book authors attempted to reconcile the role of the architect with the construction of modest houses. For instance, in their 1856 *Village and Farm Cottages*, architects Henry Cleaveland, William Backus, and Samuel D. Backus underlined the architect's particular importance to the design of small houses: "It is an error to suppose that the architect's aid is needed only by those who erect large and expensive houses. The man who in building is compelled to a close economy has, perhaps, even greater occasion for the best professional advice. . . . [Small houses require] close calculation and ingenious contrivance, to secure at once utility and good looks." They further justified this claim by suggesting the utility of bringing in an architect even before putting pencil to paper. The professional would help sort out the clients' requirements as to size, accommodation, style, and cost from their vague notions of what they wanted.[16]

These authors attempted to carve out an additional niche for themselves in the housing market by arguing that making even a *slight alteration* to a published design might "change its whole character, and destroy this value."[17] For despite their promotion of architects, their book ultimately signaled a different trend: the emergence of pattern books, or more accurately plan books, as tools for selling house plans by mail order, which would in turn ultimately lead to the availability of complete houses by mail order. *Village and Farm Cottages* includes a notice from the architects offering, at a cost of $3.00 to $5.00, lithographed working drawings and printed specifications, detailed enough "to enable any competent workman fully to understand the plans," for each of the designs in the book. In seeming contradiction with earlier statements, they also offered to answer questions that might arise in the execution of the designs but indicated no fee for this service.[18]

As would become evident in the subsequent 150 years, the small rural house was not a viable market for the architect; its design would become the domain of builders, the other audience for pattern books, aside from prospective homeowners. With the increasing availability of small-dimension, machine-milled wood and machine-made nails for wood frames, the construction of houses required less skill, enabling builders and homeowners themselves to erect houses based on simple published or mail order plans. Consequently, the publication of inexpensive, complete designs that could be constructed without hiring an architect weakened the claim of architects to a role in this housing market.

The authors of pattern books, even those advocating architects, were obviously aware that their designs would be adopted directly by builders on their own initiative or on the suggestion of clients. This ambiguity is particularly noticeable in the back cover descriptions and the introductions and prefaces of many pattern books, which often directly mention builders as being among their readership. Although such references can be dismissed as practical attempts to increase book sales, they also reflect the state of the profession, for the distinction between builder and architect in the antebellum era was fluid. Many architects were trained as builders and had made the transition into the architectural profession through self-education and courses of study organized by the trades.[19] These builder-architects also produced pattern books as demonstrations of their architectural skills and as educational tools for their fellow builders.

One of the earliest American pattern books, written by John Hall, illustrates this tendency. Its title, *A Series of Select and Original Modern Designs for Dwelling Houses: For the Use of Carpenters and Builders: Adapted to the Style of Building in the United States* (1840), leaves no doubt of the intended audience. Hall's preface stated that the carpenter would benefit from the book by using it to help his clients express their needs more clearly as well as to glean from it new ideas to suggest to his clients. He also included a one-page addendum on drawing plans and elevations, intended to expand his audience to students. Although it is unclear whether any of the designs published in this book were designed by Hall, he claims them as examples of his abilities by stating that "many of them, during their erection, [were] under the author's immediate superintendence."[20] These elements demonstrate that the aims of the book were both educational and promotional.

Oliver P. Smith in *The Domestic Architect, Comprising a Series of Original Designs for Rural and Ornamental Cottages with Full and Complete Explanations and Directions to the Builder* (1852) emphasized the educational value of his book: it was intended to educate country builders in the "science of Architecture" in order to elevate the standards of rural architecture. The principal text in this book is its "Introductory Remarks to the Student," explaining the various styles of architecture, the orders, the basic principles of construction and design and architectural drawing; it also supplies a glossary of architectural and building terms. Despite this central focus, though, Smith encourages those planning to build a house to hire an architect "of talent and experience." He justifies this digression in a book intended for builders by encouraging builders to *become* architects: "The builder should understand better the business of his profession. He should not content himself with being a mechanic, but should qualify himself as an architect."[21]

These publications constitute an important context to the understanding of *The Model Architect.* Sloan himself was trained as a builder, and the book is infused with a continued concern for builders. But as the foregoing discussion of pre–Civil War pattern books suggests, to succeed as tools for promoting the architectural profession, rather than as design source books for builders and prospective homeowners, pattern books needed to achieve a readership among people who would hire architects and supply commissions of sufficient size and frequency to support their practices. The architect-author needed simultaneously to woo these potential clients with attractive designs and to convince them of the need for an architect to execute these designs. Samuel Sloan with *The Model Architect* succeeded in this dual agenda.

The Model Architect

The Philadelphia publishing house of E. S. Jones & Co. contracted with Sloan to issue twenty-four paperback folios of designs in monthly installments.[22] The first folio of *The Model Architect: A Series of Original Designs for Cottages, Villas, Suburban Residences, etc., Accompanied by Explanations, Specifications, Estimates, and Elaborate Details, Prepared Expressly for the Use of Projectors and Artisans throughout the United States* appeared in the summer of 1851. Like other pattern books, it began as a serial publication, thereby minimizing the initial outlay of expense in establishing a readership. But rather than also adopting an inexpensive format to keep down the cost, *The Model Architect* is more lavish than many other contemporary books.[23] It is larger in size and has carefully designed page layouts with large margins, ornamented borders, and floriated initials. The plates are of higher quality than those in most early American pattern books, including full-page perspectives and six color plates. Consequently, it was more expensive than many contemporary publications. Half the folios were complete and issued as a book in 1852, the second volume in 1853.[24]

The Model Architect included designs and descriptive texts as well as essays on various subjects related to design and construction. The two-volume book presents sixty designs, primarily for houses—villas, cottages, and suburban residences—but also for multiple-unit dwellings, domestic outbuildings, several schools and churches, and architectural elements such as doors and ceilings. The designs are accompanied by twenty-six explanatory texts, in addition to a preface, an introduction, and concluding remarks in both volumes. *The Model Architect* details, in Sloan's words in the introduction, "the successive operations in the process of building."[25] A series of articles offers a primer not only of construction techniques but also of the history and use of styles, and other articles specifically address the work of the architect.

The format of articles as well as designs conveyed the importance of architects, not only in direct statements in the texts but also in the overall content. Unlike the earlier builder's guides, which provided esoteric knowledge on construction to the specialist, *The Model Architect* delineated the knowledge of the architect. It did not aim to make the reader an architect; rather, it advocated the need for professional assistance by imparting to the reader the complexities of the process: in Sloan's words, "an intelligent man will employ an Architect who is his superior in matters connected with building." The introductory statement to his article "The Architect," which describes the skills and role of the architect in the design and building process, encapsulates the importance of the profession which he wants to convey to his readers: "Designing a house is no easy matter. Such abilities, indeed, are required to do it well that it has become a business, a profession, an art. Men who have devoted their lives to it are, notwithstanding, continually making blunders; then what are we to expect from him who endeavors to build, while destitute of taste, experience, and knowledge of construction?"[26]

The clientele of Sloan's Philadelphia practice—the newly established mercantile and industrial aristocracy—was representative of the readership that the book targeted. Sloan focused on an emerging market for architects among ambitious, newly wealthy clients which had been generated by the shift during the antebellum period from an agrarian, land-based economy to a more prosperous and diverse urban economy based on speculation. Further, *The Model Architect* reflected Sloan's understanding that the outward growth of the American city was a pragmatic suburbanization driven by speculation rather than the manifestation of a bucolic ideal of rural domestic life. The players in both this suburban growth and the accompanying industrial and commercial growth were his readership and his clientele, and Philadelphia was an ideal incubator for his talents. Beginning in 1830, the city had begun to grow rapidly and expand outward, and this growth obviously required considerable new construction.[27]

The content of the articles and the designs in *The Model Architect* reflected the desires of this architectural client base. Such clients craved symbols of their new status in the form of ostentatious houses, wielded influence over institutional and ecclesiastical commissions, augmented their wealth through speculative building, and needed buildings for their new enterprises.[28] But many were also practical men who wanted sound and convenient designs. *The Model Architect* addressed both these dimensions. Sloan achieved a balance between texts on the stylistic aspects of architecture and those dealing with the practical considerations of design and construction.

The book began with an introduction that briefly explained the originality of architecture. Unlike the other arts, Sloan contended, it is not based on natural forms. He used this distinction to elevate the status of the skills and knowledge of the architect: "The architect has drawn entirely from within himself, and given material embodiment to an abstract conception of fitness." He then stressed, mirroring other pattern books, the importance of good cultivated taste to domestic architecture in America. Improved standards of taste would lead to the construction of beautiful, "appropriate and correct designs" throughout the country. He further pointed out that a house is a reflection of its owner: "A man's dwelling at the present day, is not only an index of his wealth, but also of his character. The moment he begins to build, his tact for arrangement, his private feelings, the refinements of his tastes and the peculiarities of his judgement are all laid bare for public inspection and criticism. And the public makes free use of this prerogative."[29]

The implications of this argument for the reader and potential homeowner were twofold. First, it was necessary to learn about the principles of good cultivated taste in order for one's future home to reflect them—and naturally, reading *The Model Architect* was a means of obtaining this education. Second, architects had a better understanding than other people of the principles of good taste; hence, hiring an architect would lead to a tasteful dwelling.

This two-page introduction set the tone and approach for the texts in *The Model Architect.* Rather than discussing in detail architectural principles and ideals, Sloan skimmed over the theory to focus on how it affects the wants of the future homeowner. His approach was always pragmatic rather than idealistic. He understood his audience to know already what they wanted. Unlike Downing and other authors on rural architecture, he did not attempt to persuade his readers of the desirability of a rural home or to define the type of house appropriate to their situation. Instead, Sloan made the basic assumption of the desire for a suburban residence. What he understood his readers to need was the knowledge to obtain stylish, appropriate, and well-built suburban residences. *The Model Architect* aimed to provide this knowledge.

The first articles in the book addressed the history, characteristics, and use of "Architectural Styles." Sloan suggested that, though based on "our instinctive love of the beautiful," their various forms derive from the specifics of the national origins affected by climate, customs, character, availability of materials and skills. He conceded, however, that the various styles now used throughout Europe and America no longer retain their national specificity, but he contends that the key to their tasteful use is to utilize only "pure specimens of the various styles" rather than hybrid styles. He presents the designs in *The Model Architect* as pure examples.[30]

In an article titled "Location," returning in a limited geographic sense to the nationalism of styles, Sloan stressed, as he did throughout the book, the need to choose a style appropriate to the specific location of the building. For instance, a Swiss cottage is not appropriate on the prairies, nor should an Italian villa be constructed in the mountains, for such combinations create "violent contrast with their oppositions in nature." Sloan pointed to places around Philadelphia where he was active as an architect, including Germantown and Hamilton Village (West Philadelphia), as localities where public taste was progressing, and appropriate designs in harmony with nature were being built. He concluded by asserting that the principal goal of the designs and practical suggestions in *The Model Architect* was to promote the "tasteful growth of such places, in the environs of our cities," which are being developed "under the spur of speculation." By implication, he endeavored to establish a role for architects in this growth.[31]

The content of these articles on style, as well as others in the book, was by no means original; Sloan admitted this much in his preface. He borrowed liberally, as was common in contemporary pattern books, from both British and American sources. Many other pattern books discussed the various styles as well, but Sloan was notable in focusing on the key styles that would interest his readership. Gothic, Italian, and Norman architecture were detailed in the opening articles. Grecian architecture, widely considered less appropriate to country houses, was described only much later, in the second volume in the context of the design of churches. Sloan's bias was for the Italian style as the most appropriate for suburban homes. Once again, it is apparent that he understood the self-conscious desires of the readers/clients for houses appropriate to their status: "It [the Italian

Style] speaks of the inhabitant as a man of wealth, who wishes in a quiet way to enjoy his wealth. It speaks of him as a person of educated and refined tastes, who can appreciate the beautiful both in art and nature; who, accustomed to all the ease and luxury of city life, is enjoying the more pure and elevating pleasures of the country."[32]

With the exception of one article on schoolhouses, the article on Grecian architecture, and three on architectural practice,[33] all the other articles in *The Model Architect* discuss the various elements of a house's construction sequentially, from the excavation to the roof. In Sloan's approach, the subjects of these articles illustrate how their order directly parallels the construction of a house: Excavations, Foundations, Mortar, Masonry, Brick Work, Timber, Preservation of Timber, Carpentry, Framing, Joinery, Warming and Ventilating, Plastering, Painting, Finish of Roofs, and Landscape Gardening.[34]

In these texts, Sloan's true knowledge base as a builder-turned-architect emerged. The purpose of these articles was not "for particular instruction" but "for general information."[35] They were intended not to teach readers how to build a house but rather to develop in readers an understanding of the construction process which would enable them to judge the quality of construction work and to be knowledgeable clients. The content of these articles was quite diverse varying from historical overviews of the building materials or types of construction to descriptions of component assembly (for example, the wall and floor framing) to quasi-scientific discussions on the chemical composition of materials (for instance, mortar and wood).[36] Sloan described the best construction methods and materials and the available alternatives, emphasizing the need for high-quality materials, techniques, and craftsmanship in constructing comfortable, convenient, long-lasting country dwellings. He lamented the carelessness and ignorance of many workmen and expressed a hope that American carpenters and artisans would become "a body of educated, scientific men" with theoretical and mathematical as well as mechanical knowledge of construction.[37]

Sloan's tone and approach reveal his assumptions of the book's readership, which he assumed to be, like his clients, educated or self-made men active in industry and business. As these individuals were interested in innovation and progress, Sloan's articles on the process of building catered to their attitudes in two respects. First, they incorporated the readers' interest in scientific understanding by going beyond simply describing the *mechanics* of house construction to explain the underlying *science* of construction. Second, the practical articles provided proof of the technical knowledge of the architectural profession and proved that an architect would indeed be a client's "superior in matters connected with building." Sloan made clear the practical knowledge to be expected of an architect: "The Architect must have a through appreciation of the wants of society. He must be well versed in all the arts of construction. There is no necessity for him to possess manual dexterity, but he must be a good judge of masonry, carpentry and their kindred. He must be acquainted with all the varieties of the best materials, and their prices, together with the prices of all kinds of labor. He must also be familiar with all modern improvements which add to the comforts of living."[38] The articles in *The Model Architect* demonstrate that Sloan, as a member of the architectural profession, possessed these skills.

Nevertheless, the articles on house construction and the accompanying tables and plates show that *The Model Architect* was still transitional in terms of readership. The book included a level of technical information valuable only to a builder: diagrams for laying out circular stairs, tabular descriptions of the orders, a table of the resistance of various woods to cross strains, framing drawings. The detail of technical information is not consistent; Sloan often pointed to more technical books, especially Peter Nicholson's *Carpenter's New Guide,* as sources of further information.[39] The designs are, however, accompanied by sufficient information to enable their construction. The prints themselves tend to be pictorial, giving an overall impression of the building's form, style, and layout rather than concrete information on the building's construction (figure 4.2). The lack of graphic information is counterbalanced by detailed specifications or descriptions and, in some cases, estimates with bills of goods listing building dimensions, building materials, fittings, finishes, construction techniques, configuration of spaces, and quality of work. There is no doubt that a skilled builder could, without consulting an architect, construct a house based on one Sloan's published designs.

Does the inclusion of this information for the builder weaken *The Model Architect* as a tool for promoting architects? To answer this question, it is necessary to recall part of the subtitle of the book: "Prepared Expressly for the use of Projectors and Artisans throughout the United States." In this subtitle as well as in the preface, Sloan indicated that the *artisan* was part of his intended readership. Given his continued sense of allegiance to the builder, he aimed for an audience that included both builders and the general public. Readers who were builders would construct the designs selected from the book by their clients. Other readers—projectors—would hire builders and use the designs as models for what

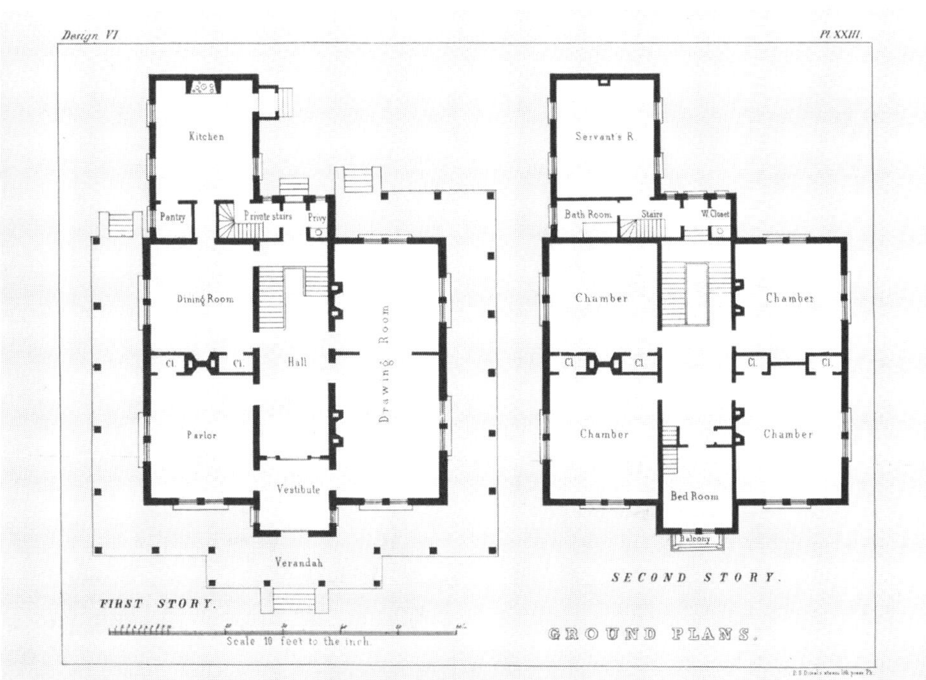

FIG 4.2 Sloan, perspective view and plans of "An Italian Villa" (design 6) from *The Model Architect*, vol. 1, plates 21 and 23.

they wanted. The intended utility of the book for builders is clear from notation in the design descriptions indicating the particular value of certain drawings to the construction of the building. In one case, Sloan stated that the details of the design "may be taken directly from this plate, without reference to others." Similarly, the acceptance of designs being used by projectors without further consultation with the architect is explicit from a warning regarding altering the published designs: Sloan cautioned that changes could cause regrettable inconsistencies in the style or affect the practicability of the house's plan. He advised that it was best to consult the architect before making changes but added that "we will, however, from time to time, mention some such changes as may be made consistently."[40]

Still, the builders and those who hired builders rather than architects were secondary audiences for the book. Sloan's stance on when an architect was needed is clear: "When a pleasing design, with all its concomitants, is found, whose source is good authority, it may be adopted without hesitation; but when a building adapted to some peculiar notions is desired, the only safe course is to communicate these to some experienced Architect, who will elaborate them."[41] This and similar comments leave no doubt of Sloan's differentiation between those who would simply copy the designs from his book and those who would heed his advice and hire an architect able to convert "peculiar notions" into tasteful and original plans for clients concerned with the image that their houses would express.

From the point of view of the "Projectors" mentioned in *The Model Architect*'s subtitle, the inclusion of highly technical information would not detract from its purpose of promoting the value of architects but emphasize their position as experts with specialized knowledge. Like the articles, the drawings in *The Model Architect,* especially in the second volume, illustrate that the technical information was intended less as information for builders than as proof of the knowledge and, thereby, creditability of architects. Sloan included elaborate atmospheric renderings of the buildings in natural settings to convey the effect of the building to the projector (figure 4.3). But he also provided isometric framing drawings for several designs (figure 4.4); these, in addition to supporting the essay on framing, are evidence that the designs are not merely pretty pictures but buildable plans. The sorts of clients whom Sloan sought to convince of the validity of the architectural profession would not be swayed solely by skill at architectural composition. The inclusion of detailed structural drawings and information on construction was evidence that architects also possessed technical knowledge that would enable them to produce not just visually appealing but also practical, viable designs.

FIG 4.3 Sloan, perspective view of "A Country Residence" (design 26) from *The Model Architect*, vol. 1, plate 106.

Clients

To understand his conception of the architect, it is helpful to look at some of Samuel Sloan's clients. Many, like Sloan himself, began work in the practical trades and advanced their careers through self-education and drive. These men believed in the advancement of American society through industrialization, which would also result in the advancement of their own social status. They were entrepreneurs who had achieved success through a combination of good business sense and innovation. In the design of houses, they were as concerned about practicalities and even innovations as they were about style. These clients demonstrate the important parallel between *The Model Architect* and the kind of architectural practice that Samuel Sloan pursued. The book was simultaneously a marketing tool for Sloan's practice

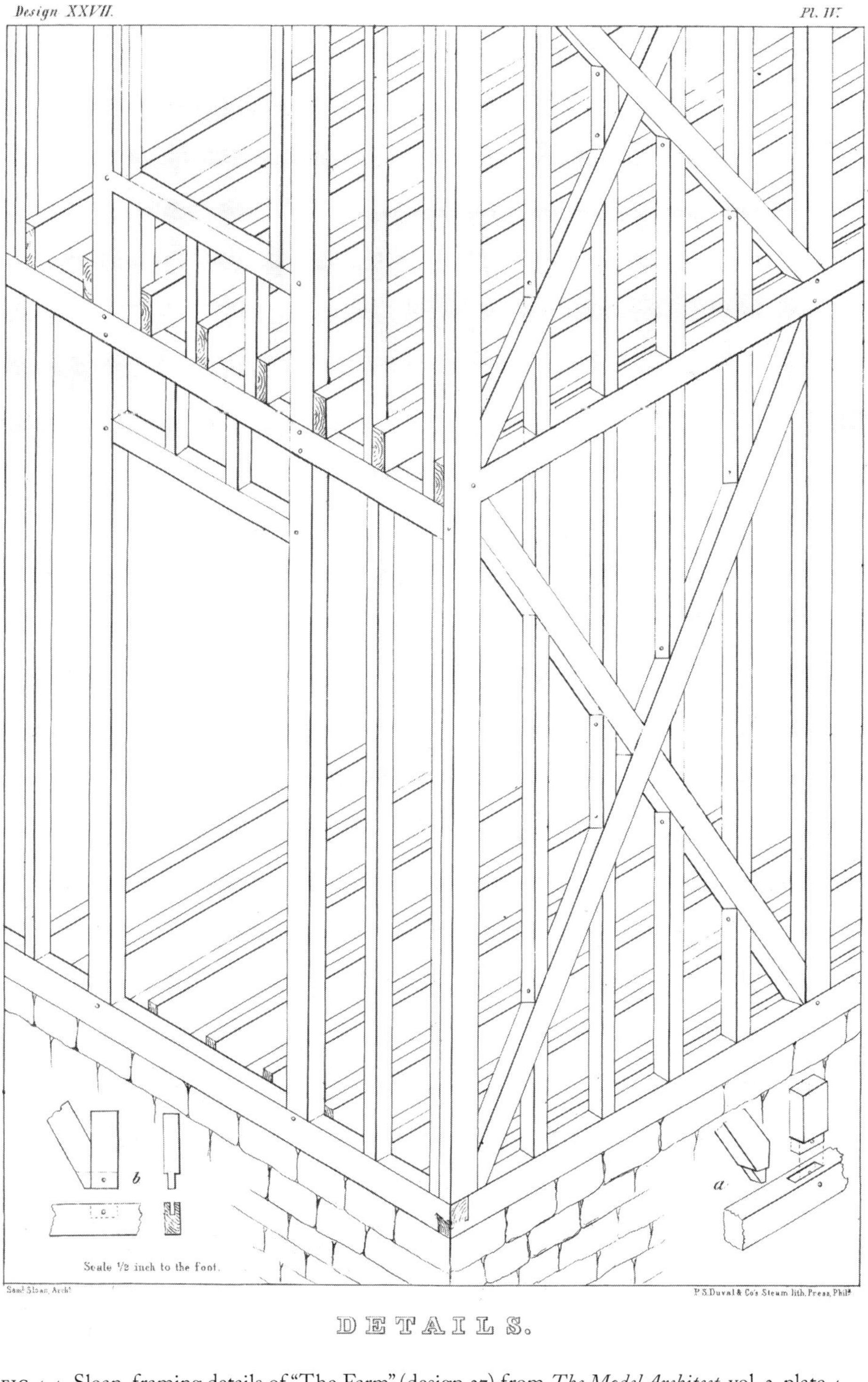

FIG 4.4 Sloan, framing details of "The Farm" (design 27) from *The Model Architect*, vol. 2, plate 4.

FIG 4.5 Sloan, perspective view of "A Norman Villa" (design 10) from *The Model Architect*, vol. 1, plate 39.

and a reflection of that practice. The projects that Sloan designed for five clients demonstrate the relationship to the themes and intentions of *The Model Architect*.

Sloan's first domestic client was Andrew McCalla Eastwick, who hired Sloan in 1850 to design a house for a suburban site on the west bank of the Schuylkill River. The house is published in *The Model Architect* as the tenth design, "A Norman Villa" (figure 4.5).[42] This substantial house is one of the most expensive in the book at a cost of about $30,000.[43] An often told story (or perhaps myth) suggests that Sloan, not yet a "built architect,"[44] gained the commission by presenting Eastwick with an unsolicited design, then modifying it to accommodate his criticisms.[45] This account, whether true or not, is very suggestive of the importance of designing and drawing to Sloan's new career as an architect. He did not offer to build Eastwick a house but presented him with a design on paper as a product separate from the construction of the house. Thus the transition from builder to architect was the difference between selling the products of one's physical labor and selling the products of one's mental skill. Sloan's ability to sell his mental skill through architectural drawings for clients and through published drawings and writings in his books were key to his success as an architect.

Eastwick was representative of the clients that Sloan would continue to attract—self-made, forward-looking businessmen. Andrew McCalla Eastwick, who was trained as a machinist, rose to fortune as a partner in the locomotive firm Harrison, Winans and Eastwick, which provided Russia with locomotives and other rolling stock for the first railroad between St. Petersburg and Moscow, constructed in the 1840s–50s.[46] Coupling business prowess with technical innovation, he was not only financially successful but also responsible for several innovations in the development of the steam locomotive.

A later client demonstrates that Sloan continued to attract a similar type throughout his career. Asa Packer commissioned his house—a substantial $14,000 Italianate villa with central cupola—in Jim Thorpe (then Mauch Chunk), Pennsylvania, in 1860–61 (figure 4.6).[47] Packer, like Eastwick and Sloan, was trained in manual skills: he had apprenticed as a tanner and a carpenter but eventually built his fortune through the construction of canals and railroads. Although without a college education himself, he established Lehigh University in 1865 in Bethlehem, Pennsylvania.

The majority of designs in *The Model Architect* are for substantial suburban and country residences. Most of these houses were estimated by Sloan to cost, based on Philadelphia prices, between $3,000 and $10,000 and to accommodate families of six to twelve plus servants. Stylistically, the designs are predominantly Gothic and Italianate, but a few more exotic examples—Swiss, Oriental, and Norman—are included as well. Sloan favored chiefly brick and stone construction but acknowledged that in certain areas of the country, wood frame was more practical. He also included landscape plans and designs for ornamental structures to enhance the grounds of these residences: summerhouses, fencing, gatehouses, observatories, a grapery, a flower stand, and even a squirrel house and a poultry house. The dominance of plans for substantial houses in *The Model Architect* provides evidence that Sloan considered a growing middle and upper class of citizens—as represented in his own practice by Eastwick, Packer, and many others—to be a core source of commissions for architects. On the surface, this view differs little from A. J. Downing's understanding of the character of architectural clients. Yet, as suggested earlier, a significant difference between the intentions of the two architects is evident in

FIG 4.6 Samuel Sloan, Asa Packer Mansion, Mauch Chunk (now Jim Thorpe), Pa., 1860–61. Historic American Buildings Survey, Library of Congress.

their respective books. Downing was a *prophet* for the advantages of rural living and offered ways in which this ideal could be achieved tastefully. Although Sloan continued to promote the need for good taste in domestic design, his book offered examples for the fulfillment of *existing* desires for rural or suburban houses.

Andrew Eastwick's house was a fulfillment of these desires. In choosing to live on the west bank of the Schuylkill River in what would become West Philadelphia, Eastwick was part of the outward movement of middle- and upper-class Philadelphian households to the north and west of the city.[48] This suburbanization would sustain Sloan's career. A significant number of his domestic commissions were constructed in the suburbs especially of West Philadelphia and Germantown.[49] Suburban growth resulted in two types of domestic commissions. Starting in the early years of the nineteenth century, wealthier Philadelphians built large, freestanding villas to be used as their own summer or year-round residences. As Philadelphia's growth accelerated, however, speculators began constructing both single-family and mutilple-unit houses to appeal to members of the middle class eager to move out of the central city.

Samuel A. Harrison, a tile manufacturer, and Nathaniel B. Browne, a lawyer (and later Philadelphia's postmaster), were involved in this speculative construction and contributed significantly to the development of West Philadelphia. Sloan, also extensively involved in the construction of speculative dwellings, undertook at least six commissions for Harrison and five for Browne. His best-known Harrison and Browne project is Hamilton Terrace in West Philadelphia (1856), which consists of two Gothic cottages and two Italianate double residences flanking (one of each on each side) Harrison's own residence in the Norman style (figure 4.7).[50] This development as well as another surviving Harrison commission—two detached Gothic cottages of 1851 (figure 4.8), now on the University of Pennsylvania campus[51]—are representative of the houses intended for middle-class buyers that Sloan was designing for speculative projects.

Sloan included in *The Model Architect* a number of designs of the sort that Harrison and Browne commissioned—double residences and cottages. Indeed, the design for the Gothic cottages was published as the second design in the book (figure 4.9). These designs differ from the single-family residences described earlier in price, size, and elaboration; including the double residences, they were generally estimated to cost under $3,000. Like the more expensive designs, they were most frequently Gothic or Italianate but with less ornamentation. In fact, a number of the designs were specified as "plain" with minimal ornament (figure 4.10).

These less expensive designs were probably the ones most frequently copied by builders from *The Model Architect*, and they were ideal for suburban houses to be constructed by speculators, who were not builders themselves and therefore hired architects to plan and oversee their projects. Several of Sloan's designs illustrate his intention of providing these as examples of speculative houses for middle-class buyers. Near the beginning of the first volume he included designs (the fourth and fifth) for double houses in the Gothic and Italianate styles. Their descriptions highlight the practicality and economical construction of duplexes—undoubtedly part of their appeal to speculators. Although Sloan acknowledged the need for economy in speculative construction, he also understood the need to appeal to the buyer with solid, tasteful dwellings. His double houses, like many of the single-family houses in the book, were to be constructed of stone, and he emphasized the importance of ornament to the designs (figure 4.11). In the second volume he broadened the

FIG 4.7 Samuel Sloan, Hamilton Terrace, West Philadelphia, Pa., 1856. Courtesy of the Atwater Kent Museum, on loan to The Athenaeum of Philadelphia with the support of The Pew Charitable Trusts through its Museum Loan Program.

FIG 4.8 Samuel Sloan, Samuel A. Harrison Cottage (Kelly Writers House), Philadelphia, 1851. Photograph ca. 1900, courtesy of the Collections of the University of Pennsylvania Archives.

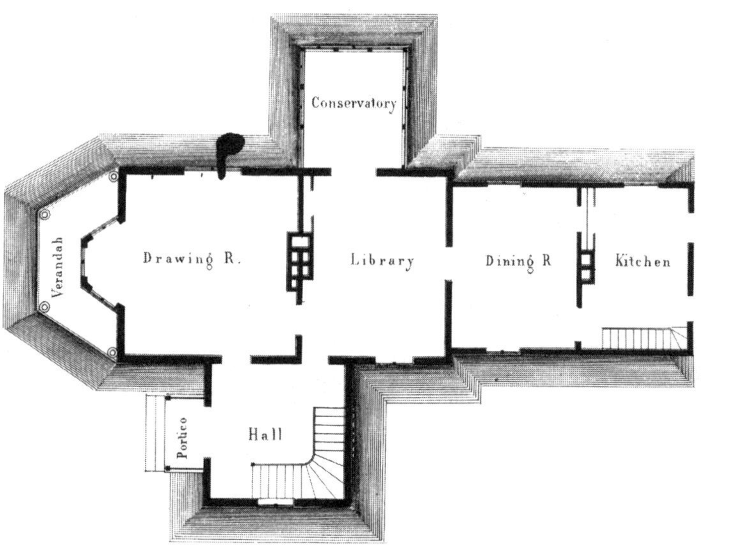

FIG 4.9 Sloan, front elevation and floor plan of the "English Gothic Style" (design 2) from *The Model Architect*, vol. 1, plates 7 and 8.

FIG 4.10 Sloan, elevation of "A Small Villa" (design 15) from *The Model Architect*, vol. 1, plate 62.

range of possibilities for double houses by offering both a more richly ornamented Italianate double house and a cheap double house. Sloan even included a design for a row of laborer's houses, which he suggested building "near to a large manufactory, for the accommodation of the hands."[52] The inclusion of accommodations for laborers with the implication that they could be constructed by the hiring manufacturer demonstrates further that the intended audience for *The Model Architect* extended beyond individuals planning to build a house for themselves.[53]

A fifth client provides a more intimate example of the role of *The Model Architect* in Sloan's practice. A wealthy southern cotton planter, Haller Nutt, approached Sloan in 1859 to design a house for him in Natchez, Mississippi; now known as Longwood, it is a monumental octagonal house left unfinished as a consequence of the outbreak of the Civil War (figure 4.12).[54] He had seen the design for an octagon-shaped Oriental villa in the second volume of *The Model Architect* (figure 4.13), and Sloan's discussion of the circumstances in which this design would be appropriate suggests why it would appeal to a planter in fashionable Natchez, where the house was crucial to one's identity within the community: "A large edifice is necessary to

FIG 4.11 Sloan, elevation of "Italian Residences" (design 5) from *The Model Architect*, vol. 1, plate 18.

give it proper force and expression. . . . [M]any persons, contemplating building, seek for a design, at once original, striking, appropriate and picturesque."[55] Nutt, like many Natchez planters, had Philadelphia connections which may have led him to choose Sloan.[56] Additionally, strong Union ties and a distrust of local southern mechanics may have influenced his choice of a northern architect. Whatever his reasons, hiring Sloan does suggest a consciousness of the architect's importance to the success of his house.

Fortunately, many of the letters between Sloan and Nutt have survived and are revealing of Nutt's attitude toward Sloan as an architect.[57] Nutt had many practical suggestions regarding his house but always expressed a willingness to defer to Sloan. The tone of his letters in general indicates that he valued Sloan's superior knowledge of architecture—key to the recognition of architects as professionals. Two examples illustrate this client-architect dynamic. Taking advantage of the octagon plan of the house, Sloan grouped the fireplaces in adjacent rooms around four chimneys. Nutt expressed concern over the size of the chimneys necessary to

FIG 4.12 Samuel Sloan, Longwood, Natchez, Miss., begun 1860. Photo by James Butters, 1936, Historic American Buildings Survey, Library of Congress.

accommodate the flues for all the fireplaces and suggested that certain fireplaces could be eliminated from the design. But he concluded, "I wrote you merely suggestions and I much prefer you following your own plans." When Sloan assured Nutt that a single flue could be used for all the fireplaces on each chimney, Nutt responded, "I feel relieved that you can conduct all the flues of each chimney into one large flue. I did not know that would work well."[58]

A second particularly interesting example demonstrates that Nutt referred back to *The Model Architect* as a guide to the building process. On 29 March 1860 he wrote to Sloan, "In looking over your Model Architect again I observe you recommend the use of a layer of slate in the foundation of walls." Naturally, Sloan responds that this is an excellent idea which his firm always uses on their good houses. A final quotation from these letters illustrates in more general terms Nutt's acknowledgment of the architect's domain. Nutt says, in a letter dated 3 February

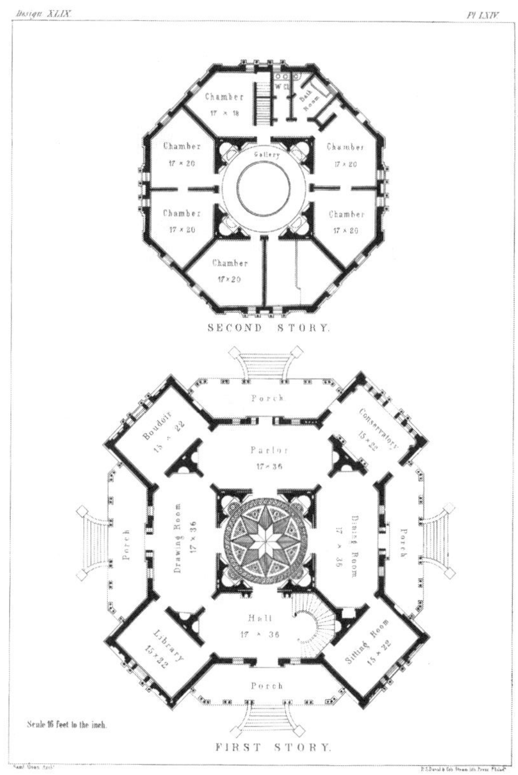

FIG 4.13 Sloan, elevation and plans for an "Oriental Villa" (design 49) from *The Model Architect*, vol. 2, plates 63 and 64.

1860, referring to unresolved aspects of the design: "In regard to architectural proportions and style of work throughout I feel sure that your taste is far better than Mrs. Nutt and my own."[59] This comment and these letters demonstrate that in this case, at least, *The Model Architect* had generated not only a client for Sloan's practice but one who respected the professional skill of architects.

* * *

Samuel Sloan was an unlikely champion of the architectural profession. Having gained entry to it through self-education, ambition, and aggressive self-promotion, he exemplified a self-promoting approach to architectural practice. Indeed, Roger G. Kennedy in *Architecture, Men, Women, and Money* characterizes Samuel Sloan as "America's fiercest architectural entrepreneur until the time of Daniel Burnham and Frank Lloyd Wright."[60] An entrepreneurial approach in this period was often construed in opposition to the contemporaneous professionalization of the field. The architectural entrepreneur was seen as solely interested in *selling* his designs through the means most advantageous to him. He was thought to lack consideration for the way his actions might reflect on the profession as a whole. But, as stated earlier, the American architectural profession prior to the Civil War was based primarily on the actions of individual architects asserting their role in the production of buildings and thereby promoting professionalization. So although Sloan may have been a self-promoting architectural entrepreneur, he nonetheless contributed to the professionalization of architects.

The Model Architect not only advanced Sloan's own career but also helped to cultivate for all architects a clientele of businessmen who controlled and influenced a range of commission types. Sloan's ambition and entrepreneurship attracted clients who shared his values. Sloan understood early how significant such clients would become to American architectural practice. In the pre–Civil War period, businessmen were building the foundations for the corporations that would emerge later in the century and further expand the market for architects.[61] Sloan was also quick to learn the value of architectural publishing to reinforce the architect's position in this market. In following the existing pattern book models, *The Model Architect* incorporated the ambiguities of readership of its predecessors in trying to accommodate both the *artisan* and the *projector*. Its original serial publication gave Sloan the opportunity to experiment with different types of designs, ideas, and formats and to explore how a pattern book could be focused on the needs of the potential client rather than of the artisan.

Sloan went on to apply the knowledge gained from the development of *The Model Architect* to his second book.[62] *City and Suburban Architecture* (1859) targets more directly and exclusively the sort of clientele he had established through his practice and his first book. In the new book he reduced the descriptive articles to a minimum, incorporating most commentary and information into the description of the designs. He eliminated all cottages and less-expensive designs not clearly intended for a middle- and upper-class clientele or, even more precisely, the businessman who required commercial buildings in the city, or a city or a suburban house (or perhaps both). Ten of the thirty designs are for commercial buildings, fourteen for city and suburban houses, four for churches, one each for a courthouse and a monumental schoolhouse. The format also reflects the needs of the reader as an architectural client. The drawings are generally pictorial in the form of plans, elevations, and ornamental details; an increased number are color-tinted plates.

Architectural publications continued to have a role throughout Sloan's career. Simultaneously with the appearance of *City and Suburban Architecture,* he published *Sloan's Constructive Architecture*, specifically targeting builders, and then, in 1861, *Sloan's Homestead Architecture*, and *American Houses: A Variety of Original Designs for Rural Buildings.*[63] After the Civil War, he introduced and edited from 1868 to 1870 the first American architectural periodical, *The Architectural Review and American Builder's Journal.* But of his publishing endeavors, *The Model Architect* remains particularly compelling for the insight that it gives into this transitional period for the American architectural profession, when the roles and relationships of architects, builders, and clients had not yet been fully formulated and formalized.

NOTES

1. Samuel Sloan, *The Model Architect* (Philadelphia: E. S. Jones, 1852–53; rpt. Dover, 1980), 1:7 (page numbers refer to Dover edition). The principal source of information on Samuel Sloan and his career is Harold C. Cooledge Jr., *Samuel Sloan, Architect of Philadelphia, 1815–1884* (Philadelphia: University of Pennsylvania Press, 1986).

2. My interpretation of American pattern books and the architectural profession in the pre–Civil War period is influenced by several key sources: Mary N. Woods, *From Craft to Profession: The Practice of Architecture in Nineteenth-Century America* (Berkeley: University of California Press, 1999); Daniel D. Reiff, *Houses from Books: Treatises, Pattern Books, and Catalogs in America, 1738–1950: A History and Guide* (University Park: Pennsylvania State University Press, 2000); and Dell Upton, "Pattern Books and Professionalism: Aspects of the Transformation of Domestic Architecture in America, 1800–1860," *Winterthur Portfolio* 19 (Summer/Autumn 1984).

3. On this view of professionalization, see Andrew Saint, *The Image of the Architect* (New Haven: Yale University Press, 1983), 73.

4. Based on listings in Henry-Russell Hitchcock, *American Architectural Books : A List of Books, Portfolios, and Pamphlets on Architecture and Related Subjects Published in America before 1895* (1946; expanded ed., New York: Da Capo Press, 1976). This figure does not include foreign reprints. It is important to remember that the format and content of these American pattern books was not original but frequently copied—indirectly and directly—British precedents.

5. Typically for contemporary pattern books, Sloan's *Model Architect* attempted to appeal to many different audiences. The preface refers to a range of readers—"experienced man," "learner," "projector," and "artisan" (1:7).

6. For more on Downing's views and books, see Adam W. Sweeting, *Reading Houses and Building Books : Andrew Jackson Downing and the Architecture of Popular Antebellum Literature, 1835–1855* (Hanover, N.H.: University Press of New England, [1996]); and John E. Crowley, *The Invention of Comfort: Sensibilities and Design in Early Modern Britain and Early America* (Baltimore: Johns Hopkins University Press, 2000).

7. Andrew Jackson Downing, *Cottage Residences; or, A Series of Designs for Rural Cottages and Cottage-Villas, and Their Gardens and Grounds: adapted to North America* (New York: Wiley & Putnam, 1842), ii.

8. Andrew Jackson Downing, *A Treatise on the Theory and Practice of Landscape Gardening, adapted to North America . . .* (New York: Wiley & Putnam; Boston : C. C. Little, 1841), 1.

9. Andrew Jackson Downing, "Hints to Persons about Building in the Country," in George Wightwick, *Hints to Young Architects. Calculated to Facilitate Their Practical Operations* (New York: Wiley, 1859), xxvii–xxviii; and Downing, *Cottage Residences,* 184–85.

10. Downing, *Cottage Residences,* 186.

11. Andrew Jackson Downing, *The Architecture of Country Houses* (New York: D. Appleton, 1850), 71. (The word "cheap" was used without the negative connotations it carries today.)

12. These terms are extracted from John Hall's preface to *A Series of Select and Original Modern Designs for Dwelling Houses: For the Use of Carpenters and Builders: Adapted to the Style of Building in the United States* (Baltimore: John Murphy, 1840).

13. John Warren Ritch, *The American Architect: Comprising Original Designs of Cheap Country and Village Residences, with Details, Specifications, Plans and Directions, and an Estimate of the Cost of Each Design* (New York: C. M. Saxton, [1849–50?]), design 2, n.p. John Warren Ritch practiced in New York from 1846; in 1857, he became a charter member and first treasurer of the American Institute of Architects. See Henry F. Withey and Elsie Rathburn Withey, *Biographical Dictionary of American Architects (Deceased)* (1956; facsimile reprint, Los Angeles: Hennessey & Ingalls, 1970).

14. Ritch, *American Architect,* design no. 4.

15. T. Thomas, *The Working-man's Cottage Architecture: Containing Plans, Elevations, and Details, for the Erection of Cheap, Comfortable, and Neat Cottages* (New York: R. Martin, 1848); O. S. Fowler, *A Home for All; or, The Gravel Wall and Octagon Mode of Building [microform] : New, Cheap, Convenient, Superior, and adapted to Rich and Poor* (New York: Fowler & Wells, 1854); and Charles P. Dwyer, *The Economic Cottage Builder; or, Cottages for Men of Small Means, Adapted to Every Locality, with Instructions for Choosing the Most Economical Materials Afforded by the Neighborhood: To Which Are Added Many Valueable Hints and Most Useful Observations: Illustrated with Tinted Designs on Stone* (Buffalo: Wanzer, McKim, 1855).

16. H. W. Cleaveland, William Backus, and Samuel D. Backus, *Village and Farm Cottages : The Requirements of American Village Homes Considered and Suggested, with Designs for Such Houses of Moderate Cost* (New York: D. Appleton, 1856), 52–53.

17. Ibid., 55. This logic recurs in other pattern books.

18. Ibid., "notice," n.p.

19. See Jeffrey A. Cohen, "Building a Discipline: Early Institutional Settings for Architectural Education in Philadelphia, 1804–1890," *Journal of Architectural Historians* 53 (June 1994): 139–83; and Jack Quinan, "Some Aspects of the Development of the Architectural Profession in Boston between 1800 and 1830," *Old-Time New England* 68 (July–December 1977): 32–37.

20. Hall, *A Series,* 3.

21. Oliver P. Smith, *The Domestic Architect: Comprising a Series of Original Designs for Rural and Ornamental Cottages*, 2nd printing (Buffalo: Phinney, 1854), iv–v, 30, 32.

22. Cooledge, *Samuel Sloan,* 35–36.

23. In format and content, *The Model Architect* may have been modeled on William Ranlett's *The Architect: A Series of Original Designs, for Domestic and Ornamental Cottages and Villas, Connected with Landscape Gardening, adapted to the United States* (New York: W. H. Graham, 1847–49). Richard C. Muehlberger in "William H. Ranlett and *The Architect*" (master's thesis, Johns Hopkins University, 1967) argued in detail the superiority of Ranlett's book, as the first American pattern book of its type, over *The Model Architect*. I contend, however, that although Ranlett's may have been the earlier of the two books, *The Model Architect*, especially in relation to Sloan's practice, is more revealing of the state of contemporary architectural practice. Ranlett seems to have been influenced in format and content Richard Brown's *Domestic Architecture: Containing a History of the Science, and the Principles of Designing Public Edifices, Private Dwelling-Houses, [etc.]* (1842). For information on Brown, see Helen C. Long, *Victorian Houses and Their Details: The Role of Publications in Their Building and Decoration* (Oxford: Architectural Press, 2002.), 41–42.

24. The format also suggests that the primary target readership was not builders. Fowler & Wells sold the whole book for $15 in 1855 (Hitchcock, *American Architectural Books*, 98). Both volumes were reprinted four times: twice by E. H. Butler, and twice by J.B. Lippincott, both of Philadelphia. The last edition was issued in 1873. (Cooledge, *Samuel Sloan*, 35–36).

25. Sloan, *Model Architect*, 1:8.

26. Ibid., 34.

27. Sam Bass Warner Jr., *The Private City: Philadelphia in Three Periods of Its Growth* (Philadelphia: University of Pennsylvania Press, 1968).

28. This fourth category of buildings is the focus of Sloan's later book, *City and Suburban Architecture* (Philadelphia: Lippincott, 1859).

29. Sloan, *Model Architect*, 1:9–10.

30. Ibid., 11–12.

31. Ibid., 26–27.

32. Ibid., 32.

33. "The Architect," "Architectural Drawings," "The Contract."

34. I have not included in this list three brief articles of a promotional nature: "Encaustic Tiles," "Building Hardware," and "Bells and Speaking Tubes."

35. Sloan, *Model Architect*, 2:71.

36. For instance, Sloan devoted almost six pages to describing the types of wood available in the United States, plus their characteristics and use, and six more pages to the importance of seasoning timber.

37. Sloan, *Model Architect*, 2:32.

38. Ibid., 1:35, 34.

39. Peter Nicholson's *Carpenter's New Guide* was first published in England in 1792 (with thirteen editions by 1857). See Long, *Victorian Houses,* 78–79. Editions of the book were published in America

beginning in 1818. Sloan contributed roof and dome designs to the 1854 edition published by Lippincott, Grambo & Co. (Hitchcock, *American Architectural Books*, 69).

40. Sloan, *Model Architect*, 1:13, 22.

41. Ibid., 34.

42. Design 53, "A Southern House," which was built for Joseph Samuel Winter in Montgomery, Alabama, is the only other house published in *The Model Architect* for which the client is named. Although not of the same fame and fortune as Eastwick, Winter was also part of the industrial advancement of America. J. S. Winter and Company was one of the earliest ironworks in the city of Montgomery (J. S. Winter and Company Records, 1851–59, Alabama Department of Archives and History).

43. As this is an actual construction cost, the amount seems to suggest that estimates in *The Model Architect* may have been lower than the actual cost of constructing the houses.

44. Construction on the Delaware County Courthouse, his first commission as an architect, was not yet complete. This project had been awarded to him by competition in 1849. Samuel Sloan was born in 1815. He apprenticed as a carpenter, and by 1833 he was working as a journeyman carpenter on the Eastern State Penitentiary, designed by John Haviland, in Philadelphia, and subsequently worked on the construction of the Pennsylvania Hospital for Mental and Nervous Diseases designed by Isaac Holden. He continued to be listed in Philadelphia directories as a carpenter until 1850, at which point he started listing himself as an architect. His practice flourished rapidly; according to his biographer, by spring 1851 he had received forty commissions for houses, a commercial block, a church, and seven public schools. In 1853 he entered into partnership with a builder, John Stewart, which lasted until 1858. He continued to practice in Philadelphia (with Addison Hutton between 1864 and 1867) until the 1870s. The focus of his commissions in his late career shifted to North Carolina: he moved to Raleigh in 1883, and died there in 1884. Biographical information based on Cooledge, *Samuel Sloan*; and Roger W. Moss and Sandra L. Tatman, "Samuel Sloan," in *Philadelphia Architects and Buildings* (www.philadelphiabuildings.org), 2003.

45. This story is first told in Cooledge's biography, based on an unidentified newspaper story from the 1890s when the house burned (Cooledge, *Samuel Sloan*, 21–22).

46. Patricia Herlihy, Review of *Russia Enters the Railway Age, 1842–1855*, *American Historical Review* 107, no. 2 (2002). Also see Roger G. Kennedy, *Architecture, Men, Women and Money in America, 1600–1860* (New York: Random House, 1985), 380–83.

47. The attribution of this building to Sloan is based on the U.S. Historic American Buildings Survey (Library of Congress, 1986) and information from the museum that now owns it.

48. His specific choice of location—the former home and gardens of John Bartram—seems actually to have been intended to save the site from further development.

49. For further discussion of the suburbanization of Philadelphia, see John R. Stilgoe, *Borderland: Origins of the American Suburb, 1820–1939* (New Haven: Yale University Press, 1988), 129–37.

50. Ibid., 137; Cooledge, *Samuel Sloan*, 60. Harold Cooledge lists fifteen of Sloan's projects as being speculative dwellings, but others not referred to as such may have also been speculative. It is not clear which projects were commissioned collaboratively and which independently by Harrison and Browne. S. A. Harrison has a small place in *The Model Architect*: a short description and plate of examples of the encaustic tiles he imported from Europe.

51. Now used by the Kappa Alpha Society and Kelly Writers House. Cf. figure 1.10.

52. Sloan, *Model Architect*, 2:28.

53. This argument is further reinforced by the school and church designs included in *The Model Architect*.

54. It is always difficult to establish the motivations that lead clients to hire specific architects, but in the case of Haller Nutt, enough documentation and circumstantial evidence exist to presume that

he commissioned Sloan as a result of having looked at *The Model Architect*. Sloan had other southern clients in this period. James Alexander Ventress of Woodville, Mississippi, commissioned him to add a second story and restyle his plantation house in an Oriental manner. This commission seems to have postdated Longwood and may well have been inspired by the design taking shape for Nutt. Given the proximity of Natchez and Woodville and the men's similar backgrounds, Ventress and Nutt most likely knew each other. See Mary Carol Miller, *Lost Mansions of Mississippi* (Jackson: University Press of Mississippi, 1996), 19–20.

55. Sloan, *Model Architect*, 2:71.

56. Nutt's daughters attended school in Philadelphia, and Natchez planters commonly had strong business ties to Philadelphia.

57. In Ina May Ogletree McAdams, *The Building of Longwood* (Austin: Published by the author, 1972). Unfortunately, Nutt's initial letter commissioning the design of Longwood has not survived.

58. Ibid., 18, 21, 24.

59. Ibid., 31, 11.

60. Kennedy, *Architecture*, 378.

61. Today, billings from business, industrial, and commercial companies and private individuals constitute 35 percent of American architects' work, ahead of government commissions at 31 percent. See *The Business of Architects: The 2003 AIA Firm Survey* (Washington, D.C.: American Institute of Architects, 2003).

62. Samuel Sloan, *City and Suburban Architecture: Containing Numerous Designs and Details for Public Edifices, Private Residences, and Mercantile Buildings: Illustrated with One Hundred and Thirty-six Engravings, Accompanied by Specifications and Historical and Explanatory Text* (Philadelphia: Lippincott, 1859).

63. Samuel Sloan, *Sloan's Constructive Architecture: A Guide to the Practical Builder and Mechanic. In Which Is Contained a Series of Designs for Domes, Roofs and Spires* (Philadelphia: Lippincott, 1859); Samuel Sloan, *Sloan's Homestead Architecture, Containing Forty Designs for Villas, Cottages, and Farm Houses, with Essays on Style, Construction, Landscape Gardening, Furniture, etc., etc. Illustrated with Upwards of 200 Engravings* (Philadelphia: Lippincott, 1861); Samuel Sloan, *American Houses: A Variety of Original Designs for Rural Buildings: Illustrated by Twenty-six Colored Engravings, with Descriptive References* (Philadelphia: Ashmead, 1861).

V

"AT THE CORE OF HIS CAREER"

Enoch A. Curtis and Architectural Books

Daniel D. Reiff

Enoch A. Curtis (1831–1907), a little-studied regional architect who designed more than sixty buildings in western New York and northwestern Pennsylvania, epitomizes the carpenter who turned architect thanks to books. It is recorded that before and after serving in the Civil War, Curtis studied architecture from books, and in 1867 he opened an architectural office in Fredonia, New York. But to put his method of designing with the prompting—or the aid—of books in context, one must first look at how essential books were to the "average" architect in the late nineteenth century. This can be determined by examining the pages of the leading architectural journal of the day, read by virtually all architects in the United States, the *American Architect and Building News* (*AABN*).[1]

Books on architectural design and theory were common aids to carpenters and architects alike in the colonial period, in the early and middle nineteenth century, and especially in the years following the Civil War.[2] Even after the establishment of schools of architecture in the United States—MIT in 1865, Cornell in 1871, Syracuse and Illinois in 1873, and so on—many architects had to rely on self-education through the study of books. The letters to the editors in the *AABN* provide a direct insight into this situation. One from the 17 November 1877 issue is especially revealing: "I have read with deep interest your articles on the subject of the technological education of architects. I have vainly hoped that some one might be prompted to champion that class of architects who owe none of their . . . ability and skill to any school, but solely to natural ability and persistent private study. . . . Should you not . . . extend the helping hand to struggling merit . . . by pointing out a judicious course of study to those who are not able to pursue any other?"[3]

This was a need recognized by the *AABN* editors; in an article titled "Architectural Students—II" (30 September 1876) they had written: "A few years ago it was difficult to give satisfactory advice to a young man in our country who wished to become an architect. There were no architectural schools in the United States; no common understanding of what an architect's training was. . . . For those who could not go to Europe to study,—of course very few could,—there was no resource but to go into some architect's office, and learn what could be got from routine-work there."

But the editors did not tell the whole story. They uniformly recommended study in professional schools and only reluctantly admitted the possibility of becoming an architect through the study of books—though books had been essential "tools of the trade" for over a century. Interestingly enough, the editors did on occasion let slip the fact that even for professionally trained architects, books were common aids: in 1880 they noted the influence of "the works of [Eugène Emmanuel] Viollet-le-Duc, which have had such extensive circulation in this country."[4] A few years later they again acknowledged, in passing, the importance to architectural education of early pattern books: in an obituary notice in 1884 for Samuel Sloan, the editors noted that "many of the younger architects throughout the country owe something of their knowledge to the excellent books in which [Sloan] sought to convey to others the results of his experience."[5]

Books, of course, were the key to private study. It is remarkable to see—despite the editors' claim in 1876 that there were "few appliances [such] as books" to aid the student—how many books indeed *were* available. A chart (figure 5.1) based on the work of Henry-Russell Hitchcock clearly shows how many architectural books were published in America, and how many were in fact published in the 1870s and 1880s—328 *new* titles![6] If one consulted volumes from England and the Continent as well, the list of available printed resources would of course be vastly greater. And the fact that so many books were published—and sold—demonstrates that such volumes were in demand.

The *AABN* readership frequently requested information on books. Here is a sampling from the 1880s and 1890s, beginning with general books and moving on to specific topics (with the number of sources suggested by the editors in parentheses).

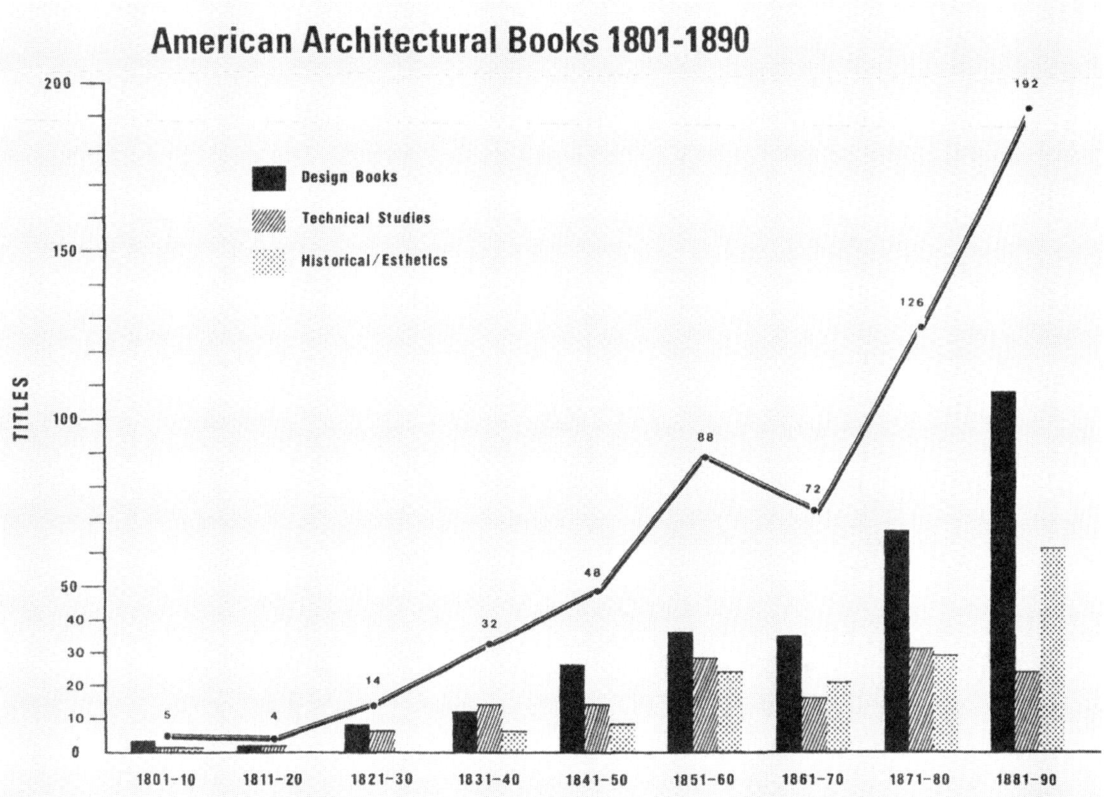

FIG 5.1 American architectural books, 1801–90. Tabulation by the author based on H.-R. Hitchcock, *American Architectural Books* (1976).

"Book for Beginners," requested 2 June 1883 (in response, the editors listed eleven volumes).

"Studies for Beginners," 23 June 1883 (three titles—in seven volumes).

"Books for Students," 16 August 1890 (six titles).

"Learning [the orders and drawing] without Teachers," 6 December 1884 (eight books).

"Books [on construction, and interior decoration]," 7 January 1888 (five titles, some multivolume).

"Books on Plumbing and Steam-Heating," 9 April 1890 (four).

"Books on School-Houses," 19 April 1890 (three).

"Books on Pompeiian Architecture," 3 May 1890 (four).

"Books on Byzantine and Renaissance Ornament," 3 May 1890 (two).

"Books [on masonry construction]" 3 May 1890 (five).

"Architectural Dictionaries," 2 August 1890 (four, two of them multivolume).
"Books [on modern church architecture]," 21 February 1891 (one).
"Books [on state house building]" 21 February 1891 (none available).
"Books on Stone-Cutting," 18 April 1891 (two).
"Books on Acoustics" [a request by none other than Cass Gilbert!], 12 January 1895 (two books—one English, one French—and references to eight articles in previous numbers of the *AABN*).[7]

In the issue of 21 February 1891 there were in fact nine separate letters requesting book information—and the geographic range of the queries is significant: they came from Massachusetts, Rhode Island, Pennsylvania, Ohio, Virginia, Michigan, Illinois, Utah, and Canada.

Further, in response to readers' requests, the *AABN* provided lists of essential books for architects to study. On 28 November 1885 it published "List of Selected Books for Professional Reference and Study," containing 168 titles. An essay "Advice to Students" on the same date listed thirty-four titles, one of them being Viollet-le-Duc's ten-volume *Dictionnaire*. In 1887 (issue of 30 July) the editors provided *three separate lists*—supplied by three different authorities—of "One Hundred Architectural Books" they considered important. And in the 12 January 1895 issue they brought to architects' attention, as a useful resource, the architectural catalogue of the Boston Public Library, which contained some 5,000 titles.

An analysis of the books that the *AABN* editors recommended, or commented on, during the 1870s and 1880s in reviews or in response to reader requests reveals that many were familiar pattern books, including (with the date of the issue in which the information was published) *Woodward's National Architect*, volume 2, 1877 (1 September 1877); H. H. Holly's *Modern Dwellings in Town and Country*, 1878 (8 June 1878); *Bicknell's Specimen Book of 100 Architectural Designs*, 1878 (6 July 1878); S. B. Reed's *House Plans for Everyone, for Village and Country Residences*, 1878 (12 September 1878); *Palliser's Useful Details*, 1881 (23 July 1881); Calvert Vaux's *Villages and Cottages*, the old classic of 1857 (8 April 1882); W. T. Comstock's *Modern Architectural Designs and Details*, 1881 (13 May 1882); W. T. Comstock's *American Cottages*, 1883 (14 February 1885)—and, a few years later, the classic F. C. Withers, *Church Architecture: Plans, Elevations, and Views . . .*, 1873 (21 February 1891). Books suggested by the editors for "general study" were more fundamental. These included (as listed by the editors) Fergusson's *History of Architecture*, Gwilt's *Encyclopaedia of Architecture*, and Trautwine's *Hand-Book for Engineers and Architects*

(2 June 1883); T. M. Clark's *Building Superintendence*, W. R. Ware's *Modern Perspective*, and Viollet-le-Duc's *Dictionnaire raisonnée* (10 November 1883); Nicholson's *Cyclopaedia of Architecture*, *Chambers' Civil Architecture*, and J. Ruskin's *Elements of Drawing* (6 December 1884).

The best indication of the sorts of books that the *AABN* editors recommended as essential to the architect "for professional reference and study" can be seen in an analysis they provided their readers by breaking up the book list of 28 November 1885 into sections. (The citations, in somewhat telegraphic form, are as given by the editors; titles do not always conform exactly to current bibliographic listings.)

The first was "History of Architecture—General History and Biography" and provided twelve titles, including Fergusson, *Illustrated Handbook of Architecture*; Gailhabaud, *Monuments anciens et modernes*; Kugler, *Geschichte der baukunst*; and of course Vasari. In the second section, "Classical," were seventeen titles, including Adam, *Ruins of the Palace of Diocletian at Spalatro*; Normand, *New Parallel of the Orders of Architecture*; Canina, *L'architettura antica*; Mauch, *Neue systematische darstellung der architecktonischen ordnungen*; and Wood, *Ruins of Palmyra*. The third section was "Byzantine," with five titles, including Texier and Pullan, *Byzantine Architecture*; Couchard, *Choix d' églises Bysantines en Grèce*; and Salzenberg, *Alt-christliche baudenkmal von Constantinopel vom V, bis XII, jahrhundert*. Next came "Mediaeval" with fifteen books, including Bloxam, *Principles of Gothic Ecclesiastical Architecture*; Caumont, *L'architecture religieuse*; Pugin, *Architectural Antiquities of Normandy*; Scott, *Lectures of Mediaeval Architecture*; and of course Viollet-le-Duc, *Dictionnaire raisonné de l'architecture française*. The fifth category, "Renaissance," contained only six titles, among them Berty, *La renaissance monumentale en France*; Ciognara, Diedo, and Selva, *Le fabbriche e i monumenti di Venezia*; and Letarouilly, *Edifices de Rome moderne*. The sixth category was "Encyclopaedias, Glossaries, Etc." and listed four titles, including Gwilt, *Encyclopaedia of Architecture*; and Parker, *Glossary of Terms Used in Architecture*. "Mouldings and Ornaments," broken down into Classical, Renaissance, and Medieval (including Byzantine and Gothic), cited among its eleven titles Chambers, *Treatise on the Decorative Part of Civil Architecture*; Albertolli, *Corso elementare di ornamenti architettonici*; and Paley, *Manual of Gothic Mouldings*. Then came eight books under "Sanitary Science," including Bailey-Denton, *House Sanitation*; Hellyer, *The Plumber and Sanitary Houses*; and Parkes, *Manual of Practical Hygiene*. The ninth category was "Materials and Construction" with eighteen titles, including Ashpitel, *Treatise on Architecture, including the Arts of Construction*; Fairbairn, *Application of Cast and Wrought Iron to Building Purposes*;

Humber, *Handy-book for the Calculation of Strains in Girders, etc.*; Rondelet, *L'art de bâtir*; and Tredgold, *Elementary Principles of Carpentry*. The tenth and final category was "Specifications and Professional Practice" with sixteen titles, among them Bartholomew, *Specifications for Practical Architecture*; Emden, *Building Leases and Building Contracts*; Leaning, *Quantity Surveying*; and Noble, *Professional Practice of Architects*. (The three separate compilations of "One Hundred Architectural Books" published in the *AABN* issue of 30 July 1887 were similar to this list.)

It is at once apparent that the journal's high-minded editors had prepared their list for professional architects of some stature—and financial wherewithal. Furthermore, many of these titles, often in multiple volumes, were available only from English or European booksellers, and though of course the illustrations were accessible to all, it seems unlikely that the average reader (or the majority of readers) of the *AABN* would have had a good enough command of French, German, or Italian to benefit from the texts of many "key works." Indeed, some readers specifically requested titles in English. A subscriber in Brooklyn asked for "books on architecture and construction (printed in English)" in the issue of 5 March 1892; another, in North Dakota, wanted to know of English translations of Viollet-le-Duc and Planat (24 March 1894).

What is interesting about the 1885 list is that the popular pattern books published in such great numbers in both England and America are nowhere to be seen on it. It appears unlikely that the average architect in America—those who wrote asking for advice—would have purchased many of the recommended tomes; their letters of request suggest that most wanted books with illustrated designs, to provide help with their own work. In fact, after 1885 the *AABN* editors essentially ceased mentioning pattern books at all, and a decade later such books had actually sunk quite low in the editors' esteem. In the issue of 3 November 1894 they noted with obvious opprobrium that "within the last few years there has sprung up in various parts of the country a brood of architects, if the name can properly be applied to such creations, who apparently make it their chief business . . . to turn out designs for houses, churches, and school-houses by the score and sell them in cheaply-bound volumes by the hundred. It is hardly possible to turn through the advertising papers or any magazine or newspaper of note without finding frequent advertisements of building plans." Yet there were indeed many architects who, not able to attend professional schools (and few indeed could), learned from books and designed with their help.

The work of a specific regional architect during this era can show just how one individual used books. Enoch A. Curtis, born in 1831 to a farming family in western

New York, was apprenticed to a carpenter in 1852 and practiced this trade for several years before entering the Union army in 1862. He was discharged in 1864 after serious injury at the Battle of Cold Harbor. His biographical sketches and obituaries note that he studied architecture from books before and after the war; alas, no source mentions which books he consulted. After his discharge Captain Curtis operated a hardware business in Fredonia, but by 1867 he had opened an *architect's* office—and practiced for the next forty years.[8]

Everyone knows that on occasion, during the eighteenth and early nineteenth centuries, builders and architects turned to illustrations in books for ideas and often copied specific features, or even whole facades, closely. In Mount Vernon, George Washington's craftsmen borrowed designs from books for plaster ceilings, fireplaces and their surrounds, and the impressive Palladian window in the banquet room; the facades of Drayton Hall, Mount Airy, and Tryon's Palace were all based on illustrations in books.[9] Even such accomplished designers as William Thornton, James Hoban, Thomas Jefferson, and Samuel McIntire relied on books for compositional ideas.[10] In the 1840s, with an upsurge in published pattern books (see figure 5.1) and a growing middle class, the use of these books increased. Whole facades copied quite literally can readily be found; architectural details drawn from books are harder to track down, but house designs based on A. J. Downing's plates are ubiquitous (figures 5.2, 5.3).[11] And copies or close adaptations of facades from Samuel Sloan, Oliver Smith, Orson Squire Fowler, Calvert Vaux, E. C. Hussey, and others, are easy to spot, confirming the widespread usefulness of these books in America.[12]

Enoch Curtis seems to have eschewed the copying of entire facade designs, a common practice with many carpenter-architects; none of the sixty-odd buildings known to be by him seems to be a direct copy, in totality, of any one plate. Rather, Curtis drew on published designs for ideas of style and overall composition, and for "correct" details. Many pattern books (such as Marcus Cummings and Charles Miller's *Architecture: Designs . . . including Details for Both Exterior and Interior* of 1868, and *Cummings' Architectural Details* of 1873) were specifically published with this approach in mind; they contained primarily design details (only a few entire facades were depicted), since that was what many local architects needed. A careful study of Curtis's buildings provides an insight into this practice on the part of a "typical" regional architect in the later nineteenth century.

Architectural books had been available from local booksellers in Fredonia for years. In 1836, books by Edward Shaw and Asher Benjamin were advertised for sale in the local paper and, in 1843, two of A. J. Downing's books.[13] Specifically which

FIG 5.2 A. J. Downing, design 2 from *Cottage Residences* (1842).

FIG 5.3 Upham-Wright house, Newark, Ohio, ca. 1848. Vintage photo, courtesy of Mary Sherwood Wright Jones.

books Curtis had in his personal collection is not known; no inventory or probate list has been found. But an examination of some of his Fredonia buildings, where motifs that are traceable to well-known books of the day can be observed, offers some idea of what sorts of books he had recourse to, as well as how he used them in the 1860s and 1870s.

One of his first houses, a stylish Second Empire building with central facade tower, was the Spencer Bailey dwelling of 1868. It appears to have been based on a Calvert Vaux design from his *Villas and Cottages*, not only in overall composition and scale but even in many features such as the paired central second-floor windows, the railing just below, and the arched window in the central tower mansard.[14]

The Putnam Brothers' Store (1868–70), a brick commercial block built on a prominent corner in downtown Fredonia (figure 5.4), originally displayed (the top is now somewhat altered) a brick cornice that seems to have come from Cummings and Miller's *Architecture* of 1868[15] (figures 5.5, 5.6).

The Odd Fellows Building of 1869–70 (figure 5.7), although composed generally like other Second Empire structures that Curtis could have seen in his travels, has many direct parallels in the same Cummings and Miller volume of 1868. Though

FIG 5.4 Putnam Brothers' Store, 1868–70 (left), and Day Building, 1878 (right), Fredonia, N.Y. Photo by the author.

FIG 5.5 Putnam Brothers' Store, cornice detail. Photo by the author.

FIG 5.6 Marcus Cummings and Charles Miller, *Architecture* (1868), plate 4, fig. 2.

FIG 5.7 Odd Fellows Building, 1868–70, Fredonia, N.Y. Photo by the author.

FIG 5.8 Architectural features from the Odd Fellows Building compared with details from Cummings and Miller, *Architecture*.

the original mansard roof burned in 1923 and was replaced by a plain parapet, other pattern book features include quoins beveled at the outer edges, beveled blocks, pedimented window caps on brackets, single arched windows, piers with alternating vermiculated blocks, keystoned hood molds, grouped arched windows, a triple-arched entrance feature, chamfered piers, vermiculated voussoirs, and even the incised rosette found on ground-floor piers (figures 5.8, 5.9).

Thus Curtis did not simply copy a business block, in totality, from Cummings and Miller (who did include a few attractive Italianate examples), but with the aid of their book—using details that were thus "guaranteed" to be the up-to-date work of professional architects—he created a Second Empire showpiece by skillfully adapting many of their high-style features. This method—eschewing the bald copying of an overall published design but gathering together numerous published motifs in a felicitous manner—is of course of long standing; it was how William Buckland had achieved such a successful design for his classic Hammond-Harwood House a century before.[16]

FIG 5.9 Architectural features from the Odd Fellows Building and details from Cummings and Miller, *Architecture*.

In the asymmetrical Second Empire house that Curtis built on East Main Street in 1872, he was probably inspired by such designs as plate 7 in E. C. Hussey's *Home Building*.[17] Although the Hussey design is, obviously, too late to be the real inspiration for the dwelling, Curtis may have studied a Second Empire design of about 1870 (an updated version of the classic asymmetrical villa in Downing's 1842 *Cottage Residences*, and its imitators) in some other pattern book.

The Clark-Johnson House, a wonderfully picturesque and colorful High Victorian dwelling of 1877–78, does seem to have been inspired by an 1875 Hussey design, his plate 35, and interior details parallel other published contemporary plates—in this case, for example, the stair newel post similar to those in Bicknell's *Designs for Newels, Hand-Rails, and Balusters* (1873), plates 39 and 40.[18]

The Horace White House of about 1878 in nearby Laona, another High Victorian dwelling with a clear pattern book legacy, is especially instructive as to Curtis's methods of "inspiration" from book designs. Two published models were apparently his main sources. His primary inspiration seems to have been the astonishing Victorian Gothic villa with lofty central facade tower found in William Woollett's *Villas and Cottages* as design 4. In Ocala, Florida, he indeed carried out that design, closely following Woollett's model, in 1877, but there Curtis used the printed image as a starting point for his less extravagant version. He omitted the central tower, replacing it with a dormer window instead; but the use of the Woollett design as his model is confirmed by the treatment of the paired gables, each with quatrefoils in circular frames flanking the central finial. Here Curtis showed his thoughtfulness as a designer, for he improved on Woollett: he transformed the blank space above the quatrefoils into three-lobed cusps, consistent with the Gothic features they surmount. Curtis seems to have had an eye on plate 36 in Hussey's *Home Building*, too, for the twin facade gables, central dormer, and full-width porch (a feature not on the Woollett model but originally found on the Horace White House) are much the same.[19]

An excellent, and more complex, example of Curtis's creative adaptation and reformulation of published designs is found in his Aaron O. Putnam House of 1878–79. The overall design seems to have been inspired by several sources, perhaps the most prestigious being a dwelling by Peabody and Stearns (published in the *AABN* for 3 January 1877) to which the Fredonia house owes its overall composition, roof form, "Stick Style" belt course, bargeboard treatment, and paired central windows. He also seems to have admired a remodeling project published in the *AABN* the following year (21 September 1878), whose side bay of two stories with chamfered edges and gabled roof is much like those of his Putnam House. This

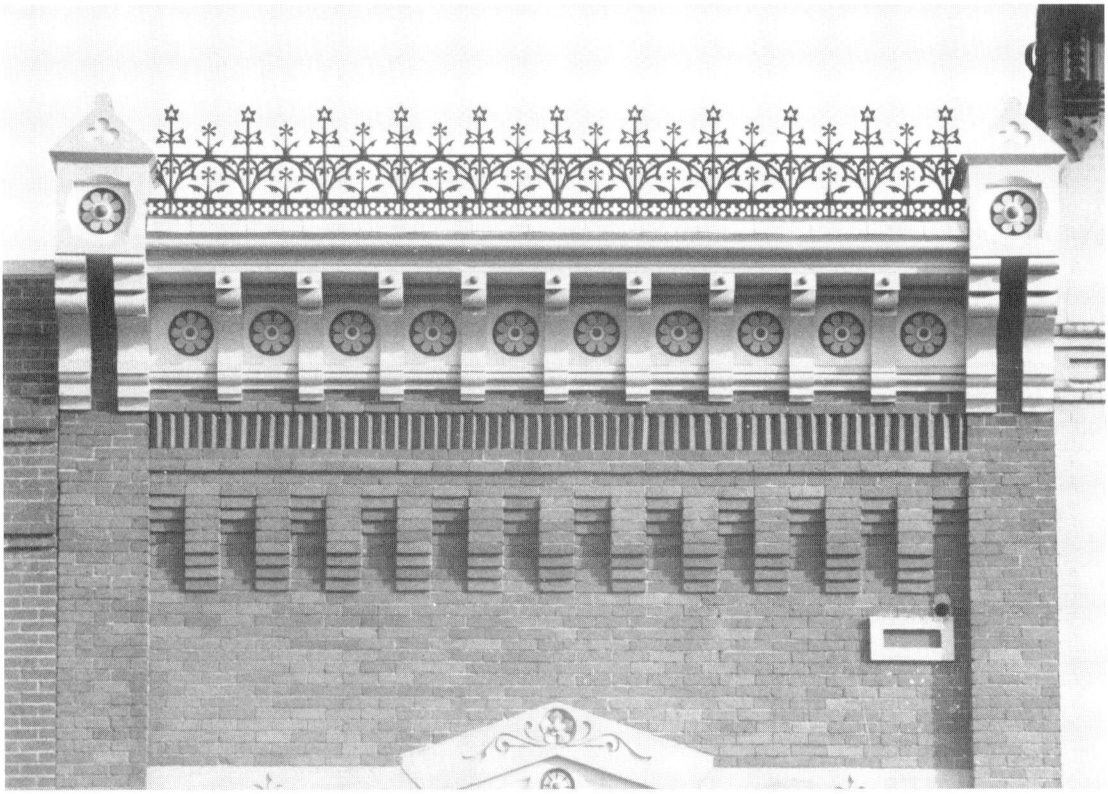

FIG 5.10 Day Building, cornice detail. Photo by the author.

design, as well as two depicted in *Palliser's Model Homes*, plates 7 and 9, seem to have provided inspiration for the full-width porch. The Palliser plates also seem to be the source for the use of two windows at each side of the central gabled bay, and the fan feature in the gable.[20] All these were creatively melded; only the porte-cochère was copied literally—well, almost literally—from plate 25 of Daniel T. Atwood's *Atwood's Modern American Homesteads*. Some details as well can be traced to plates in books: the window treatment appears to come from *Cummings' Architectural Details*. Yet the *plan* of the house is unlike any of the models cited.[21]

Curtis's Day Building, a charming commercial structure of 1878 (adjacent to his earlier Putnam Brothers store; see figure 5.4), with attractive brick and stone polychromy, reveals again his knowledge of the *AABN*, for the cornice seems to be based on a design published 24 February 1877, just a year earlier (figures 5.10, 5.11). Interestingly enough, the fine cast-iron cresting Curtis added above is similar to the "iron cresting and finials" manufactured by J. W. Fiske (of New York City) as depicted in Hussey's *Home Building* (1875) on page 392 (figure 5.12).[22]

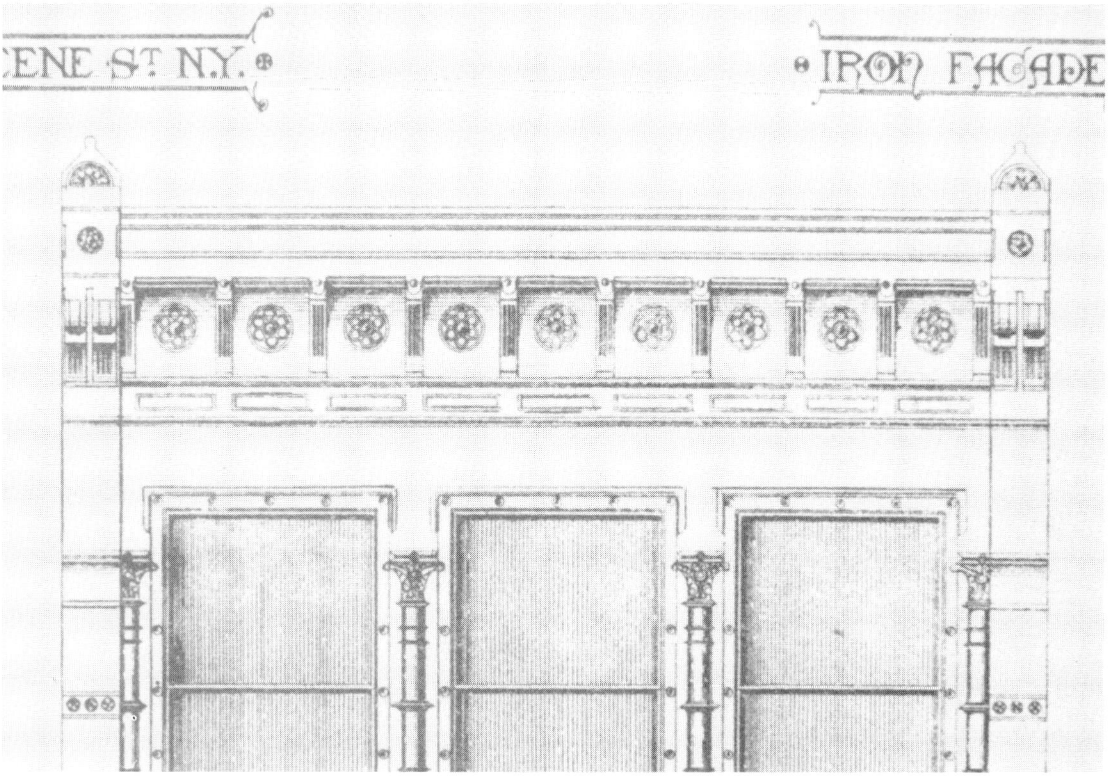

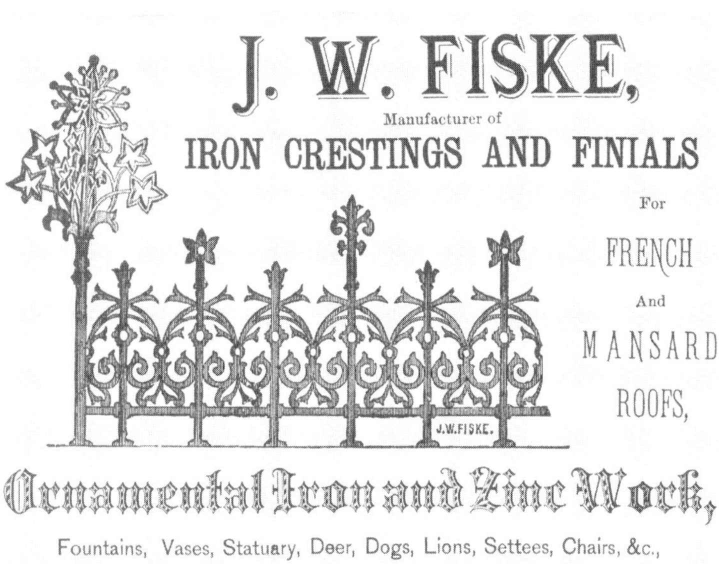

FIG 5.11 "Store No. 31 Greene Street N.Y.—Iron Façade" (G. W. Romeyn, architect), detail. From *AABN*, 24 February 1877.

FIG 5.12 "Iron Crestings and Finials" manufactured by J. W. Fiske Co., New York City. From Elisha Charles Hussey, *Home Building* (1875), p. 392.

A final example of Curtis's adaptation of published designs is the Nathan A. Putnam House of 1880. Another home with "Stick Style" features (notably the belt course), it was built for the brother (and partner in his dry goods business) of Aaron O. Putnam. The dwelling appears to be based on *Palliser's Model Homes* (1878), plate 3, but with variations of the roof shape and design of the front porch.[23]

If we needed any further confirmation that Curtis referred to books for ideas, inspiration, and motifs, we have the statement of the daughter of C. D. Ellis of Laona that when Captain Curtis discussed their proposed house (built about 1890) with her father, he brought a book of designs to show him. But then Curtis prepared his own set of drawings, which survive, and they do not match up at all closely with any published model that I have yet seen. Still, such reliance on books assured that he was designing buildings that were up to date and that reflected the published work of notable, professionally trained architects—even to the likes of Peabody and Stearns.

Curtis designed many buildings—churches, village halls, commercial blocks, schools, and others, in western New York and northwestern Pennsylvania—that do not seem to be based directly on any published models or even details. Yet in quite a number of his buildings the value of published illustrations is clear for suggesting a style, an overall design, and details and features. He must have had quite a library of architectural books, as well as issues of the *AABN*: his house still stands, and in the front room that was his office, the outlines are still visible of shelves that filled one whole wall at each side of the fireplace.[24] Each was about six feet wide and five feet tall—space for hundreds of books and periodicals. Clearly, for Curtis, publications were essential "tools of the trade," and they also would have been an impressive display of erudition—just as they were in H. H. Richardson's inner sanctum—for prospective clients.[25]

This "creative inspiration" from published sources that Curtis employed must have been common practice with self-trained architects of the day (though harder to spot than the direct, more or less complete, copying of models). This sort of creative visual assistance—in a way, getting professional advice from colleagues farther afield, thanks to their books—shows clearly that for Enoch Curtis, from his early training and throughout much of his life as an architect, books and the professional press were at the core of his career.

NOTES

1. Less than a decade after it was established in 1876, *The American Architect and Building News* had roughly 5,500 subscribers (*AABN*, 6 September 1884); at that time there were, according to the United

States census, about 8,000 individuals in the country listing themselves as architects. Thus, considering that many offices employed more than one architect yet would probably receive only one subscription to the journal, it seems likely that most architects, either individually or through their office, had access to the *AABN*. That a great many architects took an active interest in the journal is born out by the statistic, cited in the 2 August 1884 issue's editorial, that "up to the close of 1883 we had published designs contributed by four hundred and twenty architectural *firms*, while the membership of the [American] Institute [of Architects] amounted at that time to one hundred and sixty-five *individuals*." (My thanks to the West Point Academy Library for their lending me its microfilm copy of the *AABN*, from which much of this research was conducted; and to the Buffalo and Erie County Public Library, from whose copies of the *AABN* I made xerographic and photographic reproductions.)

2. On the use of architectural books in the eighteenth century, see Daniel D. Reiff, *Houses from Books: Treatises, Pattern Books, and Catalogs in American Architecture, 1738–1950, a History and Guide* (University Park: Pennsylvania State University Press, 2000), 25–38. In practice, the copying of plates in pattern books for entire facades was very rare in the colonial era before 1750, and not really common after that. During this whole period the method of design that drew on pattern books was the copying or adapting of *details* (fireplaces, door cases, window treatment, ceiling moldings, etc.) in the "standard" vernacular house types—in eighteenth-century Virginia, by the 1720s, the main one being the two-story, hipped-roof dwelling with central hallway, which I have called the "Jaquelin-Ambler Type" after the first mature version built in Jamestown about 1715. See Daniel D. Reiff, *Small Georgian Houses in England and Virginia: Origins and Development through the 1750s* (Newark: University of Delaware Press, 1986), 221–84. For the use of architectural books in the early and mid-nineteenth century, see Reiff, *Houses from Books*, 38–84; for the growth and use of pattern books after the Civil War, 85–126.

3. A most remarkable account of an architect's self-education is given in the *AABN*, 31 August 1878, as "The Studies of an Architect." The anonymous author had gone to work—and was self-supporting—at the age of *nine*, taught himself Latin and Greek, completed three years of craft training, and "studied three years with an architect"; he now had his own office, with his own students.

4. "The Condition of Architecture in the Western States, I," *AABN*, 13 March 1880, 108. Viollet-le-Duc had in fact been well known to architects many years before 1880. Henry Van Brunt published a review of the first volume of Viollet's *Entretiens sur l'architecture* (1863) in *The Nation* in 1866, and in 1869 his ten-volume *Dictionnaire raisonnée de l'architecture française* (1854–68) was reviewed by Russsell Sturgis in the same journal. English translations of his works began appearing in the 1870s—though architects were primarily interested in the cornucopia of illustrations his books provided. The *AABN* featured Viollet-le-Duc frequently, between 1876 and 1895 publishing at least seventy-one articles, reviews, excerpts, letters, serializations, and accounts by or about him. See Daniel D. Reiff, "Viollet-le-Duc and American Nineteenth Century Architecture," *Journal of Architectural Education* 42 (Autumn 1988): 32–47.

5. *AABN*, 2 August 1884. Sloan's influence was not limited to his books; the editors continue that he also was "one of the first persons in the country to perceive the deficiency in technical literature which he afterwards endeavored to supply by the publication of his *Architectural Review and Builder's Journal*."

6. The graph was prepared from an analysis of the entries in Henry-Russell Hitchcock, *American Architectural Books: A List of Books, Portfolios, and Pamphlets on Architecture and Related Subjects Published in America before 1895* (1946; Minneapolis: University of Minnesota Press, 1962). My thanks to Charlotte R. Morse for drawing up my results.

7. Although my focus here is on the importance of books for architectural inspiration and design, journals were also of great importance (as suggested in note 5 above). The editors of the *AABN* commented with amazement on how many professional journals were being published in the 1880s; in the

issue of 29 November 1890 they observed: "Looking over the 'directory' just issued by an advertising agent, we counted this week, a list of *fifty-five* journals under the heading 'Architecture, Building, and Real Estate.'" Their readership also valued journals: a subscriber asked on 7 January 1888 for the names of leading foreign, non-English, journals, and the editors obliged by listing *ten*, from publishers in France, Germany, Austria, and Russia. For additional information on American architectural journals, see Reiff, *Houses from Books*, 128–31.

8. The main sources for biographical information on Enoch A. Curtis are George D. Merrill, ed., *History of Chautauqua County, New York* (Boston: W. A. Fergusson, 1894), 503–5; "Death of Capt. E. A. Curtis," *Fredonia Censor*, 9 October 1907, 1; and B. F. Dilley, ed., *Biographical and Portrait Cyclopedia of Chautauqua County* (Philadelphia: John M. Gresham, 1891), 133. Tabulations of references to Curtis's buildings in local newspapers (prepared by Ann M. Fahnestock), and other data, can be found in the Darwin R. Barker Historical Museum, Fredonia, New York.

9. Illustrations of these four buildings (and their pattern book sources) can be found in Reiff, *Houses from Books*, figs. 35–36; 25–26; 28–29; and 30–31.

10. Illustrations of these architects' buildings (and their pattern book sources) can be found in ibid., figs. 37–38 and 49–50; 41–42; 43–46; and 39–40.

11. For Downing plates and their progeny, see ibid., figs. 79–90, 91–92, 93–97, 98–101, and 110–11.

12. For illustrations of these architects' buildings (and their pattern book sources), see ibid., figs. 108–9, 112–15, 118–25; 102–7; 128–29; 145–48, 149–50, 163–64; and 445–46, 453–54.

13. An ad inserted by a local bookseller in the *Fredonia Censor* of 8 June 1836 notified the public of "Shaw's and Benjamin's Architects, both latest editions, just received." These were probably Edward Shaw's *Civil Architecture; or, A Complete Theoretical and Practical System of Building*, 4th ed., rev. and enl. (Boston: Marsh, Capen & Lyon, 1836), and Asher Benjamin's *The Practical House Carpenter*, 4th ed. (Boston: The proprietors; New York: J. P. Peaslee, 1835). In the 23 October 1843 issue of the *Censor*, the same bookseller announced that "Downing's Landscape Gardening . . . also his Cottage Residences, both very desirable works, for every person of taste, and especially to those intending to build and improve their grounds," were now available at his shop. Downing's *A Treatise on the Theory and Practice of Landscape Gardening* first appeared in 1841, and his *Cottage Residences* in 1842; second editions of both were published in 1844. (My thanks to Douglas H. Shepard for bringing these two *Censor* items to my attention.)

14. Calvert Vaux, *Villas and Cottages: A Series of Designs Prepared for Execution in the United States* (2nd ed.; New York: Harper & Brothers, 1864). See Reiff, *Houses from Books*, figs. 453–54.

15. [Marcus Fayette] Cummings and [Charles Crosby] Miller, *Architecture. Designs for Street Fronts, Suburban Houses, and Cottages, Including Details, for both Exterior and Interior*, 4th ed. (Toledo, Ohio: S. Bailey & Eager, 1868), plate 4, fig. 2. The first edition of this large-format volume was published in 1865. It was a great success and, the authors noted, "has found its way into the hands of architects, carpenters and builders in every portion of the United States, from Maine to California, and the demand . . . continues unabated." Their fourth edition was reprinted by the American Life Foundation in 1978; its second printing (1980) has an excellent thirteen-page illustrated introduction on Cummings and Miller by Diana S. Waite.

16. Although William Buckland did adapt, as the central part of this splendid house (1773–74), the standard English archetype (two-story, hipped-roof block with central projecting pedimented frontispiece) which I call the "Kingston Lacy Type"—after the first English dwelling of this type: Kingston Lacy by Roger Pratt, designed in 1662 (see Reiff, *Small Georgian Houses*, fig. 67)—it appears that he nonetheless turned to pattern books for the overall composition, and for many of the details, which he brought together (one might say *zuzammengestohlen*) from various books: overall tripartite form of the dwelling, the central block composed with 1-3-1 fenestration, the form of the doorway, the

composition of the door with enframed widow above it, the end window with a "Gibbs surround," the pedimental window with elaborate escutcheon, and polygonal end wings. These features are drawn from James Gibbs, Robert Morris, and Abraham Swan. For the specific pattern book sources and illustrations of all these, see Reiff, *Houses from Books*, 32–33 and fig. 34.

17. E. C. Hussey, *Home Building: A Reliable Book of Facts, Relative to Building . . . Containing . . . 45 Original Designs* (New York: Published by Author, 1875). See Reiff, *Houses from Books*, figs. 455–56.

18. Reiff, *Houses from Books*, figs. 463–64; for the newel post comparison, see Daniel D. Reiff, *Architecture in Fredonia, New York, 1811–1997: From Log Cabin to I. M. Pei* (Fredonia, N.Y.: White Pine Press, 1997), figs. 150–51.

19. William Woollett, *Villas and Cottages: Plans and Elevations . . . of Twelve Villas and Ten Cottages . . .* (New York: A. J. Bicknell, 1876). See Reiff, *Houses from Books*, figs. 161–64; for the house in Ocala, Florida, fig. 160.

20. *Palliser's Model Homes: Showing a Variety of Designs for Model Dwellings* (New York: Palliser, Palliser & Co., 1878). See Reiff, *Houses from Books*, 101–3 and figs. 153–59. About 1885, Putnam had the interior of his sumptuously decorated house photographed; three of these views appear in Reiff, *Architecture in Fredonia*, figs. 140–42. For all six interior views (and biographical information on Putnam), see Daniel D. Reiff, "The Aaron O. Putnam House: A Victorian Showplace in Fredonia, New York," Society of Architectural Historians Western New York Chapter, *Little Journal* 6 (February 1982): 21–29.

21. *Atwood's Modern American Homesteads Illustrated by Forty-six Plates* (New York: A. J. Bicknell, 1876); *Cummings' Architectural Details, Containing 387 Designs and 967 Illustrations of the Various Parts Needed in the Construction of Buildings* (New York: Orange Judd, 1873).

22. The J. W. Fiske Co. is represented in Fredonia to this day by two impressive (and now fully restored) cast iron fountains, the "Mark Fountains," given to the village in 1901 and located in the east and west parts of the Fredonia Common. See Reiff, *Architecture in Fredonia*, fig. 282, for the eastern fountain.

23. See Reiff, *Houses from Books*, figs. 465–66.

24. For a view of the house, see Reiff, *Architecture in Fredonia*, fig. 184. Curtis's office was at the front right, reached from the entrance hall by sliding doors (now closed in). Curtis's skill, and cleverness as a designer is born out by the fact that his Colonial Revival home was actually a thorough remodeling of a vernacular Italianate house that he transformed in 1900–1901 while his family still occupied it! For this project, commented upon with wonder in the local paper, see Daniel D. Reiff, "House Remodeling in the Victorian Era," *Nineteenth Century* 20 (Spring 2000): figs. 7a and 7b.

25. H. H. Richardson's book-filled "inner sanctum" was illustrated in the *AABN* for 27 December 1884. At the architect's death he owned 380 volumes on architecture and art, 50 bound volumes of photographs, and nearly 400 loose photographs. In the published view of Richardson's "library and study," at least 175 books are visible. See Reiff, *Houses from Books*, fig. 200. See figure Intr. 2.

VI

EDWARD TOWNSEND MIX

Books and the Professional Architect in Nineteenth-Century Milwaukee

Chris Szczesny-Adams

Edward Townsend Mix (1831–1890), a Milwaukee architect working 1855–90, owned a variety of architectural books that enhanced his professional practice (figure 6.1). Although not commonly recognized as a major figure in American architecture, Mix designed and built structures throughout the Midwest and played a critical role in Milwaukee's architectural development. His designs encompassed various architectural styles, including Italianate, Second Empire, Romanesque, and Queen Anne, all of which were reflected in his book collection.

To understand E. Townsend Mix, his books, and his impact on Milwaukee's architectural development, one must consider a variety of issues. It is important, first, to correlate the development of Milwaukee as a city, Mix's place in it, and his architectural designs; second, to observe how his New Haven, Connecticut, background exposed him to the use of books within an architectural practice; third, to discuss the variety and substance of the architectural works in his library. Finally, one must discover how Mix's designs demonstrated the influence of his architectural book collection on his work. As Milwaukee's principal late-nineteenth-century architect, his lineage, training, and architectural books reflected his status as a professional and provided the background for his innovative and cosmopolitan designs for himself, his clients, and the upper Midwest.

Milwaukee is known for its strong cultural heritage derived from the German, Polish, Italian, and Irish communities that developed there during the nineteenth century.[1] In 1890, the year Mix died, the U.S. census identified Milwaukee as the "Most Foreign City in the United States": 72 percent of the its 285,315 residents were of German descent.[2] Its rich German heritage aided in developing Milwaukee into a modern city. Yet it is important to remember that many of its first large-scale real estate developers were *not* German, and those were the men for whom Mix worked.[3] Milwaukee's antebellum architecture was developed by Yankees with ethnic backgrounds primarily from the British Isles, who saw in the city an opportunity to obtain wealth.

FIG 6.1 Edward Townsend Mix, ca. 1880. Photo courtesy of the Milwaukee County Historical Society.

In 1856, Mix arrived in Milwaukee after working for a year in Chicago with W. W. Boyington. The city was barely ten years old, and Wisconsin had only recently (in 1848) become a state. The majority of the buildings in Milwaukee, the state's largest city, had been constructed hastily of wood and were in need of repair. In order to stay competitive in attracting desirable residents, such as the educated and entrepreneurial New Englanders and New York Knickerbockers who were among its early settlers, Milwaukee in the 1850s needed to shed its appearance as a frontier outpost and cultivate a metropolitan outlook.[4] The 1850 census indicated that of the 31,077 people residing in Milwaukee County, only 1,187 could not read, which suggests a highly educated population. The proportion of foreign-born residents in the entire state of Wisconsin was approximately 36 percent, which included a significant number of immigrants from British America and England.[5] These statistics highlight the importance of the original Yankee population that settled Milwaukee, an importance that has been eclipsed in modern memory by the predominance of later immigrant populations.

Many of Mix's commissions reflected the close relationships he had with the Yankee businessmen, industrialists, and entrepreneurs of the city, including two of the most prominent, the meatpacker John Plankinton and the banker and railroad magnate Alexander Mitchell. These men, and many of their friends and colleagues as well, employed Mix to create lavish commercial, residential, religious, and institutional structures. Mix even designed the building for the Milwaukee Club, a predominantly Yankee businessmen's organization whose membership included only a few of the leading German businessmen.[6] Of its members, approximately twenty were documented patrons of Mix—who was also a member. His association with this group reflected a system of patronage that lasted for approximately twenty-five years during the nascent city's largest period of architectural and economic expansion. It was through the patronage of such men that many of Mix's buildings were realized. For these patrons Mix created a variety of structures in cosmopolitan styles to suit their taste as well as the East Coast and European trends reflected in the books he owned.

The second area that is significant in understanding Mix is the importance of his family background and the influence of Connecticut on his architectural development. Mix came from a New Haven family with an extensive lineage tracing back to the New Haven Colony (1640–). His mother, Emily Townsend, was a niece of Hezekiah Howe, the New Haven bookseller and publisher, and a cousin to Henry Howe, the writer and publisher.[7] Uncle Hezekiah owned a bookstore that owing to its proximity "standing in the shadow of Yale college . . . was the daily resort and gathering place of the learned men of that institution, and for those from many other localities who were temporarily drawn to New Haven through its attractions as a literary and educational center."[8]

In considering New Haven as a literary and intellectual locale, it is significant to note that the first quarto edition of Noah Webster's dictionary was published in Hezekiah Howe's printing office in 1828. Hezekiah's son Henry worked in the family bookstore and learned the printing trade at an early age. Although Henry planned to attend Yale College, his father's declining financial situation made that an impossibility, and at age fifteen, in 1831, he began working full time in his father's printing office within the bookstore.[9] Also in 1831, Henry's first cousin once removed, Edward Townsend Mix, was born in New Haven. Mix lived in the city until 1836, when his father, Captain Edward H. Mix, briefly moved the family to a farm in the experimental colony of Andover, Illinois.[10] During Mix's youth, Henry Howe gave him a set of drawing cards that supposedly "awakened his genius."[11] In one of the books in Mix's collection, Robert W. Billings, *Illustrations of the Architectural Antiquities of the County of Durham* (1846), two drawing cards approximately 3 by 6 inches were glued into the end pages. It cannot be proved, but these could be the cards that engaged him.

One card contained a section and an elevation of a temple dedicated to Napoleon's army. The design combined features from the Roman Pantheon and Palladio's Villa Rotunda. The other card illustrated an ancient Roman mosaic pavement depicting Hades abducting Persephone. Unlike the previous card with its French references, this one was probably published in the United States or England, given its English title and the name of the engraver, W. Cooke. Of particular interest, at the top of the card, written in pencil, was the name "Edward," at least suggesting that this was one of the original cards given to Mix by his cousin Henry Howe.

In the 1830s, New Haven remained a relatively small community consisting of about 10,000 residents.[12] Although the Mix, Howe, and Townsend families were extensive, the previously mentioned members were close. Around 1834, Henry Howe accepted a clerkship in New York at Nevins & Townsend, which was owned by his cousin Emily's father, Ebenezer Townsend.[13] All these connections indicated strong family relationships, and it was in this New Haven environment that Mix began his life.[14]

Besides becoming an important literary site, New Haven was growing as an architectural center. Ithiel Town (1784–1844) began working in New Haven around 1813 and kept a residence there into the 1840s. Although he was a practicing architect, his patented design for a lattice truss in 1820 had made him financially secure and provided him with the means to begin his extensive collection of architectural and fine arts books. Town's library, one of the largest of its kind in the United States at the time, was open to architects, intellectuals, artists, and others. It was from research collected in this library that New Haven resident Louisa Tuthill compiled her *History of Architecture from the Earliest Times* (1848). In 1836 Town built a fire-proof home in New Haven to house his library, which became so well known that it even developed into a tourist site.[15]

Although his book collection was dispersed in the 1840s, its influence shaped the architectural profession. Town's library and his interest in architectural education changed the way architects trained and thus advanced the idea of architects as professionals. No longer would training take place completely through apprenticeship. Now it became significant for architects to study other works through books as well as to gain experience in an office and on the job site. Although no current documentation provides a specific association, it is possible that Ithiel Town trained such New Haven architects as Sidney Mason Stone (1803–1882) and perhaps Henry Austin (1804–1891).[16]

In 1846 the Mix family returned from Illinois to the East Coast, and Mix completed his education at the Collegiate School in Batavia, New York, after which he held a variety of jobs and perhaps served a brief apprenticeship with architect Richard M. Upjohn (1828–1903).[17] In the summer of 1848, Mix returned to New Haven for a visit, met with church designer Sidney Mason Stone, and stayed to begin his architectural training in Stone's office.[18] Stone, who was considered one of New Haven's "early professional architects," had been exposed to Town's extensive architectural library and recognized its importance as a tool for the profession.[19] Although not much is known about Stone's practice beyond the scant buildings that survive, several of his designs were published in various books, including *A Book of Plans for Churches and Parsonages* (1853), issued by the Congregational Churches of the United States General Convention held at Albany in 1852, and in what looks to be an undated partial reissue of that work titled *Rural Church and Cottage Architecture* (figure 6.2), of which Mix once owned a copy.[20] Stone's published designs help confirm his interest in books and provide tangible evidence of their importance in his architectural practice. (And the same might be said of Stone's New Haven contemporary, Henry Austin.)

New Haven and Mix's family background were important to his architectural and scholarly development in at least two ways. First, he was exposed by his

FIG 6.2 Sidney Mason Stone, church facade. Plate 5 from Mix's copy of *Rural Church and Cottage Architecture*, n.d. Photo by the author. Courtesy of the Milwaukee Public Library.

extended family to the importance of books in various fields. Second, his architectural mentor, Sidney Mason Stone, certainly communicated his personal interest in books through his connection to the architectural library of Ithiel Town (from which Stone acquired several books) and his own published works.[21]

Following Mix's death in 1890, Mary B. Hayes Mix, his wife, donated to the Milwaukee Public Library a collection of twenty-one architectural titles comprising nearly forty different volumes.[22] This extensive collection comprises eight books published in France, four English publications, and nine issued in the United States; they include encyclopedias, journals, books on structure, pattern books, catalogues, and architectural histories (see the Appendix to this chapter). These books provided Mix with readily accessible sources of contemporary and historical architectural designs, and since such sources were limited on the frontier, particularly before the Civil War, they also provided design examples for his clients to consider. Eight of these books offer special insight into Mix's architectural practice.

First, César Daly's *L'architecture privée au XIXme siècle sous Napoléon III* was published in three folio volumes in 1864. Daly was the "Architect of the Government" and director of the General Review of Architecture and Public Works in Paris. He dedicated his work to Baron Georges Eugene Haussmann and in the first volume discussed the importance of the architecture of Paris and Haussmann's role.[23] Following the dedication is a one-page response by Haussmann himself. Each of the three volumes highlights a different type of residential building: private mansions, apartment houses, and villas. Each design contained multiple plans, elevations, and views as well as details. The buildings illustrated were all designed by architects, and the book's index lists each building's address.

This series was particularly interesting because of its contemporary nature. Published in the midst of the renovations that Baron Haussmann was orchestrating for Paris, it reflected the city as a growing metropolis utilizing new technology and modern design. It was critical for Mix, as an architect who was transforming the midwestern frontier, to see and understand the new styles and how they could be integrated into his own designs. It seemed appropriate that this type of book would be in Mix's collection because of the contemporary nature of the innovations that were taking place in Paris in the 1860s. The volumes also suggested the importance of understanding how new technology was beginning to play a crucial role in architectural and urban design.

The second work, *Motifs historiques d'architecture et de sculpture d'ornement*, also by Daly, was published in 1869. Its two folio-sized volumes had been written when

Daly was still "Architect of the Government." In both volumes, opposite the title page, is the handwritten inscription "E. Townsend Mix, Minneapolis, Sep. 23, 1890"—the location and date of Mix's death.[24] This work focused on the history of the architecture of France from François I to Louis XVI. Both volumes illustrated architectural details showing stylistic variations and continuities between subsequent periods, encompassing everything from facade views to cornice details drawn to scale. These images were intended as a practical interpretation of how architecture, particularly historical architecture, had been developed. The elaborate French details highlighted in these volumes were a feature that Mix utilized in his commercial buildings, which again reflected his interest in cosmopolitan French design.

The third work consisted of twelve volumes of the *Encyclopédie d'architecture*, with Victor Calliat and Adolphe Lance as editors, published in Paris by Bance between 1851 and 1862. This series was less an encyclopedia than a contemporary architectural journal. It provided the reader with an up-to-date view of architectural issues in Paris and throughout France, as well as presenting images of modern design such as Henri Labrouste's Bibliothèque Ste.-Geneviève. Although most of the images did not contain numeric details, several were drawn to scale. The images offered the reader a comprehensive view of a design from elevations, sections, plans, and specific details, and many buildings were covered in multiple monthly issues, each highlighting different aspects of a design, how it could be constructed, and its overall architectural importance. This series also provided Mix with the opportunity to understand the contemporary architectural issues and designs of Paris without traveling there.

The fourth work, *L'architecture du Vme au XVIIme siècle et les arts qui en dépendent*, written by Jules Gailhabaud, was published in five volumes in 1858. Although most of the volumes focused on religious architecture, the third consisted primarily of institutional architecture in France and Italy, the building types it depicted including hospitals, baths, crypts, tombs, and funerary chapels. Overall, this series contained a wide variety of buildings and objects that were probably helpful to Mix particularly in his church designs and in adapting stylistic features.

The fifth book was Léon Isabey and Leblan's *Villas maisons de ville et de campagne*. Isabey, the author, was an architect who held the title "Inspector of the Imperial Palace." Leblan, who was known only by his last name, served as architectural draftsman for the book. Following the author's explanation of intent, he focused on the images of domestic architecture in both city and country settings in France.

Single-family dwellings were the dominant type, and most plates showed facades, plans, and roof designs. The houses highlighted in this book reflected a variety of easily recognized styles, including Tudor, Flemish, Renaissance, and Second Empire, although the author did not specifically mention any style. Wood, stucco, brick, and stone were all incorporated to suit the stylistic needs of each design. This book illustrated some of the ideals of the large-scale homes that Mix designed in the upper Midwest as well as the architect's cosmopolitan style. Mix did not seek to create every building in the same style; his book collection was also eclectic.

The sixth book, Raphael and J. Arthur Brandon's *The Open Timber Roofs of the Middle Ages*, was published in 1849 prior to the completion of Mix's professional education. The book itself was not lengthy but did contain a wealth of images showing various types of timber structures. Most were for parish churches, and each plate contained detailed measurements followed by descriptions of pitch, span, and the size of beams and rafters. This book resembled the pattern books that gained popularity and availability throughout the United States in the nineteenth century. The open timber structure Mix used in several of his churches was probably adapted from this book.

The seventh book, the previously mentioned *Rural Church and Cottage Architecture*, consisted entirely of a series of designs. It was of great interest for several reasons. First, it included designs by Mix's mentor, Sidney Mason Stone; second, marginalia were found on several designs. One by architect J. Wells bore the notations "this is our *plan* [illegible]," "A.W. Morris," and "JJG." The existence of marginalia suggests that Mix possibly used the designs in this book as a starting point for his own work. Third, there is a drawing of a new church design (figure 6.3), which Mix must have thought significant, because it is glued into the book. Although this building has not been identified as one by Mix, and no notations indicate that the design was his, the supposition is that this was one of his student works.[25] It shows the facade of a church with two flanking towers. Within each of the towers is a doorway; the central section is punctuated by seven compass-headed windows with the larger paired central windows serving as a focal point. The central section has a gabled roof and a projecting cornice. The towers are identical and separated into three stories. If this drawing was done by Mix, it may provide clues to his subsequent work. Although I have attempted to correlate the design with the work that Mix was doing in Stone's office, however, I have as yet found no connection. Still, *Rural Church and Cottage Architecture* showed contemporary American designs by important nineteenth-century architects—the professionals that Mix

FIG 6.3 Attributed to Edward Townsend Mix, church facade. Pasted into Mix's copy of *Rural Church and Cottage Architecture*. Photo by the author. Courtesy of the Milwaukee Public Library.

was acquainted with—and thus provided some basic ideas from which to begin his own church designs with reference to his mentor's work.

The final book, Minard Lafever's *The Architectural Instructor, Containing a History of Architecture from the Earliest Ages to the Present Time* (1856), extends to 526 pages. *The Architectural Instructor* was just that: a book teaching all the information an architect on the frontier could want. It discussed the historical styles from the origins of architecture to the mid-nineteenth century. It highlighted the history and proper use of the orders. It contained the basic information that was needed to construct a building and some designs to assist the architect in his work. This book, which provided a comprehensive examination of architecture from its historical interpretations to the functional aspects of building construction, was no doubt useful to its owner.

To understand how Mix utilized books within his practice, it is important to see how he translated the design ideas in his books into tangible architecture. Two of his commercial buildings, four residential commissions, and several churches can demonstrate his methods.

The Mitchell Building, designed by Mix in 1876, was considered "the pride of Milwaukee, as well as the whole Northwest," wrote James Buck.[26] Commissioned by Alexander Mitchell, one of Mix's primary patrons, this commercial structure served as the Mitchell Bank for many years. Its style was Second Empire, and when completed it was one of the tallest buildings in town. Since Mix did not travel to France, and there were no other buildings of its kind in Milwaukee, the style must have been developed from his books, many of which provided ready examples.[27] But copying was not in Mix's nature. His adaptations from the books were not mere copies, instead, he reworked the models to make sophisticated creations that were completely his own.

The facade of the Mitchell Building followed the traditional five-part French design constructed of granite and sandstone (figure 6.4). The central section incorporated elaborate gilded griffins and carved cherubs, lions' heads, garlands, and other details, the origins of some of which can be found in Mix's books. The caryatid figures near the top of the facade were similar to the atlantid figures seen in Victor Calliat's *Encyclopédie d'architecture* (figures 6.5 and 6.6). Another feature was the incorporation of faces at the top of the arches. Similar faces can be found in Daly's *L'architecture privée au XIXme siècle sous Napoléon III* and *Motifs historiques d'architecture*; although the expressions are not identical, the forms are similar (figure 6.7). Also attributable to the influence of designs in the *Encyclopédie*

FIG 6.4 Edward Townsend Mix, Mitchell Building, Milwaukee, 1876. Photo by the author.

d'architecture was the use of faces in the metopes on the lower level of the building. All these details reflected Mix's cosmopolitan nature in design and his ability to pull designs together from a variety of sources to create his own interpretation of Second Empire.

Another Mix design was the Grain Exchange Building, also known as the Chamber of Commerce Building (figure 6.8). Completed in 1879, it was at that time the world's largest grain exchange and one of the first fireproof buildings in Milwaukee. Its style was completely Mix's creation; the *Milwaukee Sentinel* referred to the building as "Modern Italian."[28] One of its main features can be found in the third volume of Jules Gailhabaud's *L'architecture du Vme au XVIIme siècle*, where a palace in Italy shows the protruding pyramidal stonework that was interspersed

FIG 6.5 Mix, Mitchell Building. Caryatid figures on the facade. Photo by the author.

FIG 6.6 Atlantid figures. From Victor Calliat and Adolphe Lance, eds., *Encyclopédia d'architecture* (1854), plate 79. Photo by the author. Courtesy of the Milwaukee Public Library.

FIG 6.7 Arch. From César Daly, *Motifs historiques d'architecture et de sculpture d'ornement* (1869). Photo by the author. Courtesy of the Milwaukee Public Library.

throughout Mix's design (figure 6.9). Further, his exterior also had a vermiculated stone arch of a type that can be seen in Daly's *Motifs historiques d'architecture* (see figure 6.7). The Grain Exchange retains one of the most complete interiors that Mix created, thanks to an accurate renovation in the late 1980s. In examining this interior with its lavish marble columns rising three stories and its series of allegorical paintings depicting "Commerce," one can experience Mix's elaborate design.

In constructing by contemporary accounts "not less than three-fourths of the most costly and ornate private residences erected in Milwaukee," Mix adapted a modified Italianate style for several of his houses.[29] This style reflected a trend that he initiated in New Haven and brought to fruition in Milwaukee. Critical elements of it can also be seen in Minard Lafever's *The Architectural Instructor*, Mansion no. 1, which looks very similar to Mix's completed Montauk House in

FIG 6.8 Edward Townsend Mix, Grain Exchange/Chamber of Commerce Building, Milwaukee, 1879. Photo by the author.

FIG 6.9 Italian palace. From Jules Gailhabaud, *L'architecture du Ve au XVIIe siècle* (1858). Photo by the author. Courtesy of the Milwaukee Public Library.

FIG 6.10 Edward Townsend Mix, Robert Patrick Fitzgerald House, Milwaukee, 1874. Photo by the author.

Iowa and the Robert Patrick Fitzgerald house in Milwaukee, both designed in 1874 (figures 6.10 and 6.11). Although he did not copy it directly, Mix referenced the drawing, transforming it into two unique compositions through modifications in the window and compositional arrangement as well as other details.

Throughout Mix's career he frequently adapted to new architectural trends, and the Milwaukee homes for Mrs. Martha Terry in 1886 and A. K. Mayhew in 1888 reveal a change in his domestic designs. These buildings comprised a mixture of styles bordering on the Queen Anne, which was one of the predominant styles Mix worked with in the 1880s. Designs in Isabey and Leblan's *Villas, maisons de ville et de campagne* reflected these stylistic trends (figure 6.12). The design for the Martha Terry House was significant beyond Milwaukee, as it was published in Chicago's *Inland Architect and Builder*, New York's *Sanitary Engineer*, and in the French periodical *La Semaine des Constructeurs* in 1886. Mix's eclectic nature allowed him to pull ideas from a variety of sources and thus cultivate designs appropriate to each new building project.[30]

The final buildings reflecting Mix's interest in architectural books were his churches. He frequently utilized open-timber roof structures for his ecclesiastical work. This can be seen in St. Luke's Episcopal Church in Racine, 1866–67; the First Baptist Church in Waukesha, 1872; and three in Milwaukee: St. Paul Episcopal Church, 1883; Holy Rosary Catholic Church, 1885; and the Grand Avenue Congregational Church, 1887. Each of these churches had a different pattern of timber framing, some more elaborate than others, but the form remained a staple of Mix's design repertoire. Although he did not specifically copy from Brandon's *Open Timber Roofs of the Middle Ages*, there were similarities between some of those designs (figure 6.13) and Mix's constructed buildings, demonstrating that he utilized his books for interior as well as exterior inspiration and construction.

The work of Edward Townsend Mix and his books shows that Milwaukee, although commonly recognized as having a predominantly German heritage, was

FIG 6.11 Mansion no. 1. From Minard Lafever, *The Architectural Instructor* (1856). Photo by the author. Courtesy of the Milwaukee Public Library.

FIG 6.12 Maison. From Léon Isabey and Leblan, *Villas, maisons de ville et de campagne* (1867). Photo by the author. Courtesy of the Milwaukee Public Library.

originally developed by a significantly Yankee population that has been overlooked. Mix's work also reflects the importance of his New Haven, Connecticut, background and early exposure to the function of books within an architectural practice. A study of the variety and content of his book collection and how it was used establishes that his designs were influenced by, although not copied from, his architectural books. These characteristics merged to provide critical visual cues confirming his status as a professional architect. Did Mix show these books to his clients in order to evoke responses to design concepts they had never seen before, or had seen in other locations and desired to emulate? As a professional architect, Mix utilized his books not to copy the drawings as a builder would but, as a designer, to prime

FIG 6.13 Timber framing. From Raphael and J. A. Brandon, *Open Timber Roofs of the Middle Ages* (1849). Photo by the author. Courtesy of the Milwaukee Public Library.

the flow of his own ideas within a traditional framework. In the mid-nineteenth century, Mix was Milwaukee's primary architect and a founding member of the Western Association of Architects, and his lineage, training, and personal library reflected his status as a professional architect and provided inspiration for his cosmopolitan and innovative designs.[31]

APPENDIX

Edward Townsend Mix Collection of Architectural Books Compiled from the List of Gifts of Mrs. E. T. Mix, 23 June 1891, to the Milwaukee Public Library (in list order)

Calliat, Victor, and Adolphe Lance, eds. *Encyclopédie d'architecture; Journal mensuel publié sous la direction de Victor Calliat; texte descriptif par Adolphe Lance.* 12 vols. Paris: Bance, 1851–62.

Daly, César D. *L'architecture privée au XIXme siècle sous Napoléon III; Nouvelles maisons de Paris et des environs, par César Daly.* 3 vols. Paris: A. Morel, 1864.

———. *Motifs historiques d'architecture et de sculpture d'ornements, pour la composition et la décoration extérieure des édifices publics et privés.* Paris: A. Morel, 1869.

Degen, Louis. *Les constructions en briques, par Louis Degen.* Paris: A. Morel, 1864.

Gailhabaud, Jules. *L'architecture du Vme au XVIIme siècle et les arts qui en dépendent: la sculpture, la peinture murale, la peinture sur verre, la mosaïque, la ferronnerie, etc.; Pub. d'après les travaux inédits des principaux architectes français et étrangers par Jules Gailhabaud.* 5 Vols. Paris: Gide, 1858.

Isabey, Léon. *Villas, maisons de ville et de campagne, composées sur les motifs des habitations de Paris moderne dans les styles des XVI, XVII, XVIII, XXIX siècles, et sur un choix des maisons les plus remarquables l'étranger par Léon Isabey et Leblan.* Paris: A. Levy, 1867.

Révoil, Henry. *Architecture romane du midi de la France, dessinée, mesurée, et décrite par Henry Révoil.* 3 portfolios. Paris: A. Morel, 1867–74.

———. *Croquis d'architect 5ème année.* Paris: G. Raulin, 1876.

Billings, Robert William. *Illustrations of the Architectural Antiquities of the County of Durham: Ecclesiastical, Castellated, and Domestic.* Durham: St. Andrews; London: T. and W. Boone, 1846.

Brandon, Raphael, and J. A. Brandon. *The Open Timber Roofs of the Middle Ages.* London: D. Bogue, 1849.

Charles, Richard. *The Cabinet Maker: A Journal of Designs. For the Use of Upholsterers, Cabinet Makers, Decorators, Carvers, Gilders, and Others, by R. Charles and Other Designers.* London: E. and F. N. Spon, 1868.

Conway Manufacturing Company. *Sixteen Designs of Fine Mantels; Selected from our Entire Line; Series A.* Milwaukee: Conway Manufacturing, 1856.

Cundall, Joseph, ed. *Examples of Ornament: Selected Chiefly from Works of Art in the British Museum, the Museum of Economic Geology, the Museum of Ornamental Art in Marlborough House, and the New Crystal Palace, Drawn from Original Sources, by Francis Bedford, Thomas Scott, Thomas Macquoid . . . [et. al.] and edited by Joseph Cundall.* London: Bell & Daldy, 1855.

De Forest, Lockwood. *Indian Domestic Architecture.* [Boston: Heliotype Printing, c. 1885].

Lafever, Minard. *The Architectural Instructor, Containing a History of Architecture from the Earliest Ages to the Present Time; Illustrated with nearly 250 Engravings of Ancient, Mediæval, and Modern Cities,*

Temples, Palaces, Cathedrals, and Monuments; also, the Greek and Early Roman Classic Orders, Their Principles and Beauties; with a Large Number of Original Designs of Cottages, Villas, and Mansions, of Different Sizes, Accompanied with Practical Observations on Construction . . . and further Designs of Churches, Monuments, and Public Buildings; Together with a Glossary of Architectural Terms . . . by Minard Lafever, Architect. New York: G. P. Putnam, 1856.

Hart, J. Coleman. *Designs for Parish Churches, in the Three Styles of English Church Architecture; with an Analysis of Each Style; a Review of the Nomenclature of the Periods of English Gothic Architecture, and Some Remarks Introductory to Church Building, Exemplified in a Series of over One Hundred Illustrations. By J. Coleman Hart.* New York: Dana, 1857.

Loudon, J. C. *Encyclopædia of Cottage, Farm, and Villa Architecture and Furniture.* London: Warne, 1869.

Low, J. G., and J. F. Low. *Illustrated Catalogue of Art Tiles Made by J. G. and J. F. Low.* Chelsea, Mass.: J. G. & J. F. Low, 1884.

Talbert, Bruce J. *Examples of Ancient and Modern Furniture, Metal Work, Tapestries, Decorations, etc. by B. J. Talbert.* Boston: J. R. Osgood, 1877.

———. *Gothic Forms Applied to Furniture, Metal Work, and Decoration for Domestic Purposes by B. J. Talbert, Architect, London.* Boston: J. R. Osgood, 1873.

Upjohn, Downing, Renwick et al. *Rural Church and Cottage Architecture: Comprising a Series of Designs for Churches, Parsonages, and Cottages Exemplified in Plans, Elevations, Sections, and Details with Practical Descriptions by Upjohn, Downing, Renwick, Wheeler, Wells, Austin, Stone, Cleveland, Backus, Reeve, Etc.* Chicago: Northwestern Publishing House, n.d.

NOTES

I thank librarians Pat DeFrain and Virginia Schwartz of the Milwaukee Central Library for all their assistance in tracking down the accession numbers and books provided to the library by Mrs. E. Townsend Mix.

1. Milwaukee's ethnic legacy is still evident in the architecture and cultural associations that survive. According to Kathleen Neils Conzen, "The German community was to color Milwaukee's urban development and crucially mediate the adjustment of several generations of immigrant residents to American life. It was not only the numbers of Germans who settled there that gave Milwaukee its reputation as the most German of American cities nor their proportionate strength in the city's population, but also the solidity and character of the community they created." Conzen, *Immigrant Milwaukee 1836–1860* (Cambridge, Mass.: Harvard University Press, 1976), 2.

2. U.S. Bureau of the Census, *Eleventh Census of the United States: 1890* (Washington, D.C.: GPO, 1891), 372.

3. John Burrows, "The Work of E. Townsend Mix from 1856 [to] 1890" (master's thesis, University of Virginia, 1978).

4. William G. Bruce, "Old Milwaukee's Yankee Hill," *Wisconsin Magazine of History* 30 (March 1947): 289.

5. U.S. Bureau of the Census, *Seventh Census of the United States: 1850* (Washington, D.C.: Robert Armstrong, Public Printer, 1853), 917, 929. It is important to note that in the early census records, a person who had been born in the "colonies" was noted as being from British America.

6. The German members of the Milwaukee Club included Frederick Pabst, Guido Pfister, Emil Schandein, and August Uihlein. See *The Articles of Association, the Milwaukee Club* (Milwaukee, Wis.: Cramer, Aikens & Cramer, 1883).

7. Margaret Townsend, *Townsend-Townshend 1066–1909: The History, Genealogy, and Alliances of the English and American House of Townsend* (New York: Broadway Publishing, 1909), 39–40.

8. Joseph P. Smith, "Henry Howe, the Historian," *Ohio Archaeological and Historical Quarterly* 4 (1895): 314.

9. Ibid., 315–16.

10. On Andover, Illinois, see Mike and Sue Otto, *Our Future Is in Our Heritage* (Orion, Ill.: Evans Printing and Publishing, 1985); and Ronald E. Nelson, "The Role of Colonies in the Pioneer Settlements of Henry County, Illinois" (Ph.D. diss., University of Nebraska, 1970).

11. Louis Conard, *History of Milwaukee County from Its First Settlement to the Year 1895* (Chicago: American Biographical Company, 1895), 446.

12. New Haven Free Public Library, "Historical Population," <http://www.cityofnewhaven.com/library/population.htm> (5 December 2003).

13. Smith, "Henry Howe," 316.

14. It should be noted that although Mix lived the majority of his life in Milwaukee, he was buried in the Grove Street Cemetery in New Haven.

15. Jane B. Davies, "Town, Ithiel," in *MacMillan Encyclopedia of Architects*, ed. Adolf Placzek (New York: Free Press, 1982), 220, 222; Francis S. Drake, *Dictionary of American Biography, Including the Men of the Time* (Boston: James R. Osgood, 1872; rpt., Detroit: Gale Research, 1974), 611; Sarah Allaback, "Louisa Tuthill, Ithiel Town, and the Beginnings of Architectural History Writing in America," in *American Architects and Their Books to 1848*, ed. Kenneth Hafertepe and James F. O'Gorman (Amherst: University of Massachusetts Press, 2001), 199, 203.

16. Henry F. Withey and Elsie Rathburn Withey, *Biographical Dictionary of American Architects (Deceased)* (Los Angeles: New Age Publishing, 1956), 577; Rexford Newcomb. "Ithiel Town of New Haven and New York," *The Architect* 2 (1929): 523.

17. *Commemorative Biographical Record of New Haven County, Connecticut, containing Biographical Sketches of Prominent and Representative Citizens of Many of the Early Settled Families* (Chicago: J. H. Beers, 1902), 1:416. According to Alexander Guth, "Early Day Architects in Milwaukee," *Wisconsin Magazine of History* 10 (September 1926): 27, Mix served an apprenticeship with Richard M. Upjohn; I have found no other documentation either to support or to disclaim this statement.

18. Conard, *History of Milwaukee County*, 447. We know from the 1850 Census that the family was then residing in New Haven and that E. T. Mix listed his profession as architect.

19. Withey and Withey, *Biographical Dictionary*, 577.

20. For the Congregational Convention publication, see Henry-Russell Hitchcock, *American Architectural Books* (New York: Da Capo Press, 1976), #282. There is a copy of *Rural Church and Cottage Architecture*, formerly owned by Mix, at the Milwaukee Public Library (see the appendix).

21. According to George Dudley Seymour, *New Haven* (New Haven, Conn.: self-published, 1942), 245, Stone purchased several books from the collection of Ithiel Town, including a set of large volumes by William Chambers.

22. Milwaukee Public Library, *Card Catalog of Gifts*, Noted 383, 14 May 1891. Mrs. Mix also came from an extensive Connecticut family; the earliest recorded member was George Hayes, who was residing in Connecticut in the 1680s. Mary's great-grandfather, Ezekiel Hayes, was the grandfather of President Rutherford B. Hayes. See *Commemorative Biographical Record of New Haven County, Connecticut*, 1:415.

23. César Denis Daly's, *L'architecture privée au XIXme siècle sous Napoléon III* (Paris: A. Morel, 1864), 1:2. For more information on Daly, see Richard Becherer, *Science plus Sentiment: César Daly's Formula for Modern Architecture* (Ann Arbor: UMI Research Press, 1984).

24. César Denis Daly, *Motifs historiques d'architecture et de sculpture d'ornement* (Paris: A. Morel, 1869), 1 (end leaf).

25. Burrows, "Work of E. Townsend Mix," 100.

26. James S. Buck, *Pioneer History of Milwaukee* (Milwaukee: Swain & Tate, 1881), 2:134.

27. Mix had been experimenting with Second Empire elements such as the mansard roof in earlier structures but nothing to the extent represented in the Mitchell Building.

28. "Chamber of Commerce, Milwaukee," *American Architect and Building News* 9 (January 1, 1881): 7; *Milwaukee Sentinel*, April 5, 1879.

29. *U.S. Biographical Dictionary and Portrait Gallery: Eminent and Self-Made Men, Wisconsin Volume* (Chicago: American Biographical Publishing, 1877), 655. In studying Mix, I have not found any references to buildings that he constructed or designed for wealthy German patrons in Milwaukee.

30. Marcel Daly, "*Villas et Maisons de Campagne Amèricaines*," *La Semaine des Constructeurs* 10 (1886): 594–96.

31. This essay is based on my forthcoming doctoral dissertation from the University of Virginia, "Cosmopolitan Design in the Upper Midwest: The Nineteenth Century Architecture of Edward Townsend Mix."

VII

THE ARCHITECTURAL LIBRARY OF HENRY A. SIMS

Michael J. Lewis

Two charges used to be made against Victorian architects, and both cannot be true: it was said that they copied their designs from books *and* that they made them up out of their heads. But if someone cannot simultaneously be a shameless copyist and a capricious fantasist, he may combine aspects of each. The peculiar mixture of bookishness and originality is perhaps the most distinctive trait of the High Victorian era. It is not always clear, however, what the extent of this bookishness was, for although we know in copious detail what books architects had at their fingertips, in many cases we know shockingly little about when they were used, or how.

Which books were routinely consulted for reference, or folded flat so that a detail might be traced, or merely browsed for inspiration? Or were they used at all? The study lined with bound journals and folios was itself an object of prestige, bespeaking sophistication and refinement. Daniel Burnham and John Wellborn Root had themselves photographed in their library, whereas H. H. Richardson had his photographed for its own sake, letting the books serve as surrogate for the man.

The library of Henry A. Sims (1832–1875) offers an unusual case study. Although now obscure, Sims was prominent in his day, a passionate Gothic Revivalist who practiced in Canada and Philadelphia before his untimely death by a stroke.[1] His is not the only Philadelphia architectural library known from the era—there are fairly good inventories of the architectural libraries of T. P. Chandler, James H. Windrim, and Joseph Koecker—but it is the only one cut short by sudden death, so that there is none of the pruning and updating that most working libraries undergo.[2] The timing is propitious, for it depicts an intelligent and quirky library on the eve of the American centennial, when so much changed so quickly in American architecture: the enthusiasm for Queen Anne and Old English, the rediscovery of the colonial, the first Japanese currents—all of which displaced the High Victorian.

Sims came to architecture belatedly, after a detour as a civil engineer. Born in Philadelphia, he moved to Canada in 1851 and served four years on the staff of the Bytown and Prescott railroad; he spent another year in Brunswick, Georgia, as an engineer for the Brunswick and Florida Railroad. In 1858, after some false starts, he permanently renounced engineering for architecture, practicing first in Prescott, Ontario, and then in Ottawa. He returned to Philadelphia in 1866, after the Civil War, where he hoped his prominent family might throw commissions his way.[3]

From the first, Sims was "a warm admirer of the Gothic styles."[4] So he declared in a public lecture of 1860, liberally peppered with extracts from the writings of John Ruskin and John Henry Parker. His earliest churches were archaeologically fastidious affairs, so much so that upon his arrival in Philadelphia he was dismayed by the low quality of its medievalism. "I am the only architect here making any pretensions to a knowledge of Gothic," he confided to his diary in early 1867.[5]

This was not quite true. Charles M. Burns (1838–1922), George Hewitt (1840–1916), and Frank Furness (1839–1912) were all Philadelphia architects and capable medievalists, as Sims must have known; in short order he was on intimate terms with each of them. But Sims was understandably defensive, for his "pretensions" to Gothic proficiency were exactly that. He had not seen Europe and never would; his conception of medieval architecture remained secondhand and bookish. Still, his scholarliness seems to have impressed itself on his colleagues. After he joined the American Institute of Architects in 1869, helping to establish its Philadelphia chapter, he became the organization's first foreign correspondent. (Evidently, having lived in Canada made one sufficiently international.)

Sims worked primarily for Episcopalian clients, who were sympathetic to High Church ritual and symbolism, yet ironically, his most important church with his richest iconographic program was built for a fashionable Presbyterian congregation. This was Philadelphia's Second Presbyterian Church (planned 1867–68; built 1869–72).[6] A vibrant High Victorian performance, it took the form of a basilica with transepts and a polygonal apse, overawed by an emphatic corner tower, planned to rise as high as the church was long (figures 7.1 and 7.2). Its daring spire was never

FIG 7.1 Henry A. Sims, design for Second Presbyterian Church, Philadelphia, 1867–72 (Now First Presbyterian Church of Philadelphia.)

FIG 7.2 Henry A. Sims, Second Presbyterian Church. Tower added by Frank Furness, 1900. Photo by Ralph Lieberman.

built, however, and thirty years later Frank Furness brought the tower to an abrupt end with a rather antagonistic belfry.

The church's iconography was a lively mixture of the ethnic and the patriotic, conflating Presbyterianism, Americanism, and a kind of fictitious pan-British identity: on the north portal was an interlace of the Scottish thistle, English rose, Welsh leek, and Irish shamrock, while the western bays depicted the principal crops of America, showing corn, wheat, grapes—and tobacco, about which the pastors evidently had no qualms. The carving was by Alexander Kemp, who was assisted on the interior by Alexander Milne Calder, the young Scottish émigré who would subsequently win fame for his vast sculptural program at Philadelphia's City Hall.

Sims's work was by no means exclusively Gothic, or even exclusively medieval. An unbuilt design for the main hall of the Centennial Exhibition, for which he won a $1,000 premium, was a rangy Romanesque affair of considerable monumentality (figure 7.3). A proposal for a combined town hall and market in Prescott, Ontario, was less successful, a freakish jumble of Second Empire and Neoclassical

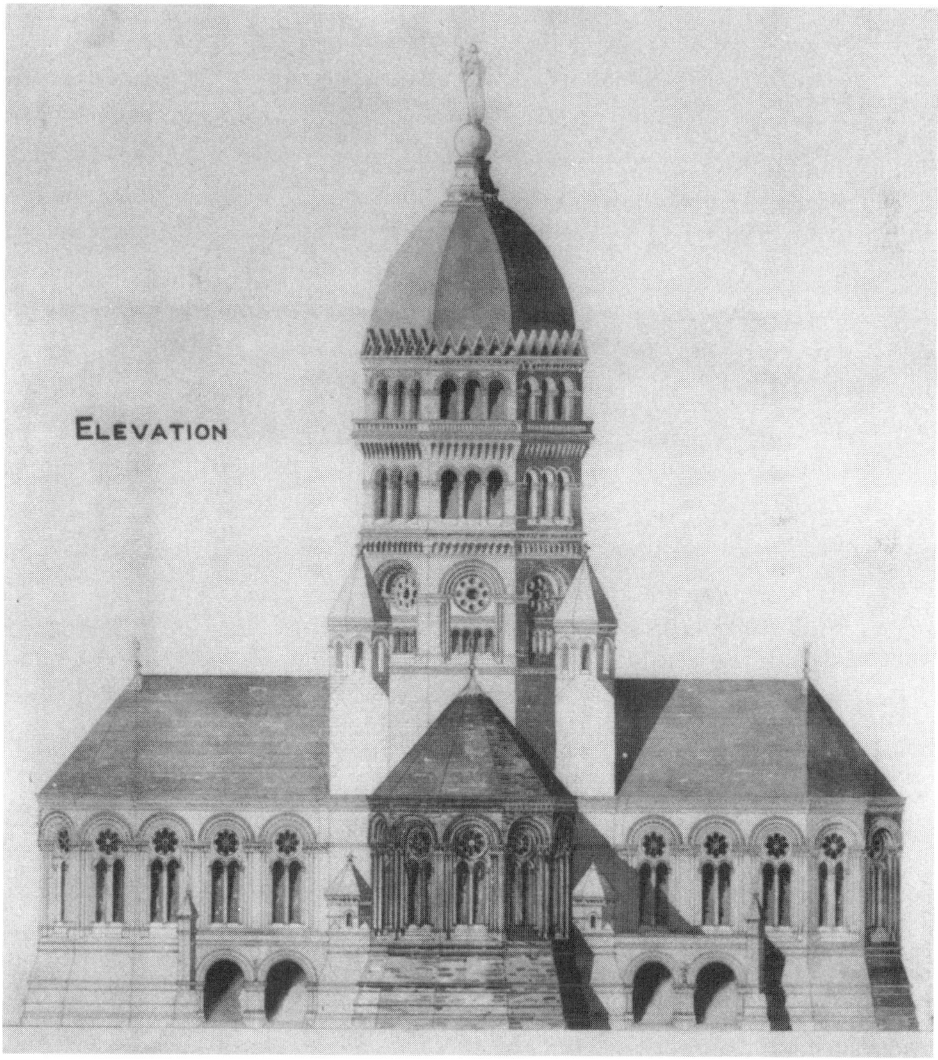

FIG 7.3 Henry A. and James P. Sims, Proposal for the Centennial Exhibition Hall, Philadelphia, 1873. Historical Society of Pennsylvania.

ideas that stubbornly refuse to coalesce (figure 7.4). Here Sims was sadly out of his depth. In a Gothic design this sort of rambling, additive composition could be pleasantly picturesque, but for a Classical design the consequence was too often a kind of fidgeting incoherence. Both projects were designed in collaboration with his younger brother, James Peacock Sims (1849–1882), who became a partner in early 1872.

Even on more familiar Gothic turf, Sims was often a hapless competitor. In 1871 he was invited to submit a design for the Pennsylvania Academy of the Fine Arts and told that "it will be found desirable to break the straight line of a front on so great a length." Sims obligingly produced a facade of alarming restlessness and assured the building committee—quite unnecessarily—that its "outline was as much broken as possible" (figure 7.5).[7] Here again Sims followed Gothic Revival convention, deriving his external composition from the internal arrangement of volumes and functions. The method may have guaranteed architectural truth, but it did not guarantee beauty, as Sims found to his dismay. His 1871 pocket notebook shows him brooding over the point. An entry made around the time of his academy design proposed several possible mottos for his work, none of them especially elegant: *Design with Beauty/Build in Truth* and *Beauty in the Design/Truth in Execution*.[8]

Occasionally, though, his moral convictions and his architectural gifts aligned, and the result could be splendid indeed, as in his Holy Trinity Chapel. This was an early Gothic basilica in the muscular William Burges mode, reveling in its broad swaths of unrelieved rugged masonry. But above the conventional torso was an astonishing display of flying buttresses, executed in slender iron girders rather than stone arches. Here the railroad engineer of the nineteenth century came to the aid of the stonemason of the thirteenth (figure 7.6). Sims had already seen Furness's exposed iron truss alongside the new Pennsylvania Academy of the Fine Arts. For once he was able to top his friendly rival, allowing his structural iron to caper freely in space. One wonders what he would have done had he lived longer.

If Sims's achievement was chronically uneven, his book collection, sold at auction shortly after his death on 10 July 1875, might suggest why. A printed inventory survives, listing a large collection of fiction and history as well as seventy-odd architectural items. Besides books, these include bound journals and several lots of loose photographs. It is odd that the architectural library did not remain with the firm, which was continued by James P. Sims, but perhaps Henry's widow, who had two children, needed the money. Had her brother-in-law wanted the books, he would have had to bid against other architects and pay full market value.

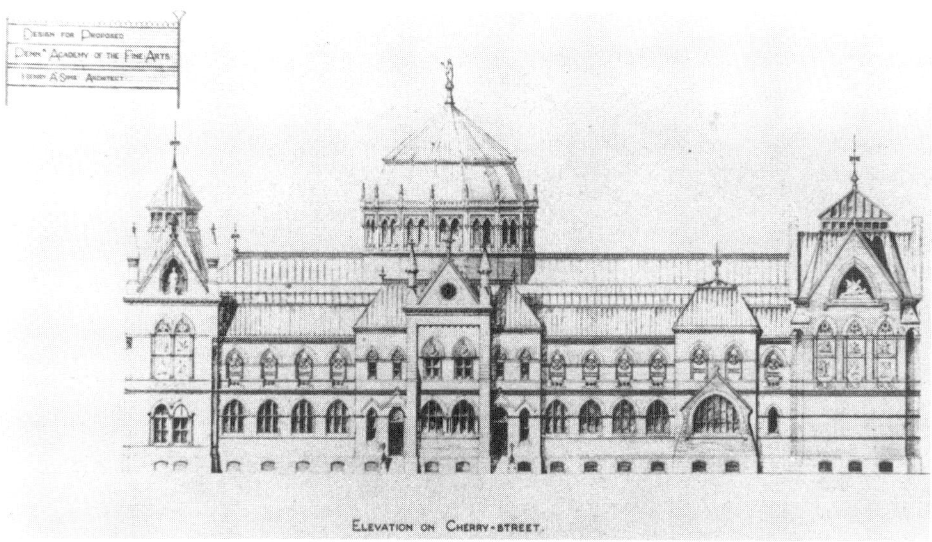

FIG 7.4 Henry A. and James P. Sims, Proposed Town Hall and Market, Prescott, Ont., 1874. National Archives of Canada, Picture Collection, ACC. C 5832.

FIG 7.5 Henry A. Sims, Competition entry for Pennsylvania Academy of the Fine Arts, north elevation, 1871. Pennsylvania Academy of the Fine Arts.

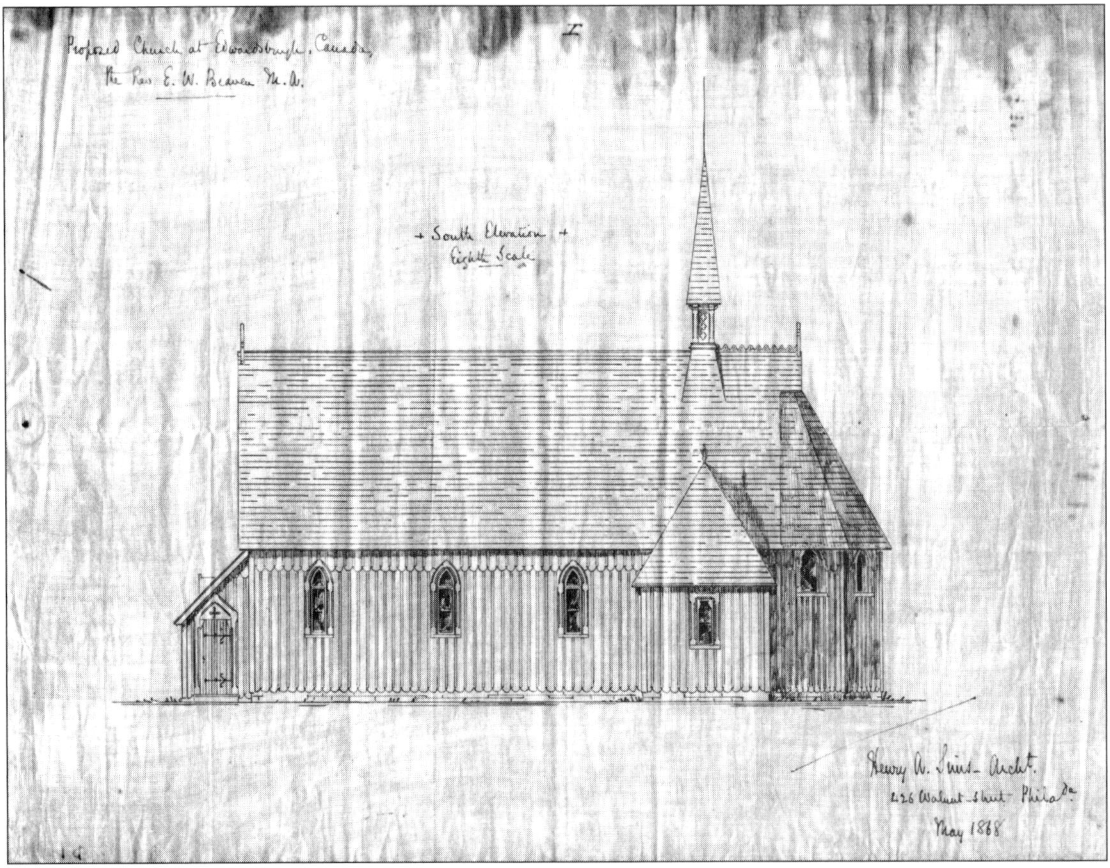

FIG 7.6 Henry A. and James P. Sims, Holy Trinity Chapel, Philadelphia, 1874–75. Photo by Ralph Lieberman.

The printed auction inventory is scrupulous in including frequent notes on condition and rarity; unfortunately, it is irregular in giving dates and full titles. It is impossible, for example, to know whether the item listed as Humphrey Repton's *Landscape Gardening* refers to his *Sketches and Hints of Landscape Gardening* (1798), his *Observations on the Theory and Practice of Landscape Gardening* (1805), or his *Fragment on the Theory and Practice of Repton's Landscape Gardening* (1816). But even in its abbreviated form (reproduced in the Appendix below), the inventory is revealing.

Sims's books fall into four broad categories: those of antiquarian interest; English books, almost exclusively medieval in scope; American books; and a smattering of miscellany, mostly German. Of French literature there was none, although Sims was an astute observer of recent French architecture. The inventory lists neither Eugène Emmanuel Viollet-le-Duc's *Dictionnaire raisonné de l'architecture française*

(1854–68) nor his *Entretiens sur l'architecture* (1863–72)—books that Sims, who wrote perceptively about French architecture, obviously knew.

The antiquarian books seem to have stood on Sims's shelves for prestige value. His few works by Andreas Palladio, Leon Battista Alberti, and Vitruvius were in editions that were venerable rather than valuable. These were apparently haphazard acquisitions: for example, he owned Palladio's study of ancient Roman baths but not his *Four Books of Architecture*. He scarcely had the minimal reference library necessary to design in Greek or Renaissance Classicism; he had neither Stuart and Revett's *Antiquities of Athens* nor Paul Letarouilly's *Edifices de Rome moderne*. His one classical compendium, Domenico de Rossi's *Studio d'architettura civile*, was presumably a stray.

The largest category of books, about forty of the seventy, were English and formed an exemplary compendium of Gothic Revival theory and practice. Besides the principal theoretical works of Ruskin, Sims owned key works by George Gilbert Scott, John Henry Parker, and F. A. Paley, as well the *Instrumenta Ecclesiastica*, the comprehensive manual of church furnishing published by the Ecclesiological Society. Here too, though, were some odd gaps: there was not a single number of *The Ecclesiologist*, the articulate and acerbic journal that was the mouthpiece of High Church medievalism. Likewise, George Edmund Street's *Brick and Marble in the Middle Ages* (1855), Owen Jones's *Grammar of Ornament* (1856), and Christopher Dresser's *Principles of Decorative Design* (1873) are all conspicuous by their absence. There was nothing by Edmund Sharpe and, strangest of all, not a single work by A. W. N. Pugin (although Sims did own Benjamin Ferrey's biography). This gap is baffling, for Pugin's *True Principles* was the ultimate source of Sims's constant mantra of architectural truth. Is it possible that he had bequeathed these Gothic Revival essentials to his brother?

Sims was assiduous in collecting books that would assist him in the design of suburban or country houses. He owned Robert Kerr's *The Gentleman's House*, C. J. Richardson's *The Englishman's House*, and Thomas Morris, *A House for the Suburbs*, popular works that went through several editions. Books such as Kerr's provided practical suggestions for designing houses on the largest scale, establishments requiring platoons of servants and capacious service wings to operate. It is not clear how Sims made use of these texts; although his obituaries credit him with several large country houses, none have been identified.[9]

The pride of Sims's library was his collection of illustrated English periodicals. He had nearly complete runs of all three English architectural journals: *The*

Builder (1850–75), *Building News* (1864–75), and *The Architect: A Journal of Art, Civil Engineering, and Building* (1869–75). With their regular woodcuts of English architecture, he would have been as well informed about the new buildings of London as those of New York or Boston, and perhaps more so. He even bought a complete run of J. C. Loudon's *Architectural Magazine* (1834–38), although it was long since defunct. So enthusiastic was Sims about the usefulness of journals to the professional health of architecture that he tried to persuade the American Institute of Architects to launch one; however, it came to grief on the sensitive issue of illustrating the work of nonmembers.[10]

Although Sims came of age architecturally during the 1850s, his library showed a keen alertness to the latest currents of thought. He was aware of William Burges, whose 1866 design for the London Law Courts competition created a sensation. He was also aware of Richard Norman Shaw and W. Eden Nesfield, who urged the Gothic Revival in the direction of a gentler pictorial picturesque and who helped bring about the Queen Anne fad of the 1870s. All were represented on Sims's shelves.

The other pillar of Sims's library was his collection of American books. Of course, American architectural literature was on a much less sophisticated plane than that of Europe and consisted almost entirely of illustrated pattern books, but here he purchased diligently. He owned A. J. Downing's five most important books, as well as volumes by Richard Upjohn, Gervase Wheeler, and A. J. Bicknell. He owned Martin Field's *City Architecture* (New York, 1853), a comparatively rare work. He even owned Orson Squire Fowler's *A Home for All; or, The . . . Octagon Mode of Building*, which foisted the short-lived fad for octagonal houses on the American public, but though he bought avidly, he did not buy indiscriminately. Strangely, for a man who loved books, he owned none by Philadelphia's most assiduous producer of architectural literature, Samuel Sloan. Sloan's national reputation was based on his pattern books, but Sims—evidently put off by Sloan's freewheeling eclecticism and vulgar self-promotion—had no use for him. Or so his behavior suggests: Sims once asked facetiously in a lecture before the local AIA if "the architect of Horticultural Hall" (i.e., Sloan) should, for reasons of its architectural sins, be hanged.[11]

Sims's smattering of German books is intriguing. Since the failed revolution of 1848, which brought a considerable number of German architects to the United States as refugees, German sources had enjoyed a certain vogue. Because of the language barrier, however, publications that consisted chiefly of images rather than text were most popular. The *Architektonisches Skizzenbuch*, a periodical with generous color plates of picturesque palaces and country villas, was particularly coveted during the 1850s and 1860s, and it shows up in the libraries of an extraordinary variety of American architects.[12] But not that of Sims—his curiosity extended rather to those German Goths who were exploring the relationship between the materials of construction and architectural form, above all Georg Gottlob Ungewitter (1820–64). He owned Ungewitter's pioneering *Vorlegeblätter für Ziegel und Steinarbeiten* (Model designs for brick and stonework), published in Leipzig by Romberg, 1849, which showed how forms of extraordinary vigor and plasticity might be extracted from the facts of construction (figure 7.7).[13] He also owned *The Workshop*, a Hanover-based journal published by Ungewitter's disciples who applied Gothic Revival dogma to furniture and the decorative arts.

One must be careful when speculating from an inventory: the mere presence of a book on Sims's shelf was no endorsement. He owned *Builder's Jewel* (1768) by Batty Langley even though he savagely mocked its author in print; apparently the book was there for laughs.[14] On the other hand, even Gothic heroes such as George Gilbert Scott were not guaranteed a read: his *Remarks on Secular and Domestic Architecture, Present and Future* (1858) was the most cogent argument for the applicability of the Gothic to the problems of the modern world, yet it is listed in Sims's inventory as "an uncut copy."

* * *

Such were Sims's books, but how did he use them? Here, alas, our evidence is only indirect and anecdotal. Even for architects within Sims's immediate circle, there was great variety in the amount of emphasis placed on books. Furness and Hewitt—two of his closest friends among the Philadelphia architectural fraternity—showed completely opposite attitudes. Louis Sullivan, who came to know them during his 1873 stint in their office, mocked Hewitt "as a man who kept his nose in books" and devised his architectural essays "as per the English current magazines and other English sources." Furness, by contrast, shunned books and "made buildings out of his head." John Harbeson, who met him nearly four decades later, confirmed Furness's utter contempt for books and singled out Viollet-le-Duc's *Dictionnaire raissonné* as the one publication Furness found useful.[15]

Obviously, Sims's temperament was closer to that of Hewitt. Moreover, the two were happy to exchange books, as we know from at least one occasion. On 1 February 1868 he recorded in his diary that he "borrowed Brandon's *Open Timber Roofs of the Middle Ages* from Hewitt. Read it tonight."[16] Sims was not looking for

FIG 7.7. Details from Georg Gottlob Ungewitter, *Vorlegeblätter für Ziegel und Steinarbeiten* (1849).

bedtime reading; shortly thereafter he designed a crisp board-and-batten church for Edwardsburgh, Ontario, distinguished by a mighty exposed wooden roof truss (figure 7.8) and must soon have bought the book, for it shows up on his inventory.

Sims's consultation of Brandon might suggest the way that an earlier generation consulted Stuart and Revett to determine the correct proportions of a Greek order, yet there is a qualitative difference. It is one thing to peruse a compendium of roof trusses for a felicitous model and quite another to refer to a set of prescribed proportions. The reference books of the previous generation were authoritative manuals of propriety and rectitude. The library of Joseph Koecker, for example, a near contemporary of Sims, was conspicuously heavy in compendia such as Paul Letarouilly's *Edifices de Rome moderne* (Liege, 1849–53); Sebastian Serlio's *Tutte l'opere* (Venine, 1600); A.-C. d'Aviler's *Cours d'architecture* (Paris, 1750), and Isaac Ware's *Complete Body of Architecture* (1756). By mining these books intelligently for the details of doors, windows, cornices, and pediments, architects had found them sufficient to compose the vast array of houses, storefronts, and churches demanded by mid-Victorian practice.[17]

Sims's library, rich and comprehensive as it was, offered nothing comparable. To be sure, he might crib the construction of a truss from Brandon or the profile of a molding from F. A. Paley's treatise, but in the High Victorian system, such copyism was limited to incidental details. The larger aspects of design—the overall arrangement of masses and volumes, the character of a masonry wall, its pattern of openings and solids, the signature of the roofline against the sky—were not to be determined by any reference source whatsoever but left to the architect's judgment and eye. An architect like Sims would have been horrified by the prospect of not being original. In 1867, when he was frantically lobbying to make a design for Philadelphia's Masonic Temple, he was offered a look at the project of John

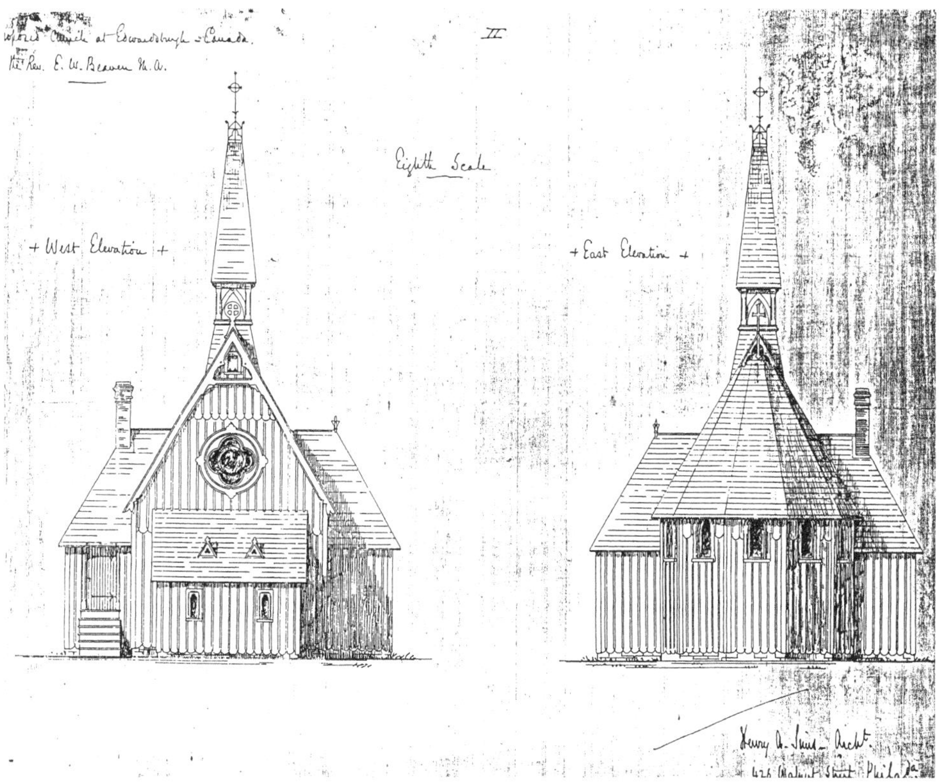

FIG 7.8 Henry A. Sims, proposed church at Edwardsburgh, Ont., west and east elevations, 1868. Ontario Archives.

McArthur. He categorically refused, evidently reluctant to see anything that might prejudice his own effort, however unconsciously.[18]

Architectural design was for Sims a kind of controlled improvisation, guided by intuition and principle. Such a method was fundamentally abstract, worked out in terms of volumes and masses. The form of his Second Presbyterian Church, for example, was shaped less by any specific English model than by the general principles proclaimed in Ruskin's *Seven Lamps of Architecture*, such as his plea for large areas of sheer unadorned masonry.

For all of Sims's pedantry, his conception of design was hardly bookish at all. His posthumous article "Architectural Fashions" compares the competing merits of Gothic architecture and the French *néo grec*, but it does so on the basis of purely visual critiera. The questions of ultimate meaning and validity that were of burning urgency in the stylistic battles of the 1840s and 1850s held no interest for Sims. He reserved his fascination for the abstract visual properties of each style, criticizing the French *néo grec* not for its pagan Classicism—the trump card of Pugin and Ruskin—but on purely optical arguments, its lack of "heavy vertical shadows" and of "chiaro oscuro."

Because Sims's criteria were essentially visual, it is not surprising that the most forward-looking component of his collection was not literature but photographs, purchased from commercial photographers or given to him by the architects themselves. Besides photographs of commercial buildings in Boston by the firm of Cummings & Sears and Memorial Hall by Ware & Van Brunt, he owned a photograph of H. H. Richardson's Grace Church in Medford, Massachusetts, one of the architect's earliest works (figure 7.9). The brawny masonry, dramatically belted by smooth courses in the tower, would have captivated Sims, who was then experimenting with masonry texture in his Second Presbyterian Church. But Richardson had not yet achieved national celebrity, and Sims was unusually prescient to recognize the inherent promise in the design.

An even more adventurous choice was Sims's photograph of the tomb of the Duc du Morny, at the cemetery of Père Lachaise, Paris (figure 7.10). Designed in 1866 by Viollet-le-Duc, it is a remarkable synthesis of *néo grec* and Gothic motifs, and closer to the work of Furness than perhaps any other single work of European architecture. It is telling both that Sims owned the photograph, and that Furness did not see fit to buy it at auction.[19]

Photographs such as Sims's were usually treated as ephemera; unless collected in albums or otherwise cared for, they were likely to be discarded. Since it is unusual

FIG 7.9 Henry Hobson Richardson, Grace Church, Medford, Mass., 1868. Architectural Archives, University of Pennsylvania.

FIG 7.10 Eugène Emmanuel Viollet-le-Duc, Duc du Morny Monument, Père Lachaise Cemetery, Paris, 1865–66. Architectural Archives, University of Pennsylvania.

for them to be noted in detail in an inventory, they have been systematically underestimated in favor of books and periodicals. Here scholars have made the pardonable error of assuming that the distribution of the surviving evidence corresponds roughly to what was then available. But Sims's collection shows that by 1875, architects were relying heavily on purchased photographs, both American and European, and that some of their most important inspiration and design impulses came this way.

Taken together, Sims's library and his buildings present the picture of a gifted and charmingly earnest naïf. Given his peculiar education, it could hardly have been otherwise. As a seasoned railroad engineer, charged with superintending the construction of minor service buildings as well as viaducts, embankments, and trestles, Sims had a thorough education in construction before he lifted his thoughts to architecture. When he did, at some point in the mid-1850s, it was through the bracing and urgent literature of the Gothic Revival, which gave a sense of vital purpose and meaning to the forms he designed. But it was not a substitute for a systematic architectural education in which design, construction, ornament, and theory were treated as parts of a comprehensive whole. As a result, the theoretical and the practical lobes of Sims's architectural mind were not integrated, and all his piety about architectural and structural truth, sincere as it was, could not make it so.[20]

APPENDIX

The Architectural Library of H. A. Sims

Because the auction catalogue usually does not specify which edition of a book Sims owned, it has not been possible to arrange the titles entirely chronologically. They are listed here in approximate order, although for ease of comparison, works by the same author are grouped together.

Antiquarian Books

Andrei Putei, *Perspectiva Pictorum et architectorum Andrea Putei e Societate Jesu* (Rome, 1693). Bound with Leon Battista Alberti, *Della Pittura, della Statua.*
Domenico de Rossi, *Studio d'architettura civile, &c.* (Rome, 1721).
Le Fabbriche e i disegni di Andrea Palladio (Vicenza, 1796).
Andrea Palladio, *Le terme dei Romani* (Vicenza, 1797).
Dell' architettura di M. Vitruvio Pollione (Perugia, 1802).
Francesco Milizia, *The Lives of Celebrated Architects, Ancient and Modern* (London).

English Books

Batty Langley, *Builder's Jewel* (Dublin, 1768).
George Saunders, *A Treatise on Theaters* (London, 1790).
Archibald Alison, *Essay on the Nature and Principles of Taste.*

Humphrey Repton, *Landscape Gardening.*
James Hall, *On Gothic Architecture* (London, 1813).
M. H. Bloxam, *Principles of Gothic Architecture.*
Thomas Rickman and John Henry Parker, eds., *Gothic Architecture* (London).
John Henry Parker, *Introduction to the Study of Gothic Architecture* (London).
———, *Architectural Guide to the Neighborhood of Oxford* (London).
———, *Glossary of Architecture*, 3 vols. (Oxford).
[William Butterfield], *Instrumenta Ecclesiastica,* Ecclesiological Society (London).
Henry E. Kendall Jr., *Designs for School and School Houses, Parochial and National* (London).
John Ruskin, *The Seven Lamps of Architecture.*
———, *The Stones of Venice.*
———, *The Political Economy of Art.*
———, *The Crown of Wild Olive; Work, Traffic, and War.*
R. and J. A. Brandon, *The Open Timber Roofs of the Middle Ages* (London).
———, *Analysis of Gothic Architecture* (London).
F. A. Paley, *A Manual of Gothic Architecture* (London).
———, *A Manual of Gothic Moldings* (London).
A. J. B. Beresford Hope, *The English Cathedral of the XIX Century* (London).
Thomas Morris, *A House for the Suburbs* (London).
Robert Kerr, *The Gentleman's House* (London, 1864).
C. J. Richardson, *The Englishman's House* (London).
Thomas H. King, *The Study-Book of Medieval Architecture and Art; Being a Series of Working Drawings of the Principal Monuments of the Middle Ages* (London, 1868).
Owen Jones, *702 Monograms* (London, 1864).
J. Gwilt, *Encyclopaedia of Architecture* (London, 1867).
Benjamin Ferrey, *Recollections of A. N. Welby Pugin.*
W. Eden Nesfield, *Specimens of Medieval Architecture.*
Richard Norman Shaw, *Architectural Sketches from the Continent* (1858).
C. L. Eastlake, *Hints on Household Taste* (London, 1868).
George Gilbert Scott, *Church Restorations.*
———, *Remarks on Secular and Domestic Architecture, Present and Future* (London)
———, *Executed Examples by Sir Geo. Gilbert Scott and others,* 26 plates (London).
William Burges, *Architectural Drawings* (London, 1870).
M. A. Racinet, *Polychromatic Ornament. One Hundred Plates . . .* (London, 1873).
William Fairbairn, *Cast and Wrought Iron.*

German Books

Byzantine Capitals, 36 plates (Munich).
Georg Gottlob Ungewitter, *Vorlegeblätter für Ziegel und Steinarbeiten.*
L. Degen, *Der Ziegel-Rohbau.*
The Workshop, in 4 numbers (Hanover).

English Periodicals

Building News (1864–75).
The Builder (1850–75).
The Architect: A Journal of Art, Civil Engineering, and Building (1869–75).
J. C. Loudon, *Architectural Magazine*, 5 vols. (London [1834–38]).

American Books

Asher Benjamin, *Elements of Architecture.*
A. J. Downing, *Country Houses.*
———, *Landscape Gardening and Rural Architecture.*
———, *Cottage Residences.*
———, *Rural Essays.*
Downing and Vaux, *Villas and Cottages.*
Richard Upjohn, *Rural Architecture: Designs, working drawings, and specifications for a Wooden Church, and other rural structures.*
O. S. Fowler, *A Home for All; or, The . . . Octagon Mode of Building.*
Robert Dale Owen, *Hints on Public Architecture.*
Martin Field, *City Architecture.*
John Bullock, *The American Cottage Builder.*
Gervase Wheeler, *Homes for the People.*
———, *Rural Homes.*
R. G. Hatfield, *American House Carpenter.*
A. J. Bicknell & Co., *Wooden and Brick Buildings, with Details, containing 160 plates.*
Henry Barnard, *School Architecture.*
Frank J. Scott, *The Art of Beautifying Suburban Home Grounds of Small Extent* (New York, 1870).
The New York Sketch Book of Architecture (1874).
Philadelphia Sketch Club Portfolio (1874).

NOTES

1. An inventory of the library of Henry A. Sims, 1875, is in my collection.

2. The Henry A. Sims Papers are on deposit at the National Archives of Canada, M-5480, MG, -29-B-36. These include two diaries (1863–64; 1866–68), two notebooks (1871 and 1875), and miscellaneous correspondence. A microfilm of the collection is available under RG-11, microfilm C-12801. Also see Barbara Humphreys and Stephen Otto, "Henry Augustus Sims, 1832–1875," *Society for the Study of Architecture in Canada: Selected Papers* 5 (1982): 41–47; and "Henry A. Sims," in *Drawing toward Building: Philadelphia Architectural Graphics*, ed. J. F. O'Gorman (Philadelphia: University of Pennsylvania Press, 1986); Sandra L. Tatman and Roger W. Moss, *Biographical Dictionary of Philadelphia Architects, 1730 to 1930* (Boston: G. K. Hall, 1985). The library of T. P. Chandler is recorded in the collection of the Athenaeum of Philadelphia. For Windrim, see *Books on Architecture and the Fine Arts, including Works on Sculpture, Paintings, Furniture, Decoration, Iron and Metal Work and Gardens: The Library of the late John T. Windrim, Phila., Pa., to be dispersed at public sale, Nov. 6, by order of the administrators* (New York: American Art Association, Anderson Galleries, Inc., 1935); a copy is at the Library of Congress. Although many of the books listed were owned by the son of James H. Windrim, those published before about 1890 can be presumed to have belonged to the elder Windrim. An inventory of the library of Joseph Koecker is at the Houghton Library, Harvard University; this is the most conservative of the three and reflects his training in the office of Thomas U. Walter.

3. Even after moving to Philadelphia, Sims continued to work in Canada and with Canadian architects. In 1869 he entered the competition for Philadelphia City Hall together with Thomas Fuller and Augustus Laver, the principal designers of the Canadian Parliament Buildings; their joint

design, now lost, placed third and received a $1,000 premium. See Michael J. Lewis, "'Silent, Weird, Beautiful': Philadelphia City Hall," *Nineteenth Century* 11, nos. 3–4 (1992): 13–21.

4. Henry A. Sims, "Gothic Architecture," a public lecture delivered in 1860 (the manuscript is in the Sims Papers), quoted in Humphreys and Otto, "Henry Augustus Sims," 43.

5. Sims Diary, Sims Papers.

6. Because of a subsequent merger, it is now confusingly known as the First Presbyterian Church.

7. Michael J. Lewis, *Frank Furness: Architecture and the Violent Mind* (New York: Norton, 2001), 93–94; Michael J. Lewis, "The Pennsylvania Academy of the Fine Arts as Building and as Idea," in *The Pennsylvania Academy of the Fine Arts: 200 Years of Excellence, 1805–2000* (Philadelphia: Pennsylvania Academy of the Fine Arts, 2005), 63–73.

8. Sims Notebook, 1871, Sims Papers.

9. It is possible that he designed the first wing of the Haverford country house of A. J. Cassatt, with whom Sims consulted repeatedly in 1871. See George E. Thomas, Jeffrey A. Cohen, and Michael J. Lewis, *Frank Furness: The Complete Works* (New York: Princeton Architectural Press, 1996), 344B.

10. [Henry A. Sims], "The American Institute of Architects," *Penn Monthly* 4 (1873): 499–505.

11. The minutes of the Philadelphia chapter of the American Institute of Architects are on deposit at the Athenaeum of Philadelphia.

12. A partial list of owners of *Architektonische Skizzenbuch* includes Richard Morris Hunt, P. B. Wright, E. T. Potter, Addison Hutton, T. P. Chandler, and Frederick Graff Jr.

13. Karen David-Sirocko, *Georg Gottlob Ungewitter und die malerische Neugotik: In Hessen, Hamburg, Hannover und Leipzig* (Petersberg, 1997). Sims was not the only Philadelphia architect to own volumes by Ungewitter. T. P. Chandler owned the *Vorlegablätter für Holzarbeiten* (1860) as well as the *Lehrbuch der gotischen Konstruktionen* (1890–92). Collection of the Athenaeum of Philadelphia.

14. Henry A. Sims, "Architectural Fashions," *Penn Monthly* 7 (September 1876): 700–711.

15. Louis H. Sullivan, *The Autobiography of an Idea* (1924), 190–196; John Harbeson, "Philadelphia's Victorian Architecture, 1860–1980," *Pennsylvania Magazine of History and Biography* 77 (July 1943): 266ff.

16. Sims Diary, 1 February 1868, Sims Papers.

17. Joseph Koecker's architectural library also included Charles Perrault, *Vitruvius* (1673); Le Muet, *Palladio* (1676); Isaac Ware, *Palladio's Four Books of Architecture* (1738); Andrei Putei, *Perspectiva pictorum* (Rome, 1741); C. A. D'Aviler, *Cours d'architecture* (Paris, 1750); Isaac Ware, *The Complete Body of Architecture* (1756).

18. Sims Diary, 1 October 1867, Sims Papers.

19. This photograph, along with several others from the Sims estate, was glued into an album that was donated to the University of Pennsylvania Architectural Archives by John Harbeson. It has been suggested that the photographs had been purchased by T. U. Walter.

20. From Stephen Otto comes late word that some of Sims's books were a fortunate purchase. On 21 April 1866 he noted in his diary that he "Bought a lot of books and drawings which an English architect named Edmunson left with him for his board." Edmunson is not further identified; "him" seems to have been the landlord of Sims's boarding house in Ottawa. At least two other books were sent to him by Thomas Curtis Clarke (1827–1901), his roommate in Prescott for nine years and later his collaborator on the Girard Street Bridge. On 10 September 1866 Sims recorded that he had a note from Clarke accompanying the copies of William Fairbairn, *On the Application of Cast and Wrought Iron to Building Purposes* (1857) and John Henry Parker, *Introduction to the Study of Gothic Architecture* (1849). Both were later sold at auction.

Books he is known to have owned but were not in the auction include E. W. Godwin, *A Handbook of Floral Decoration for Churches* (1865; acquired 31 January 1868), Bruce J. Talbert, *Gothic Forms Applied to Furniture* (1867; 31 August 1868), and Maw & Company's catalogue (31 August 1868). Among titles he borrowed were John Ruskin, *Lectures on Architecture and Painting* (1854; 20 December 1863), Ruskin, *Two Paths* (1859; 23 September 1867), and Edward Peacock, *English Church Furniture* (same date). It is not clear whether he owned or borrowed Edward Lacy Garbett, *Rudimentary Treatise on the Principles of Design in Architecture* (1850), which he read in January 1864.

VIII

"EITHER IN BOOKS OR ARCHITECTURE"

Bertram Grosvenor Goodhue in the Nineties

James F. O'Gorman

In a letter of 28 June 1894, Bertram Grosvenor Goodhue (1869–1924) reported to the photographer-publisher F. Holland Day that he was experiencing a momentary lull in his labors, "either in books or architecture."[1] Within three years of his arrival in Boston, then, Goodhue was looking for work in two specialized fields, the two on which his fame principally rests, and the lull he then remarked was the last he was to enjoy for many years.

In preparing a brief profile that emphasizes his double-barreled career in the 1890s, I have visited some of his major buildings, held in hand some of his finest volumes, and cast an eye on some of his original decorative drawings at the Grolier Club and elsewhere, but I must confess to having drawn primarily on the work of other, more specialized scholars. Whoever seeks the historical Goodhue must use and acknowledge the contributions of such recent students as the late Richard Oliver, whose monograph of the architecture is currently definitive; Susan Otis Thompson, writing on the influence of William Morris in American book arts; Estelle Jussim on the career of that "slave to beauty" F. Holland Day; Beverly Brandt on the local Society of Arts and Crafts; and Nancy Finlay in her fine exhibition catalogue on artists of the book in Boston.[2] Collectively, these publications provide an indispensable context for Goodhue's career. In short, I hold no special brief in the study of design in Boston in the mid-1890s; I draw upon the work of others and here attempt merely to make whole again that which specialized scholarship has tended to pull asunder.

We generally split art history in a way that separates fields such as architectural design from book decoration, and rarely do we discuss the two at the same time. But Goodhue was not the first to excel in both areas (I am thinking particularly of his Boston progenitor, Hammatt Billings),[3] and in his case, at least, books and buildings must be thought of as variant flowers from a common stem. One cannot approach his bookwork without recognizing his origins, early development, and ultimate career as an architect as well.

Born in Pomfret, Connecticut, Bertram Goodhue was the scion of old New England stock.[4] He was from his early years a student of design in all its phases, with special attention to the medieval. Oliver reports that at the age of ten, Goodhue set up a studio in the attic of his parents' house and painted its windows in imitation of stained glass. Although allowed to grow up unburdened by much formal learning, he was bookish, reading the Arthurian legends and other romantic literature. His precocious talent as a graphic artist led him at fifteen to an apprenticeship in New York with the architectural firm of Renwick, Aspinwall & Russell, whose principal partner, James Renwick Jr., was, with Richard Upjohn, a leading figure in the early Gothic Revival in this country.[5] Renwick has provided Manhattan with two of its finest midcentury medieval churches: Grace on lower Broadway, begun in the 1840s; and Saint Patrick's Roman Catholic Cathedral on Fifth Avenue, begun in the 1850s and completed a few years before Goodhue's arrival in New York. It was this neo-Gothic world into which the budding designer plunged in 1884.

Grace and Saint Patrick's, like Upjohn's Trinity at the head of Wall Street, represent the earliest phase on this side of the Atlantic of a design movement that originated in England, so far as Americans were concerned. Its chief voice was that of Augustus Welby Pugin, whose vision of an exclusively Gothic world (filled with churches of his own design) appears as frontispiece to his *Apology for the Revival of Christian Architecture* (1843). Through Renwick, Goodhue's professional lineage reached back to Pugin, the theoretical rock upon which rested the English medievalism of the later nineteenth century, whether championed by Ruskin or Morris, the High Victorians, or the Arts and Crafts movement. Pugin's influence went far beyond mere building design. In his view, reform was all-encompassing, and from his feverish talent stemmed drawings for churches and everything they contained. Another plate in the *Apology* drives home his program (figure 8.1). In

FIG 8.1 "Church Furniture Revived at Birmingham." A. Welby Pugin, *An Apology for the Revival of Christian Architecture* (1843).

it Pugin displays his wares, his designs for a spectrum of medieval liturgical hardware ranging from miters and incense burners to altar cloths and book covers.

Pugin died seventeen years before Goodhue's birth. One might suppose that his influence had weakened by the 1880s, when Goodhue joined Renwick, but in fact it remained for the younger man focused and potent. We know from Goodhue's early partner, Ralph Adams Cram, that Pugin's books were an important source for Goodhue's designs in architecture.[6] And we have visual confirmation of continuity in the realm of the decorative arts in sheets of sketches such as the one that contains studies for the seal of the Society of Arts and Crafts, Boston, founded in 1897 (figure 8.2). Here Goodhue's pen explores a host of design problems, ranging from buildings to ecclesiastical furniture to book covers, all of medieval inspiration. On such a page, and on others like it, Goodhue practices the profession of total design prescribed by Pugin and reiterated by the English Arts and Crafters.

Goodhue was, then, an all-round designer, but at least through the 1890s he wore two principal hats. In the one guise, as he is portrayed in a grotesque in his chapel at West Point, he practiced architecture; in the other, he embellished books for the trade and the private presses of Boston.

While still a teenaged apprentice to Renwick, Goodhue was publishing pen sketches of Pomfret buildings in professional magazines. At twenty he entered a Richardsonian Romanesque project in the competition for the Anglican Cathedral of Saint John the Divine in New York. This early perspective already shows the low angle of vision characteristic of his presentation drawings. Although his scheme for Saint John's went unnoticed, two years later—now aged twenty-two—he won a competition for the cathedral of Saint Matthew in Dallas. Recognizing his lack of experience in actual building, Goodhue associated himself in 1891 with the Boston architectural firm headed by Cram. By the next year he was Cram's partner.

The firm's first triumph was All Saints' in the Ashmont section of Boston, a stylistically transitional work combining the seemingly irreconcilable characteristics of Richardsonian robustness and Gothic grace.[7] Winning the competition for the major additions to West Point in 1903 established the firm on a national basis. Goodhue's drawing for that project, showing cliffs of architecture rising sublimely above the Hudson's waters, their picturesque silhouettes darkly emphasized against the blank sky, is an enhanced version of the low angle of vision in the perspective of Saint John the Divine (figure 8.3). This trademark of Goodhue's graphics recurs

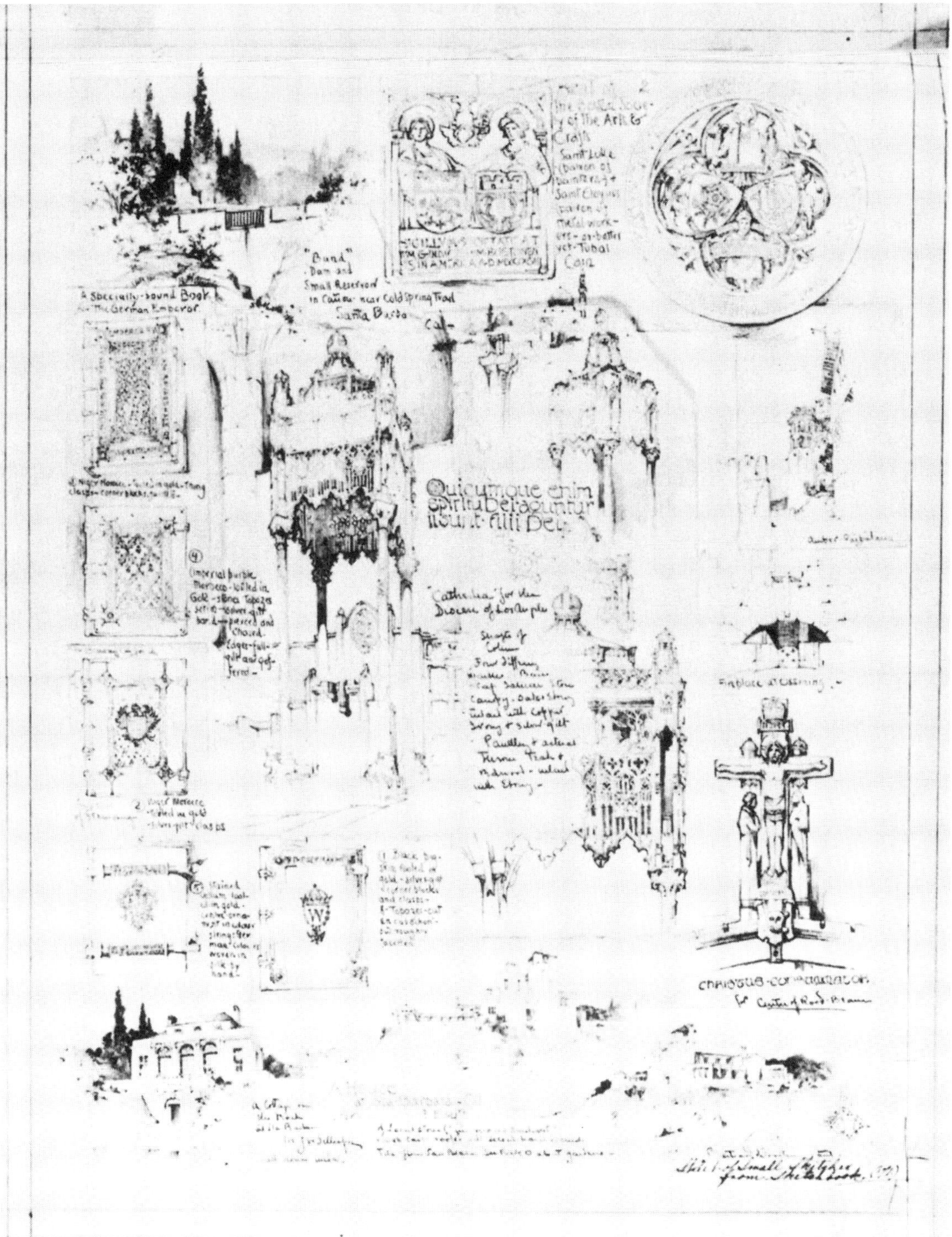

FIG 8.2 Bertram Grosvenor Goodhue, miscellaneous sketches for architecture and decoration, various dates. Private collection.

FIG 8.3 Goodhue, presentation drawings for the U.S. Military Academy, West Point, N.Y., 1903. Courtesy of the U.S. Military Academy.

over and over—for example in the drawing for the Frederick Peterson House of 1915 at Brewster, New York. The low eye level dramatizes the image, urging the building to body upward from its geological base. This viewpoint is also characteristic of architectural perspectives in English romantic book illustration, such as the view of Ludlow Castle, after J. M. W. Turner, in an 1858 Boston edition of Milton's poetry (figure 8.4). The sublime may have been tempered somewhat in Goodhue's presentation, but it remained the underlying aesthetic assumption on which his sensibilities rested. As Cram reported, "The sense of romance possessed him . . . and made him a Mediaevalist in all things."[8]

With the need to supervise the work at West Point, Goodhue moved to New York, where, starting in 1905, the firm created in Saint Thomas's Church on Fifth

FIG 8.4 After J. M. W. Turner, Ludlow Castle. From John Milton, *The Poetical Works* (1858).

Avenue (across and down from Renwick's Saint Patrick's Cathedral) one of the glories of turn-of-the-century urban Gothic. Goodhue's creative energy lingers in the smallest detail, and in such decorative accents as the ornamental door hardware the spirit of Pugin lives on into the early twentieth century. When Saint Thomas was completed in 1913, Goodhue split with Cram and began a period of stylistic experimentation in architecture that eventually materialized in buildings such as the Nebraska State Capitol in Lincoln, begun in 1920, in which Gothic drive joins Classic calm to emerge as modern synthesis. Goodhue died as its tower began to rise above the prairie.

Goodhue's winning design for the cathedral at Dallas was never built, but it represents a pivotal moment in his career. It took him to Boston and into a circle called by various recent writers the "local bohemian intelligentsia,"[9] or "those brilliant young men of the nineties,"[10] who took for granted the totality of the design reform stemming from Augustus Welby Pugin and reinvigorated by William Morris. The circle included the architect and polemicist Cram, the aesthete publisher-photographer F. Holland Day, Day's partner Herbert Copeland, the designer-printer D. B. Updike, the poet Bliss Carman, the architects and designers who collectively formed in 1897 the earliest Arts and Crafts Society on this side of the Atlantic, and the intellectuals who gathered into such social clubs as the Pewter Mugs and the Visionists. It was a heady world for a twenty-two-year-old, even one as gifted as Goodhue. In this ripe atmosphere his abilities and inclinations flowered in memorable works of architecture and book design. Nor was he merely one of the crowd. As Cram wrote in the 1925 memorial volume to his former partner: "It was he, more than any one else, who was instrumental in bringing together that extraordinary group of young men who found such joy in life. . . . He would design a font of type or a sumptuous set of initials as quickly as he would clothe an architectural form with the splendid vesture of intricate Gothic ornament."[11]

* * *

In his *Decorative Illustration of Books* (1896), Walter Crane distinguished between what he called a volume's "pictorial statement" and its "decorative treatment": that is, between illustration and ornamentation.[12] If artists of the book in Boston are divided into such camps, then Hammatt Billings falls into the pictorial fold, and Goodhue must be counted a decorator. His illustrations, though significant, take second place to his borders and full-page designs, covers, bookplates, printers' marks and seals, miscellaneous decorations, initials, tailpieces, endpapers, and printing types.[13]

If Goodhue's architecture of the 1890s was deeply rooted in the English medieval revival, his work as book designer stemmed from both old and new layers of the same soil. The cover of the *Knight Errant*, that evanescent art magazine edited by Goodhue and Cram, with contributions by Day, Walter Crane, Bliss Carman, and others of the crowd, visually conveys their editorial stance (figure 8.5): Sir Knight, somewhat hesitantly, to be sure (for he glances back toward a kerchief being waved from the open window of the castle-keep), rides forth to do battle with the forces of materialism and ugliness, represented by snakes, turtles, toads, and other crawling things. The failures of previous aesthetes are graphically depicted by the skull half submerged in the dank tarn lying athwart his path. This image reeks of Scott or Tennyson while it anticipates Howard Pyle; it is the illustrative equivalent of the romantic associations of Goodhue's architecture. At the same time, the cover's heavy black-and-white design punched up with red, and the magazine as a whole—a large quarto on handmade paper set in old-style type with wide margins and embellished with initials and tailpieces by Goodhue—shows an early awareness of the English Arts and Crafts book, especially of William Morris's new Kelmscott Press.

His high-minded, high-art *Knight Errant* having succumbed to the forces of materialism within a year, Cram retreated to the opposite extreme, producing in 1893 a call to idleness titled *The Decadent: Being the Gospel of Inaction.* We might think of it as the 1890s mild equivalent of the 1960s call by Timothy Leary for a dropout drug culture. Copeland & Day published it; it was dedicated to Goodhue, who provided the cover, three initials, and a frontispiece. This last reflects Cram's change of mood, for here the designer is toying with a variant stream of current English art, the Aesthetic movement. This linear, flat, sanguine, asymmetrical, Japanese-influenced plate shows Aurelian Blake, the opium-beclouded hero (if a tract on inaction can be said to have a "hero"), lounging in a hammock full of books and flowers, smoke from his hookah swirling around Shiratsuyu, his Oriental serving girl. The art of Aubrey Beardsley comes to mind, but this is Beardsley denatured and, in truth, made banal. Cram's fin-de-siècle text and Goodhue's derivative illustration do nothing to enhance the reputation of either, and from this moment on, with notable exceptions, Goodhue stuck largely to decoration, leaving illustration to others.

Susan Thompson sees the frontispiece to *The Decadent* as clearly an Aesthetic creation, but she finds the book as a whole, with its heavy black letter scarcely relieved by a few historiated initials, decidedly Arts and Crafts. Arts and Crafts

FIG 8.5 Goodhue, cover design. *The Knight Errant* (1891).

books were known in Boston as early as 1892, the very year Morris opened his Kelmscott Press; in October, five months after Morris's *The Story of the Glittering Plain* was published in Hammersmith, the Boston trade publisher Roberts Brothers issued it in photofacsimile. The heavy type, engraved initials, and swirling vegetable borders were to become standards of Morris's work. The speed of the arrival of *The Glittering Plain* in Boston attests to the anglophilia of local taste; and the speed with which Morris's example affected the Boston publishing world in general and the work of Goodhue in particular attests to the permeation across the ocean of the Arts and Crafts spirit.

By 1892 this spirit had generated a native design, although neither one from a fine art press nor one by Goodhue. The first American book to show Morris's influence was a collection of sketches by F. Hopkinson Smith published by Houghton Mifflin and designed by D. B. Updike.[14] This has a title page border drawn by Harold Van Buren Magonigle, a man better known as a Gothic Revival architect than as a book decorator.[15] Two years passed before Goodhue's more accomplished emulation appeared, in Dante Gabriel Rossetti's *The House of Life*, from the house of Copeland & Day. According to the colophon, this exists in five hundred copies on French handmade paper, plus fifty on Michallet paper, with three borders and 114 initials by Goodhue. It is dated 1894, although printed in 1893 and—again according to Susan Thompson—probably designed in 1892. A review in the *Knight Errant*, while recognizing the origin of Goodhue's inspiration in this work, self-consciously sought to distance its editor from his source and concluded that "while Mr. Goodhue's style would hardly have been possible without Mr. Morris, it cannot be justly said that he has copied him."[16] I leave it to others to decide the size of Pugin's American follower's debt to Pugin's English successor.

After *The House of Life*, Goodhue turned out one Arts and Crafts book after another for Copeland & Day, Updike's Merrymount Press, and other Boston publishers. In some work—such as the title page to the ballad of Saint Kavin, Goodhue's tiny 1894 masterpiece of the guild of Visionists who are shown in apostolic assembly at the top (figure 8.6); the page spread for Louise Imogen Guiney's *Nine Sonnets Written at Oxford* (Copeland & Day, 1895); or the *Description of the Pastoral Staff . . . at Albany* (Merrymount, 1900)—Goodhue's use of architectural rather than floral borders seems to penetrate through the Kelmscott influence to its Puginesque roots. Other work, such as the folio *Altar Book* published in 1896, achieves, despite the noticeable stylistic differences between illustrations and decoration, a kind and

FIG 8.6 Goodhue, title page for [Bliss Carman], *Saint Kavin: A Ballad* (1894).

quality of design equal to that of the master of Hammersmith himself (figure 8.7a and 7b). *The Altar Book* was a collaborative effort overseen by Updike, with heraldic designs by Charles Sherman of London, illustrations by Robert Anning Bell of Liverpool, and borders, initials, and type by Bertram Goodhue (the first of two fonts to his credit).

Goodhue's work as book decorator seems largely a function of his Boston days and milieu. His design for the cover of the *Knight Errant* is dated 1891 in the lower right corner, the year he joined Cram; his last works are dated 1903–4, the year he moved to New York. Thereafter, lacking the stimulation of the Boston crowd and increasingly becoming slave to a burgeoning architectural practice, with few exceptions (for example, a drawing for initials at the Grolier Club dated 1924), he abandoned his second design career.

Goodhue's output in both books and architecture was far richer than suggested here, but the medievalist roots and characteristics that I have emphasized are fundamental in any attempt to understand his historical position as a designer. It is possible, in fact, to envision him at work looking something like the man in figure 8.8, at least during the first decade of his career—perhaps not dressed in a robe but totally immersed in a world of Gothic things. The fact is, this is not Goodhue but Pugin; at any rate, this is the frontispiece to Pugin's *True Principles of Pointed or Christian Architecture* (1841), depicting the medieval designer at work. Perhaps the parallel is forced, perhaps not. Goodhue shows (presumably) himself looking a lot like that medieval designer in his personal bookplate (figure 8.9); he would certainly have acknowledged his descent from the English polemicist.

But this bookplate suggests another dimension, a decidedly macabre one, of Goodhue's self-image. Here Death stays the designer's hand, just as death did in fact stay Goodhue's hand in 1924, when he was only fifty-five. In his biography of Goodhue for the *Macmillan Encyclopedia of Architects*, Richard Oliver characterized Goodhue's death as coming at an "awkward moment." It can be argued that many deaths are inconveniently scheduled, but what Oliver meant to emphasize was that Goodhue died just as he had begun to emerge in architecture from the Gothic Revival of his origins to a twentieth-century interpretation of historical materials in buildings such as the Lincoln State House. Goodhue's work in the book arts was cut off even earlier and more awkwardly, not by death but by the press of architecture. If we wish that he had had more time to work out his reinterpreted architectural style, what can we say of his potential as a book designer? All is speculation of course, but one piece of evidence at least suggests

FIGS 8.7A and B Verso and recto of facing pages in *The Altar Book* (1896).

THE NATIVITY OF OUR LORD, OR THE BIRTHDAY OF CHRIST, COMMONLY CALLED CHRISTMAS-DAY.

ALMIGHTY God, who hast given us thy only-begotten Son to take our nature upon him, and as at this time to be born of a pure virgin; Grant that we being regenerate, and made thy children by adoption and grace, may daily be renewed by thy Holy Spirit; through the same our Lord Jesus Christ, who liveth and reigneth with thee and the same Spirit ever, one God, world without end.

Heb. i. 1.

GOD, who at sundry times and in divers manners spake in time past unto the fathers by the prophets, hath in these last days spoken unto us by his Son, whom he hath appointed heir of all things, by whom also he made the worlds; who being the brightness of his glory, and the express image of his person, and upholding all things by the word of his power, when he had by himself purged our sins, sat down on the right hand of the Majesty on high; being made so much better than the angels, as he hath by inheritance obtained a more excellent name than they. For unto which of the angels said he at any time, Thou art my Son, this day have I begotten thee? And again, I will be to him a Father, and he shall be to me a Son? And again, when he bringeth in the firstbegotten into the world, he saith, And let all the angels of God worship him. And of the angels he saith, Who maketh his angels spirits, and his ministers a flame of fire. But unto the Son he saith, Thy throne, O God, is for ever and ever: a sceptre of righteousness is the sceptre of thy kingdom. Thou hast loved righteousness, and hated iniquity; therefore God, even thy God, hath anointed thee with the oil of gladness above thy fellows. And, Thou, Lord, in the beginning hast laid the foundation of the earth; and the heavens are the works of thine hands: they shall

ADAM·PROTOPLAS
TVS·ABRAHAM·PAT
RIARCHA·MOYSES·LEG
ISLATOR·DAVID·REX

ISAIAS·PROPHETA
IEREMIAS·PROPHETA
DANIEL·PROPHETA
EZECHIEL·PROPHETA

SIBYLLA·PERSICA
SIBYLLA·LYBICA
SIBYLLA·ERYTHRÆA
SIBYLLA·DELPHICA
SIBYLLA·CVMANA

FIG 8.8 Frontispiece. A. Welby Pugin, *The True Principles of Pointed or Christian Architecture* (1841).

that Goodhue would have continued to develop in the realm of the book arts too. The work that stands out from the line of Arts and Crafts designs listed earlier is his contribution, including endpapers, illustrations, and covers, to Emily Delafield's play *Alice in Wonderland*, printed by Updike at the Merrymount Press and published by Dodd, Mead in 1898 (figure 8.10). Here, as at the beginning of the decade, Goodhue worked as both pictorial and decorative artist, to reiterate

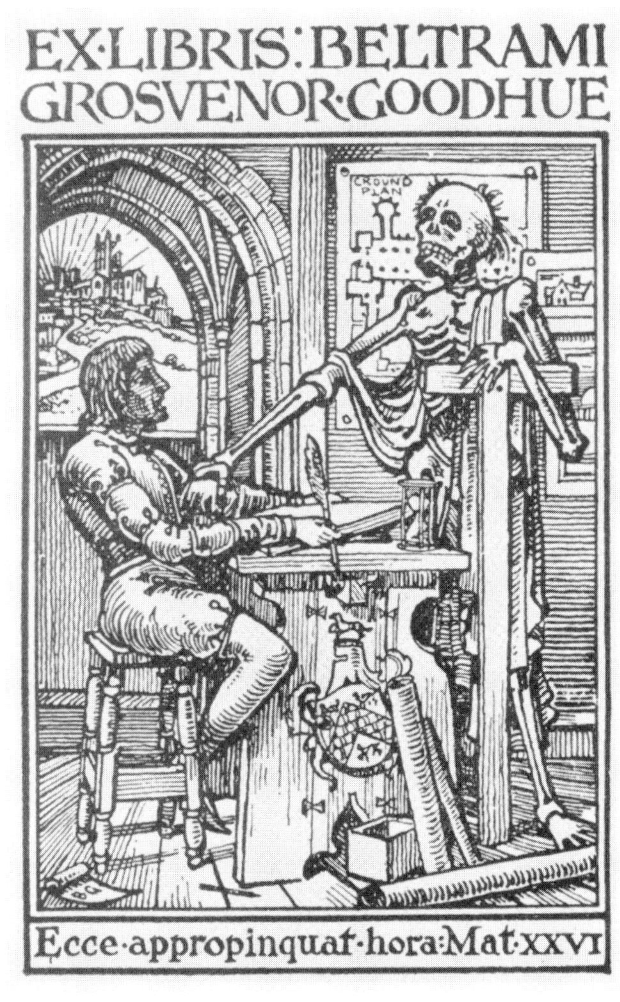

FIG 8.9 Goodhue, bookplate. After *Bertram Grosvenor Goodhue, Architect and Master of Many Arts*, ed. Charles H. Whitaker (1925).

Crane's distinctions, and has broken out of the black and white straitjacket of his coeval production. He works in the firm, flat, colorful style that marks and perhaps anticipates the product of contemporaries such as Maxfield Parrish. Here, in the book arts, he seems to prefigure the modernized medievalism that was to mark his last works in architecture. As I hope this brief essay suggests, a full study of his achievement in book design is a necessary concomitant to any study of his achievement in architecture.

FIG 8.10 Goodhue, cover for Emily P. Delafield, *Alice in Wonderland: A Play* (1898).

NOTES

1. Houghton Library, Harvard University, MS Am 800.14. This essay is adapted from a talk delivered in the Houghton Library on 30 October 1985 at a symposium, "Artists and the Book," in Boston. It is reprinted here by permission and with only slight changes from the *Harvard Library Journal* 30 (Spring 1987): 165–83.

2. Richard Oliver, *Bertram Grosvenor Goodhue* (New York: Architectural History Foundation, 1983); Susan Otis Thompson, *American Book Design and William Morris* (New York: R. R. Bowker Co., 1977); Estelle Jussim, *Slave to Beauty* (Boston: Godine, 1981); Beverly Brandt, "The Essential Link: Boston Architects and the Society of Arts and Crafts," *Tiller Magazine* 2 (1983): 7–32; and Nancy Finlay, *Artists of the Book in Boston, 1890–1910* (Cambridge Mass.: Houghton Library, Harvard College Library, 1985).

3. James F. O'Gorman, *Accomplished in All Departments of Art: Hammatt Billings of Boston, 1818–1874* (Amherst: University of Massachusetts Press, 1998).

4. Oliver, *Bertram Grosvenor Goodhue*, 2 ff.

5. William H. Pierson Jr., *American Buildings and Their Architects*, vol. 2, *Technology and the Picturesque* (Garden City, N.Y.: Doubleday, 1976), 206–19.

6. R. A. Cram, *My Life in Architecture* (Boston: Little Brown, 1936), 78.

7. Douglass Shand-Tucci, *All Saints' Ashmont* (Boston: Published by the Parish, 1975); and Douglass Shand-Tucci, *Boston Bohemia, 1881–1900: Ralph Adams Cram, Life and Architecture* (Amherst: University of Massachusetts Press, 1995).

8. R. A. Cram, "Partnership," in *Bertram Grosvenor Goodhue, Architect and Master of Many Arts*, ed. Charles H. Whitaker (New York: Press of the American Institute of Architects, 1925), 31.

9. Oliver, *Bertram Grosvenor Goodhue*, 26. See also Shand-Tucci, *Boston Bohemia*.

10. Thompson, *American Book Design*, xiii.

11. Cram, "Partnership," 30–31.

12. Walter Crane, *Of the Decorative Illustration of Books Old and New* (1896; London: Bell, 1916), v.

13. See *Book Decorations by Bertram Grosvenor Goodhue* (New York: Grollier Club, 1931).

14. Thompson, *American Book Design*, 77–78.

15. Finlay, *Artists of the Book*, 4.

16. *Knight Errant*, January 1893, quoted in Thompson, *American Book Design*, 44.

IX

JOHN CALVIN STEVENS'S ARCHITECTURAL LIBRARY

Earle G. Shettleworth, Jr.

*In 1997, Paul S. Stevens presented the 400-volume architectural library of his great-*grandfather, John Calvin Stevens (1855–1940), to the Maine Historical Society in Portland. This impressive collection of eighteenth-, nineteenth-, and twentieth-century architectural books had been owned by three subsequent generations of architects before joining the historical society's Stevens collection of drawings, specifications, sketchbooks, and photographs given in 1973 by Paul's father, John Calvin Stevens II (1908–1990). Thus, the library completed an extensive archive devoted to Maine's leading architect of the late nineteenth to early twentieth century, now widely appreciated for his work in the Shingle Style.

The collection had been started almost a century and a quarter before, when John Calvin Stevens, not quite eighteen years old, entered the office of Francis H. Fassett (1823–1908) in Portland in the fall of 1873. A carpenter who began practicing architecture in Boston in 1850, Fassett had moved to Portland at the age of forty in 1863 and emerged as the city's most prominent designer after the Great Fire of 1866. In a memoir written in 1935, Stevens recalled with pleasure that "Mr. Fassett had an excellent library, and his boys had ample opportunity to make use of it, so that the office boy had only himself to blame if he did not profit by what was at his hand."[1] Stevens further recollected spending "most of my evenings in the office among the books. . . . Reading and drawing during those evenings 'all by my lonesome' really gave me my start."[2]

Largely self-educated except for a brief period of early training with architects in Boston and New York, Francis Fassett was a man of vigorous intellect who enjoyed studying architectural history and had experienced firsthand the great buildings of England and the Continent through two extended tours. His sizable library of design and technical books ranged from eighteenth-century works by William Pain and Jacques-François Blondel to recent titles by Augustus Welby Pugin and Eugène Emmanuel Viollet-de-Duc. After Fassett's death in 1908, his library passed to his son Edward F. Fassett (1848–1922), an architect who had worked in partnership with his father at different times during their careers. When the younger Fassett died in 1922, some of the books were sold by the local antiquarian bookman A. J. Huston, giving John Calvin Stevens the opportunity to purchase volumes such as William Pain's *Practical Builder* (Boston, 1792) and Stuart and Revett's *Antiquities of Athens* (London, 1825) from the very library that had surrounded him during his formative years almost a half-century before.[3]

The nucleus of Stevens's own architectural library was formed during his apprenticeship in Fassett's office from 1873 to 1880. The earliest datable acquisition is a copy of *The English School of Painting in Water Colours* by Adam Penley (London, 1874), which bears the inscription "Presented to John C. Stevens By F. H. Fassett, October 8, 1875" (figure 9.1). This gift, received from his employer on his twentieth birthday, is significant in view of Stevens's early facility as an artist who used watercolors for both architectural rendering and landscape painting. Four other titles acquired in the course of his training are of a practical nature: *The Builder's Guide* by Asher Benjamin (Boston, 1839); *The Text Book of Modern Carpentry* by Thomas W. Silloway (Boston, 1858); *Orthographic and Isometric Projection* by Ellis Davidson (London, n.d.); and *The Sanitary Drainage of Houses and Towns* by George E. Waring (Boston, 1879). When Stevens purchased the 1839 edition of Benjamin's *Builder's Guide* from the Portland book collector George Doane Rand in 1878 (figure 9.2), the Greek Revival designs would have been considered out of fashion, but those plates devoted to the Classical orders as well as the technical information in the text would have been appreciated for their reference value.

As John Calvin Stevens joined the vanguard of young American architects developing the Shingle Style and the Colonial Revival in the 1880s, the English and American builders' guides of the Georgian, Federal, and Greek Revival periods took on added meaning and usefulness as sources of historical inspiration and design material. The opportunity to acquire an important group of such books came to Stevens shortly after he formed a partnership with Francis Fassett in 1880. That year the younger architect opened a branch office in Boston for the purpose of supervising the construction of the Hotel Pemberton at Nantasket Beach. During the eighteen months Stevens spent in Boston he also assisted Winslow Alden, an architect in West Randolph, Massachusetts. Family tradition holds that Alden paid Stevens in books that he had purchased during his career.[4] Among the twenty-one

FIG 9.1 John Calvin Stevens commemorated the gift of *The English School of Painting in Water-Colours* by Adam Penley (1874) from his employer, Francis H. Fassett, with this decorative water-color inscription on the flyleaf of the book. Collection of the Maine Historical Society, Portland.

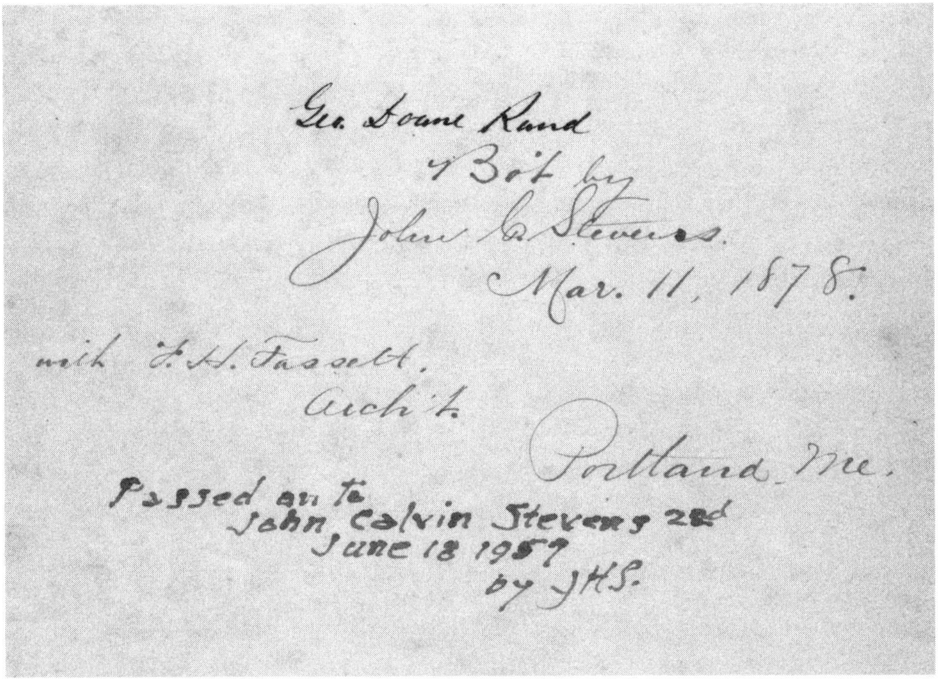

FIG 9.2 Flyleaf inscription showing that Stevens acquired his copy of *The Builder's Guide* by Asher Benjamin (1839) from George Doane Rand of Portland in 1878. Collection of the Maine Historical Society, Portland.

titles bearing Alden's name in Stevens's library, two from the Georgian period are *The Calculator* by James Dodson (London, 1747) and *New and Complete System of Architecture* by William Halfpenny (London, 1759). Books used in the Federal period include *The Practical House Carpenter* by William Pain (London, 1794) and *The Young Carpenter's Assistant* by Owen Biddle (Philadelphia, 1805). Alden's strongest holdings were in the Greek Revival with such American classics as Asher Benjamin's *Practice of Architecture* (Boston, 1836), Edward Shaw's *Rural Architecture* (Boston, 1850), Chester Hill's *The Builder's Guide* (Hartford, 1834), and Minard Lafever's *The Beauties of Modern Architecture* (New York, 1839) and *The Modern Builder's Guide* (New York, 1852).

Although John Calvin Stevens's acquisitions from Winslow Alden's library in the early 1880s constituted his largest holding of early builders' guides, his interest in such books continued throughout his life. In 1903 he received a gift of four exceptionally well-documented Georgian and Federal volumes from Mrs. Charles F. Kimball upon her husband's death. A noted stairbuilder and a gifted landscape artist, Kimball had been a close friend and painting companion of the architect as well as the son and grandson of prominent Portland architect-builders of the late eighteenth and early nineteenth centuries. Grandfather John Kimball Sr. had been credited with the design and construction of the Hugh McLellan House of 1800–1801, now part of the Portland Museum of Art. The four Kimball books, three English and one an American edition of a British work, are rich in provenance (see figures 9.3, 9.4). For example, the copy of *The British Architect* by Abraham Swan (London, n.d.) contains an ink inscription that traces its history through five owners:

The property of John Kimball, Ipswich, Massachusetts, 1779
John Kimball Jr., Portland, 1810
William G. Kimball, Portland, 1865
Charles F. Kimball, Deering, 1892
John Calvin Stevens, Portland, 1903

Other friends as well as clients were a valuable source of old books for Stevens's library. In 1908 the Portland carver and fellow landscape painter Edward S. Griffin gave the architect two English architectural reference books published in the 1850s. In honor of a birthday, the Portland Rotary Club presented Stevens, a prominent member, with a copy of *The Country Builder's Assistant* by Asher Benjamin (Worcester, 1798). When Mrs. Frank B. Comins of Cape Neddick wanted to thank Stevens for an unbilled consultation in 1929, she sent him *The American Builder's General Price Book and Estimator* by James Gallier (Boston, 1836). John Howard Stevens (1879–1958) responded for his father that "the interesting old 'Price Book' which you left with me is a sufficient reminder of a very pleasant interview and I am glad that you feel I was at all helpful in bringing your plans to a successful conclusion. I assure you that anything more is entirely unnecessary."[5]

John Calvin Stevens's antiquarian interests are also reflected in his early membership in the Society for the Preservation of New England Antiquities, which was founded by William Sumner Appleton in Boston in 1910 to preserve historic buildings and related collections. In 1921, Stevens responded positively to the society's call to New England architects to contribute $5.00 each toward the purchase of a group of architectural drawings by Asher Benjamin.[6] In 1935, Appleton wrote Stevens "to bear in mind in case you come across anything that can be turned into our collections, which often take on gladly what is to others mere junk headed for the waste paper basket or the ash barrel."[7]

Much of John Calvin Stevens's architectural library comprises books that were published during the period of his practice from 1880 to 1940. These contemporary volumes reflect the Romanesque Revival, Shingle Style, Colonial Revival, and Classical Revival trends of the six decades in which he was active. H. H. Richardson is represented by his *American Architect and Building News*

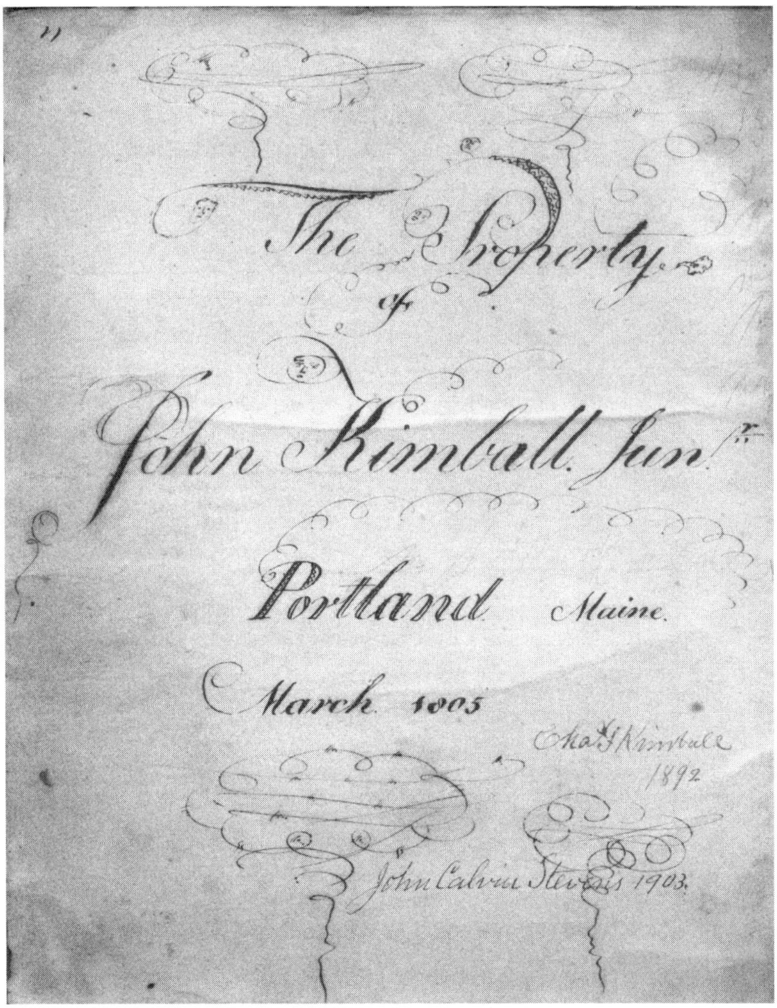

FIG 9.3 Elaborate pen-and-ink inscription on the inside cover of volume 1 of *The Builder's Magazine* (1800) documenting a chain of ownership from John Kimball Jr. in 1805 through his son Charles F. Kimball to Stevens in 1903. Collection of the Maine Historical Society, Portland.

FIG 9.4 Inscription on the inside cover of *The British Architect* by Abraham Swan (n.d.) tracing the book's ownership from John Kimball Sr., of Ipswich, Mass., in 1779 through the Kimball family of builders to Stevens in 1903. Collection of the Maine Historical Society, Portland.

monographs on Austin Hall, the Ames Memorial Building, and Trinity Church. The Colonial Revival is found in E. E. Soderholtz's photographic portfolios of Colonial architecture in Maryland, Virginia, Georgia, and South Carolina; in John Mead Howells's *Lost Examples of Colonial Architecture*; and in J. Frederick Kelly's *Early Domestic Architecture of Connecticut*. Monographs on major architects include those about Frank Forster, the firm of Mellor, Meigs & Howe, and Charles Platt. Stevens's interest in domestic architectural trends is reflected in four volumes of *American Country Homes of Today* (1912, 1913, 1915, 1922); three titles by Aymar Embury, including *One Hundred Country Houses* (1909); and books published by William Comstock on bungalows and camps. New building types of the time are addressed in *The Tenement House Problem* (1903) and *The Planning and Construction of High Office Buildings* (1898); Stevens may have consulted the latter in designing an eight-story office building project in 1907. Considering the architect's own talent for creating Romanesque- and Colonial-inspired ornament, it is not surprising to find also one of the great twentieth-century treatises on the subject, Louis Sullivan's *A System of Architectural Ornament with a Philosophy of Man's Powers* (1924).

Architectural annuals and periodicals emerged in the late nineteenth century as a significant means of communicating design ideas as well as technical information. Like many architects of the day, Stevens contributed to and collected annuals, yearbooks, and exhibition catalogues from architectural clubs in Boston, Chicago, Detroit, Los Angeles, New York, Philadelphia, Pittsburgh, Portland (Oregon), Seattle (Washington), and London (England). Fifty-four such volumes are found in his library.

Stevens also subscribed to several weekly and monthly American and English architectural periodicals and frequently submitted drawings and photographs of his own work for publication. An inventory made after his death documents his ownership of long runs of seven American and four English magazines from the period 1867 to 1905.[8] The individual issues were bound in leather with two volumes usually comprising a year. When John Howard Stevens became his father's partner in 1904, the practice of binding and retaining the periodicals in their entirety changed in favor of the younger architect's system of maintaining a file of tear sheets of selected articles and illustrations. This extensive file survives as part of the Stevens Collection at the Maine Historical Society, whereas the bound volumes of periodicals were discarded after the elder Stevens's death, probably in the interest of space in one of his successor firm's office moves. To the best of my knowledge, the bound volumes are the only major missing element of Stevens's library, and we do have their titles and years, thanks to a 1942 listing.

John Calvin Stevens himself created a personal system of albums for retaining and retrieving architectural sketches and photographs. Sketches were organized by categories such as doorways and mantles and pasted into large bound scrapbooks labeled "Sugs" for suggestions. He decorated the covers of these volumes with his own distinctive lettering and ornament.

By 1890, technological advances in printing resulted in a shift from line drawings to photographs in the architectural publications of the day. John Calvin Stevens and his contemporaries continued to produce sketches and renderings for internal office use, for presenting designs to clients, and for entering competitions and exhibitions. Increasingly, however, publicity for their completed buildings depended upon high-quality photographs. For these, Stevens turned primarily to Thomas Ellison, an architectural photographer active in Boston from 1905 to 1923. Ellison was responsible for many of the photographs used in early twentieth-century articles about Stevens's work. In addition to their promotional value, these photographs served other purposes. Carefully arranged in oblong black leather albums, they were shown to prospective clients as examples of the firm's recent work. The albums also functioned as reference books for the architect and his staff. Examples of both the suggestion scrapbooks and the photograph albums survive in the Stevens Collection.

For much of his career, Stevens maintained his office on the top floor of the Oxford Building at 183–187 Middle Street in Portland, an 1887 Romanesque Revival commercial block of his own design. Early photographs reveal that Stevens's drafting room and that of his staff contained large built-in shelves to store both drawings and published folios. When the office was redesigned in 1912, Stevens replaced these shelves for himself with two large folio cases. An adjoining room designated for consulting with clients also served as a library, with books kept on shelves that lined two walls. Off the sample room was a small walk-in book vault, perhaps to house rarer volumes. (Frontispiece)

Throughout the sixty-five years in which John Calvin Stevens amassed his architectural library, he clearly enjoyed leaving his personal mark on his books. Francis Fassett's 1875 gift of the English watercolor book is commemorated on the flyleaf with a decorative painted inscription by Stevens. Most of the books acquired before 1906 bear the architect's first bookplate (figure 9.5), an open folio illuminated by a wax candle in an antique holder. The tools of the trade are also present: a quill pen dipped in an inkwell and a compass laid across a pencil. Below this Colonial

Revival motif appears the bold signature of John Calvin Stevens. In 1906, Stevens adopted a new bookplate (figure 9.6) in the form of an Arts and Crafts block print showing the architect doing plein air painting under an umbrella, a direct reference to Stevens's long-standing Sunday ritual of joining fellow Portland artists in making oil sketches of local scenes.

FIG 9.5 Stevens's bookplate prior to 1906. Collection of the Maine Historical Society, Portland.

In addition to developing at least two other bookplate designs for himself (see figure 9.7), John Calvin Stevens used his artistic talent to create bookplates for family members, friends, and clients. Within his immediate family he designed bookplates for his daughters Caroline and Margaret as well as Margaret's husband, Neal W. Allen Sr. Longtime secretary Jeannette M. Craig received a striking Arts and Crafts thistle design; client General John Marshall Brown, an avid bibliophile himself, was favored with an intricate foliate motif of pine boughs and cones. But most delightful of all is the bookplate that son John Howard Stevens sketched in

FIG 9.6 Stevens's bookplate, 1906. Collection of the Maine Historical Society, Portland.

1914 for *his* six-year-old son, John Calvin Stevens II: a toy electric train running through tunnels of books.

John Calvin Stevens's appreciation for books is reflected in the design of *Examples of American Domestic Architecture*, which he published in 1889 with his partner, Albert Winslow Cobb. Cobb wrote a stirring text that called for reform in American architecture in the socialistic terms of the day; Stevens worked with publisher William T. Comstock of New York to create one of the most visually attractive architectural books of the period. It is presented in an oblong format measuring 10 by 14 inches; the "examples" are Stevens's sketches interspersed with the text, plus

FIG 9.7 Stevens's bookplate ca. 1919. Collection of the Maine Historical Society, Portland.

FIG 9.8 Stevens derived his design for the elegant Palladian window that graces the High Street facade of the L. D. M. Sweat Memorial of 1911 in Portland from this documentary photograph of the early nineteenth-century Palladian window of the Union Hall in Free Street in Portland (see FIG 9.9). Collection of the Maine Historical Society, Portland.

FIG 9.9 Both the historical view of the Union Hall window (see FIG 9.8) and this one of Stevens's Sweat Memorial window are part of a large group of architectural photographs of the architect's work which he kept in oblong black albums both for office reference and to show to prospective clients. Collection of the Maine Historical Society, Portland.

fifty-nine full plates of his elegant pen-and-ink renderings, many shown individually on a page and others in composite groupings. In addition, ornamental lettering devices begin each section of the text. Although it may be debated, as it was in 1889, where doctrine ends and self-promotion begins in a book such as Stevens and Cobb's, no one, then or now, would criticize the aesthetic achievement of *Examples of American Domestic Architecture.*[9]

The question remains, to what extent did John Calvin Stevens rely directly on his library for designing his work? All the evidence points to his innate ability to absorb the vocabulary of the architectural styles in his books and then create his own expression, rather than making precise copies. For example, a suggestion scrapbook may contain a dozen drawings for Federal mantelpieces, but not one will match exactly those shown in Pain or Benjamin. One exception is the photograph of the Palladian window of Union Hall on Free Street in Portland, which Stevens paired in an album with a picture of his own Palladian window on the Sweat Gallery of the Portland Museum of Art (figures 9.8, 9.9). Clearly, the Federal example was the basis for his Colonial Revival design.

Perhaps John Calvin Stevens's approach to design is best illustrated by a story told of his bicycle sketching tour of France in 1892. A former draftsman in his office, Ellis F. Lawrence, wrote of Stevens in 1932: "Another illustration of his extraordinary power of visualization—he is at Chinon. After visiting the chateau he sits in the shade of the awning at the café and sketches his impressions. His pals, admiring the composition, go off in a mad scurry to find it, but it was never there, yet the sketch is clearly Chinon."[10]

Using his powers of visualization, John Calvin Stevens remained actively engaged in the design process until his death in 1940 at the age of eighty-four. When John Calvin Stevens II joined the family firm in 1933, one of his duties was to drive his grandfather to work as well as to job sites. As soon as the senior architect took his place in the front passenger seat, he would produce a used envelope or a scrap of paper and commence sketching for a current project.[11] In true Maine fashion, Stevens never wasted either time or drafting materials in his lifelong pursuit of architectural excellence.

NOTES

1. John Calvin Stevens, three-page typescript memoir, 1935, Stevens Collection, Maine Historical Society, Portland.
2. John Calvin Stevens to Ellis F. Lawrence, 11 December 1931, Stevens Collection.

3. A. J. Huston, *Books New and Old, Part I: Art and Architectural Library of E. F. Fassett*, Catalogue 39, Maine Historical Society, Portland, 1922.

4. John Calvin Stevens II to the author.

5. John Howard Stevens (writing for John Calvin Stevens) to Mrs. Frank B. Comins, n.d., in response to Mrs. Comins's letter of 29 October 1927, Stevens Collection.

6. John Calvin Stevens to Lawrence Park, 28 May 1921, Historic New England Archives, Boston.

7. William Sumner Appleton to John Calvin Stevens, 25 March 1935, Stevens Collection.

8. John Howard Stevens, "A list of books from the library of John Calvin Stevens, F.A.I.A., consisting of architectural magazines bound in leather," typescript dated 27 October 1942, Stevens Collection.

9. For a discussion of Stevens and Cobb, *Examples of American Domestic Architecture*, see Earle Shettleworth and William Barry's introduction to the 1978 reprint of the book by American Life Foundation (Watkins Glen, N.Y.).

10. Ellis F. Lawrence, "John Calvin Stevens," *Architecture*, July 1932, 2.

11. John Calvin Stevens II to the author. Jane Gregory, in "The Shingle Style" (*Down East*, February 1986), wrote that Stevens "was continually working on architectural problems, according to grandson Neal W. Allen, Jr., a noted historian and retired Union College Professor. 'A pencil was always at hand; out of a jacket pocket would come a slip of paper, a used envelope, or the back of a sheet of stationery. Sitting there, he would attack some design problem that had not yet been resolved to his satisfaction; the detail of a mantelpiece, the rendering of a molding, a doorway or a window. His pencil worked rapidly, catching in a few sure strokes, it seemed to me, the desired results.'"

X

BOOKS AND LIBRARIES IN FRANK LLOYD WRIGHT'S OAK PARK DAYS

Elaine Harrington

Before Frank Lloyd Wright devoted his long life to architecture, he had discovered books and reading. They were central themes throughout his career. Since his death in 1959, Wright's legacy remains an American cultural heritage of buildings and a wealth of books about that architecture. Indeed, books *about* Wright are a growth industry for scholarly and popular historians, inspiring several bibliographies.[1] During his architectural career, Wright also produced and wrote books himself, many about his architectural thinking and work.

Wright went from reading books to making books to writing books. He owned and used books important to his professional development and marked some of them with a distinct personal stamp. He gave books an honored place in his home and in more than one room. He saw the book as a design problem to be addressed, and he used the book, and publication in general, to convey his architectural ideas to others. Books influenced Wright as a child and an adult, and his interests in the book arts included printing, photography, and the collecting of Japanese prints.

Additionally, Wright had an appreciation for library spaces, as had Boston architect Henry Hobson Richardson, whose architecture Wright knew well, and Chicago architect Louis Sullivan, whom Wright thought of as mentor. Wright designed both family and professional library rooms in his own Oak Park home and studio. With these interests as background, he designed handsome rooms and spaces for books in the homes of many of his early clients (highlighted below).

Frank Lloyd Wright was born in 1867 in Richland Center, Wisconsin. His exposure to architecture began at an early age when his mother, Anna Lloyd Jones Wright, hung images of English cathedrals, taken from a "pictorial periodical," in his room.[2] He had two younger sisters: Maginel, who became a children's book author and illustrator, and Jane, who became a teacher. His father, William Cary Wright, was a minister, music teacher, and organist; however, Wright's parents divorced in 1885 while they were living in Madison, Wisconsin. Life was difficult financially, and at a young age Wright worked summers on the farms of his grandfather and uncles near Spring Green, Wisconsin.[3]

But he always read: "ever since boyhood . . . omnivorous reading" was the way Wright characterized his lifelong interest in books. Boyhood favorites mentioned in his autobiography were *The Arabian Nights* (the genie and his lamp from this book were later the focus of Wright's own children's playroom mural), John Ruskin's *Seven Lamps of Architecture*, and novels of derring-do from the Nickel Library.[4]

His mother also owned many classics of literature and poetry which he presumably read as a child and a young adult. Examples are *Selected Poems* of Robert Browning, *Birds and Poets* by John Burroughs, Ralph Waldo Emerson's *Essays*, Washington Irving's *Sketch Book*, writings by his Unitarian minister uncle Jenkin Lloyd Jones, Rudyard Kipling's *Ballads*, *The Travels and Surprising Adventures of Baron Munchausen*, and Shakespeare's plays. The list of her books also included poetry by William Morris, James Whitcomb Riley, Friedrich Schiller, Alfred Tennyson, Walt Whitman, John Greenleaf Whittier, and William Wordsworth.[5]

Not only was Wright an avid reader as a youngster; he became interested in printing when he and a friend in Madison, Robie Lamp, operated a small hand press with seven type fonts.[6] This interest would expand for him as an adult, first into the book arts of designing, illustrating, and printing, and then into writing and publishing. These small-press printing projects also helped him appreciate the wood block process of the Japanese prints he later collected.

Wright developed his literary interests further while he was an engineering student at the University of Wisconsin–Madison. He read Carlyle, Plutarch, Ruskin, Shelley, Goethe, Blake, and Viollet-le-Duc's *Raisonné de l'architecture,* which he credited in his autobiography as the "only really sensible book on architecture." His son, John Lloyd Wright, recorded that his father told him he would find "all the architectural schooling you will ever need" in the two-volume set of *Discourses on*

Architecture written by Viollet-le-Duc in 1860: "What you cannot learn from them, you can learn from me."[7]

When he was almost twenty, and without completing college, Wright decided to travel to Chicago to seek his fortune as an architect. He largely financed this trip of 1887 by pawning some of the family's books, including even one of his favorites, the edition of Plutarch's *Lives* left behind by his father, and a finely bound set of Gibbon's *Decline and Fall of the Roman Empire*.[8] He found a drafting position with Joseph Lyman Silsbee, an architect formerly from New York state, who is credited with bringing the residential Shingle Style to the Midwest and was then designing a new church for Wright's uncle, Rev. Jenkin Lloyd Jones. While working for Silsbee, Wright read Owen Jones's *Grammar of Ornament*, Viollet-Le-Duc's *Habitations of Man in All Ages*, and Victor Hugo's *Notre Dame*—all borrowed from his uncle's church, All Souls Unitarian, located on Chicago's south side.[9] As an architectural apprentice, no doubt he read the "enigmatic words . . . the book will kill the building" in the chapter entitled "This Will Kill That" in Victor Hugo.[10] He later observed, "And the book is becoming to you and me what the cathedral was to the middle ages"—that is, he thought the book emblematic of its time.[11]

In 1888 he became draftsman, and then chief draftsman, with the Chicago firm of Dankmar Adler and Louis Sullivan. In 1889 he married Catherine Tobin, who was from Kenwood, also on the south side of Chicago. In the same year he purchased land in Oak Park—the streetcar suburb just west of Chicago—at the corner of Chicago and Forest Avenues. There, financed by a loan from Sullivan, he built a small but significant, shingled home of his own design in 1889; he expanded this honeymoon cottage into a larger home in 1895 and added an architectural studio in 1898. His mother and sisters moved into the Gothic Revival cottage already on the site, just beyond the Wrights' back garden. In or after 1892, Wright left the employ of Sullivan (the firm was located in Sullivan's Auditorium Building) and then opened his own architectural office, first in Chicago in the Sullivan-designed Schiller building.[12]

When considering the place of books on architecture in Wright's early professional life, it is necessary to mention both his mentor, Louis Sullivan, and his and Sullivan's early interest in Boston architect H. H. Richardson. It was in Sullivan's library that Wright pored over published illustrations of Richardson's architecture (Sullivan owned portfolios of photographs of Richardson's Austin Hall at Harvard and of his buildings for the Ames family in North Easton, Massachusetts, and also Mariana Griswold Van Rensselaer's 1888 biography of Richardson).[13]

Both architects served as exemplars to Wright because of their interest in architecture books, especially the books they initiated about their own buildings and architectural ideas. Richardson had understood the importance to his architectural success of getting his work published; Sullivan would write influential books about his architectural ideas and drawings. He gave Wright a copy of his essay "Inspiration," a pale tan, slim pamphlet published in 1886 which identifies nature as inspiration to art. Wright said that Sullivan gave him also a copy of Herbert Spencer's *Synthetic Philosophy* "to take home and read," and that they both enjoyed the work of Walt Whitman.[14]

Both Sullivan and Richardson were book collectors and owned important volumes in the fields of art, decorative arts, and architecture, with Sullivan also having books on plant materials.[15] By 1909, the end of the time Wright lived in Oak Park, he too had gathered a professional library and started to enhance his professional accomplishments by publishing both his own work and his ideas. Wright acknowledged the influence of these two men by featuring their photographs in the first edition of his autobiography of 1932, (along with photos of other men important to his early career: engineer Dankmar Adler, architect and friend Cecil Corwin, and his uncle, Jenkin Lloyd Jones).[16]

Well before he wrote about his own life, Wright used information in books to inform or reinforce his knowledge of both design and life. From the decorative windows in his home, the rugs on his floor, the sculpture in his rooms, and the boughs in his vases to the Japanese prints he collected, he absorbed the contents of his books and applied them to his own ideas. From compiled booklists, as well as his autobiography, it is clear that he read literature for both pleasure and contemplation. As for architecture books, the few he said were most significant to him and the publications he saw (known from the evidence present in his own home, often used as an architectural test laboratory) are telling examples.

Early in his career he was familiar with volumes relevant to the building construction trades and showing architectural components. The Oak Park home he designed in 1889 for himself and wife Catherine, with an open verandah and bay-windowed facade under a sheltering gabled roof, shows a strong resemblance to a residence designed by Bruce Price, located in Tuxedo Park, New York, and published in 1886.[17] He based the art glass windows for his family's dining room, in the 1895 addition to their home, on a design in an 1886 German art glass publication that he owned.[18] (Wright used the same art glass pattern for the upper part of the double-hung windows on the second floor of one of his first independent

FIG 10.1 Frank Lloyd Wright, William Winslow House, River Forest, Ill., ca. 1893. Previously unpublished watercolor by Paul Lautrup. Wright and Winslow printed *The House Beautiful* (1896–97) in the basement and stable of this house. In this view the decorative frieze is shown as cream colored. The Frank Lloyd Wright Preservation Trust Museum Purchase, 1991.07a. Photo by Philip Mrozinski.

commissions after leaving Sullivan's employ, the Winslow House of 1894 in River Forest; see figure 10.1).

The dining room addition made it possible to turn the original dining room of 1889 into a functional study, necessary for a growing family of children (there were four in 1895)[19] and a growing collection of books. These volumes likely would have included the atlas, dictionary, and encyclopedia that a Unitarian minister, Rev. William C. Gannett, listed in his essay *The House Beautiful* (c. 1895) as necessary for the well-equipped home library. He wrote that a family's thought and taste could be known from its books.[20] Gannett was a friend of Jenkin Lloyd Jones, and Wright admired his essay, so with assistance from his friend and client William Winslow, he undertook to design and print it in a limited edition of ninety copies. This was accomplished over a period of time in 1896 and 1897 in the Winslow basement and later in the stable (also designed by Wright). A handsome, large, thin volume bound in olive green leather, the work featured tall, narrow photographs printed on Japanese tissue, of weed arrangements photographed by Wright. In addition to binding these in at the front, he designed a flat, conventionalized pattern of leaves to ornament full pages throughout the book and a related design to surround panels of Gannett's words. He and Winslow, along with friend and client

Chauncey Williams, had already printed an edition of poetry earlier in 1896, *The Eve of St. Agnes* by John Keats, with title page designed by Wright.[21] There must have been a positive reception for these efforts, because during the years 1890–1910 there was a renaissance in the graphic arts and small-press printing, and Chicago was one of the centers of activity.[22]

Although Wright well understood the artistic value of a beautifully designed and printed book, his family's own library was not a collection of fine bindings and unread pages. With few exceptions, the books known to have been in their own home in the Oak Park years were covered in book cloth and were used for information or read for enjoyment. The books owned by Frank and Catherine and their children were primarily literature, both fiction and poetry, essays, and volumes about nature and the decorative arts. There were also a number of small, illustrated Japanese books.

Three built-in, glass-fronted cupboards in the Wrights' home study housed the family's books. Some of their titles were particular to Wright's interests, including three on Oriental rugs, published circa 1901, 1902, and 1904, with both black-and-white pictures and many colorful plates. One by Rosa Belle Holt, *Rugs: Oriental and Occidental, Antique and Modern*, has a tan cloth binding embellished with an oriental rug pattern in dark blue and rust colors; it was inscribed as a Christmas gift to Wright from his family in 1901.[23] He enjoyed the appearance in his own home of rugs in the geometric patterns of Middle Eastern tribal and village rugs with designs in tan, rust, and blue tones.[24]

Another family book, *The Japanese Floral Calendar* (ca. 1904), a small volume with a green spine published by Open Court in Chicago (noted for its books on Oriental topics), has black-and-white photographic illustrations of flowers similar in character to Wright's own nature photographs. He often printed his nature photographs on Japanese tissue, including those of a leafy branch of prickly ash and one of morning glories, comparable to a photograph in the *Floral Calendar* (figures 10.2, 10.3). The Wright children, too, had books on nature, including *Our Insect Friends and Foes: How to Collect, Preserve and Study Them* (1904), and Ernest Thompson Seton's *Wild Animals I Have Known* (1898).[25]

Many of the family's books are marked with a red square chop mark, a personal stamp that was one among many souvenirs of Frank and Catherine Wright's trip to Japan in 1905. The Wrights traveled to Japan with Mr. and Mrs. Ward Willits, clients and also Japanese print collectors. The black lacquerware (soup bowls with covers, a large rectangular serving tray, and a *jubako*—a Japanese picnic basket composed of black lacquer trays and a carrying support) purchased by the Wrights

FIG 10.2 Frank Lloyd Wright, Morning Glory, ca. 1904. Colotype printed on tissue, 10⅝ × 11⅞ in. This is close to a photograph in one of the Wright family books, *The Japanese Floral Calendar*, ca. 1904. He used similar photos of weed arrangements in his design of William C. Gannett's *The House Beautiful* (1896–97). The Frank Lloyd Wright Preservation Trust, Gift of David and Gladys Wright, 1990.34.196.01. Photo by Philip Mrozinski.

on this trip was also marked with a red square outlined in gold on the lacquer. When Wright stylized this red square, it became the basis for his professional architectural symbol.

Up in the children's barrel-vaulted playroom, part of the 1895 addition to the Oak Park house, there were ample places for books—and music rolls for the family's piano player—in shelves on either side of the entrance doorway and in cupboards with art glass doors on either side of the fireplace, over which was the mural of the genie and the lamp. The ceiling featured a pierced-wood design of prickly ash leaves with concealed lighting. There were high open shelves over the large bay window seats for books and toys, as well as cupboard spaces for games below the seats. A photograph dated to 1895–96 shows Catherine Wright reading to two of their children in her dayroom, the former nursery expanded in this renovation.

FIG 10.3 Frank Lloyd Wright, Prickly Ash, ca. 1904. Colotype printed on tissue, 10⅝ × 11⅞ in. Such a study, and Wright's perusal of conventionalization from nature in Owen Jones's *Grammar of Ornament*, is reflected also in the architect's design for the ceiling of his children's playroom in Oak Park. The Frank Lloyd Wright Preservation Trust, Gift of David and Gladys Wright, 1990.34.196.05. Photo by Philip Mrozinski.

In Japan she had collected a scrapbook full of colorful Japanese paper robes, many examples of Japanese decorated art papers called Chiyogami (printed by woodblock process just like Japanese prints), small illustrated Japanese books, and stencils for Japanese fabrics. She used some of these materials for art play with her own children and likely for the small kindergarten she organized in the large playroom for them and for the children of neighbors.[26]

In 1898, Wright built a whole new wing for an architectural studio attached to the house by a wide hallway (with a willow tree on the site incorporated through one wall and out the roof). In addition to shelf storage for paper and tools in four cupboards, the two-story-high drafting workroom had shelves at eye level on two walls for books used by his draftsmen. The entry, facing Chicago Avenue, featured bas relief panels of paired storks above which was "the tree of life" and "the book of knowledge" (from which hung an architectural plan similar to that of the studio itself). Visitors and clients stepped into a gold-walled entrance with a large rectangular yellow and green art glass skylight, from which they might be ushered through a small connecting hall into Wright's professional library space.

This was a skylit octagonal library (an octagon in rotation: woodwork elements of cabinets, shelves, and cornice molding alternate their angled corners and straight lines five times from floor to ceiling) that featured intriguing storage with an interplay of open shelves toward the top of the space.[27] Wright used these for displays of figurines, ceramics, books, treasures and arrangements of boughs of needles and leaves. Around the octagon were storage cupboards fronted by movable swinging cork bulletin boards. There were bookshelves just above these cupboards, two of the sections with art glass–fronted doors. (More cupboards with solid wood doors located on both sides of the small connecting hall may have stored architect's materials and samples, or overflow from other bookshelves.)

Wright decorated this library to make a statement about his architectural interests and a persuasive, artistic setting in which to talk to clients. Distinctively, at the doorways of the small hall leading into this personal library he hung portieres of a woven wool fabric, called "Campion," that William Morris, of British Arts and Crafts fame, had designed in 1883. These are shown in a photograph taken by Wright dated to about 1898 (figure 10.4) but do not appear in later photos of the same doorways, perhaps indicating that his interest in Morris designs was brief. H. H. Richardson also had William Morris portieres, including one in this same pattern, in his own studio library.[28] (Wright may have purchased the Morris fabric from Marshall Field's department store in Chicago, where the designer's goods

FIG 10.4 Frank Lloyd Wright, entrance to his architectural library in Oak Park. The architect shows his library as an artistic space, with portiers made from a woolen fabric woven by William Morris. Photograph, ca. 1898. Courtesy of The Frank Lloyd Wright Foundation, Scottsdale, Ariz.

were available and where the family shopped. Indeed, Field's was the source of their fine china, white Limoges with a gold unit design border.)[29]

In his studio rooms as well as his home, Wright displayed a number of plaster casts of Classical sculpture, purchased from the Caproni Company of Boston either through a catalogue or from an outlet on Wabash Avenue in Chicago.[30] A contemporary visitor to the studio noted decorations of "jars of wildflowers and choice bits of plaster."[31] In the office of Wright's studio he displayed a bas-relief of "Boys Singing from a Book," a copy of a Luca Della Robbia sculpture (from the choir balcony of the cathedral in Florence), probably from Caproni. Richardson had this same sculpture in the library of his studio.[32] Richardson's architectural studio and library attached to his Brookline home had been pictured in 1884 in the *American Architect and Building News*, a copy of which was in Sullivan's professional library.[33]

Richardson and Wright are noted as likely the first two architects in the United States to have studios attached to their homes, where they worked with a staff of employees.[34] (These two architects also shared the same number of precocious children, four boys and two girls each.) As Wright added wings to his family's home, it became more modern in that books were located in several rooms around the residence and in the studio, rather than just in one room, and were therefore more available to everyone.

Wright's own studio was featured in *House Beautiful* magazine (founded in Chicago in 1896) in 1899, and the family's home had been discussed in the same magazine in 1897. With both articles written by Chicago architect Alfred H. Granger, they were excellent public relations support for a young architect such as Wright.[35]

In the new century his ideas for homes for prospective clients were shown in three significant articles in the *Ladies Home Journal*, two in 1901 and one in 1907. These were primarily directed toward possible builders of smaller and middle-size homes.[36]

During his early career, Wright participated in Chicago's active Arts and Crafts scene. As a practitioner he designed copper and terra cotta vases and urns as well as furniture for both his own and clients' homes. His lecture "The Art and Craft of the Machine," delivered originally for Hull House in 1901, was published as an essay in the *Catalogue of the Fourteenth Annual Exhibition of the Chicago Architectural Club* in 1901. His copy of this catalogue, from his professional library, is filled with notes and changes entered directly in ink in his own handwriting. The idea of machine-produced architectural details and furnishings was actually in opposition to the Arts and Crafts philosophy of hand craftsmanship, but it was a theme he returned to when he used it to introduce lectures of the same title delivered in 1930.[37] He also reworked other writings and revisited another early published work, "In the Cause of Architecture." This had first appeared in the *Architectural Record* in 1908 and was continued by Wright in the same journal in 1914. Moreover, he reused that title in two series of articles in 1927 and 1928, also published in the *Record*).[38]

In his book design and production and the early decorative arts of his studio, as well as the essay "The Art and Craft of the Machine," Wright participated in and responded to the Arts and Crafts movement. He also was familiar with the literature of the arts and crafts. He owned a copy of *The Complete Poetical Works* of Dante Gabriel Rossetti in dark brown cloth binding with gold-stamped decoration; Wright's name appears inside. The British poet was a painter as well, and also an art glass designer for the firm of William Morris.[39] Among visitors to the Wrights' home around 1900 were two friends associated with the Arts and Crafts movement in Britain and in the United States who were especially interested in the book arts. One was Charles Robert Ashbee, English architect and an Arts and Crafts designer (who created two typefaces). He and his wife became friends with the Wrights when Ashbee was in Chicago to give lectures in 1900.[40] Wright's sons David and John and daughter Catherine all remembered the Ashbees as dinner guests.

David and John also recalled another visitor, Elbert Hubbard, as a dinner guest. Hubbard, the originator of the Roycroft Shop (an Arts and Crafts effort in the town of East Aurora, southeast of Buffalo, New York), was a writer, lecturer, and publisher of popular Arts and Crafts–styled books. Son John wrote humorously about Hubbard and Wright bragging to each other as great orator and great architect. Even though the books produced by the Roycroft were directed to a mass market, compared with the artistic Arts and Crafts publications in England, Wright talked to makers of both. He shared a further interest with Hubbard in literary and self-created mottoes, which Wright sometimes displayed in the buildings he designed.

Daughter Catherine accompanied her father on a trip to Hubbard's Roycroft. At the same time they visited the Martin and Barton (Mrs. Barton was Martin's sister) families in Buffalo, likely when Wright was working out the details of his residences for these two clients, built in 1904 and 1903.[41] In 1904, Wright also designed a house for Hubbard's sister Mary and her husband William Heath, called by Hubbard "your fine new home." Wright specified for it a large sandstone panel over the living room fireplace on which was this motto:

> THE BEAUTY OF THE HOUSE IS ORDER
> THE BLESSING OF THE HOUSE IS CONTENTMENT

THE GLORY OF THE HOUSE IS HOSPITALITY
THE CROWN OF THE HOUSE IS GODLINESS.[42]

All these homes, including Wright's Davidson House of 1908, were built in Buffalo for executives of the Larkin Soap Company. Hubbard had formerly been a founding partner of the firm, for which Wright also designed the administration building of 1903, later razed.

The books in Wright's collection identify his primary interests, especially in Japan. One large volume covered in green book cloth is Josiah Condor's *The Floral Art of Japan*, published in Tokyo in 1899. His book detailed flowers of spring, summer, and autumn seasons in lists, line drawings, and fourteen colored plates. It suggested arrangements not only of flowers but also of bamboo, plum, willow, pine, and maple branches. Wright liked these arrangements, and photographs he took of his Oak Park home and studio show many informal arrangements of branches. Condor was a professor of architecture in the Engineering Department of Tokyo Imperial University for eleven years, starting in 1877.[43] Another significant book about Japan in Wright's collection is a Japanese-bound, grasscloth-covered album of photographs from his storied first trip there in 1905. It is an important glimpse through his eyes into the country he found so meaningful.[44] Wright took many of the photographs of buildings, gardens, and vistas himself during this trip. The album also includes a few images of waterfalls which he likely purchased there.

The family owned *A History of the Arts of Wood-Cutting and Color Printing in Japan* by Edward F. Strange (1904), which was inscribed with both Catherine's and son John's names.[45] This red book cloth–bound standard source, showing sixty-one examples of print artists' work and the wood-block process, was central to Wright's interest in Japanese prints; the appreciation may have been stimulated while he worked for Silsbee, who collected East Asian works of art and was first cousin to Ernest Fenellosa of Boston, a scholar of Japanese art and influential tastemaker in promoting it to Americans. It is known that Fenellosa visited Chicago while Wright was working for Silsbee, and Wright may have purchased his first Japanese prints from him.[46]

Between 1895 and 1899, Wright had started collecting Japanese prints; a photograph of the children's playroom from those years shows several displayed on the wall.[47] These lively and color-filled woodblock-printed images became a lifetime passion for Wright. He hosted print parties in his studio, which included a vault where his own fine collection of prints was stored, and he purchased prints for other collectors. (Those that he sold eventually became part of the collections of the Art Institute of Chicago, the Boston Museum of Fine Arts, the Metropolitan Museum of Art, and the Elvehjem Museum in Madison, Wisconsin.)

As a later outgrowth of this early interest in Japanese prints, Wright wrote his own book in 1912, *The Japanese Print: An Interpretation*, published in Chicago by the Ralph Fletcher Seymour Company. In this appreciation of prints and Japanese aesthetics, he engages in a wider discussion of art and design topics, such as the elimination of the insignificant, conventionalization, and the relation of colors in prints to those in Oriental rugs. He also names here his favorite sculptures, the Winged Victory and the Venus de Milo, plaster casts of which he had placed in his own and clients' homes, calling them "true sculpture."[48]

Wright and several other Japanese print collectors in Chicago, including Frederick Gookin, a banker and consultant on Japanese prints, were members of the Caxton Club, which was devoted to the study and production of the artistic printed book and also offered programs on prints. In 1913, Gookin published *Japanese Colour-Prints and Their Designers*, of which Wright owned a copy. Other members of the Caxton Club suggest architectural connections to Wright: clients William Winslow, Chauncey Williams, and George Millard; architects Joseph L. Silsbee and Daniel H. Burnham; and industrialist John J. Glessner (for whom H. H. Richardson had designed a home in Chicago). In his journal Glessner wrote that young architects would ask to see this house.[49]

In Wright's octagonal studio, a balcony around all sides at the second-floor level was part of the tall drafting room. At the top of the stairs to the balcony was a dark room for developing photographs, and the balcony furnished additional work areas for drafting, sculpture, and other design work. Milwaukee interior and furniture designer George Niedecken (1878–1945) worked here, circa 1904, for convenience while he was assisting with decorative portions of Wright's architectural programs.[50]

In the early years of the twentieth century, Wright's sister Maginel (1877–1966), a commercial artist, also worked on the drafting room balcony "after hours and weekends." She became a well regarded children's book illustrator known for her pictures in *Hans Brinker; or, The Silver Skates*, *Heidi*, and books by L. Frank Baum. She also both wrote and illustrated *Weather Signs and Rhymes*, *Animal Airs,* a baby's record book, and children's stories in magazines. Her illustrations were used in a number of women's magazines and on their covers as well. Her pictures featured delightful children and animals, often drawn in a colorful but flat style without much shading, much like the flat style used in the design of the Japanese prints she had seen in her brother's collection.[51]

Although they were in different programs, both Niedecken and Maginel Wright had attended the School of the Art Institute for the same year, 1897–98.[52] Niedecken designed murals, furniture, and decorative elements for a number of Wright projects, from before 1904 to about 1917.[53] Perhaps during the time when Niedecken was designing the fireplace surround for the Coonley House of 1907, which features scenes of ferns and birch trees (figure 10.5), some cross-fertilization took place, possibly the influence of a shared teacher or book: the ferns and birches (and prickly ash) of Maginel's illustrations for a book published in 1927, *Lost Village* by Alberta Bancroft (figure 10.6), are similar in both their general appearance and their details.[54] (The book arts also called to Maginel Wright Enright Barney's daughter, Elizabeth Enright Gilham (1909–68), who both wrote and illustrated award-winning children's books, including *Thimble Summer*, which won the Newbery Medal for 1939).[55]

Also in the Wright family's collection of books from their Oak Park days was a bittersweet two-volume set of daily reminder books that Catherine created for Frank for the last year they were together, 1909. Leather bound, about 5-by-7 inches tall,[56] including daily pictures relevant to the season and short entries of poetry, admonitions, and reminders, they were to be used together as a daily appointment calendar. The contents of many pages make it clear that she knew she was losing him and was trying to change that potential outcome.[57]

In October 1909, Wright put his practice in the care of architect Herman Von Holst.[58] He went abroad with Mamah Borthwick Cheney (who with her husband Edwin had been Wright's client for a new house in Oak Park in 1903). They both had book projects to complete, and this work was accomplished in Italy in the city of Florence and nearby Fiesole. Hers was the authorized translation from the Swedish of *The Morality of Woman and Other Essays*, by Ellen Key (published by the Ralph Fletcher Seymour Company in 1911; in Wright's mother's book collection was another Key title, *The Woman Movement*, 1912).[59]

Wright's book was the collection of drawings and floor plans to be published by Wasmuth, which would become an influential source on the important work of his early career. His eldest son Lloyd and fellow draftsman Taylor Woolley completed the drawings with crow quill on tracing paper, working in a cold courtyard apartment south of the Arno River in Florence in 1910.[60] The striking Wasmuth plates printed in Germany were wide but not tall in proportion, perfect for depicting Wright's horizontal Prairie School buildings. A few images made in a tall and

FIG 10.5 Frank Lloyd Wright, Avery Coonley house, Riverside, Ill., 1907. Long bookcases flank the living room fireplace beneath a mural of ferns and birches by George Niedecken. From *Ausgeführte Bauten und Entwürfe von Frank Lloyd Wright* (1911). The Frank Lloyd Wright Preservation Trust.

narrow format, including that of the interior of the Larkin Building's large open workroom, were reminiscent of the proportion of some Japanese prints. It was printed on tissue as were a small number of these images, while many were printed in brown ink on a light-toned gray paper stock. It was a handsome portfolio publication in dark green book-cloth-covered boards and was published in 1910 with an introduction by the architect. "Mr. Wright's text is by no means negligible" was the rare praise critic Montgomery Schuyler gave to Wright's words.[61] Wasmuth also published a noteworthy separate volume of photographs in 1911 that detailed Wright's architectural work to that date, with an introduction by Charles Robert Ashbee, his English friend. These two publications introduced Wright's work to a larger audience, the first aimed to an elite readership, the second more to students both at home and abroad.[62] (Still another volume in Wright's collection published by Wasmuth, a monograph on Persian tiles and decoration, may have been acquired while he was in Germany working on his own publication.[63] He continued to buy rare books into the 1950s.) A later, major work including Wright's Oak Park architectural career was the volume published in 1925 which collected seven issues of the Dutch periodical *Wendingen* (originally seen primarily by Europeans).[64]

These major publication efforts graphically showed the significant buildings that were the culmination of the early work he accomplished while living in Oak Park. Many of the clients' residences delineated included rooms designated as libraries, separate from parlors or living rooms; other homes that Wright designed merely had areas, spaces, or nooks with built-in bookshelves, but all reflected his understanding of the production, pleasure, and function of books. Wright's provision for

FIG 10.6 Maginel Wright Enright Barney, illustration in Alberta Bancroft, *Lost Village* (1927), following p. 52. The treatment of ferns and birches (and prickly ash) is similar to the Coonley House mural by Niedecken and may stem from a teaching aid used at the School of the Art Institute of Chicago, where both artists were trained. The Frank Lloyd Wright Preservation Trust.

FIG 10.7 Frank Lloyd Wright reading in a wicker chair on the front veranda of his house in Oak Park (detail), ca. 1890–1900. Courtesy of the Frank Lloyd Wright Foundation, Scottsdale, Ariz.

bookcases throughout many of his residential designs indicates the broad social acceptance of the role of books in all aspects of domestic life. The twenty years that Wright lived in Oak Park, 1889 to 1909, parallels the first half of the era from 1890 to 1930 which historians now call "halcyon days of book buying, of book collecting, and of the development of the home library" in the United States.[65] Wright's interests in books and libraries well prepared him to design book spaces for both his own and his clients' homes (figure 10.7).

Although public libraries with purpose-built wooden bookshelves (*armaria*) for storing library materials (scrolls) were known during Roman times, and royal and religious libraries were prized in the Middle Ages and the Renaissance, home libraries were not common until the eighteenth century and then were found only in homes of the very wealthy.[66] Early in the nineteenth century, home libraries were still limited to upper-class homes. Not all citizens knew how to read, and books were expensively handcrafted. By 1830, however, advances in book production and distribution of both domestic and imported books were making them available in larger quantities at more accessible prices. By 1840, most of the adult population in the northeastern and midwestern United States could read. The parallel rise of education and literacy in the nineteenth century created larger numbers of readers who could borrow books from public libraries (the first was founded in 1852 in Boston), rent books, purchase them from bookstores and general stores, or find them serialized within magazines.[67]

By the 1880s, homes of large size often had a special room to house all these books. An architectural journal suggested that a fireplace "indicates true comfort," and that window seats, easy chairs in "cosey corners and well lighted alcoves," and a library table ("an essential piece of furniture") were all desirable. Decorations on top of the bookshelves indicated further literary, artistic, scientific, or travel interests. Although all members of the household might use it, this library room could also serve as a study for the man of the house. Even more modest-sized homes would have at least a book corner with a cupboard for books, suggesting refinement and culture.[68]

Wright's early residential work adopted some of the foregoing suggestions, and they were incorporated in a seminal home with an exemplary library that also functioned as a parlor. The Charnley House of 1892 was designed by the firm of Adler and Sullivan when Wright was still the company's chief draftsman, just before he left the firm. Though not a large home, the quartersawn oak woodwork for this room included two full walls of open bookshelves, interrupted only by two windows with window seats, one centered in each wall. Part of the third wall contained closed cabinets with wood doors. The fourth wall featured a centered fireplace with a foliate-design wood surround, similar to other acanthus patterns designed by Sullivan; bookshelves on each side of it had glass doors of a geometric design, probably by Wright and similar in effect to windows in the two street facades of his Blossom House. (The art glass overdoor and sidelights surrounding the inner front door of the Charnley House, featuring ribbed yellow ribbons and a flat opaque shield shape, are remarkably similar in theme and materials to the art glass stair windows at the Blossom House, especially at its third-floor ballroom level. In both houses, these windows are Colonial Revival in appearance and look like neither architect's characteristic designs. They may have been purchased through a commercial art glass supplier.)

The Charnley oak bookshelves on each side of the parlor-library were connected at the top at a height of four feet, six inches. This was also a height for built-in bookcases used by Richardson.[69] And it is similar to the proportion of the bookshelves of other libraries in large homes of the period (e.g., the Glessner and Winslow Houses). This placement allowed for wall decorations above the books: murals, special wallpaper, or wall colors selected to show off pictures and objects—a treatment suggested in the tastemaking 1878 book *The House Beautiful* by Clarence Cook, in which an even lower bookcase height was encouraged.[70] At the Charnley House this measurement of four feet, six inches continued as a datum line throughout the principal rooms of the first floor as a dado molding, with the top line of two other fireplaces, and with a front hall cabinet.

Although the Charnley House remains a conundrum for architectural connoisseurs trying to decide who accomplished what parts of the design, it points the way to Wright's earliest designs after he left the Adler and Sullivan firm, dating to this same period. The Winslow House (1894) in River Forest, just west of Oak Park, vies for competition with the Harlan House (1892, razed) as his first independent commission. (Many architectural writers name the Winslow House as the first, but Wright claimed the Harlan House as the "first house built my own way.") The Winslow commission was for a larger home than the Charnley and had a separate room for just a library; oak bookshelves on three sides are shown in the floor plan, featuring murals above them.[71]

Although Wright's Blossom House (1892) in Chicago's Hyde Park neighborhood had a small corner room to the left of the front door indicated as the library, there were only two built-in shelf units. The current owner believes that early on, the small balancing room to the right of the front door (perhaps originally a receiving room) was turned into the library and that the plain-glass-fronted bookcase that now extends along the back wall of the room was there then. Next door, in the McArthur House (also 1892), there was a large, plain open bookcase located in the living room which the current, longtime owner moved to the smaller music room, also at the front of the house. This bookcase is thought by the owner to have been in the house early on.

The handsome spaces that Wright provided for books, from separate rooms to inviting nooks, were distinguished from others of the time by their lighting, both from artificial sources and from large windows. He made comfortable areas in which to sit on built-in seats or chairs, and he designed library tables and ample bookshelves. During the Oak Park years, Wright preferred oak for most of his residential woodwork and furniture, stained a medium to darker brown.

In all, Wright designed about eight-five homes for clients from 1891 through 1913 (this count does not include house renovations and summer cottages).[72] In common with many large houses designed by other architects in the latter part of the nineteenth century for upper-middle-class and wealthy clients, a good number of the larger homes by Wright in the years before 1900 had separate libraries, including those in eleven other pre–Prairie School houses.

Wright designed the first houses usually called Prairie in 1900, with the last of these from his Oak Park period usually taken to be the Harry Adams House of 1913 in Oak Park. Fourteen of the homes in these thirteen years had libraries as separate rooms. One of the first of these, the Hickox House of 1900 in Kankakee, Illinois, had a library open to the living room, balancing the dining room of equal size; that of the Willits House, 1901, in Highland Park, Illinois, was on the landing, halfway to the second floor. The Martin House, 1902, in Oak Park contained a large library room, as did the Martin House, 1904, in Buffalo, where the library was as big as, and located on the opposite side of the living room from, the dining room, a balance Wright frequently used. The Dana House, a large residential complex of 1902 in Springfield, Illinois, featured a sizable library with built-in book cupboards and two oak print tables of Wright's design in the gallery above it. It should be noted that during the forty-six years of Wright's career after 1913, he designed just six, primarily large, homes with libraries.[73]

Toward the end of the Prairie School period, instead of a library, Wright's house designs are just as likely to have a smaller room, in addition to the living room, called a den or study, which had space for books. One example is the small (compared with the living room) study of the Boynton House of 1908 of Rochester, New York. The Coonley House, a large complex of 1907 in Riverside, Illinois, had both a small study and, on either side of the living room fireplace, long bookshelves with the fern and birch mural above them, providing ample book space (see figure 10.5). In designs without either a library or a smaller study as a separate room, Wright usually made an area for books as part of the living room: for example, the Thomas House of 1901 in Oak Park had two walls of its living room assigned to bookshelves. Wright also designed a number of houses in this period that had only small spaces for books. These include the Fricke House of 1901, with two enticing nooks for books, one on either side of the large living room front window across from the fireplace wall.

Although libraries as separate rooms were not as common in Wright's smaller home plans, he urged all his clients to have his designs for movable "furniture and furnishings . . . built-in as integral features of the building."[74] Most of his residential designs, whether large or small, had built-in storage units. Although other architects' homes of this time did have some built-in furniture—window seats, drawers, cupboards, or shelves—this was part of the design philosophy that Wright encouraged his clients to adapt. His spaces for books and reading were the perfect showcase for this kind of solution, reinforcing his idea that books as well as his built-ins and furniture designs were integral to his architecture.

Wright's built-ins often took the form of open or glass-fronted shelf units and cabinets, such as the double-sided, glass-doored cabinets in the Mrs. Thomas Gale House of Oak Park, finished in 1909. These provided storage for china and glass on the dining room side, with books and objects displayed toward the living room. Wright encouraged clients to select movable pieces of furniture of his design as well. In libraries, these could include chairs and, especially, purpose-built library tables with special shelves and compartments for various-sized books and other publications. Three of these are the oak library tables for Charles Roberts (1896), for the Darwin Martin House (1904), and for the second Francis Little House (1913).[75]

The architecture that Wright created while he was associated with Oak Park coincided with the advent of electricity. He took advantage of this new source of illumination to design innovative ceiling, wall, and freestanding lighting fixtures for his own and clients' homes, some of which were used in the libraries and other reading areas. As he refined his own thinking about the interior spaces in homes during this time, he started to promote a more "spacious" living room. Rather than walls separating rooms for various functions, he advocated "screening various portions in the big room, for certain domestic purposes—like dining or reading, or receiving a formal caller."[76] This gathering of the activities of the formerly separate dining room, library, and reception room into one large space with areas for eating, reading, and entertaining is a connection from his Prairie homes to, and presages, the open floor plans of his later Usonian residential designs.

Wright never built a public library (although he had participated in a library competition in 1893, entering a drawing of a large, classically derived facade),[77] but during the Oak Park period he was the architect also of a bookstore, presenting not a space for the home enjoyment of books but rather a handsome shop from which to market them. In 1907 he designed the interior of Browne's Bookstore, located on an upper floor of the Fine Arts Building of 1898 on Michigan Avenue in Chicago, which had been redesigned by Solon S. Beman from his original 1885 showroom for Studebaker carriages into an artistic center. This is the same building where Wright's architectural office was located in 1908 and 1910, after he returned from abroad (before he moved it to Orchestra Hall, designed by Daniel Burnham) and where the clubroom of the Caxton Club was also located. Wright designed window seats and long library-style tables for the store as well as special bookshelves with the lower shelves slanted for ease in viewing the titles. Even though the store was not successful (because it lacked street traffic), it showed Wright's skill in designing a purpose-built interior especially for the display and sale of books.[78]

For Wright, what began as an "omnivorous" lifelong passion for books as a reader, continued with the design of special places for them in his own home. His book interests flourished as he made his own book designs, collected Japanese prints, and became a published author of books about his artistic and architectural ideas. Throughout his long architectural career, Frank Lloyd Wright made fine large library rooms and intriguing, smaller built-in book spaces for his residential clients, but never more than during his Oak Park days.

NOTES

Special thanks to Valerie Harris and Rebecca Hyman of the Frank Lloyd Wright Preservation Trust for assistance with photographs and research, and to Donald Davis, Don Kalec, Meg Klinkow, Mary Alice Molloy, and Kevin Harrington for reading earlier versions of this essay.

1. Donald Langmead, *Frank Lloyd Wright: A Bio-Bibliography*, Bio-Bibliographies in Art and Architecture, no. 6 (Westport, Conn.: Praeger, 2003); Robert L. Sweeney, *Frank Lloyd Wright: An Annotated Bibliography* (Los Angeles: Hennessey & Ingalls, 1978); Augusto Rossari, *Frank Lloyd Wright: bibliografia e opere* (Florence: Alinea Editrice, 1992). These are, respectively, the newest, the standard, and a good one on European sources.

2. One such cathedral print is in the collection of the Frank Lloyd Wright Foundation Archives, Scottsdale, Ariz. See Frank Lloyd Wright (hereafter FLW), *An Autobiography* (1932; rpt. New York: Horizon Press, 1977), 31, 52. When Wright first published his autobiography in 1932, he appeared to present himself in the best light, as he was starting his Taliesin Fellowship of architectural student apprentices at his home and studio in Wisconsin that same year. Although scholars have since found discrepancies in his own account of his life, I have drawn on this autobiography (citing the Horizon Press reprint unless otherwise noted) for his presumably noncontroversial recollections of books he read as a young person.

3. Robert C. Twombly, *Frank Lloyd Wright: His Life and His Architecture* (New York: Wiley, 1979), 4–11.

4. FLW, *Autobiography*, 187, 53, 54.

5. Margaret Klinkow, *The Wright Family Library* (Oak Park, Ill., FLW Home and Studio Foundation Research Center, 1994), 6–21.

6. FLW, *Autobiography*, 53.

7. Ibid., 73, 97; John Lloyd Wright, *My Father, Frank Lloyd Wright* (New York: Dover, 1992), 69.

8. Thomas S. Hines Jr., "Frank Lloyd Wright—The Madison Years: Records versus Recollections," *Journal of the Society of Architectural Historians* 26 (December 1967): 227–33.

9. FLW, *Autobiography,* 97, 100.

10. Victor Hugo, *Notre-Dame de Paris* (1831; Oxford: Oxford University Press, 1999), bk. 5, 192.

11. Bruce Brooks Pfeiffer, ed., *Frank Lloyd Wright: Collected Writings* (New York: Rizzoli, 1992), 1:29.

12. Twombly, *Frank Lloyd Wright,* 30.

13. James F. O'Gorman, *Three American Architects: Richardson, Sullivan, and Wright, 1865–1915* (Chicago: University of Chicago Press, 1991), 4–6, 113–32.

14. Collection FLW Preservation Trust Research Center, Oak Park, Ill.; FLW, *Autobiography*, 125.

15. James F. O'Gorman, "Documentation: An 1886 Inventory of H. H. Richardson's Library, and Other Gleanings from Probate," *Journal of the Society of Architectural Historians* 41 (May 1982): 151–55; Williams, Barker and Severn Co., *Auction Catalog No. 5533* (Chicago, 29 November 1909), inventory list of Sullivan's Chicago books, Art Institute of Chicago (AIC), Burnham Library; list (microfilm) of books left at Sullivan's vacation home in Ocean Springs (books now in the collection of the AIA, Washington, D.C.), AIC, Burnham Library; and B. Koppany III, *Educating Frank Lloyd Wright, 1885 to 1899* (Los Angeles: Striking Impressions, 2005), 3:569–71.

16. Frank Lloyd Wright, *An Autobiography* (New York: Longmans, Green, 1932), photographs following 371.

17. "A Cottage at Tuxedo Park, N.Y., Bruce Price, Architect, 74 West 23rd Street, New York City," *Building: A Journal of Architecture* 5 (18 September 1886): following 138.

18. David Hanks, *The Decorative Designs of Frank Lloyd Wright* (New York: Dutton, 1979), 53–55.

19. Twombly, *Frank Lloyd Wright*, 113.

20. Reprinted in Wright, *My Father, Frank Lloyd Wright,* 159; List of Published Writings by William C. Gannett, WCG Papers, Box 39, University of Rochester (N.Y.) Archives.

21. John Arthur, foreword to *The House Beautiful* (San Francisco: Pomegranate , 1996), 3.

22. May Jane Hamilton, *Frank Lloyd Wright and the Book Arts* (Madison: Department of Special Collections, Memorial Library, University of Wisconsin, 1993), 59, 35.

23. Collection FLW Preservation Trust Research Center.

24. Conversation with Joseph Fell, Oriental rug dealer, Chicago, 22 September 1995.

25. Margaret Klinkow, "Wright the Collector," in Melanie Birk, ed., *Frank Lloyd Wright's Fifty Views of Japan: The 1905 Photo Album* (San Francisco: Pomegranate Artbooks, 1996), 108, 109; Klinkow, *Wright Family Library*, 14, 15.

26. Collection FLW Preservation Trust Research Center; FLW, *Autobiography*, 133; Klinkow, "Wright the Collector," 105.

27. Elaine Harrington, *Frank Lloyd Wright Home and Studio, Oak Park* (Stuttgart: Edition Axel Menges, 1996), 8, 50; Zarine Weil, ed., *Building a Legacy: The Restoration of Frank Lloyd Wright's Oak Park Home and Studio* (San Francisco: Pomegranate, 2001), 112–16.

28. Elaine Harrington, "Frank Lloyd Wright and Dress Reform," *Positions in Architecture: The Chicago Architectural Journal 9*, ed. Tarry Tatum (Chicago: Chicago Architectural Club, 2000), 137; Linda Parry, *William Morris Textiles* (New York: Viking, 1983), 155; Linda Parry to Elaine Harrington, c.1991, curator's files, FLW Preservation Trust Research Center.

29. David Wright to Carla Lind, 6 October 1983, FLW Preservation Trust Research Center.

30. Harrington, FLW *Home and Studio*, 9.

31. Alfred H. Granger, "An Architect's Studio," *House Beautiful* 7 (December 1899): 39, 40.

32. James F. O'Gorman, "The Making of a 'Richardson Building,' 1874–1886," in *H. H. Richardson and His Office* (Boston: Department of Printing and Graphic Arts, Harvard College Library, 1974), 33.

33. "Studio and Office of Mr. H. H. Richardson, Architect, Brookline, Mass.," *American Architect and Building News* 16 (27 December 1884): 304.

34. Author's conversations with David Van Zanten, spring 1987 and 23 March 2006.

35. Alfred H. Granger, "Successful Houses," *House Beautiful* 3 (February 1897): 64–69; and "An Architect's Studio," *House Beautiful* 7 (December 1899): 36–45.

36. "A Home in a Prairie Town," *Ladies Home Journal* 18 (February 1901); "A Small House with 'Lots of Room in It,'" *Ladies Home Journal* 18 (July 1901); and "A Fireproof House for $5,000," *Ladies Home Journal* 24 (April 1907).

37. Collection FLW Preservation Trust Research Center; Margaret Klinkow, "Frank Lloyd Wright's Art and Craft of the Machine, 1887–1902" (master's thesis, University of Illinois–Chicago, 1997); FLW, "Machinery, Materials and Men," in "Modern Architecture, the Princeton Lectures, 1930," in *The Future of Architecture* (New York: New American Library, 1953), 78–102.

38. Twombly, *Frank Lloyd Wright,* 425, 426.

39. Collection FLW Preservation Trust Research Center.

40. Hamilton, *Frank Lloyd Wright and Book Arts*, 81, 82.

41. Wright, *My Father, Frank Lloyd Wright,* 32; interview files for David and Catherine Wright, FLW Preservation Trust Research Center.

42. Mary Hubbard Heath, *The Elbert Hubbard I Knew* (East Aurora, N.Y.: Roycrofters, 1929), 214; William Allin Storrer, *The Frank Lloyd Wright Companion* (Chicago: University of Chicago Press, 1993), 104. I have transcribed the motto accurately. It is difficult to read in most photographs.

43. Josiah Condor, *Landscape Gardening in Japan* (New York: Dover, 1964), v.

44. Negatives, Archives of the FLW Foundation at Scottsdale, Ariz.; album in Collection FLW Preservation Trust Research Center (a gift from Wright's last surviving son, David, and his wife, Gladys, to the Frank Lloyd Wright Home and Studio Foundation in Oak Park, which published them in 1996 as *Frank Lloyd Wright's Fifty Views of Japan, the 1905 Photo Album*).

45. Collection FLW Preservation Trust Research Center.

46. I am grateful to the late Irma Straus, who first pointed out this relationship to me. See Kevin Nute, *Frank Lloyd Wright and Japan: The Role of Traditional Japanese Art and Architecture in the Work of Frank Lloyd Wright* (New York: Van Nostrand Reinhold, 1993), 22–25.

47. Edgar Kaufman Jr., "Crisis and Creativity: Frank Lloyd Wright, 1904–1914," *Journal of the Society of Architectural Historians* 25, no 4 (1966): 292–96; photograph, Collection FLW Preservation Trust Research Center.

48. Collection FLW Preservation Trust Research Center; FLW, *The Japanese Print, An Interpretation* (1912; rpt. New York: Horizon Press, 1967), 24, 32.

49. Hamilton, *Frank Lloyd Wright and Book Arts*, 3, 73, 74; Elaine Harrington, *Henry Hobson Richardson, J. J. Glessner House, Chicago*, (Tubingen/Berlin: Wasmuth, 1993).

50. Hanks, *Decorative Designs*, 215.

51. Maginel Wright Barney, *The Valley of the God-Almighty Joneses* (Spring Green, Wis.: Spring Green Publications, 1986), 135; Collection FLW Preservation Trust Research Center; Mary Jane Hamilton, "Maginel Wright Barney: An Artist in Her Own Right," *Wisconsin Academy Review*, Fall 1992, 4–11.

52. Art Institute of Chicago, *Circular of Instruction for 1898–99 with Catalog of Students* (Chicago: Art Institute of Chicago, 1899), 140, 149, 168.

53. Hanks, *Decorative Designs*, 215–17.

54. Alberta Bancroft, *Lost Village* (New York: George H. Doran, 1927), following 52. Collection FLW Preservation Trust Research Center.

55. Maginel Wright Enright Barney file, assembled 1991, FLW Preservation Trust Research Center.

56. David Wright to Donald G. Kalec, 11 November 1975, Collection FLW Preservation Trust Research Center.

57. Private collection, viewed by the author, November 1988.

58. A copy of the contract between the two, dated 22 September 1909, supplied in 1951 by architect and friend William Gray Purcell, is in the collection of the Burnham Library of the Art Institute of Chicago; Anthony Alofsin, *Frank Lloyd Wright, the Lost Years, 1910–1922: A Study of Influence* (Chicago: University of Chicago Press, 1993), 311, 312, is an excellent source for Wright's years immediately following Oak Park.

59. Klinkow, *Wright Family Library*, 18.

60. Alofsin, *Frank Lloyd Wright, the Lost Years*, 41–43.

61. Montgomery Schuyler, "An Architectural Pioneer: Review of the Portfolios Containing the Works of Frank Lloyd Wright," *Architectural Record* 31, no. 4 (1912): 427.

62. Frank Lloyd Wright, *Ausgeführte Bauten und Entwürfe von Frank Lloyd Wright* (Berlin: Ernst Wasmuth, 1910); and Frank Lloyd Wright, *Frank Lloyd Wright: Ausgefuhrte Bauten*, no. 8 in the series Sonderheft der Architectur des XX Jahrhunderts (Berlin: Ernst Wasmuth, 1911). See Langmead, *Frank Lloyd Wright*, for the many editions of these two titles.

63. Collection FLW Foundation Archives, Scottsdale, Ariz., communication from Bruce Brooks Pfeiffer, director, 12 January 2005.

64. Th. Wijdeveld, ed., *The Life Work of the American Architect Frank Lloyd Wright* (Santpoort, Holland: C. A. Mees, 1925).

65. Linda M. Kruger, "Home Libraries: Special Spaces, Reading Places," in *American Home Life, 1880–1930: A Social History of Spaces and Services*, ed. Jessica H. Foy and Thomas J. Schlereth (Knoxville: University of Tennessee Press, 1997), 94–95.

66. Lionel Casson, *Libraries in the Ancient World* (New Haven: Yale Nota Bene, 2001), 82.

67. Candace M. Volz, "The Modern Look of the Early Twentieth Century House: A Mirror of Changing Lifestyles," in Foy and Schlereth, *American Home Life*, 35; Mary Lynn Stevens Heininger, *At Home with a Book: Reading in America, 1840–1940* (Rochester, N.Y.: Strong Museum, 1986), 3–5.

68. "Suggestions for Interior Decoration, Part IV, The Library," *Building* V (September 11, 1886): 123–24; Heininger, *At Home with a Book*, 17–19, 28.

69. James F. O'Gorman, "Catalog," in *H. H. Richardson and His Office*, 74.

70. Clarence Cook, *The House Beautiful* (New York: North River Press, 1980), 165–68.

71. Carla Lind, *Lost Wright: Frank Lloyd Wright's Vanished Masterpieces* (New York: Simon & Schuster, 1996), 40; Winslow House file, FLW Preservation Trust Research Center.

72. Storrer, *Companion*, 10–180.

73. Ibid., 181–467.

74. FLW, *Autobiography*, 169.

75. Hanks, *Decorative Designs*, 34, 93, 115.

76. FLW, "The Cardboard House," in *The Future of Architecture*, 153.

77. Jonathan Lipman and Neil Levine, *The Wright State: Frank Lloyd Wright in Wisconsin* (Milwaukee: Milwaukee Art Museum, 1992), 12, 13.

78. Hamilton, *Frank Lloyd Wright and Book Arts*, 66–70, 74; Alofsin, *Frank Lloyd Wright, the Lost Years*, 308, 309.

XI

WRIGHT AND MELVILLE'S CHIMNEY

James F. O'Gorman

As is well known, between 1889 and 1909, Frank Lloyd Wright developed a suburban, middle-class domestic building type known as the Prairie House.[1] Simply described, this was a hearth-centered, frequently cruciform or quasi-cruciform plan realized in three dimensions as a broad masonry core from which low, floating, horizontal roofs covering the arms of the house radiated out into a typically wooded surrounding landscape. The type appeared in embryonic form in the house he designed for his own family in Oak Park, Illinois (1889) and in the Winslow House in nearby River Forest (1893); it was unveiled in its full maturity in the *Ladies' Home Journal* in 1901; it characterized many of his suburban works of the next decade—including the Willits House in Highland Park, Illinois (1902), the Martin House in Buffalo (1904), the Coonley House in Riverside, Illinois (1908)—and it reappeared in a blaze of glory in the Johnson House of 1937 in Racine, Wisconsin. Since these houses represent as a group some of Wright's finest domestic work, it is of more than passing interest to look at the sources and context of the form and meaning of this house type.

It has been argued—though less and less as we know more and more about Wright's roots—that the Prairie House was a revolutionary phenomenon and therefore presumably without significant indigenous sources and parallels. But although Wright gave the hearth-centered, spreading, cross-planned house its most dramatic expression, it was not in its general plan or in its symbolic content a new idea. In fact, it can be found in one manifestation or another over and over again in American architecture and American literature. In architecture it probably came to Wright directly from the Shingle Style in which he began his career, and thus ultimately from the seventeenth-century New England house with its huge central chimney stack. The origins of the Shingle Style coincide with the rediscovery, about the time of the celebration of the nation's centennial in Philadelphia, of the country's colonial heritage. Buildings such as the Parson Capen House in Topsfield, Massachusetts, were the inspiration for the domestic wooden architecture of the 1880s and 1890s. But the central hearth had not entirely disappeared in the early eighteenth century with the introduction of the Georgian house and its imposing central hall. In fact, it is of no little significance that Thomas Jefferson's first plan for Monticello was cruciform and hearth-centered. I have suggested elsewhere that the Prairie House and other of Wright's work, including his own Taliesin, were distant cousins to Monticello.[2] Nor is it insignificant that the core of the house can be found occupied by the heating unit—a furnace or a stove perhaps replacing the masonry fireplaces—over and over again in the tastemaking pattern books for domestic architecture published from the middle of the nineteenth century on by A. J. Downing, Gervase Wheeler, Catherine Beecher, and many, many others. Indeed, the type was so common in this country in the nineteenth century that the general plan of the Prairie House should probably be described as traditional.

Wright himself thought of it as suburban—if not antiurban—and regional. It was his gift to the dormitory suburbs that ringed the growing cities of the late nineteenth century. It was also a house for the prairie, a conventional representation of our flat midlands. Ideally it had to have room to spread its wings. It had to be low and horizontal in order to pick up the dominant line that for Wright, at least abstractly, characterized the landscape of the midwestern plains. In the architect's mind the Prairie House enjoyed the freedom of the American land, if only the suburban middle landscape, and thus represented the appropriate abode for the free American citizen.

The context of the Prairie House was, however, more than architectural. Wright's stated attitude toward the past always stressed ideas rather than form. He drew inspiration from those nineteenth-century authors who had struggled with the problem of defining America and urged that her distinct qualities be recognized in her society, culture, and politics. When Wright built, he tried to follow their lead; he sought an American and therefore a democratic architecture.

He once listed the sources he would acknowledge. The last page of the second edition of his *Autobiography* (1943) contains what Wright idiosyncratically called an "Index." We would call it a selected bibliography of his intellectual sources, for it lists a few of those writers whose works he had "long ago consulted and occasionally remembered." It contains a mixed assortment but hardly a complete inventory of the thinkers and authors he admired, beginning with the ancient philosopher Pythagoras and ending with the liberal economist Silvio Gesell. It includes the Americans Walt Whitman, Henry George, Thoreau, and Thorstein Veblen but omits Emerson, a man we know he read. The only architect mentioned is Louis Sullivan, Wright's *lieber Meister*, and he is included for his thought, not his writings or his buildings. No other document so succinctly shows that Wright's aims were ideological, not merely formal; and no other document so clearly warns the critic who seeks to evaluate Wright's work that one must go beyond mere formal analysis. Wright subscribed to the idea that architecture is a language.

I do not know whether anyone has subjected this list to detailed scholarly analysis, whether anyone has read every one of these authors and systematically tried to trace the origins of Wright's thought, as Sherman Paul once attempted to do for Louis Sullivan.[3] I have no intention of attempting that here, but I *can* demonstrate a parallel between Wright and another of his indexed sources. I neglected to mention above that he also listed Herman Melville, who in specific terms would seem to offer an architect little usable material (unless he were a naval architect, perhaps), although Vicki Litman long ago pointed out "Melville's symbolic use of architecture."[4] But there is one minor work by that writer in which the formal and ideological program of the Prairie House is anticipated. I think of it not as a "source" of Wright's ideas but as an element of context for those ideas.

In 1850 Melville moved into a farmhouse called Arrowhead in the shadow of Mt. Graybock, near Pittsfield, in far western Massachusetts; there, between 1853 and 1856, he wrote all his short stories. One of those stories deals with the domestic strain of living within a house that is based on Arrowhead. "I and My Chimney," published in *Putnam's Monthly* for March 1856, describes a domestic feud between the narrator and his wife and daughters about the removal of a mountainous chimney stack that takes up most of the interior. This proto-Thurberesque, seriocomic battle of the sexes is rendered in architecturally symbolic terms, because the wife and daughters want to replace the chimney stack, this symbol of the narrator's manhood, with a grand, central, open, and (we post-Freudians would say) female hallway. The narrator wins in the end, but only at the cost of continuous and total vigilance.[5]

But there was more on Melville's mind when he wrote this short story than the eternal battle between the sexes. The farmhouse, described in detail, is an ancient one. The description suggests the typical New England dwelling that is Arrowhead. In bulk the wood-frame structure is two stories high, broader than tall, and its original gable roof has been replaced at some previous date by a flat or sloping one. The first and most obvious feature of the interior is its huge, pyramidal brick chimney stack which, writes Melville, "among other things, has the center of the house to himself. . . . From the exact middle of the mansion it soars from the cellar, right up through each successive floor, till, four feet square, it breaks water from the ridge-pole of the roof, like an anvil-headed whale." A door in the middle of the front facade gives access to a small entry before the stack from which a stair climbs to the upper floor. The rooms are grouped around the stack: "On all four sides, nearly all the chambers sidled up to the chimney for the benefit of a fireplace. . . . Going through the house, you seem to be forever going somewhere, and getting nowhere. . . . [R]ound and round the chimney you go, and if you arrive at all, it is just where you started." The parallels to the Prairie House are obvious, and so are the differences.

Such old farmhouses were common enough in New England, so despite the similarities between the narrator's home and the Prairie House, we might pay no attention to this story if it were not for the fact that Melville goes far beyond mere description to imbue this domestic establishment with social and political meanings. These, too, coincide with those of Wright. We learn from the first sentence of the story that this is a country house type, and subsequent passages demonstrate not only Melville's pro-rustic but his antiurban bias.[6] Cities are confining and dehumanizing, he tells us; there, men and their architecture forget their places in the natural order. "In the cities, where lots are sold by the inch, small space is to spare for a chimney constructed on magnanimous principles; and, as with most thin men, who are generally tall, so with such houses, what is lacking in breadth must be made up in height. . . . In towns there is a large rivalry in building tall houses. If one gentleman builds his house four stories high, and another . . . builds five stories high, then the former . . . claps a fifth and a sixth story on top of his previous four. . . . Such folks, it seems to me, need mountains for neighbors." Melville's fictional narrator's house is by contrast relatively low and spreading: "For wide houses hereabouts there is plenty of room, and cheap." But cheap as is the land, "I, for one, am proud of it for what it bears; and chiefly its three great lions—the Great Oak, Ogg Mountain, and my chimney, . . . a free citizen of this free land." Over and over again Wright echoed these sentiments, that the city dweller was a prisoner, that the freedom of the American could be expressed only through rural or semirural architecture, that a free man could find fulfillment only around the focal hearth in the center of a spacious, natural environment. These ideas found visible form in Wright's Prairie and later Usonian houses and in the utopian noncity he called Broadacres.

But Melville's house is not only a defiantly antiurban type. It is one in which, ironically enough in view of the struggle that is the central action of the story, domestic intercourse is reinforced and symbolized. The hearth is the focal point of the domestic life; in fact, it takes on an almost religious significance. The chimney is a "grand high altar . . . right worthy for the celebration of High Mass before the Pope of Rome and all his cardinals." In houses with a central hall and multiplicity of chimney stacks, the family is divided: "While one member of the household is warming himself at a fire built into a recess of the north wall . . . [his brother] may be holding his feet to the blaze before a hearth in the south wall—the two thus fairly sitting back to back. Is this well? . . . Has it not a sort of sulky appearance?" The hearth-centered house has the opposite effect. Melville's narrator's home has "one grand chimney, upon all four sides of which are hearths—two tiers of hearth—so that when, in various chambers, my family and guests are warming themselves of a cold winter's night . . . though at the time they may not be thinking so, all their faces mutually look towards each other, yea, all their feet point to one center; and, when they go to sleep in their beds, they all sleep round one warm chimney, like so many Iroquois Indians in the woods, round one heap of embers."

Not only is the oversized chimney stack in the Prairie House the quasi-religious—Norris Kelly Smith called it "sacramental"[7]—and age-old symbol of familial domesticity, as Melville uses it here, but Wright could almost have had these passages in mind when he described the very late Prairie House built for the Herbert Johnsons near Racine. The house "is of the common 'prairie type' of earlier years," he wrote. "At the center of the four zones [wings] forming a cross, a spacious wigwam of a Living Room stands. A tall central brick chimney stack with five fireplaces on four sides divides this roomy . . . space into four spaces for the various domestic functions. . . . Extending from this greatly dignified, lofty central wigwam are the four wings. This extended . . . plan lies, very much at home, quiet and integral with the prairie landscape which is, through it, made more significant and beautiful."[8] The Johnson House was not only the last of the Prairie Houses in Wright's work; it was also a recapitulation in the architect's mind of that architectural type.

I must repeat that I do not see in Melville's story the "source" of Wright's iconography. Since "I and My Chimney" was published in a periodical long before Wright's birth, and not republished as far as I know until after Wright had developed, and temporarily abandoned, the Prairie House type, it is doubtful that he could have known this specific story in the early years of his career. Melville was scarcely read before his "rediscovery" in the 1920s by Lewis Mumford and others. Yet the ideas expressed there were widespread in the second half of the nineteenth century, not only within the confines of the architectural world but in literature as well. The very personal relationship between man and hearth, for example, is expressed over and over again. At midcentury Thoreau (who, as we have seen, also appears in Wright's "Index") wrote in *Walden* of the fireplace as "the most vital part of the house.... It was I and the Fire that lived together."[9] In "The Fireplace," a short story published in 1906, midwesterner Hamlin Garland echoed, with less humor but greater poignancy, Melville's earlier tale of a man seeking domestic peace at his hearth.[10] Melville, Thoreau, Garland, and a host of other writers were merely expressing in verbal language a common attitude of the nineteenth century. In the Prairie House, Wright summed up that attitude in a dramatic architectural statement.

NOTES

1. The literature on Wright is vast and yet ever expanding. For an overview, see Neil Levine, *The Architecture of Frank Lloyd Wright* (Princeton: Princeton University Press, 1996).

2. James F. O'Gorman, *Three American Architects: Richardson, Sullivan, and Wright, 1865–1915* (Chicago: University of Chicago Press, 1991); this essay is summarized on page 139.

3. Sherman Paul, *Louis Sullivan: An Architect in American Thought* (Englewood Cliffs, N.J.: Prentice-Hall, 1962). Vincent Scully, with characteristically sweeping veracity, once wrote that "Wright was heir, in architecture ... of a tradition, in part Jeffersonian, which had previously found its best expression in the works of Melville, Whitman, and Mark Twain." Scully, *Frank Lloyd Wright* (New York: George Braziller, 1960), 11.

4. Vicki Halper Litman, "The Cottage and the Temple: Melville's Symbolic Use of Architecture," *American Quarterly* 21 (1969): 630–38.

5. Herman Melville, *Billy Budd and Other Prose Pieces* vol. 13 of *The Works of Herman Melville*, ed. R. W. Weaver (London: Constable, 1924), 276–311. See also Stuart C. Woodruff, "Melville and His Chimney," *Publication of the Modern Language Association* 75 (June 1960): 283 et seq. My thanks to John McCoubrey for bringing Melville's story to my attention. There are many scholarly interpretations of it, such as that in William Dillingham, *Melville's Short Fiction* (Athens: University of Georgia Press, 1977). I prefer my own.

6. Morton and Lucia White discuss Melville's antiurban bias but do not mention this story in *The Intellectual versus the City from Thomas Jefferson to Frank Lloyd Wright* (Cambridge, Mass.: Harvard University Press, 1962), 46 et seq.

7. Norris Kelly Smith, *Frank Lloyd Wright: A Study in Architectural Content* (Englewood Cliffs, N.J.: Prentice-Hall, 1966), 68–72.

8. Frank Lloyd Wright, *An Autobiography*, 2nd ed. (New York: Duell, Sloan & Pearce, 1943), 476.

9. Quoted in T. M. Brown, "Thoreau's Prophetic Architectural Program," *New England Quarterly* 38 (March 1965): 3–20.

10. Hamlin Garland, *Main-Travelled Roads* (New York: Harper & Row Perennial Classic, 1956), 241–59.

XII

EXOTIC AND AESTHETIC

The Library of Charles Sumner Greene

Edward R. Bosley and Anne E. Mallek

Within these plain and unpretentious houses there are often to be seen marvels of exquisite carving, and the perfection of cabinet work; and surprise follows surprise, as one becomes more fully acquainted with the interior finish of these curious and remarkable dwellings.

Edward S. Morse, *Japanese Homes and Their Surroundings*, 1895 ed.

As principal designer in the southern California firm of Greene & Greene (1894–1922), Charles Sumner Greene (1868–1957), with his younger brother Henry Mather Greene (1870–1954), created compelling works of domestic architecture and decorative arts that today define a rarified niche within the American Arts and Crafts movement. During the first decade of the twentieth century the firm rose from local obscurity to international prominence through the strength of their designs for refined wooden houses and furnishings that celebrated the inherent visual and tactile beauty of superbly crafted materials. A quiet man of slight stature, Charles Greene had a probing curiosity and highly developed intellect. He found inspiration in part through a personal library of books and periodicals that allowed him to explore exotic cultures, contemplate alternative spiritual paths, and satisfy his steady thirst for creative stimuli in art, architecture, and design. Based near Los Angeles in the suburb of Pasadena, neither Charles nor his brother ever traveled to

Japan, yet his investigations of that country through numerous books, popular and obscure, informed the unique amalgam of Occidental and Oriental design themes that permeate the firm's most noted work. Equally important to Charles Greene were his periodicals, particularly *The International Studio*, which he annotated with references to design motifs and methods of fabrication. The firm's own work was also published in the monthly magazine. We seek to identify important themes and influences that emerge from the books, magazines, and other bibliographic evidence that remain following the dispersal of Charles Greene's library and personal papers into institutional and private hands after his death.

Through Western Eyes

Among the most demonstrably influential texts in Charles Greene's library was his second-edition copy (1895) of *Japanese Homes and Their Surroundings* by Edward Sylvester Morse. A renowned naturalist, Morse (1838–1925) had traveled initially to Japan in 1877 to study brachiopods. While there, he was offered a position as professor of biology at Tokyo Imperial University, where he taught until 1879. Becoming an avid scholar of Japanese culture and art, Morse amassed and meticulously catalogued a significant collection of rare Japanese ceramics and other artifacts which today form the basis of major holdings at the Museum of Fine Arts, Boston, and the Peabody Essex Museum in Salem. He also recorded his observations of Japanese life and illustrated hundreds of details typical of urban and rural domestic construction. Charles Greene's copy of *Japanese Homes and Their Surroundings* is signed in his distinctive hand and dated "Dec. 1, '03." By that date, the Greene & Greene firm had been active in Pasadena for ten years, garnering commissions among elite, mostly midwestern families who wintered there.[1]

Interestingly, the significance of the book's date of purchase relates directly to the firm's work in progress at that moment. Greene & Greene had recently designed its first house in the Arts and Crafts idiom. The James Culbertson House of 1902 was modeled on an American adaptation of an English country house designed by the Boston architect Ralph Adams Cram.[2] Filled with Gustav Stickley's newly marketed United Crafts furniture, the house was a showcase of the emerging Craftsman style. But merely to replicate the accepted Anglo-American Arts and Crafts aesthetic would not satisfy the Greenes for long. By the following year, just before Charles signed and dated his copy of *Japanese Homes*, they had begun design work on the Arturo Bandini House in Pasadena, a family residence with a U-shaped, courtyard

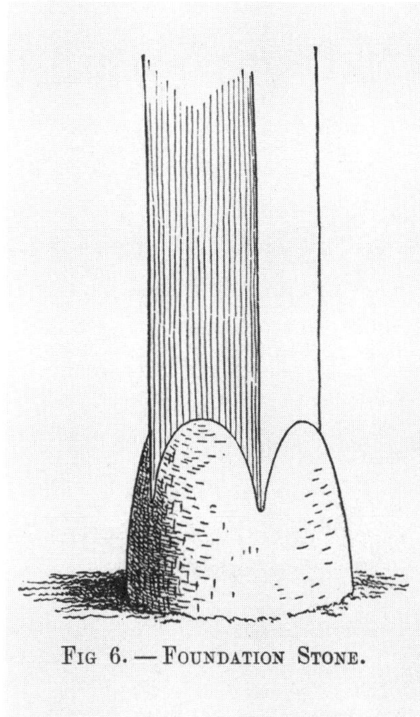

FIG 12.1 Greene & Greene, Arturo Bandini House, Pasadena, Calif., 1903. Exterior detail. Greene & Greene Archives, The Gamble House, University of Southern California.

FIG 12.2 From Edward S. Morse, *Japanese Homes and Their Surroundings* (1895), p. 16. Charles Sumner Greene's copy. Greene & Greene Archives, The Gamble House, University of Southern California.

plan that recalled the Spanish Colonial heritage of its owner. The construction details, however, revealed features common to Japanese homes almost exactly as they were illustrated in Morse. The book had instantly become a design resource for Greene & Greene. The covered walkway that defines the interior of the courtyard plan, for example, is nearly identical to the Japanese use of covered walkways as shown in Morse, even to the supporting posts whose bases are carved out to rest on irregularly shaped stones (figures 12.1, 12.2). According to Morse, "Nearly all the houses have a verandah, which is protected by the widely-overhanging eaves of the roof, or by a light supplemental roof projecting from beneath the eaves. . . . The uprights rest directly, and without attachment, upon single uncut or rough-hewn stones, these in turn resting upon others which have been solidly pounded into the earth."[3]

In the following year, 1904, the Greenes designed a house for Jennie Reeve in Long Beach, California, which also drew from Morse, this time in its treatment of a stone path in the garden. Later work for James Culbertson seems likely to have caused Charles Greene to refer to Morse again in 1909 in his design for a carved redwood panel that depicts overlapping mountain ranges. It is very nearly identical to one described in Morse: "At Nagoya, in the house of a poor man, I saw a simple and ingenious form of *ramma*, in which two thin boards, one of light and the other of dark cedar, had been cut in the form of mountain contours. These were placed in juxtaposition, and from either side the appearance of two ranges of mountains was conveyed" (figures 12.3, 12.4).[4]

Though influential, Morse's book was not Charles Greene's sole source of Japanese inspiration. He also owned a copy of *The Ornamental Arts of Japan* by George Ashdown Audsley, a folio-sized publication with hundreds of plates from which he could glean details of the fine and decorative arts, including drawing, painting, engraving, printing, embroidery, lacquer, metal work, cloisonné enamel, and carving. Of particular interest to Greene may have been an illustration for the essay "Incrusted Work," which depicts a decorated panel with inlay that is uncannily reminiscent of the Greenes' work for their most favored clients (figure 12.5). Portions of the brief text that accompanies the illustration may have piqued Charles Greene's interest:

> Who, in our country of sand-paper finish and French polish, would dream of adopting a decayed and weather-worn piece of wood as a groundwork for elaborate and costly ornamentation? Yet we see that the Japanese artist not only adopts such a groundwork when it naturally comes to his hand, but that he sets himself, as in the present instance, to laboriously cut and carve a fresh plank into a marvelous imitation of weather-worn timber; and when he has produced a result which delights his eye with its richness of texture, its light and shade, and a total absence of regularity in its lines, he proceeds to incrust it with carved mother-of-pearl, tortoiseshell, stained ivory, and highly raised gold lacquer.[5]

For his decorative panel designs, Charles Greene scrupulously selected old-growth timber with interesting grain and the distinctive character of age. On these he would sometimes use inlay of fruitwoods and semiprecious stones, as he did in 1909 for David and Mary Gamble's bedroom suite in black walnut. On others he would employ bits of ivory, jade, contrasting woods, or metal wire, as he did to decorate the Gambles' living room letterbox in 1912. Greene also designed redwood boards at the frieze level in the Gambles' living room which were carved to let the

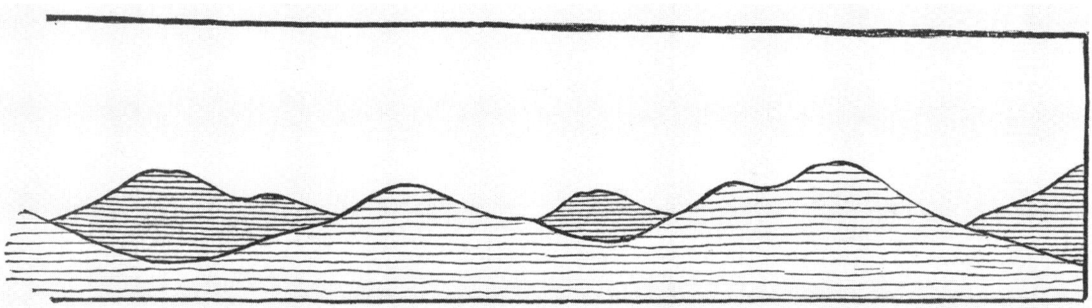

FIG 12.3 Greene & Greene, James A. Culbertson House, Pasadena, 1902–10. Interior detail. Greene & Greene Archives, The Gamble House, University of Southern California.

FIG 12.4 *Ramma* from Morse, *Japanese Homes*, p. 174.

character of the grain express directly the composition of the scenic representations. Still other panels, such as the frieze in the second-floor hallway of the R. R. Blacker House (1907), were brushed with wire to bring the darker, late-season grain of the redwood into low relief. Methods such as these were described in the slim volume on Greene's shelf titled *A Course of Instruction in Wood-Carving according*

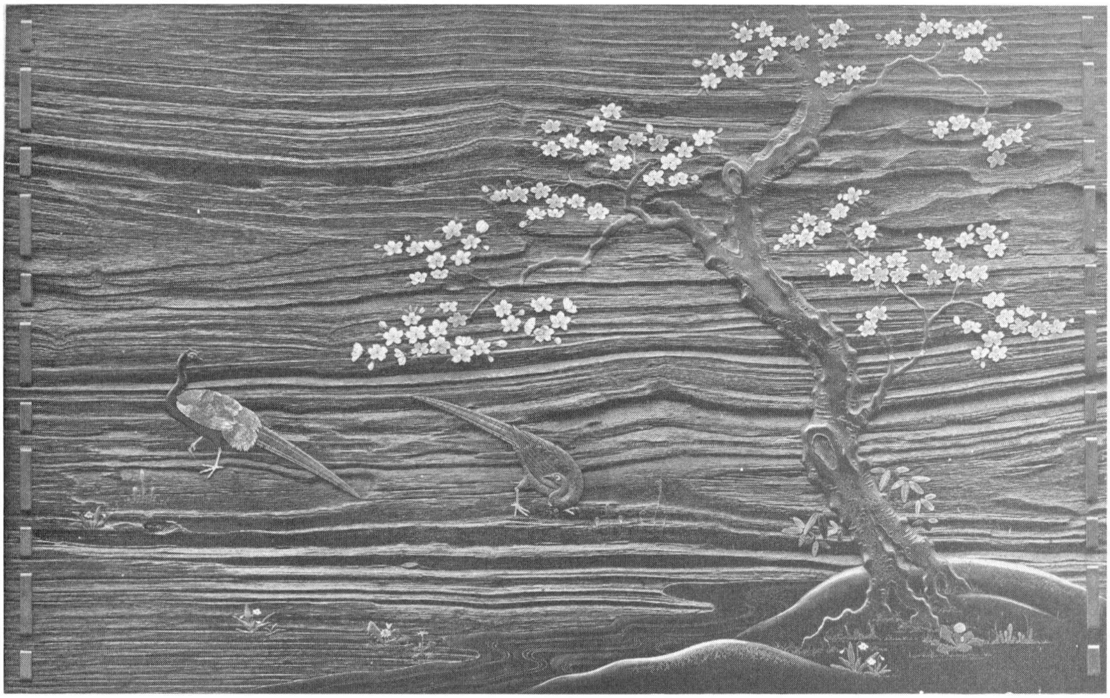

FIG 12.5 George Ashdown Audsley, *The Ornamental Arts of Japan* (1882), sec. 5, plate 6. Greene & Greene Archives, The Gamble House, University of Southern California.

to the Japanese Method, published in London in 1899. Other ideas may have come from numbers of *The Kokka: An Illustrated Monthly Journal of the Fine and Applied Arts of Japan and Other Eastern Countries*, of which Charles Greene collected several examples from the years 1907–14.

Although Japanese art and design were of particular interest to Charles Greene, he did not neglect to study the Japanese people themselves. Greene owned seven books by Lafcadio Hearn (1850–1904), an American author of Irish-Greek descent who made Japan his home for the last fourteen years of his life, married the daughter of a Samurai family, became a Japanese citizen, and adopted the name Yakumo Koizumi. Because he took on his exotic identity with particular zeal, he was sometimes said by the Japanese to be at least as Japanese as the Japanese themselves. Greene's books by Hearn included both volumes of his classic *Glimpses of Unfamiliar Japan*; *Kokoro: Hints and Echoes of Japanese Inner Life*; *In Ghostly Japan*; and *Japan: An Attempt at Interpretation*, which reflected the author's struggle to explain the inner mind of the Japanese.[6]

Hearn's evocative and atmospheric observations doubtless provided Greene with a sense of mystery and wonder about the country, but another book in his library, *A History of the Japanese People* by F. Brinkley, would have augmented subjective impressions with historical fact. Brinkley's text is dense with detail, including an analysis of each imperial era, leading up to and including the political and social climate that had brought about trade agreements between Japan and the outside world by the 1850s and 1860s. Other titles related to Japan on Charles Greene's shelves included both a particularly beautiful portfolio of eighty lithographs of Japanese designs for textiles, *Etoffes Japonaises*, and the popular *European and Japanese Gardens*, which included essays on English gardens by Greene's one-time employer R. Clipston Sturgis and an essay on French gardens by John Galen Howard, dean of the University of California's Department of Architecture and later a close friend of Charles Greene. The chapter "Japanese Landscape Gardening" by K. Honda describes the codification of types, such as "flat" and "hill" gardens, with illustrations of garden features not unlike those the Greenes designed for their client Adelaide Tichenor in Long Beach, California (1904), and the Gambles in Pasadena (1908).[7]

Application and Practice

Beyond Japonism, Greene's book-collecting interests encompassed science, aesthetics, religion, the building arts, and—to a more modest degree—literature. His reputation as a dreamy and distractible artist-architect is founded in reliable documentation, but it would be careless to underestimate his practical side. Among the books in his library that reflect an underlying pragmatism was *Rational and Applied Mechanics*, rev. ed. (St. Louis: Nixon-Jones, 1915) by Calvin Milton Woodward, founder of the Manual Training School of Washington University in St. Louis. Woodward had been the first to bring manual training to teenage boys in America. In teaching polytechnic courses at the university level in the late 1870s, he was alarmed to discover that most young men had an inadequate knowledge of tools, how to make and use them. He set out to correct this lack by offering a course of study to boys aged fourteen to seventeen which would include machine toolmaking, woodworking, and other practical instruction alongside the academic subjects typically covered at the secondary level. Both Charles and Henry Greene attended Woodward's school in St. Louis before enrolling at the Massachusetts Institute of Technology in Boston to study architecture, and they credited their later success partly to the practical training they had received at the hands of Woodward. The date of the book, twenty-eight years after Charles had left the school, suggests that Woodward's influence persisted well into the Greenes' professional lives.[8]

Practical books on building constituted a significant portion of Greene's library, among them the classic *Builder's Golden Rule* by William Pain (London, 1787), and John Crunden's *Carpenter's Companion* (London, n.d.), which was inscribed in 1799 by Greene's great-grandfather, the Boston housewright Thomas Waldron Sumner. Later works typical of this genre included *Rules for Grading of California White Pine and Sugar Pine Lumber* (San Francisco, 1916), *Natural Woods and How to Finish Them* (n.p., 1894), *Hints and Practical Information for Cabinet-Makers, Upholsterers, and Furniture Men Generally* (New York, 1899), and *Mixed Metals or Metallic Alloys* by Arthur H. Hiorns (London, 1901), which was purchased by Greene in London in August 1909. Greene's interest in the life sciences was primarily mainstream and included Charles Darwin's *Expression of the Emotions in Man and Animals* (New York, 1892). He owned copies of Eadweard Muybridge's two classics, *Animals in Motion* and *The Human Figure in Motion*, as well as Ernest Brucke's *The Human Figure* (London, 1891). Most notable among Greene's books treating the intersection of art and science was the influential nineteenth-century treatise on color theory, *The Principles of Harmony and Contrast of Colours, and Their Applications to the Arts*, by Michel-Eugène Chevreul (1786–1889), who trained as a chemist and supervised the preparation of dyes at Gobelin, the French carpet- and tapestry-maker. He submitted that optics played a greater role than chemistry in affecting how colors were perceived, which led him to the notion that adjacent colors will always appear to be as dissimilar as possible. Charles Greene paid close attention to color harmony in his work, often experimenting until a visually sympathetic effect was achieved.[9]

Aesthetics and Spirit

Greene's books devoted to the fine and applied arts and related subjects show a robust and wide-ranging interest in painting and engraving, pottery and porcelain, garden design, Gothic cathedrals, Classical orders, and architectural decoration. Charles Greene was tempted by the picturesque, as evidenced by his copy of Peter H. Ditchfield's *English Cottages and their Doorway Gardens* (Philadelphia, 1905). In 1915 he journeyed to San Francisco to see the Pan-Pacific International Exposition, and his supplier of architectural terra cotta, Gladding McBean &

Company, gave him a signed copy of Louis Christian Mullgardt's *Architecture and Landscape Gardening of the Exposition,* published by Paul Elder. While in San Francisco he purchased *Gardening in California*, written by John McLaren (1909), the Scottish-born horticulturist who developed Golden Gate Park, transforming it from 1,100 acres of sand dunes into verdant meadows and forests over his fifty-six-year tenure as park superintendent. Greene was interested in the antique, as well, having on his shelf titles such as *Old Greek Life* (New York, n.d.), and *Dictionary of Greek and Roman Antiquities* (London, 1842). Like William Morris, interested in forgotten technologies as they related to the arts, he owned a copy of *Stained Glass of the Middle Ages* by Hugh Arnold and Lawrence B. Saint (this title was also in the library of William Morris's firm).[10]

Titles in religion and mysticism attracted Greene, too, especially following his move in 1916 from Pasadena to the central California artists' colony of Carmel-by-the-Sea. In Carmel, Charles distanced himself from the practice of architecture (with the notable exception of the D. L. James House, 1918–22), and by the early 1930s he had chosen to devote himself to the study of Buddhism, theosophy, and other contemplative disciplines. Author T. W. Rhys-David's *Buddhism* and *Buddhist Birth Stories* were among the books Greene bought during this period, as was G. I. Gurdjieff's tract, *The Herald of Coming Good*, published in Paris in 1933. In its preface the Gurdjieff text promises, among other things, to show the reader "how to attain the knowledge of the way leading to Real Being," which reflected Charles Greene's state of self-observation and searching at that time. *Amulets and Superstitions* by E. H. Wallis-Budge shared Greene's shelf space with the same author's *Babylonian Life and History* (London, 1925) and *From Fetish to God in Ancient Egypt* (Oxford, 1934). Charles Greene took part in the social and artistic culture of Carmel alongside such luminaries as writers Robinson and Una Jeffers and photographer Edward Weston. His copy of Weston's 1932 folio of images, produced by fine-press publisher Merle Armitage, is inscribed "Charles; artist, friend. Edward." The occasional salons on Buddhism and theosophy that were held in Greene's Carmel studio were attended by local figures, including Dora Hagemeyer, whose privately published poem *Songs of the Green Flame* (Oceano, Calif., 1930), she inscribed to Charles "With sincere friendship." Perhaps foremost among the titles that captured his attention during this period, however, was Claude Bragdon's *The Beautiful Necessity: Seven Essays on Theosophy and Architecture.* Greene transcribed significant portions of the book, including illustrations with embedded text, apparently during the late 1920s or early 1930s. These transcriptions remained among his personal papers until his death.

Bragdon sets out for the reader specific "laws of beauty," which, in his theoretical framework, use nature to suggest proportion and decoration in architecture.[11] This framework must have appealed to Charles Greene, whose Carmel studio (1923–24) shows the influence, particularly in the symbols such as waves, crabs, and shells that he carved into the studio's redwood doors and beams.[12] In Bragdon, the crab demonstrates the "Law of Radiation," whereas the wave form and spiral shell illustrate the "Law of Rhythmic Diminution" (figure 12.6).[13]

The International Studio

In a letter to his client James A. Culbertson, in October 1902, Charles Greene wrote, "The suggestions enclosed in your letter for the living room pleased me very much, as I am in thorough sympathy with the Wm. Morris movement, in fact the whole inside of the house is influenced by it in design."[14] Although William Morris had died six years before, the achievements of his decorative arts firm and the legacy of his theories concerning the purpose and production of beautiful objects were evident across Europe, even extending overseas to influence the work of a young architect in southern California.[15] The spate of international exhibitions that had begun in 1851 with London's Great Exhibition of the Industry and Works of All Nations (familiarly known as the Crystal Palace) greatly facilitated the transmission of Morris's ideas. In addition, art periodicals sprang up in many countries, further encouraging design cross-fertilization and allowing architect-designers such as Charles Greene to keep abreast of developments in international architecture and design.

The London-based publication *The Studio: An Illustrated Magazine of Fine and Applied Art* may have been the most qualified periodical to disseminate the ideals of William Morris and the Arts and Crafts movement.[16] As well as possessing an international distribution, it was also one of the most widely read of the contemporary art periodicals, being of interest to the professional artist as well as the artistically curious. Articles in the *Studio* ranged from reports on current exhibitions to explanations of new artistic processes and art movements. It was frequently the first magazine to publish the work of such artists as C. F. A. Voysey, M. H. Baillie Scott, Aubrey Beardsley, Josef Hoffmann, and Peter Behrens, in addition to the output of minor and unknown artists through magazine-sponsored competitions. All were keen to model themselves on Morris's example: Gustav Stickley was acclaimed as "the American William Morris"; C. R. Ashbee, the Cotswold

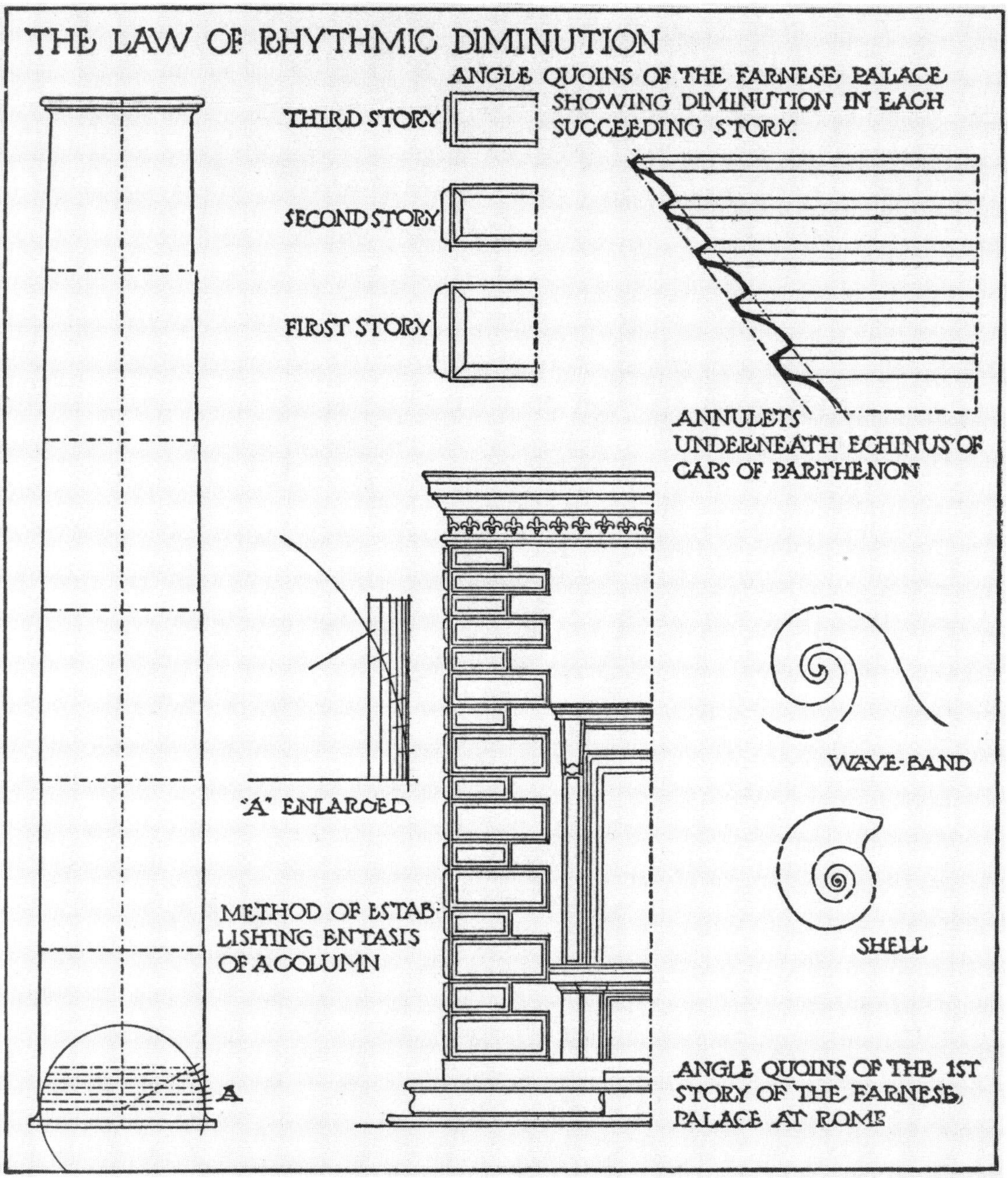

FIG 12.6 "Laws of Beauty" from Claude F. Bragdon, *The Beautiful Necessity* (1910), p. 57.

craftsman who would visit Charles Greene in Pasadena in 1909, also styled himself as the successor to William Morris. It seems no surprise, then, that the founder of the *Studio*, Charles Holme (1848–1923), a merchant-venturer who traded in goods from India and Japan, was uniquely positioned to report on the Arts and Crafts or "Morris Movement": in 1889 he had become the proud owner of Morris's iconic Red House, often cited as the first major work of Arts and Crafts architecture, and the embodiment of one of the central tenets of Morris's philosophy: that the useful could coexist in harmony with the beautiful.[17]

The magazine that Holme created became a kind of artistic scrapbook of its time, an eminently useful resource for the display and discussion of beautiful things. This appears to have been precisely the purpose its issues served for Charles Greene, whose library included a nearly fifteen-year run of the *Studio*'s American counterpart, *The International Studio* (*IS*) (figure 12.7).[18] In almost every volume from 1897 until 1912, Greene inserted place markers noting subject matter and design styles, or instructive articles on such subjects as enameling, carving, or monotyping. The papers he used to bookmark pictures or articles of interest bear his comments, sketches, block prints, and attempts at calligraphy. From some notes and his use of dated materials as markers, it is possible to deduce that Greene did not necessarily look through these volumes in a timely or even chronological fashion; rather, they were a resource to be continually revisited for new ideas and instruction.[19] Their significance, then, is not only as a record of developments in the art world of the late nineteenth and early twentieth centuries but as documentation of Charles Greene's own artistic career.

It seems likely that Greene's own subscription began in 1905, not long after he visited the 1904 Louisiana Purchase Exposition in St. Louis with his client Adelaide Tichenor.[20] At the German and Austrian pavilions there, Greene had seen the work of Peter Behrens and Koloman Moser, purveyors of their countries' innovative lines of industrial art. Behrens's work seems to have been of continuing interest to Greene as he looked through his issues of *IS*, whether for the composition of his interiors or articles of furniture or even garden ornament. Behrens was unique among the seven members of the German Darmstadt Colony for designing the structure, as well as the interior decoration and furnishings, for his home. In a volume from 1901, Greene marked a series of interiors by Behrens, illustrating the article "The Artists' Colony of Darmstadt."[21] One example is the studio door and music room from Behrens's own house. As a graphic artist, Behrens possessed a keen eye for detail that may have held particular appeal for a man like Charles

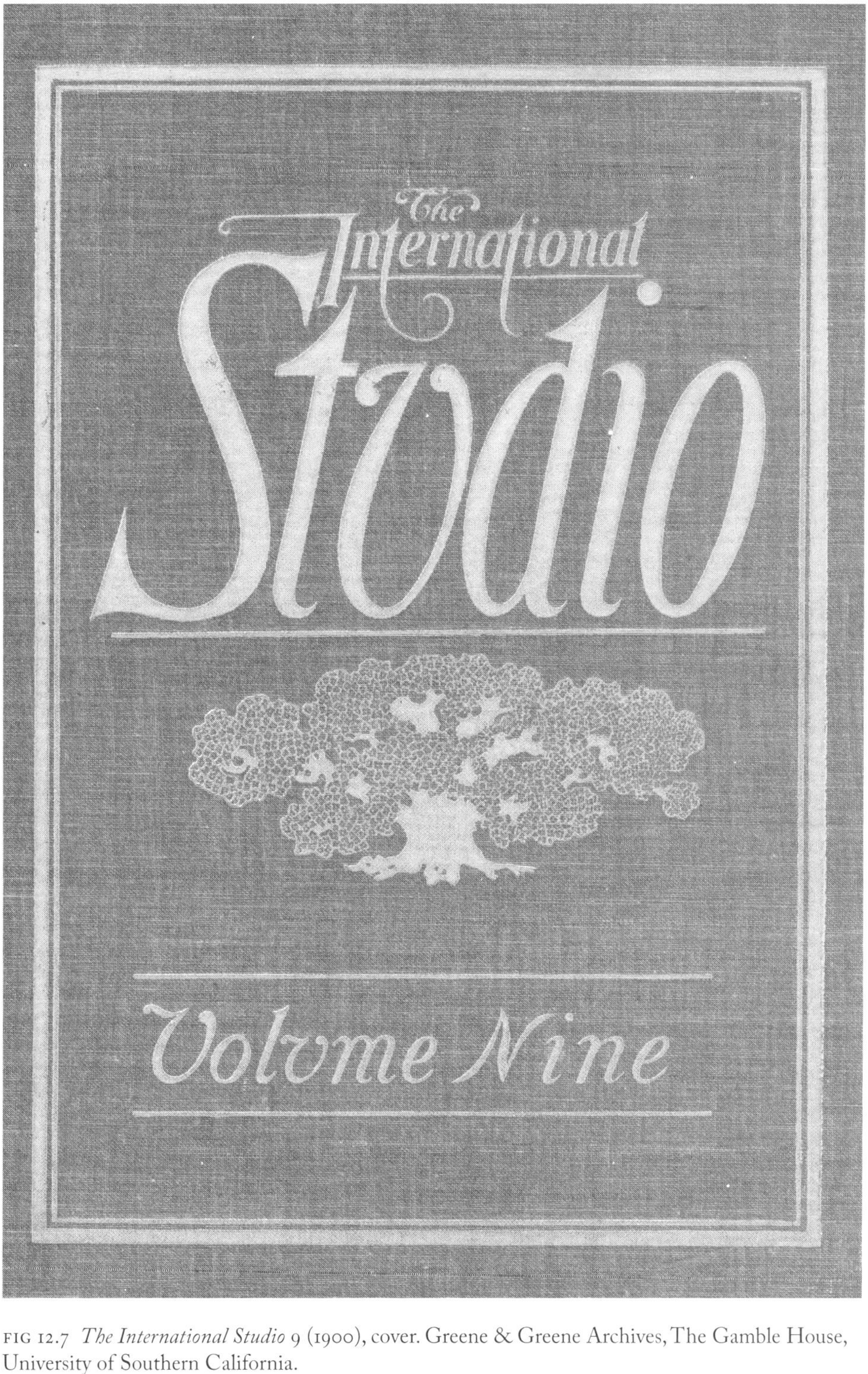

FIG 12.7 *The International Studio* 9 (1900), cover. Greene & Greene Archives, The Gamble House, University of Southern California.

Greene, who felt his true vocation to be that of an artist rather than that of an architect. It may have been the carved motif on the door which caught Greene's eye, especially given its symbolic resonance in relation to the poster produced for the opening of Darmstadt, which had also been Behrens's design: the poster portrays a woman reaching toward a crystal, the shape of it exactly matching that of the carved ovoid shape in the studio door. The attainment of beauty, to give pleasure through the creation of beautiful objects, was the ultimate goal of these artists as it had been for Morris. Years later, Greene wrote to a client about the importance of "this art of helping make living pleasurable and beautiful beyond the merely useful."[22]

Although beauty was often to be found in the intricate details, it was as important to consider the form of an object as it was its substance or decoration. In the *IS* volumes relating to 1904, Greene was especially attuned to the work of Behrens, Baillie-Scott, and Cotswold craftsmen C. R. Ashbee and Ernest Gimson, marking beautifully inlaid cabinets, lanterns, tables, and chairs. In at least two instances he appears to have had certain commissions in mind, specifically the Robert Roe Blacker House and the David B. Gamble House in Pasadena, as in his notes regarding images from the 1902 International Exhibition of Modern Decorative Art at Turin. Although he did not select any examples from that exhibition's Austrian, English, or Scottish sections illustrated in the previous volume, Greene seemed once again keenly interested in the interiors designed by Behrens, as well as others by Anton Huber, Josef Olbrich, and Carl Spindler. One of the notes he used to mark this section reads "RRB," perhaps for Robert Roe Blacker, whose Pasadena home was designed by the Greenes in 1907. On the same note, Greene sketched the posts and backboard of two of the beds illustrated, one by the Italian U. Ceruti, and the other by Spindler (figures 12.8, 12.9). It is possible that the Greenes considered designing beds for the Blacker House as they designed its other bedroom furnishings, especially given the abstract tree motif used for the inlay in the master bedroom, which has previously been attributed to the influence of architect-designers Charles Rennie Mackintosh and C. F. A. Voysey.[23] But it is also very similar to the sketch Charles Greene made, inspired by the designs of Spindler and Ceruti, and thus may demonstrate Greene's talent for synthesizing various styles and motifs, especially as he would be aware of the work of all designers, both from illustrations in *IS* and from international exhibitions.

On the page illustrating the bed by U. Ceruti, Greene notes "Bed and Box / Gamble" (David B. Gamble was another of the Greenes' Pasadena clients, whose house they designed only one year after completing the Blacker House). The beds for the Gamble House are the only ones known to have been designed by the Greenes, though they do not follow the design of either of the beds marked by Charles Greene except that David and Mary Gamble's beds include decoration on both head- and footboards. The "box" or chest also noted does not seem to have been completed, but Greene marked many such chests throughout the *IS* volumes, both carved and inlaid, contemporary and antique, and is known to have employed this form in at least one other commission.[24] Interior design schemes are also marked, which speaks to Greene's focus on holistic design: the idea of each room as a composition, with its own unique theme or motif.

FIG 12.8 Sketch by Charles Sumner Greene on note used to mark page 276 in *The International Studio* 18 (see FIG 12.9). Greene & Greene Archives, The Gamble House, University of Southern California.

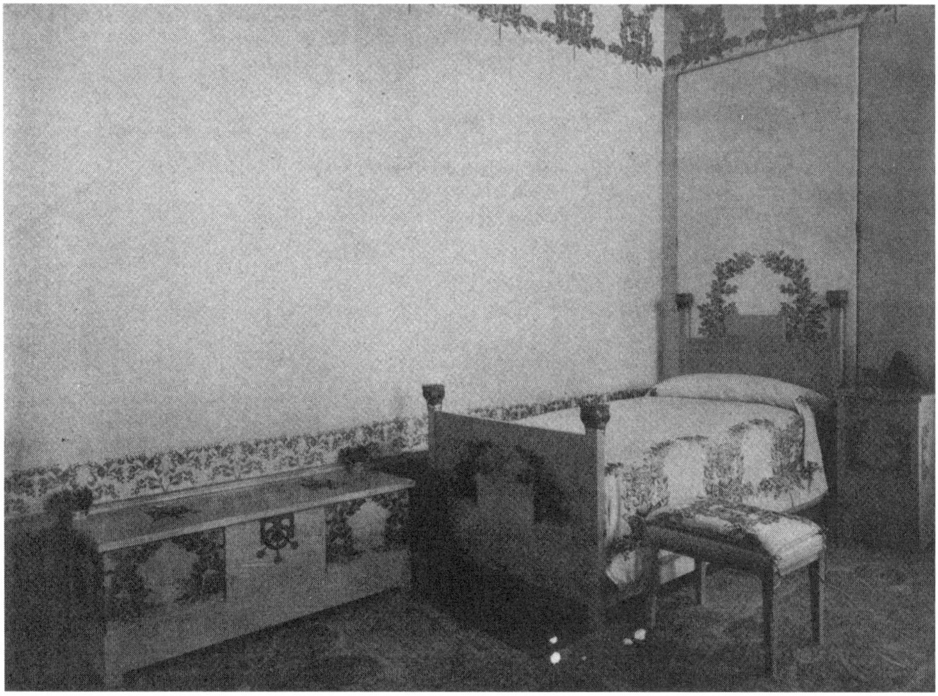

FIG 12.9 U. Ceruti, bedroom. From "The International Exhibition of Decorative Art at Turin (Austrian and Italian sections)," *The International Studio* 18 (1902): 276. Greene & Greene Archives, The Gamble House, University of Southern California.

Also for the Gamble House, for which the Greenes designed some of the only willow furniture of their career, Greene has marked a variety of "wicker work"—Austrian, German, and British—over a series of *IS* issues from 1904 to 1908. These dates are in keeping with the timing of the commission in 1908, and the apparent profusion of wicker illustrations are evidence both of its popularity and of the fact that it merited the attention of other important designers. As well as presenting a design challenge, the materials were relatively inexpensive, allowing for that ideal combination of the useful with the beautiful, and all for a moderate price. None of the chairs illustrated is an exact match with the Gamble chairs, but similar styles such as that of the couch were in Greene's designs.

In the quest for beauty, nothing was too insignificant to be considered; that a simple carved motif in a door could be endowed with such symbolic resonance is testimony to this fact. Nor was large-scale work ignored. It has been suggested that upon his return from a four-month honeymoon traveling around Britain and Europe, Greene may have begun to follow the latest designs in *IS* with renewed interest, having visited Glasgow and the Lake District, where the work of Voysey, Baillie Scott, and Mackintosh would have been in evidence.[25] Charles Greene seems to have shared a great deal with these architects, who brought that remarkable "infinite care and thought" to bear "upon the multiplicity of detail."[26] Even though no notes exist to testify to his interest in some of the architectural plans presented in *IS*, it is possible to assume that Charles would have looked at such articles as "Architectural Gardening" and "Recent Designs in Domestic Architecture," each of which ran as a series in *IS*, showing the work of Baillie Scott, Olbrich, and others. These articles address architecture as an art, a concept taken up by Greene in his 1917 article "Architecture as a Fine Art." The article on the Darmstadt Colony quotes Behrens echoing this sentiment: "Architecture is the art of building, and comprises in its name two ideas: the mastery of the practical, and the art of the beautiful."

The idea of integration or holism was essential to Arts and Crafts philosophy, as so many of its participants followed Morris's example of cultivating the skills of an architect as well as those of a craftsman and even landscape designer. The architect M. H. Baillie Scott, no exception to this rule, was a great proponent of the integration of housing and site. In fact, he had initially trained at the Royal Agricultural College in preparation for managing his father's estates in Australia, before his interest in architecture emerged. Charles Greene also made an effort to integrate prominent environmental features in his architectural plans (e.g., the accommodation of eucalyptus or oak trees in the design of a roof line or patio). The planning and decoration of a garden were equally essential, for they were seen as an extension of the living space, as "home in the big, fine sense of the word that leaves the horizon, not four walls, for the boundary lines."[27] This transition was facilitated in many Greene and Greene designs by an open but sheltered sleeping porch. While Greene marked formal garden lanterns designed by Peter Behrens for the Fine Arts and Horticultural Exhibition at Dusseldorf in 1904, he also looked at ancient gardens, many of which, such as that of the Villa d'Este, he had seen first during his honeymoon trip to England and the Continent in 1901. The fountain and water garden were an inspiration for those he designed in 1911–13 for Cordelia Culbertson and her sisters in Pasadena's Oak Knoll neighborhood (figures 12.10, 12.11).[28]

The concept of the leitmotif was not unique to the work of Charles Greene, but he used it to great effect in the homes of some of his wealthier clients, employing

FIG 12.10 Alinari photograph of the Villa d'Este. From "Italy's Private Gardens," *The International Studio* 16 (1902): 182. Greene & Greene Archives, The Gamble House, University of Southern California.

the lotus flower or dogwood blossom to distinguish one room from another. In *IS*, Greene jotted "Grape leaves" in reference to a bacchanalian scene of female nudes situated among grapevines.[29] This may have been an inspiration for the grapevine motif in the stained glass used in the Blacker House stairwell. Another marker in a 1901 volume may refer to the cherry blossoms used in a chandelier for the Laurabelle A. Robinson House (1905–6). The penchant of Japanese watercolor artists for portraying abstracted plant forms or portions of a branch or tree seem to have attracted Greene particularly, as he returns to them over several volumes. This is in keeping with the interest in Japanese architecture and design evidenced by his purchase of Edward Morse's book in 1903, not long before he began subscribing to *IS*.

Another recurring motif in Charles Greene's designs, and one frequently illustrated in *IS*, is the image of the galleon or sailing ship. Indeed, that Greene seemed generally drawn to the rusticity and "practical sentiment" of Scandinavian work is shown in his marking of engravings, carvings, and glass in the Viking Revival

FIG 12.11 Greene & Greene, Cordelia A. Culbertson House, Pasadena, 1911–13, rear terrace, garden, and fountain. Avery Architectural and Fine Arts Library, Columbia University, New York, N.Y.

style.[30] The galleon, a symbol of discovery and conquest, was used by Greene in a variety of media: for the bronze silhouette in the lampshade designed for Adelaide Tichenor;[31] in the gate for the William R. Thorsen House in Berkeley;[32] and finally in the elegantly carved panel that Greene carried out himself in 1923 for Mrs. Willis Walker, illustrating Christopher Columbus's three ships, the Niña, the Pinta, and the Santa Maria.[33] The meaning of such motifs could not have escaped Greene, and even though he might in some instances have been guided by a client's preferences, it is likely that he also chose to portray subject matter for its symbolic resonance as well as its aesthetic potential.

The significance of the integration of the home with its environment cannot be underestimated, as it was this idea of the necessary integration of things natural, material, and spiritual which defined Charles Greene's personal symbolism, "the oneness of all that exists." He goes on in his diary to say that "A symbol, by expressing the knowledge of the laws of unity, has at the same time expressed the path to it"—it is the ultimate form of communication and is "more perfect" than contemporary language.[34] It is perhaps for this reason that Greene identified so closely with the professions of artist and painter versus that of architect, though he made the attempt to define it, too, as "a Fine Art."[35] A series of drawings by Victor Hugo marked by Greene in a 1904 volume demonstrate his interest in the ability of the imagination to extend and magnify a landscape. He also selected a number of what he termed "decorative landscapes," hazy romantic scenes of mountainscapes sprinkled with the blurred forms of trees (figures 12.12, 12.13). Many of the paintings he made in England in 1909 show a similar preoccupation, and it is likely that he would have identified with the description of the work of landscape painter Leon Dabo in a 1909 volume of *IS*: "To give the character of nature, not the feature, by means of the familiar symbols of trees and rocks, of land and sea, of azure vaulting skies and star-bejeweled firmament; to render up the intimate and evasive spirit of things, and to make visible these secret laws by means of line and color—that would seem to be the highest function of the landscape painter."[36]

In addition to painting, woodcarving was a serious interest in Charles Greene's later years, and he utilized some of the themes he marked in *IS* in projects in both media. Greene took his carving very seriously, constructing his own tools and studying books on Japanese carving methods.[37] He marked and made use of trees, fish, birds, mist, clouds, sea foam, and mountain scenes; these became integral to his later design commissions, especially the D. L. James House (1918–22) in the

FIG 12.12 Charles Walter Stetson, *Decorative Landscape*. From "Studio Talk," *The International Studio* 23 (1904): 255. This illustration was included in a review of the annual show organized by the Società Amatori e Cultori, Palazzo delle Belle Arti. Greene & Greene Archives, The Gamble House, University of Southern California.

Carmel Highlands and his own studio in Carmel. The significance of this last work seems to have been to Greene much like that of Red House to William Morris, the only substantial difference being that Greene's studio was created at the end rather than at the beginning of his career. Both buildings symbolize the imaginative and creative achievements of these two men and provided the opportunity to synthesize their work in a variety of media, all imbued with a very personal meaning and created through collaborative effort.

For Charles Greene, issues of *IS* continued to be a resource as late as 1928 and perhaps later still, though his subscription was discontinued after 1912. As an aesthetic and philosophical point of departure, its significance cannot be in doubt. His architecture, his furniture, his personal art and philosophy all seem to have drawn significantly on this resource, though it was one of many. What made it unique among the other reference materials in his library was the fact that it was able to offer such a diverse representation of decorative and fine arts, theory and instruction. This may be why, even forty years after Greene's subscription ended, the *IS* volumes were still to be found on his shelves, not only as a record of his own work but as a reminder of what it shared with other work of its time.

FIG 12.13 Charles Sumner Greene, *Landscape with Trees*, n.d. Ink on paper, 7 × 4 ¾ in. Greene & Greene Archives, The Gamble House, University of Southern California

NOTES

Several of the titles mentioned in this essay are in the collection of The Gamble House, University of Southern California, housed in the Greene and Greene Archives at the Huntington Library's Art Division in San Marino. Other titles were shown on a list published by Cecil Whale Books, Carmel, Calif., in association with a sale at the California International Book Fair in 1993. These had come from the estate of Charles Greene's son, Nathanial Patrickson Greene, after his death. Still others are in the collection of the Environmental Design Archives, University of California–Berkeley. Our sincere thanks go to Cecil Whale; to Ann Scheid, archivist at the Greene and Greene Archives; and to Waverly Lowell, director of the Environmental Design Archives at the University of California–Berkeley, for their cooperation.

1. Edward R. Bosley, *Greene & Greene* (London: Phaidon Press, 2000), chaps. 2–3 describe the brothers' early years in practice in Pasadena.

2. Ibid., 47.

3. Edward S. Morse, *Japanese Homes and Their Surroundings* (1888; New York: Harper, 1895), 15.

4. Ibid., 173–74.

5. George Ashdown Audsley, *The Ornamenal Arts of Japan* (London: Sampson Low, Marston, Searle & Rivington/Scribner's, 1882), vol. 2, sec. 5, plate 6.

6. Lafcadio Hearn, *Glimpses of Unfamiliar Japan* (Boston: Houghton Mifflin/Riverside Press, Cambridge, 1894); *Kokoro: Hints and Echoes of Japanese Inner Life* (Boston: Houghton Mifflin/Riverside Press, Cambridge, 1896); *In Ghostly Japan* (Boston: Little, Brown, 1905); and *Japan: An Attempt at Interpretation* (New York: Macmillan, 1905).

7. F. Brinkley, *A History of the Japanese People* (New York: Encyclopaedia Britannica, 1915); *Etoffes Japonaise: Tissees et Broches* (Paris: Librairie Centrale des Beaux-Arts, n.d.); and *European and Japanese Gardens: Papers Read before the American Institute of Architects*, ed. Glenn Brown (Philadelphia: Henry T. Coates, 1902).

8. Bosley, *Greene & Greene*, 13.

9. Laboratory analysis of paint and stain samples, undertaken during the course of conservation of the Gamble House, have revealed the complex pigment recipes that were used to achieve the desired colors.

10. The copy of Arnold and Saint, *Stained Glass of the Middle Ages* (London: Adam and Charles Black, 1913) once belonging to Morris & Company is at the Huntington Library, San Marino, Calif.

11. Claude Bragdon, *The Beautiful Necessity* (Rochester, N.Y.: Manas Press, 1910; New York: Alfred A. Knopf, 1939), 63.

12. Bosley, *Greene and Greene*, 205.

13. Bragdon, *Beautiful Necessity*, 57 and 59. For more on Bragdon's influence on Greene, see Travis Culwell, "The Spirituality of Charles Sumner Greene" (master's thesis, College of Environmental Design, University of California, Berkeley, 1995).

14. Charles Sumner Greene to James A. Culbertson, Kenilworth, Ill., 7 October 1902; Greene & Greene Archives, Huntington Library, Art Collections, and Botanical Gardens.

15. Morris, Marshall, Faulkner & Company, established 1861, became Morris & Company in 1874. It would have been operating for nearly forty-one years when Charles Greene wrote his letter.

16. Morris was a dominant presence in most art periodicals of the time, including Gustav Stickley's *The Craftsman*, which dedicated its first issue to Morris in October 1901.

17. Holme lived in the house for approximately fourteen years.

18. *International Studio* began in 1897 (simultaneously with the issue of volume 10 of the *Studio*). Charles Greene owned volumes 1–45, covering the years 1897–1912; only volumes 42 and 44 are absent.

19. In volume 9 (1900), Greene used a booklet dated 1903, "Steel Mill Buildings and the Calculation of Stresses in Framed Structures," to mark illustrations from the Arts and Crafts Exhibition of 1899. In volume 14 (1901) he inserted a pamphlet, "1928 Voting Recommendation on Amendments for Monterey County," to mark an article on enameling. Greene thus seemed very willing to look back at these issues, even as long as twenty-seven years after their publication.

20. Charles Greene's set of *International Studio* includes two different bindings. Volumes 1–25 are bound in green cloth, volumes 26–45 in brown cloth, stamped with "C. Sumner Greene," which would seem to suggest that Greene's subscription began in 1905, the issue date of volume 26. This is further substantiated by the fact that Greene's marking is at its most intense over volumes 22 to 25, those issues just preceding the potential date of his subscription. In addition, the fact that he notes such commissions as "Gamble" and "RRB" for Robert Roe Blacker in the 1904 issues shows that he might have been looking at them concurrently with the Blacker House commission in 1906 and with the Gamble House commission in 1908.

21. In 1899 the Grand Duke Ernst Ludwig sponsored the founding of a colony of artists in Darmstadt, Germany. The first exhibition of the colony's work was held in 1901. W. Fred, "The Artists' Colony at Darmstadt," *International Studio* 15 (1901): 22–30.

22. Charles Greene to Mrs. Francis Fleury Prentisss, 15 February 1928.

23. Edward S. Cooke Jr., "Charles Sumner Greene and Henry Mather Greene," in *"The Art That is Life": The Arts & Crafts Movement in America, 1875–1920*, ed. Wendy Kaplan (Boston: Bulfinch Press, 1987), 406.

24. A photograph of the living room in the Laurabelle A. Robinson House in Pasadena, 1905–6, shows a simple wooden chest to the left of the fireplace.

25. Cooke, "Charles Sumner Greene," 406.

26. G. LL. Morris, "Edwin L. Lutyens, FRIBA, Architect of Houses and Gardens," *International Studio* 37 (1909): 274.

27. "The California Bungalow," *Craftsman,* 13 (October 1907): 80.

28. Bosley, *Greene & Greene,* 159.

29. The illustration by Leon V. Solon appeared in *International Studio* 22 (1904).

30. "Studio Talk," *International Studio* 21 (1904): 170. The Viking Revival style developed in response to the archaeological excavations of Viking ships in Norway during the late nineteenth century. Illustrations in *IS* show both new work inspired by the Viking style and antique Viking furniture from the thirteenth and fourteenth centuries.

31. Interestingly, the Chinese vase acquired in St. Louis for use as a lamp base is also illustrated in "The Possibilities of Clay," an article in *International Studio* 32 (1907), though it is not marked by Greene.

32. Thorsen's father had left Norway at the age of fourteen, eventually becoming a sea captain.

33. An illustration in volume 9 showing a carving of the *Pinta* was not specifically marked by Charles, but is part of an article that he did mark: "British Decorative Art in 1899, the Arts & Crafts Exhibition."

34. Notes in Greene's diaries in the Greene & Greene Library, San Marino, Calif.

35. "Architecture as a Fine Art" was the title of an article that Greene wrote in 1917, published in the *Architect* 13 (April 1917): 217–22.

36. J. Nilsen Laurvik, "Leon Dabo—Landscape Painter," *International Studio* 39 (1909): lv–lxii.

37. Charles Holme had a keen interest in the subject as well, having published *A Course of Instruction in Wood Carving according to the Japanese Method* in 1899.

CONTRIBUTORS

JHENNIFER A. AMUNDSON earned a Master of Architecture degree at the University of Illinois, Champaign-Urbana, and a Ph.D. at the University of Delaware. An associate professor of architecture at Judson College, she teaches, writes, and publishes on the history and theory of nineteenth- and twentieth-century architecture. She is the editor of *Thomas Ustick Walter: The Lectures on Architecture.*

EDWARD R. BOSLEY is James N. Gamble Director of the Gamble House in Pasadena, a program of the University of Southern California School of Architecture, located in one of the finest Arts and Crafts houses in America. His publications include *Greene and Greene* and other books and articles related to the Arts and Crafts movement. He lectures widely on the Greenes and on historic preservation.

TED CAVANAGH is an architect in Nova Scotia and chair of the School of Architecture at Clemson University in South Carolina. He holds an architectural degree from McGill University and a doctorate in the history of technology from Lehigh University. His research applies historical understanding of technological innovation to contemporary construction and design.

ELSPETH COWELL holds a Master of Environmental Design degree from Yale University. Her research specializations are architectural working drawings and the professionalization of architects in America. She currently works for the Canadian Centre for Architecture.

KENNETH HAFERTEPE holds a doctorate in American Civilization from the University of Texas at Austin and is now associate professor in the Department of Museum Studies at Baylor University. He is the author of *America's Castle: The Evolution of the Smithsonian Building and Its Institution*, and *Abner Cook: Master Builder on the Texas Frontier*.

ELAINE HARRINGTON holds a master's degree from the Cooperstown Graduate Program. She is the former curator of the Frank Lloyd Wright Home and Studio, Oak Park, Illinois, the Glessner House, Chicago, and the Campbell-Whittlesey House in Rochester, New York. A consultant to the Clarke and Charnley Houses in Chicago and Hemingway's birthplace in Oak Park, Illinois, she has written or lectured about these places as well as about the J. J. Glessner family library, William Morris, and Paisley shawls.

MICHAEL J. LEWIS studied at the University of Pennsylvania and at the University of Hannover and teaches the history of American art and architecture at Williams College. Among his many books are *The Politics of the German Gothic Revival* (which won an Alice Davis Hitchcock Award of the Society of Architectural Historians), *The Gothic Revival,* and *Frank Furness: Architecture and the Violent Mind.*

ANNE E. MALLEK is curator of the Gamble House in Pasadena. In 2002 she organized the exhibition *William Morris: Creating the Useful and the Beautiful* at the Huntington Library, and she helped research and prepare the 2004 exhibition and publication *The Beauty of Life: William Morris and the Art of Design.* She has lectured on Morris and the Arts and Crafts movement in Britain and America.

JAMES F. O'GORMAN is Grace Slack McNeil Professor Emeritus of the History of American Art at Wellesley College and currently chair of the Maine Historic Preservation Commission. He has authored, coauthored, edited, or translated many books and articles on the history of American and European art and architecture. His *Living Architecture: A Biography of H. H. Richardson*, with photographs by Cervin Robinson, won the 1997 Henry-Russell Hitchcock Prize of the Victorian Society in America.

DANIEL D. REIFF is SUNY Distinguished Service Professor Emeritus in the visual arts at Fredonia State University. He is the author of numerous books and articles on American architecture from the eighteenth through the twentieth century, with special interest in the origins of architectural designs. In 2001 his *Houses from Books* received the Historic Preservation Book Prize from the Mary Washington College Center for Historic Preservation.

EARLE G. SHETTLEWORTH, JR., who was appointed to the first board of the Maine Historic Preservation Commission in 1971 and has served as its director since 1976, has written and lectured extensively on Maine history and architecture, especially the work of Portland's John Calvin Stevens. In Augusta he sits on the Blaine House Commission and the State House and Capitol Park Commission, and he chairs the Capitol Planning Commission. In 2004, Governor John Baldacci appointed him the Maine State Historian.

CHRIS SZCZESNY-ADAMS is assistant professor of art history at the Milwaukee Institute of Art and Design. She received a doctorate in architectural history at the University of Virginia. She has researched and written about various aspects of American architecture and historic preservation on the East Coast and in the Midwest. Her master's thesis was titled "Americanization in a Greenbelt Town: The Colonial Revival in Greendale, Wisconsin."

INDEX

Page numbers in italics refer to illustrations.